Budgeting for the Military Sector in Africa

The Processes and Mechanisms of Control

sipri

Stockholm International Peace Research Institute
Signalistgatan 9, SE-169 70 Solna, Sweden
Telephone: 46 8/655 97 00
Fax: 46 8/655 97 33
Email: sipri@sipri.org
Internet URL: http://www.sipri.org

Budgeting for the Military Sector in Africa

The Processes and Mechanisms of Control

Edited by
Wuyi Omitoogun and Eboe Hutchful

sipri
OXFORD UNIVERSITY PRESS
2006

OXFORD
UNIVERSITY PRESS

Great Clarendon Street, Oxford OX2 6DP

Oxford University Press is a department of the University of Oxford.
It furthers the University's objective of excellence in research, scholarship,
and education by publishing worldwide in

Oxford New York

Auckland Cape Town Dar es Salaam Hong Kong Karachi
Kuala Lumpur Madrid Melbourne Mexico City Nairobi
New Delhi Shanghai Taipei Toronto

With offices in

Argentina Austria Brazil Chile Czech Republic France Greece
Guatemala Hungary Italy Japan South Korea Poland Portugal
Singapore Switzerland Thailand Turkey Ukraine Vietnam

Oxford is a registered trade mark of Oxford University Press
in the UK and in certain other countries

Published in the United States
by Oxford University Press Inc., New York

© SIPRI 2006

British Library Cataloguing in Publication Data
Data available

Library of Congress Cataloging in Publication Data
Data available

Typeset and originated by Stockholm International Peace Research Institute

Printed in Great Britain
on acid-free paper by
Biddles Ltd., King's Lynn, Norfolk

ISBN 0–19–926266–7   978–0–19–926266–3

1 3 5 7 9 10 8 6 4 2

Contents

To
Rocky Williams
1960–2005

Colleague and friend

*Member of the Advisory Group of the
SIPRI/ASDR Project on Military Budgetary
Processes in Africa (2001–2005)*

Preface

The barriers between security and sustainable development, as subjects both for study and for policy formation, are rapidly crumbling today. Most people would already agree that the wisdom of both disciplines needs to be combined for purposes of successful conflict prevention and post-conflict peace-building. The issues of security–development interface in the field of resource use have not yet been so thoroughly revisited and remain in some part contentious, yet certain truths seem evident. For developing countries to spend too much, and in the wrong way, not just on traditional defence but under other security headings can damage internal and external stability as well as withholding vital funds from development. For outside powers to encourage this by actions taken with one hand, like the promotion of arms sales, while claiming to guide responsible development policies with the other is unconscionable. Conversely, however, to starve a country (or make it starve itself) of the means to secure its territory and its people's safety is tantamount to gambling with the survival, not just the sustainability, of any development gains achieved. Donor policies of this type in the past have often ended with the recipient continuing to spend large sums on defence but doing so through hidden or disguised channels, which merely adds damage to democracy and transparency to all the other ill effects.

The present volume is the fruit of a multi-year research project driven by the idea of exposing the above contradictions—and finding better policy solutions—through the empirical study of military budgeting processes in eight African countries. The analyses offered in its country case studies dig deep in both historical and systemic terms, and follow a consistent route of enquiry so that the cases can be more easily compared. Recurring themes in many of them are the general weakness of national budgetary systems, compounded by a lack of the bureaucratic capacities needed for efficiency and the parliamentary rights and skills needed for democratic control. The situation is typically worse in the military sector than elsewhere, as a result of factors ranging from inter-service rivalry to political corruption, and from internal suppression of criticism to the obscure end-use of aid received and revenues earned from abroad. It might be thought that the severe internal and external conflicts suffered recently by many of the states in question should also be cited as an explanation for bad management and bad conduct among the military: yet, interestingly, countries' current performance seems to depend less on the gravity of conflict experienced than on the quality of post-conflict reforms. Sierra Leone offers one case where donors' and local efforts at post-conflict renewal have actually given a chance for a fresh start based on (in principle) much higher governance standards.

In general, this book does not content itself with the exposure of bad and weak practices, sensational though some of them may be. A constructive spirit runs through it, as reflected in the detailed treatment given to good practice models (notably in South Africa); in the specific advice offered at the end of every country chapter; and in the general template of a coherent, modern, defence planning and budgeting system provided in chapter 2. What is perhaps most significant about the latter is that it is a model that any developed country could be proud to follow, and indeed covers much of the same ground that NATO has covered in trying to promote better defence practices among its applicant countries and partners. Put more bluntly, the recipe for 'good' (effective but not excessive, transparent and democratic) defence is no different in developing regions than for any other nation in the world. The illogicality of double standards in this respect is steadily becoming clearer as thinking about peace-building points to the need to help afflicted countries get their own security back under control as fast as possible, and as nations within developing regions are increasingly expected to provide resources for local peace missions themselves. If this book carries any single big policy message, it is that outside actors will best help security and development in regions like Africa by judging local countries' defence policies on the quality of the processes involved—and measuring that quality in no different way then they would do for themselves—rather than by dictating arbitrary resource ceilings while holding themselves aloof from any real understanding of local struggles.

The project that created this book was led by Wuyi Omitoogun of SIPRI and Eboe Hutchful of African Security Dialogue and Research of Accra, Ghana (SIPRI's main partner in this project). In the project, 'the medium was the message' inasmuch as a major aim was to create a community of African experts capable of independently assessing their own countries' defence planning and budgeting standards. The success of that effort is shown not just by the quality of the writings in this collection but also by the warm welcome the study has received from leading figures of the African Union and the Economic Community of West African States and by the many other ideas that have arisen for making use of the expert capacities and the habits of cooperation built by this project. Special credit for these achievements should go to Wuyi Omitoogun himself, to Eboe Hutchful, Elisabeth Sköns and the other members of the Advisory Group—Bayo Adekanye, Nicole Ball, Kwabena Gyimah-Brempong, Boubacar Ndiaye, Nadir Mohammed, Thomas Ohlson and Rocky Williams—who provided expert guidance throughout the project, and to all other authors and contributors. The kind support of the Swedish International Development Cooperation Agency and the International Development Research Centre of Canada, which secured the financial foundations for the work, is deeply appreciated. Last but not least I wish to thank SIPRI editors David Cruickshank and Connie Wall for the long and complex effort that has gone into the preparation of this highly original and, it is to be hoped, productive volume.

Alyson J. K. Bailes
Director, SIPRI
Stockholm, January 2006

Acknowledgements

Thanks are due to a number of individuals and organizations without whose help, support and cooperation it would have been a lot more difficult to complete this project. First and foremost is the project's Advisory Group, which provided substantial and invaluable intellectual support for the project. Apart from their collective support and guidance, individual members gave additional assistance: Nicole Ball provided guidance at the early stages of the project and also commented on the initial drafts of the case studies and the synthesis chapter; in spite of his very tight schedule and other personal commitments, Thomas Ohlson engaged me in many hours of discussions that raised the level of analysis in key chapters of the book; Rocky Williams provided extensive comments and shared his vast experience of the defence sector in Africa with the project at every opportunity; Boubacar Ndiaye provided insights into the public sector practices of francophone countries and provided moral support at crucial moments in the course of the project; Bayo Adekanye, Kwabena Gyimah-Brempong and Nadir Mohammed provided comments and suggestions on how to improve the quality of the case studies.

The project which resulted in this publication was jointly organized by SIPRI and African Security Dialogue and Research (ASDR) of Accra, Ghana. This publication is a testimony to the fruitful nature of that collaboration and thanks are due to all the staff of ASDR. Special thanks are due to ASDR's Executive Director, Eboe Hutchful, co-editor of this volume, who ensured that the two critical workshops that were held to initiate this project and discuss its findings were efficiently organized and had optimal results. Eboe also contributed greatly as a member of the Advisory Group and his comments and suggestions on earlier drafts of the chapters were of great help.

Thanks are also due to the authors of the chapters for their immense contributions and sacrifice, working against great odds. Jinmi Adisa of the African Union facilitated contacts with the AU and provided support at the dissemination seminars. The Inter-Africa Group of Addis Ababa, Ethiopia, and the Centre for Democracy and Development of Lagos, Nigeria, were worthy local partners for the dissemination seminars in Ethiopia and Nigeria.

David Cruickshank, SIPRI editor, did an excellent job editing the whole manuscript to get it ready for publication. David not only refined some of the chapters, he searched for and found some of the often difficult to find references. Without his efforts and those of Connie Wall, SIPRI senior editor, this volume would not be in its current reader-friendly form.

I wish to thank Daniel Rotfeld, former SIPRI Director for his strong support and efforts in securing the initial funding for the project. Since becoming SIPRI Director, Alyson Bailes has also strongly backed the project and has been personally involved in the dissemination of the study findings. Anna Helleday, SIPRI's Head of Finance and Administration, has given a great deal of moral support during the project, for which I am grateful.

This project was carried out in SIPRI's Military Expenditure and Arms Production Project. This book and the initial study that gave rise to it were written in furtherance of the objective for which SIPRI's military expenditure project was established: to increase public knowledge of the resources committed to military activities. This book helps to achieve that objective. It could not have done so without the support and cooperation of my colleagues in the Military Expenditure and Arms Production Project. Wale Ismail provided research assistance which improved several of the case studies. Natasza Nazet provided secretarial support. Catalina Perdomo provided insight into the processes in Latin America. Eamon Surry helped with the project website. Petter Stålenheim not only supported the project generally but also helped to resolve statistical problems in addition to being generous with his time whenever I ran into difficulty with incongruent data. Last, but not least, Elisabeth Sköns, leader of the SIPRI project, supported me at every level and phase of this project. She provided leadership (intellectual and otherwise) throughout the course of the project, including during Advisory Group meetings, and provided invaluable comments and suggestions on how to improve the case studies and the synthesis chapter. Her efforts are reflected in the quality of the chapters. She was an inspiration throughout the project and without her support it would have been a lot harder to complete this project.

Finally, special thanks are due to the sponsors of this project, the Swedish International Development Cooperation Agency (SIDA) and Canada's International Development Research Center, for their generous support of both the initial study and the dissemination activities that followed. Without their support both activities, let alone this publication, would have been impossible. To them and everyone associated with the project in one way or another, I say thank you.

Wuyi Omitoogun
Project co-coordinator, SIPRI
Stockholm, January 2006

Abbreviations

AIE	Authority to incur expenditure
ANC	African National Congress
AU	African Union
BCC	Budget Call Circular/Budget Circular Call
CDS	Chief of Defence Staff
CGS	Chief of General Staff
DFC	Defence Financial Comptroller
DFID	Department for International Development
DHQ	Defence Headquarters
DICN	Defence Industries Corporation of Nigeria
DOD	Department of Defence
DPBEC	Departmental Planning and Budgeting Evaluation Committee
EAC	East African Community
ECOMIL	ECOWAS Mission in Liberia
ECOMOG	ECOWAS Military Observer Group
ECOWAS	Economic Community of West African States
EPRDF	Ethiopian Peoples' Revolutionary Democratic Front
FADM	Forças Armadas de Defesa de Moçambique (armed defence forces of Mozambique)
FAM	Forças Armadas de Moçambique (armed forces of Mozambique)
FMF	Federal Ministry of Finance
FMIS	Financial management information system
FRELIMO	Frente de Libertação de Moçambique (liberation front of Mozambique)
FY	Financial year
GAF	Ghana Armed Forces
GDP	Gross domestic product
GHQ	General Headquarters
GNP	Gross national product
GST	General Staff Target
GSU	General Services Unit
IEA	Institute for Economic Affairs
IGAD	Intergovernmental Authority on Development
IMF	International Monetary Fund
KAF	Kenya Air Force
KANU	Kenya African National Union
KAR	King's African Rifles
MDAs	Ministries, departments and agencies

MinComBud	Ministers' Committee on the Budget
MOD	Ministry of Defence
MODV	Ministry of Defence and Veterans
MOEF	Ministry of Economy and Finance
MOF	Ministry of Finance
MOFED	Ministry of Finance and Economic Development
MOND	Ministry of National Defence
MOPF	Ministry of Planning and Finance
MTEA	Medium-Term Expenditure Allocation
MTEC	Medium-Term Expenditure Committee
MTEF	Medium-term expenditure framework
NEPAD	New Partnership for Africa's Development
NGO	Non-governmental organization
NMS	New Management Strategy
NPC	National Planning Commission
NPP	New Patriotic Party
NSSWG	National Security Sector Working Group
OAcGF	Office of the Accountant-General for the Federation
OAU	Organization of African Unity
OAuGF	Office of the Auditor-General for the Federation
OECD	Organisation for Economic Co-operation and Development
OpTraLog	Operational, Training and Logistics
PDSC	Plenary Defence Staff Council
PER	Public expenditure review
PIP	Performance Improvement Programme
PTF	Petroleum Savings Trust Fund
REAN	Royal East African Navy
RENAMO	Resistência Nacional Moçambicana (Mozambican national resistance)
RSLAF	Republic of Sierra Leone Armed Forces
RUF	Revolutionary United Front
SADC	Southern African Development Community
SANDF	South African National Defence Force
SISE	Serviço de Informação e Segurança do Estado (state information and security service)
SWG	Sector working group
TLBH	Top-level budget holder
TPLF	Tigrayan People's Liberation Front
UEMOA	Union Économique et Monétaire Ouest Africaine (West African economic and monetary union)
UN	United Nations
UNAMSIL	United Nations Mission in Sierra Leone
UNOMSIL	United Nations Observer Mission in Sierra Leone
USAID	US Agency for International Development

1. Introduction

Wuyi Omitoogun

I. Background and rationale

Two interrelated developments gave rise to this study. The first was the result of a SIPRI study on the military expenditure of African states. This study concluded that an examination of the processes of budgeting for the military sector in African countries would provide a better understanding of the influences on the levels of military spending in those countries than a simple search for the final budget figure for the military sector.[1] The second was the initiation of the security sector reform debate at the February 2000 symposium organized by the British Department for International Development (DFID).[2] The emphasis of this new debate was on the process of managing military expenditure, in place of donors' earlier, narrow focus on the level of military spending.

While these developments provided the immediate motivation for under-taking this study, the central role played in the 'African problem' by security—or its absence—meant that the need for a study of military budgetary processes in Africa went much deeper, being intertwined with the whole problem of governance and development in Africa. Issues such as the diversion of resources for defence purposes and the proper balance between expenditure on security and on development were part of the disarmament discourse in the developing world as far back as the 1970s. These issues returned to the centre stage from the late 1980s as a result of widespread conflict on the continent, the phenomenon of failed states, the international financial institutions' public expenditure management reforms and bilateral donors' concerns about how their economic assistance was used by poor states.

Donors attempted to impose a predetermined ceiling (or 'acceptable level') on the military expenditure of states. These attempts were directed especially at those states deemed to be engaged in 'excessive' or 'unproductive' expenditure on the military at the expense of the social sector and economic development, and they paid little regard to local security concerns. They also failed to yield the expected results. Instead they led to two unintended consequences: (*a*) the deliberate manipulation of military expenditure figures; and (*b*) the resort to

---

[1] Omitoogun, W., *Military Expenditure Data in Africa: A Survey of Cameroon, Ethiopia, Ghana, Kenya, Nigeria and Uganda*, SIPRI Research Report no. 17 (Oxford University Press: Oxford, 2003).

[2] British Department for International Development (DFID), *Security Sector Reform and the Management of Military Expenditure: High Risks for Donors, High Returns for Development*, Report on the Security Sector Reform and Military Expenditure Symposium, London, 15–17 Feb. 2000 (DFID: London, June 2000), URL <http://www.dfid.gov.uk/pubs/files/ssrmes-report.pdf>.

off-budget spending, which further compounded the problem of public expenditure management. These unintended consequences arose primarily because recipient countries disagreed with the donors on the issue of overspending on the military. In addition, the recipient countries did not accept that their military expenditure constituted unproductive spending.

To promote an understanding of the problems caused by this approach, donors convened several meetings between 1990 and 2000 with a specific focus on the issue of military expenditure and development in developing countries.[3] These meetings and commissioned studies[4] reached fundamental conclusions, which can be summarized as follows.[5]

1. The data on military expenditure, on which judgement on excessive military expenditure was based, were very weak and needed improvement.[6]

2. Even though it could be excessive or inappropriate, military expenditure is not necessarily unproductive expenditure if it leads to an improvement in the well-being of citizens.

3. The focus should be on the process that decides the level of military expenditure rather than on the level of spending per se.

4. Defence should be treated no differently from other parts of the public sector in terms of policy formulation, budgeting, implementation or monitoring. In other words, the key governance principles of transparency, accountability, discipline and comprehensiveness in planning should apply to the military sector just like any other sector.

These conclusions found some resonance at the International Monetary Fund (IMF) and the World Bank, which had started to use the opportunities provided by the end of the cold war to take a critical look at the issue of military expenditure in member countries. By the mid-1990s, both organizations had started to include military expenditure issues in their dialogue with recipient countries. Given the pre-eminent roles played in development cooperation by the IMF and the World Bank, this development encouraged other donors, especially member

---

[3] In 1992 and 1993, 4 donor meetings were held, in The Hague, Tokyo, Berlin and Paris, to discuss the issue of military spending in developing countries. Since the policy of imposing a limit on military spending in recipient countries was just beginning, its impact could not be assessed. By the time of the donor meeting held in Ottawa in 1997, however, evidence was beginning to emerge of the failure of the policy. The report of the Ottawa meeting emphasized the need to strengthen the budgetary decision-making processes in recipient countries and to consider their legitimate security needs when deciding on spending limits. Organisation for Economic Co-operation and Development, Development Co-operation Directorate, 'Final report and follow-up to the 1997 Ottawa Symposium', Paris, June 1998, URL <http://www.oecd.org/dataoecd/16/48/1886718.pdf>.

[4] One such study is Lamb, G. with Kallab, V. (eds), *Military Expenditure and Economic Development: A Symposium on Research Issues*, World Bank Discussion Papers 185 (World Bank: Washington, DC, 1992), URL <http://www-wds.worldbank.org/>.

[5] Of course, not all these meetings reached all of these conclusions. In particular, the 4th conclusion was not reached until the 2000 DFID meeting.

[6] Michael Brzoska and Nicole Ball had earlier discussed the major weaknesses of military expenditure data. Brzoska, M., 'The reporting of military expenditures', *Journal of Peace Research*, vol. 18, no. 3 (1981), pp. 261–75; and Ball, N., *Third-World Security Expenditure: A Statistical Compendium* (Swedish National Defence Research Institute: Stockholm, 1984).

countries of the Organisation for Economic Co-operation and Development (OECD), to do the same with the recipients of their development assistance.[7] Partly as a result of this and, more significantly, of the problems of widespread conflict and post-conflict public security, donors began to understand the central role played by security in development.[8] Donors realized that some level of military expenditure is needed by states to meet their legitimate security needs and to provide the secure environment necessary for the sustainable development that is the goal of development assistance.[9]

The 'process' approach

The conclusion of the 2000 DFID meeting on Security Sector Reform and Military Expenditure—that an integrated approach should be taken to the management of military expenditure in particular, and of the security sector in general—proved to be a major reason for the shift in some donors' approach to military expenditure. The new approach, known as the 'process' or 'governance' approach, combines good governance practices and sound financial management principles with security considerations and 'focuses attention on the institutional framework for both managing trade-offs between different sectors and for the effective management of the resources devoted to the defence sector'.[10] There is no guarantee that the new approach will lead to an immediate reduction in military expenditure; on the contrary, in the short to medium term military expenditure may appear to increase, as previously off-budget military spending is brought on budget, and expenditure may rise in real terms as the armed forces are made more professional through training and the modernization of equipment. Ultimately, however, reduced military expenditure may be achieved once proper governance principles are entrenched in the system.

The process approach offers three main potential advantages to both donors and recipient countries. First, it has the potential to reveal the exact process of budgeting for the military sector, the actors involved and the kinds of trade-off made between the military and other sectors. Ultimately, it can show whether the level of resources allocated to the military is justifiable. Transparency in the decision-making process can also reveal how reliable data are. Second, for recipient countries the process approach provides a unique opportunity to justify—to donors and their own citizens—the level of military expenditure and the extent of military needs, especially where spending limits imposed by

[7] The majority of the members of the OECD are the major shareholders of the International Monetary Fund and the World Bank.

[8] See, e.g., the World Bank's PovertyNet, URL <http://www.worldbank.org/poverty/voices>.

[9] Short, C., British Secretary of State for International Development, Keynote address at the DFID Security Sector Reform and Military Expenditure Symposium, London, 17 Feb. 2000, reproduced in Annex 1: Speeches in British DFID (note 2), pp. 24–27.

[10] British Department for International Development, 'Security sector reform and the management of defence expenditure: a conceptual framework', Annex 3: Discussion Paper no. 1 in British DFID (note 2), p. 47.

donors mean that the basic security needs of the state cannot be met. Third, if donors focus on the application to the military sector of good governance principles, rather than the level of spending, the argument of political interference in domestic affairs of recipient countries carries much less weight and even becomes less sensitive.

These new ideas are gradually gaining ground, although donors still hesitate to adopt an approach that involves greater engagement out of fear of being accused of interfering in the internal political affairs of recipient states or of becoming entangled in their often complex security situations.[11] An increasing number of donors are becoming involved in efforts to improve the security sector in recipient countries. An indication of how far this process has developed is the fact that such engagement is now discussed at meetings of the OECD's Development Assistance Committee. At these meetings, the possibility of counting support for the security sector as part of official development assistance is becoming a major issue.[12]

II. The objective and focus of the study

The objective

This study is a pioneering effort to apply the process approach to an assessment of military expenditure management. Eight countries are used as case studies: Ethiopia, Ghana, Kenya, Mali, Mozambique, Nigeria, Sierra Leone and South Africa. The study is concerned not so much with the level of spending in these countries—even though this is touched on—as with the processes by which these countries arrive at their levels of spending. In using this approach to examine the processes of allocating resources to the military sector, the extent of adherence to the principles of defence planning and programming and sound public expenditure management is a major focus. The guiding principle for the book is that the military sector should be treated no differently from the other parts of the public sector and should be subjected to the same standards, rules and practices. Various studies have shown that military budgets in Africa lack scrutiny by the various oversight bodies and are often protected against cuts when there is a shortfall in expected government income, making the military sector better resourced in comparison to other sectors.[13] While the military

---

[11] Hendrickson, D., 'A review of security-sector reform', Working Paper no. 1, Centre for Defence Studies, King's College, London, 1999.

[12] Organisation for Economic Co-operation and Development (OECD), Development Assistance Committee (DAC), 'Annex 5: ODA coverage of certain conflict, peace building and security expenditures', *DAC Statistical Reporting Directives* (OECD: Paris, 28 Apr. 2004), URL <http://www.oecd.org/dac/stats/dac/directives/>. See also OECD, DAC, 'Conflict prevention and peace building: what counts as ODA?', DAC High Level Meeting, Paris, 3 Mar. 2005, URL <http://www.oecd.org/dataoecd/32/32/34535173.pdf>.

[13] Gyimah-Brempong, K., 'Do African governments favor defense in budgeting?', *Journal of Peace Research*, vol. 29, no. 2 (May 1992), pp. 191–206; Mohammed, N. A. L., *What Determines Military Allocations in Africa: Theoretical and Empirical Investigation* (African Development Bank: Abidjan, 1996); Gyimah-Brempong, K., 'Is the tradeoff between defense spending and spending on social welfare an illu-

sector does differ from other sectors in that certain aspects require some form of confidentiality, this should not confer any special status upon it in terms of resource allocation, transparency, accountability and oversight.

Thus, the main objective of this study is to critically examine the military budgetary processes of a sample of African states with a view to identifying the main actors and institutions in the budgetary process and their roles. Different actors and institutions play different roles in the budgetary process which affect both the level of expenditure and the reporting and auditing of expenditure. The other objective of this study has been to contribute to building local (African) capacity in the area of defence analysis through the use of local researchers.

These two broad objectives are set against the background of: (a) highly unreliable official military expenditure data; (b) presumed off-budget military expenditure; and (c) the scarcity of local researchers with expertise in defence analysis.

The focus

Two issues about this study's use of the process approach need to be flagged from the outset. One is the seemingly narrow focus of the study on the *military* budgetary process. A focus on the wider security sector could have been more appropriate and would perhaps have provided a slightly different set of conclusions. However, since this is a ground-breaking study and since what is true for the military sector is largely true for the whole security sector, nothing has been lost by focusing on the military, which, in any case, is generally assumed to consume the most resources and to be the least transparent of the security forces. Indeed, to ensure that the study did not lose its focus, it was decided early in the project to use a word with an unambiguous meaning to describe the section of the security sector on which research attention was to be directed: hence the use of the term 'military' rather than 'defence', which has a much broader meaning in many African states.[14] Where, following local terminology in particular countries, the term 'defence' is used in this book, it refers to the military as defined here.

The second issue is that the adoption of the process approach should not be assumed to imply general support for the belief subsisting in many circles, including the donor community, that African states spend, relatively speaking, too much on the military sector. Across Africa, there is a general underfunding of the public sector, including the military sector. While other sectors in poor states receive support from external sources, the military sector receives little such support, especially since the end of the cold war. Yet African military forces are increasingly being used for internal security purposes and inter-

sion?: Some evidence from tropical Africa', *Eastern African Economic Review*, vol. 5, no. 2 (Dec. 1989), pp. 74–90; and Omitoogun (note 1), in particular chapters 8 and 9.

[14] Many African governments use the term 'defence' very loosely to cover a broader concept of state security which includes paramilitary forces and the customs service.

Table 1.1. Military expenditure per capita in 2004 and as a share of gross domestic product in 2000–2003, by region and by income group

Per capita expenditure figures are in US$, at current prices and exchange rates.

Region/income group (GDP/GNI per capita)[a]	Military expenditure per capita, 2004	Military expenditure as a share of GDP (%)			
		2000	2001	2002	2003
World ($6019)	162	*2.3*	*2.3*	*2.4*	*2.5*
Region					
Africa ($775)	18	*2.2*	*2.1*	*2.1*	*2.1*
Americas ($16 599)	597	*2.7*	*2.8*	*3.0*	*3.3*
North America ($36 464)	1 453	*2.9*	*2.9*	*3.2*	*3.6*
Latin America ($3406)	47	*1.3*	*1.5*	*1.4*	*1.3*
Asia ($2651)	45	*1.6*	*1.6*	*1.6*	*1.6*
Europe ($15 397)	351	*2.1*	*2.0*	*2.1*	*2.1*
Western Europe ($23 971)	530	*2.0*	*2.0*	*2.0*	*2.0*
Central and Eastern ($3133)	112	*2.8*	*2.9*	*2.9*	*3.0*
Middle East ($4513)	248	*7.0*	*7.5*	*6.9*	*6.7*
Oceania ($24 145)	516	*1.8*	*1.8*	*1.8*	*1.8*
Income group					
Low income (≤$765)	20	*2.3*	*2.0*	*1.8*	*1.8*
Lower-middle income ($766–$3035)	46	*2.6*	*2.7*	*2.7*	*2.7*
Upper-middle income ($3036–$9385)	136	*2.5*	*2.6*	*2.4*	*2.4*
High income (≥$9386)	867	*2.2*	*2.2*	*2.4*	*2.5*

GDP = Gross domestic product; GNI = Gross national income.

[a] The figures in parentheses after regions are 2003 GDP per capita. The ranges in parentheses after income groups are 2003 GNI per capita.

Source: Sköns, E. *et al.*, 'Military expenditure', *SIPRI Yearbook 2005: Armaments, Disarmament and International Security* (Oxford University Press: Oxford, 2005), table 8.2, p. 316.

national peacekeeping operations without any corresponding increase in resources. One of the reasons for the prolonged conflicts in weak African states is the national armies' lack of superior firepower that could put down armed rebellions at an early stage.[15] Indeed, the ramshackle state of many military establishments in Africa is as much evidence of underfunding as a reflection of mismanagement of resources. The lack of adequate resources for the armed forces is glaring in some of the African states that are undertaking reforms of their military sectors. For instance, Uganda's defence review showed the need for reform in several key areas of the military sector. However, the costs of the

---

[15] For an elaboration of the state of African military establishment see Howe, H. M., *The Ambiguous Order: Military Forces in African States* (Lynne Rienner: Boulder, Colo., 2001) . Herbst, J., 'African militaries and rebellion: the political economy of threat and combat effectiveness', *Journal of Peace Research*, vol. 41, no. 3 (May 2004), pp. 357–69.

reforms are quite high and Uganda cannot carry them out without external support.[16]

Table 1.1 compares the proportion of Africa's gross domestic product (GDP) absorbed by military expenditure with that in other regions of the world. Compared with Asia, Latin America, Oceania and Western Europe, Africa's military burden is high. However, it should be borne in mind that a handful of Africa's 53 states account for a disproportionate share of its military expenditure, while the majority are barely able to take care of their militaries due to a dearth of resources. As the table shows, Africa's military expenditure per capita is the lowest in the world; below the average for low-income countries, the category to which the majority of countries on the continent belong. In their resource-constrained environment, many African states feel that they cannot afford both security and development. Although it is commonly acknowledged that military means are not the only way to provide security, the link between security and development is well established and so critical choices have to be made between investing available resources in security and in other sectors and on how best to synthesize security and development objectives. The trade-offs that are inevitable in the process may not meet the expectations of donors but may be unavoidable given domestic realities. Within the context of resource constraints, however, there is a need to ascertain the level of mismanagement of resources: what proportion of the, sometimes bloated, military budget actually goes towards the maintenance of the military, and what proportion falls into private hands owing to opaque management practices.

The adoption of the process approach, with its emphasis on adherence to sound public expenditure management principles and due consideration of the security environment, may aid the resolution of this dilemma.

III. Methodology and scope of the study

The study's analytical model

In order to apply the process approach to the study, a framework of an ideal process is needed. The study uses an analytical framework (see chapter 2) that is an amalgamation of: (*a*) internationally accepted standards of sound public expenditure management,[17] which includes good governance principles and sound financial management practices; and (*b*) an ideal policy, planning, pro-

---

[16] 'Uganda to spend $630 million to restructure military', *New Vision* (Kampala), 25 July 2005.

[17] Ball, N. and Holmes, M., 'Integrating defense into public expenditure work', Commissioned by the British DFID, London, Jan. 2002, URL <http://www.gfn-ssr.org/document_result.cfm?id=6>. See also World Bank, *Public Expenditure Management Handbook* (World Bank: Washington, DC, 1998), URL <http://www1.worldbank.org/publicsector/pe/handbooks.htm>; and Ball, N., 'Managing the military budgeting process: integrating the defence sector into government-wide processes', Paper presented at the SIPRI/ASDR workshop on Budgeting for the Military Sector in Africa, Accra, 25–26 Feb. 2002, URL <http://www.sipri.org/contents/milap/milex/mex_afr_publ.html>.

gramming and budgeting framework for armed forces.[18] In other words, it combines economic and security considerations as the basis for determining and managing military expenditure. This balance is important for both the finances and the security of the state. The overarching principle of the framework is that the military sector should be treated no differently in terms of policy development, planning and budgeting from any other part of the public sector. It requires an integrated set of policy principles that involve the military and other sectors in the national policy framework and reflect the country's social, economic and political environment. The translation of this policy into a defence plan allows for the appropriate allocation and efficient use of resources. This framework is based on the assumption that all armed forces have a constitutional role, which enjoins them to serve as guarantors of the territorial integrity and the sovereignty of the nation.

According to this analytical framework, the budgetary process involves a number of institutions and actors that differ from country to country. In an ideal situation, however, the stages involved in the process remain basically the same. The overall policy direction and economic policy framework of the government have a major influence on the process. The objective is to ensure that government allocates resources appropriately to the military sector within the bounds of what the state can afford. It is also important that the process is transparent and participatory—since the approach will be most successful in a democratic environment—and that the military sector competes on an equal footing with all other government sectors.

A participatory process means that economic managers and oversight bodies such as the legislature and the auditor-general play a central role and that non-state actors are consulted. The various stakeholders in the process should receive the amount and type of information required to ensure that appropriate decisions are made. They also need to receive it in timely fashion. Accountability and control are essential; thus, the last three stages in the process outlined below—output monitoring, accounting for expenditure and evaluating results—are an important part of the process approach. The following are the main elements of an acceptable budgetary process for the military sector.

1. The financial envelope for the security sector is defined by the government and communicated to those responsible for overseeing strategic planning for the defence sector.

2. The security environment is analysed.

3. The constitutional and legal framework within which the decision is to be made and implemented is identified.

4. The challenges for the armed forces are defined. These are usually articulated in a defence White Paper or similar policy paper.

---

[18] Le Roux, L., 'The military budgeting process: an overview', Paper presented at the SIPRI/ASDR workshop on Budgeting for the Military Sector in Africa, Accra, 25–26 Feb. 2002, URL <http://www.sipri.org/contents/milap/milex/mex_afr_publ.html>.

5. The types of military capability required to manage the challenges are identified and the options weighed.

6. The size, shape and structure of the armed forces are defined.

7. Resources are allocated and the military budget prepared.

8. Planned activities are implemented and functional areas aligned and rationalized in order to produce an effective defence organization.

9. Outputs (results) are monitored.

10. Expenditure is accounted for properly.

11. Outputs are evaluated and audited, and results are fed into future plans and reported to the relevant legislative and executive bodies.

While it is recognized that the framework described above may not be applicable in its entirety to all existing military budgetary processes across Africa, two compelling reasons make the use of an ideal process framework attractive (in this case for research). One is the need for a standard measure of good practice in the military policy, planning and budgeting process that will serve as the basis for assessing practice in a number of Africa states. Without such a measure it becomes difficult to assess performance in the sector. The other is that it provides conceptual support for the study on which to anchor the analyses in the case studies. A common conceptual approach provides a good basis for a comparative analysis in the whole study and helps point the way to how processes might be strengthened.

In a number of African states the gap between formal and actual processes for determining military expenditure is currently significant. The study therefore examines both the de jure and de facto processes of decision making for military budgeting.

Research design

In view of the perceived sensitive nature of the study and the need to gain access to information, two researchers were commissioned for each case study: an academic researcher and a military practitioner, serving or retired. This proved quite useful in three seemingly difficult case studies. Two workshops were held as part of the study. The first, at the beginning of the study, was to familiarize the researchers with the methodology of the study, in particular the analytical framework, the research questions and what to expect in the field. The second was to discuss the findings of the study at the completion of the country studies.

To define the conduct of the actual research, a set of research questions was discussed and refined at the first workshop. These questions served as the main guide for the conduct of the research in the countries. The researchers supported the structured questions with documentary analysis and interviews with key actors in the budgetary process.

The essence of the structured approach was to provide a basis for the comparative analysis of the country studies according to the respective adher-

Table 1.2. Key background facts about Ethiopia, Ghana, Kenya, Mali, Mozambique, Nigeria, Sierra Leone and South Africa

	Ethiopia	Ghana	Kenya	Mali	Mozambique	Nigeria	Sierra Leone	South Africa
Area (km²)	1 133 880	238 537	582 646	1 240 140	799 380	923 768	71 740	1 219 090
Location	Horn of Africa	West Africa	East Africa	West Africa	Southern Africa	West Africa	West Africa	Southern Africa
Date of independence	–	1957	1963	1960	1975	1960	1961	1910/1994
Colonizing country	–	UK	UK	France	Portugal	UK	UK	UK/white minority
Institution or restoration of democracy	1994	1993	1992	1992	1994	1999	1996/1998[a]	1994
Constitutional form	Parliamentary, federal	Presidential, unitary	Presidential, unitary	Semi-presidential, unitary	Semi-presidential, unitary	Presidential, federal	Presidential, unitary	Parliamentary, mixed federal/unitary
Form of rule before democracy	Transition from one-party rule	Military	One-party	Military	One-party	Military	Military	Minority
Proportion of seats in legislature held by ruling party, Aug. 2005[b] (%)	54	51	58	53[c]	64	59[d]	74	70
Approximate size of armed forces, 2004	182 500	7 000	20 000	7 350	10 700	80 000	12 500	55 750
Estimated population, 2005	77 431 000	22 113 000	34 256 000	13 518 000	19 792 000	131 530 000	5 525 000	47 432 000
GDP, 2004 (US$ m.)[e]	8 208	8 833	15 615	4 928	5 548	71 326	1 070	212 898
GDP per capita, 2004 (US$)[e]	116	434	482	404	292	500	201	4 500

[a] President Ahmad Tejan Kabbah of Sierra Leone, elected in 1996, was deposed by a coup in May 1997. He was restored to office in Mar. 1998.

[b] In Ethiopia, Nigeria and South Africa, this refers to the lower house of the legislature. Ghana, Kenya, Mali, Mozambique and Sierra Leone have uni-cameral legislatures.

[c] President Amadou Toumani Touré of Mali was elected as an independent candidate and the Prime Minister, Ousmane Issoufi Maïga, is not affiliated to a political party. This figure refers to the alliance of ADEMA-PASJ and RPM, which hold 44 and 35 seats, respectively, in the 147-seat National Assembly.

[d] In the Nigerian Senate, which has extensive powers, 70% of the seats are held by the ruling People's Democratic Party.

[e] Figures for gross domestic product (GDP) are in current prices.

Sources: **Area**: *The Times Comprehensive Atlas of the World*, 11th edn (Times Books: London, 2003); **Legislature**: 'Ethiopian PM wins disputed poll', BBC News Online, 9 Aug. 2005, URL <http://news.bbc.co.uk/2/4135408.stm>; Parliament of Ghana, 'About the Parliament: who is where?', URL <http://www.parliament.gh/about_whoiswhere.php>; Parliament of Kenya, 'Composition and functions of Parliament', URL <http://www.parliament.go.ke/com position.php>; 'Mali', *Europa World Year Book 2005* (Routledge: London, 2005), p. 2868; 'New Mozambican leader hails win', BBC News Online, 22 Dec. 2004, URL <http://news.bbc.co.uk/2/4115869.stm>; Nigeria Congress, 'The House of Representatives: members', URL <http://www.nigeria congress.org/reps/repslist2003.asp>; 'Sierra Leone', *Europa World Year Book 2005*, p. 3829; Parliament of South Africa, 'National Assembly: state of parties', URL <http://www.parliament.gov.za/>; **Armed forces**: chapters 3–10 in this volume; **Population**: United Nations, Department of Economic and Social Affairs, *World Population Prospects: The 2004 Revision* (United Nations: New York, 2004), URL <http://esa.un.org/unpp/>; **GDP**: International Monetary Fund, *World Economic Outlook* Database, Apr. 2005, URL <http://www.imf.org/external/pubs/ft/weo/2005/01/data/>.

ence of the eight countries to the principles of defence planning and programming and public expenditure management. Their adherence is categorized as 'high', 'medium' or 'low' and is used to identify patterns, find explanations and develop recommendations on how to improve the level of adherence (see chapter 11).

Throughout the project an international advisory group, comprised of experts in security analysis, supported the study team. The advisory group helped in many respects, including the initial drawing up of research questions, the identification of country researchers from their existing networks and the review of earlier drafts of the chapters.

Regional and country coverage

This study covers eight African countries: Ethiopia, Ghana, Kenya, Mali, Mozambique, Nigeria, Sierra Leone and South Africa. Key background facts about these countries are given in table 1.2. These countries do not fully reflect the diversity of the African continent in linguistic, cultural or geographic terms. Nor do they adequately capture the various budgetary traditions or practices found in Africa. Their choice became inevitable owing to the severe constraints encountered while conducting the study in the 14 countries which formed the ideal selection for the original project plan.

First, there was a dearth of qualified researchers to carry out the study in a number of the countries. Second, there were indications that some of the countries were hostile to the conduct of this kind of research. As well as the researchers' safety being put at risk if the study were to continue in those countries, access to information seemed likely to be denied. As a result, a number of countries where research proved impossible were either dropped or replaced. Given the circumstances, the original criteria for selecting case studies—geographical distribution, language (both anglo- and francophone), data availability, the nature of the state and the availability of researchers—were amended: the availability of researchers and of an environment conducive to research became the two most important criteria.

Regardless of the criteria, South Africa was chosen as a subject for study because of its success in the post-1994 transformation of its government in general and its budgetary process in particular.

IV. The structure of this book

This book is divided into 12 chapters. After this introduction, chapter 2 describes good practice in military budgeting, setting out the main principles and the ultimate objective of such good practice in military budgeting. Chapters 3–10 feature the eight country studies. In a comparative analysis, chapter 11 examines the extent of adherence in the country studies to the principles in the analytical model. It also offers a set of explanations for the level and pattern of adherence. In conclusion, chapter 12 provides recommendations both for national governments in Africa on how to improve their military budgetary processes and for the international community on how to contribute to this aim.

V. A note on the study findings

The majority of the eight countries in this study fall into the category of low adherence to the best practices of military budgeting. However, it is important to point out that the standards in the analytical model against which these countries are assessed are high. If the same standards were applied to developed countries, very few would qualify for the 'high' category. To a great extent, therefore, in a comparative perspective, the current situation in the countries studied is not as bad as the classification may suggest. Indeed, most of the countries in this study are making great efforts to reform their military management systems, a development that is too recent to assess. The fact that it was possible to carry out the study at all in these countries, with access to top government officials, is in itself a reflection of an increasing openness that would have been difficult to imagine a few years ago.

2. A model for good practice in budgeting for the military sector*

Nicole Ball and Len le Roux

I. Introduction

Sound financial management of a country's entire security sector is essential if the country is to have effective, efficient and professional security forces that are capable of protecting the state and its population against internal and external threats. Highly autonomous security forces that are able to act with impunity in the economic and political spheres are invariably professionally weak and bad value for money. This chapter provides a perspective on how good practice can be achieved. It emphasizes adherence to public expenditure management principles and various elements of defence planning and budgeting.

Section II describes good practice in military budgeting. Section III shows how the military budgetary process can be linked to the government-wide budgetary process. Section IV examines in some detail the defence planning process, which is central to the entire military budgetary process. The chapter concludes in section V with a discussion of three key characteristics of successful defence resource management: efficiency, transparency and accountability. Good practice in military procurement and acquisition is discussed in appendix 2A. Strategic defence planning is considered in appendix 2B, and appendix 2C presents a practical model for the determination of defence capabilities.

II. Good practice in the military budgetary process

From the perspectives of public policy and budgetary process, the military sector shares many of the characteristics of other sectors of government. This means that the citizens of any country will benefit from a military sector that is subject to the same broad set of rules and procedures that are applied to other sectors. It is therefore essential to give a high priority to principles such as transparency, accountability to elected civil authorities and comprehensiveness of budget coverage. In that respect, military budgeting should be no different from budgeting for other governmental sectors.

* An earlier version of parts of this chapter was published in Ball, N. and Fayemi, K. (eds), 'Managing financial resources', *Security Sector Governance in Africa: A Handbook* (Centre for Democracy and Development: Lagos, 2004), pp. 91–109.

At the same time, it is often argued that the military sector is different from other parts of the public sector in at least two ways. The first is the need for confidentiality in the area of national security. The second is the highly political nature of expenditure decisions relating to the military sector, especially arms acquisition decisions.

It is clear that some degree of confidentiality is necessary in the area of national security. However, this should not be used to justify a lower level of oversight or a lack of adherence to internationally recognized standards of public expenditure management. Different forms of oversight may be necessary for some areas relating to national security. It is also important to be clear about the distinction between confidentiality and the lack of public scrutiny. It is possible to retain a high degree of confidentiality in highly sensitive areas without compromising the principle of democratic accountability. A subject may be sensitive—off-budget activities, for example—but it should not be kept secret. War plans, on the other hand, should be confidential. Even so, holding war plans in confidence does not mean an absence of democratic accountability. It simply requires appropriate systems of clearance and procedures for consulting the legislature and other oversight bodies.

All budgeting involves political decisions and trade-offs, but it is often argued that political considerations carry greater weight in defence than in other sectors. To the extent that this is true, provided that the political system is open, it should still be possible to contest the basis on which decisions are made and, in particular, to ensure that the principles of sound financial management are not violated. Thus, the highly political nature of decisions concerning the military sector should not prevent that sector from adhering to the important principles of transparency, oversight and accountability.

What constitutes good practice in military budgeting?

In order to develop an appreciation of good practice in the military budgetary process, it is important to consider: (*a*) the relevance of good practice; (*b*) the principles of sound public expenditure management; and (*c*) the key principles of democratic governance in the security sector.

The relevance of good practice

Good practice is based on adherence to principles of sound public expenditure management. One might well question the relevance of somewhat abstract principles when dealing with an issue like military spending, where actual practice diverges significantly from good practice and the conditions for achieving good practice are frequently not present, as is the case throughout much of Africa.

The purpose of starting with good practice is that it provides a clear vision of the objectives of policy reform—in this case, a democratically governed military sector under civilian leadership that adheres to the principles of sound budgeting and financial management. Without such a vision, it is impossible to

---

Box 2.1. Ten principles of public expenditure management

1. *Comprehensiveness.* The budget must encompass all financial operations of government; off-budget expenditure and revenue are prohibited.

2. *Discipline.* Decision making must be restrained by resource realities over the medium term; the budget should absorb only those resources necessary to implement government policies; and budget allocations should be adhered to.

3. *Legitimacy.* Policy makers who can change policies during implementation must take part in the formulation of the original policy and agree with it.

4. *Flexibility.* Decisions should be made by those with access to all relevant information; this means, operationally, that managers should have authority over managerial decisions and, programmatically, that individual ministers should be given more authority over programme decisions.

5. *Predictability.* There must be stability in general and long-term policy and in the funding of existing policy.

6. *Contestability.* All sectors must compete on an equal footing for funding during budget planning and formulation.

7. *Honesty.* The budget must be derived from unbiased projections of revenue and expenditure.

8. *Information.* A medium-term aggregate expenditure baseline against which the budgetary impact of policy changes can be measured and accurate information on costs, outputs and outcomes should be available.

9. *Transparency.* Decision makers should have all relevant information before them and be aware of all relevant issues when they make decisions; these decisions and their basis should be communicated to the public.

10. *Accountability.* Decision makers are responsible for the exercise of the authority provided to them.

Source: Poverty Reduction and Economic Management Network, *Public Expenditure Management Handbook* (World Bank: Washington, DC, 1998), URL <http://www1.world bank.org/publicsector/pe/handbooks.htm>, pp. 1–2.

---

develop either a strategy for reaching the ultimate objectives or benchmarks to measure progress along the way. It is also impossible to determine where the problems lie with existing policy and practice.

The principles of sound public expenditure management

The 10 principles of public expenditure management presented in box 2.1 are widely accepted as the basis for budgeting processes.[1] It is important to understand that these are the ideals that public officials should have in front of them as a guide. No public expenditure system anywhere in the world gets top marks on all 10 principles. The point is to progressively improve adherence to them.

There is no justification for the military sector to violate any of these principles. The way in which it implements some of them may be a little different

---

[1] See, e.g., United Nations Development Programme, *Human Development Report 2002: Deepening Democracy in a Fragmented World* (Oxford University Press: New York, 2002), URL <http://www.undp.org/hdr2002/>, box 43, p. 90.

from some other sectors, but the principles themselves must not be violated: they are all relevant to a well-managed budgetary process.

The principles most frequently cited in relation to the military sector are transparency and accountability. As the above remarks on confidentiality suggest, transparency is the cornerstone on which an accountable military budgetary process is built. Transparency and accountability are crucial issues in the allocation and management of defence resources for all levels of planning, programming and budgeting. If the allocation and management of defence resources are not transparent, the military sector will never be able to achieve public support or the cooperation and support of broader government. If it is not accountable to government and the people, the military becomes a cause unto itself and will not be aligned with national interests and priorities. It will easily be corrupted and decision making will be easily diverted towards self-interest.

Civil involvement in and control of overall budget decisions, as well as careful auditing at all levels, can help ensure that resources are actually used to accomplish policy objectives. The most effective way to achieve this is to obtain at all levels a commitment to national interests and objectives and to develop clear and transparent planning, programming and budgeting processes and systems to implement them. These processes must of necessity be aligned with the national financial management framework.

Transparency and accountability can be enhanced through a system of performance agreements. Such agreements rely on the definition of clear output objectives and performance standards and on agreement on the required resources. The system is also based on negotiation, ensuring better insight, understanding and cooperation.

Important as transparency and accountability are, it is essential not to lose sight of the other principles of public expenditure management. In particular, attention should be given to: (*a*) the *comprehensiveness* of the budget; (*b*) the *predictability* of the level of revenues backing that budget and the macro-economic policies on which those revenues depend; (*c*) the *contestability* of the budget process; and (*d*) the *honesty* with which estimates of revenue and expenditure are developed.

The key principles of democratic governance in the security sector

The 10 principles of democratic governance in the security sector listed in box 2.2 are increasingly widely accepted. They reflect the mutual obligations that civil authorities and security personnel have towards each other. Security forces have a responsibility to be accountable to civil authorities; to uphold the rule of law, including the protection of human and civil rights; and to carry out their professional duties to the best of their abilities. Civil authorities have the responsibility to avoid politicizing security bodies; to respect their professional prerogatives; and to provide them with a clear mandate and adequate resources and training to carry out that mandate. As in the case of the principles of public

---

Box 2.2. Ten principles of democratic governance in the security sector

1. The security forces should be accountable to elected civil authorities and civil society.
2. The security forces should adhere to international law and domestic constitutional law.
3. There should be transparency in security-related matters.
4. The security sector should adhere to the same principles of public expenditure management as the other sectors of government.
5. There should be an acceptance of the clear hierarchy of authority between civil authorities and security forces, and a clear statement of the mutual rights and obligations of civil authorities and security forces.
6. The civil authorities should have adequate capacity to exercise political control and constitutional oversight of the military sector.
7. There should be adequate capacity within civil society to monitor the security sector and to provide constructive input into political debate on security policies.
8. The political environment should be conducive to civil society playing an active role.
9. The security forces should have access to professional training consistent with the requirements of democratic societies.
10. High priority should be accorded to regional and sub-regional peace and security by policy makers.

---

expenditure management, there is no justification for the military sector to violate these principles.

III. Integrating the military budgetary process into government-wide processes

There are five crucial, interrelated components of the management of expenditure in any sector: (*a*) strategic planning; (*b*) review of the previous year's performance; (*c*) determination of what is affordable; (*d*) allocation of resources both between and within sectors; and (*e*) efficient and effective use of resources. The linkages between these components are shown in figure 2.1 in the case of the military sector, with reference to the broader security sector.

For the budgetary process to be effective, every sector needs to follow good practices internally and to link with the broader, government-wide financial management and oversight process. All of this must occur within the framework of democratic governance and the principles of sound budgeting and financial management.

Strategic planning in the security sector

As in any other part of the public sector, military budgets should be prepared in accordance with a sectoral strategy. This involves identifying the needs and key objectives of the security sector as a whole and the specific missions that the defence forces will be asked to undertake.

As shown in figure 2.2, the starting point for developing policies and strategies for the security sector is an understanding of the causes of insecurity and the identification of the instruments that government wants to employ to enhance security. Governments have various tools for strengthening security. Key among these are diplomacy; economic and political tools to reduce economic and social inequalities and tensions; mediation to resolve conflict domestically and regionally; and, of course, the country's security bodies. Once the broad areas of responsibility for the security forces are identified, governments should agree on the tasks that will be undertaken by the different bodies: armed forces, police, gendarmerie or paramilitary forces, and intelligence bodies. Based on these assessments, governments should develop a formal defence policy framework. This policy then informs planning, programming and budgeting (see figure 2.3). The planning and programming process is described in more detail in section IV below, along with the linkages to the military budgetary process.

While it is true that 'policy is what government does, not what it says it wants to do', formal policies and plans to implement these policies are important. In the absence of well-thought-out and clearly articulated policies, it is impossible to manage the finances of the military sector in a rational manner. Budgeting becomes ad hoc. In the absence of a clear statement of which activities undertaken by the armed forces are included in the 'defence' function, it is impossible to develop adequate functional breakdowns of expenditure and to understand how much it costs to provide adequate military security. In addition, it is difficult to develop performance benchmarks and thus to assess the efficiency and effectiveness of expenditure in the military sector. In the absence of a strategic plan, countries risk not obtaining a level of military security commensurate with their financial outlays.

As the case studies in this volume illustrate, few governments in Africa have undertaken thorough, participatory strategic review processes of the sort outlined in figure 2.3. What is more, defence policy and planning processes are rarely based on a broad evaluation of a country's security environment and a detailed assessment of the specific tasks that should be undertaken by the country's various security forces. A counterexample is Uganda, which undertook a broad security assessment in 2002–2003. It identified 134 'threat agents', of which three were specific to the military.[2] This result underscores the importance of not attempting to undertake defence planning in a vacuum, but of linking it with planning for the police, paramilitary forces, civilian intelligence and other state security forces, as well as with the country's economic and developmental objectives.

In highly resource-constrained countries, such as those in Africa, it is extremely important for governments and societies to use resources as effi-

---

[2] Rusoke, R. (Col.), director-general of the Defence Reform Unit, Uganda Peoples' Defence Forces, 'The Uganda Defence Review', Presentation to the South–South Dialogue on Defence Transformation, Accra, 26–29 May 2003.

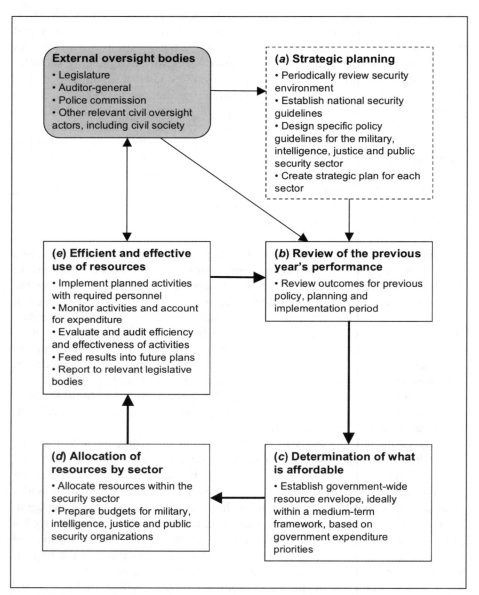

Figure 2.1. A generic financial management process for the security sector

Source: Based on the policy, planning and budgeting process as applied to the military sector in British Department for International Development (DFID), 'Annex 3: Discussion paper no. 1, Security sector reform and the management of defence expenditure: a conceptual framework', *Security Sector Reform and the Management of Military Expenditure: High Risks for Donors, High Returns for Development*, Report on the London Symposium on Security Sector Reform and Military Expenditure, 15–17 Feb. 2000 (DFID: London, 2000), URL <http://www.dfid.gov.uk/pubs/files/ssrmes-report.pdf>, pp. 41–54.

Box 2.3. Information to be captured by a financial management information system

• Approved budget allocations for both recurrent and capital outlays
• Sources of financing for programmes and projects
• Budget transfers
• Supplementary allocations
• Fund releases against budgetary allocations
• Data on commitments and actual expenditure against budgeted allocations

Source: Poverty Reduction and Economic Management Network, *Public Expenditure Management Handbook* (World Bank: Washington, DC, 1998), URL <http://www1.world bank.org/publicsector/pe/handbooks.htm>, p. 65.

ciently and effectively as possible. The first step in this process is to engage in strategic planning. In doing so, it is important to ensure that the defence review process takes place in a manner consistent with the country's economic object-ives and capacities. As figure 2.3 demonstrates, economic considerations need to be taken into account at the beginning, the middle and the end of the review process. A defence force costs money. A country will not be secure if it develops a defence policy for which it cannot provide resources in an open, accountable and sustained manner. Thus, part of the guidance for the review process should include the financial framework for the security sector in gen-eral and the military sector in particular. Throughout the entire process, the finance minister and other key economic managers need to be informed and consulted. Options for force structures need to be developed within the context of the financial parameters and the risks associated with buying a certain level of defence (see the discussion in appendices 2B and 2C). The final decisions must reflect economic realities.

Review of the previous year's performance in the security sector

While strategic reviews occur infrequently in African countries, it is important that the outcome of the previous year's financial planning and implementation period be reviewed at the beginning of the annual budget cycle. The efficient and effective management of resources in any sector, including the security sector, requires that information on performance be fed back into the budgeting process, as shown in figure 2.1. While defining and measuring performance for the military sector is more difficult than for many other sectors, a focus on readiness or capability has been shown to be helpful for any discussion of the role, structure, performance and resource needs of the defence forces.

However performance is defined, the review of the previous year's budgetary performance will be facilitated by a well-functioning financial management information system (FMIS). The types of information that should be captured by the FMIS are shown in box 2.3.

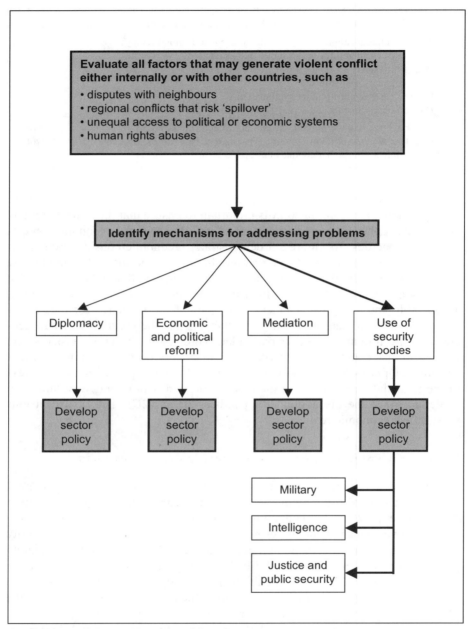

Figure 2.2. Security environment assessment

Source: Ball, N., 'Managing the defense budgeting process', Paper prepared for the conference on Security Sector Reform: Moving the Agenda Forward, Lancaster House, London, Mar. 2003, URL <http://www.eldis.org/static/DOC16685.htm>, figure 2, p. 9.

Determination of what is affordable in the security sector

Government policies, whether in the security or any other sector, must be affordable. Affordable policies require a sustainable macroeconomic balance, which is critical to the long-term economic health of a country. To attain a sustainable macroeconomic balance, governments must give a high priority to exercising discipline over public expenditure.

Overall financial discipline is also critical because a ceiling on funding that can be easily raised allows governments to avoid firm decisions on priorities. At the other end of the spectrum, without a solid floor to the budget, resources become unpredictable and operational performance suffers. It is therefore extremely important to have in place institutions that can achieve long-term macroeconomic stability, determine the overall resource envelope for public expenditure and enforce government decisions on expenditure priorities and levels.

Financial discipline is weak in many African countries. While the military is by no means the only body that exceeds the agreed limits of the financial allocation in the course of the financial year, it frequently enjoys a privileged position. Government officials, military officers, and heads of state and government have intervened in the resource-allocation process with flagrant disregard for established procedures and predetermined spending priorities. Military officers have presented the treasury with invoices for expenses incurred outside the budget framework. Defence ministers have refused to share the details of defence spending with finance ministers and parliament. The full financial implications of arms-acquisition decisions, including debt incurred for military purposes, are often not reflected in budgets, which may eventually destabilize financial policy. This sort of behaviour contributes to the widespread problem in Africa of military budgets that cannot fully fund the defence function.

As far as the failure to respect lower limits on expenditure, the armed forces are less likely to have their allocations reduced during the course of a financial year than other security forces, such as the police or gendarmerie. Nonetheless, it is important to develop clear rules for any reallocation of resources during the financial year—including those occasioned by shortfalls in revenue—and to apply them across the board.

Medium-term expenditure frameworks (MTEFs) are one mechanism that can help reduce incentives to evade financial discipline. MTEFs have become popular with the development assistance agencies because they can help: (*a*) improve the linkage between policies and objectives and between inputs and outputs; (*b*) make the budgetary process more transparent, especially by improving monitoring; (*c*) focus on outputs and service delivery; and (*d*) increase ownership by sectoral ministries.

As several of the case studies in this book demonstrate, it can be difficult for African governments to develop realistic multi-year plans, given the lack of predictability in government revenues and the reliance on a strong institutional base. However, something like an MTEF is important because the military

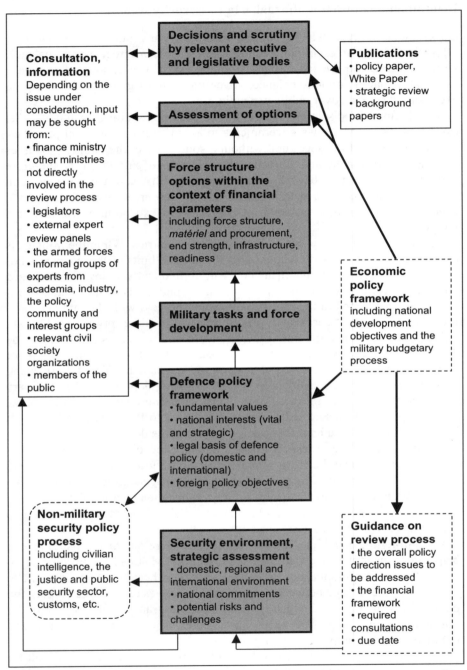

Figure 2.3. The process for conducting defence reviews and developing defence policy frameworks

sector needs a time frame for planning and budgeting of longer than one year. As the case of South Africa demonstrates, adopting a multi-year framework is not impossible in the African context.

A specific benefit to the military sector of adopting a medium-term framework is that it encourages full costing of defence programmes, particularly outlays on arms acquisition and major construction projects. Irrespective of the difficulty in implementing an MTEF, it is still important to have a full costing of the different components of the defence programme. Full costing will help make the case for a particular level of funding. It will also clarify the sustainability of individual programmes and it will help maximize efficiency and effectiveness in those cases where budget cuts become necessary. Full costing is therefore critically necessary for the operational effectiveness of the defence forces.

Allocation of resources for the military sector

Once the overall resource envelope is agreed, resources must be allocated according to priorities both within the military sector and between the military sector and other sectors. Sectoral strategies and information on performance (outputs and outcomes) are critical components of the allocation process. It is important that assessments of past performance be fed into planning for the coming year (or years in the case of multi-year budgeting cycles). The key financial and economic managers plus the legislature must have the capacity to be fully involved in the resource-allocation process and the process must include all relevant actors. The central budget office should assess the appropriateness of the defence ministry's budget. The armed forces must compete fully with other sectors for funding. The legislature must have adequate time to review and comment on the proposed defence budget before the beginning of the financial year. Methods of incorporating public input into the allocation process can help build public support for the final budget.

In many African countries the conditions required for the effective allocation of resources are not present. Institutional capacity for military budgeting is weak in both the executive and legislative branches of government. Financial management and oversight within the armed forces are correspondingly inadequate. The military sector holds a highly privileged position compared with other sectors when the overall resource envelope is divided among sectors. Arms acquisition requests include neither justification nor full costing. The legislature frequently receives even less information on the defence budget than on budgets for non-security activities, and input from the public on spending priorities is actively discouraged or ignored. Box 2.4 describes the challenges facing legislative oversight of the armed forces in West Africa.

While the military often enjoys a privileged position in terms of resource allocation, financial constraints have led some African governments to fail to provide the armed forces with adequate resources to carry out their assigned

---

Box 2.4. The legislative capacity to oversee the military sector in West Africa

In April 1999, the National Democratic Institute (Washington, DC) sponsored a seminar in Dakar aimed at encouraging a more active role for legislatures in overseeing the military sector in West African countries. The challenges facing West African legislatures were summarized in the seminar report in the following way.

Legislatures in the region face many challenges as they seek to exercise their oversight functions. These include: a dearth of technical expertise in military issues; lack of communication with their military counterparts; inefficient use of the committee system; and inexperience with drafting legislation on defense issues. Prior to the advent of political pluralism and competitive politics in the region, defense policy and legislation drafting were traditionally the domain of a strong executive branch that also monopolized interactions with the military. Legislatures, where they existed, simply 'rubber-stamped' initiatives forwarded to them by the executive.

Most of these challenges remain in 2005.

Source: National Democratic Institute, 'The role of the legislature in defense and national security issues', Report of a seminar held in Dakar, 19–22 Apr. 1999, URL <http://www.accessdemocracy.org/library/048_sn_roleoflegis.pdf>, p. 3.

---

missions. This not only places at risk the safe and secure environment that is necessary for both economic and political development, but also creates frustration and resentment within the armed forces. Participants in a workshop on democratic governance in the security sector held in Dakar in October 2001 argued that adequate transparency in the military sector is critical so that the serious underfunding that afflicts armed forces throughout the region is clear for all to see.[3] They suggested that there is both disdain for the military among civilians and a belief that military security is a comparatively low priority among those who control their countries' financial resources. In their view, this not only leads to inadequate defence budgets and thus inadequate external security but can also heighten internal insecurity through a threat of coups.

For reasons of both financial and political stability, it is important that the military sector competes on an equal footing with other sectors and that the process of allocating resources among sectors takes place in a transparent and accountable manner.

Efficient and effective use of resources in the military sector

Once a budget has been approved by the legislature and monies have been appropriated, the goal is to ensure the efficient use of resources to implement sectoral priorities. This requires careful monitoring and evaluation of operational performance both within the armed forces and by civil servants. As the case studies in this volume demonstrate, there are often significant deviations between the approved budget and actual expenditure in African countries.

---

[3] See Ball, N. and Fayemi, K. (eds), *Security Sector Governance in Africa: A Handbook* (Centre for Democracy and Development: Lagos, 2004), appendix 1.

Box 2.5. Causes of deviations between budgeted and actual expenditure

There are a number of factors that can explain why actual expenditure deviates from the levels approved at the beginning of the financial year in any sector. It is important to be explicit about which factors produce expenditure deviations in order to make the budgetary process more predictable. The reasons for deviations may vary over time. Some of the more common causes are:

- deviation in aggregate expenditure;
- reallocation of fund during budget implementation;
- policy changes during the year;
- an inability to implement policies, programmes and projects;
- donor funds not being available; and
- a lack of financial discipline.

Source: World Bank, 'Toolkit for assessing public expenditure institutional arrangements', Microsoft Excel spreadsheet, URL <http://www1.worldbank.org/publicsector/toolkitspe. htm>, sheet 'L2 Performance', heading 2.6.

Box 2.5 lists some of the reasons why such deviations may occur in any part of the public sector.

A well-functioning FMIS is critical if decision makers and public-sector managers are to obtain the financial data they require to control aggregate expenditure, prioritize among and within sectors, and operate in a cost-effective manner. Additionally, it is extremely important that irregularities identified in the course of monitoring are addressed, lest a climate of non-compliance be created or reinforced. Particular attention should be given to ensuring the transparency of procurement and acquisition processes and their conformity to good practices (see appendix 2A for a brief description of good procurement and acquisition practices).

Accounting standards in the military sector should not deviate from those in other sectors. Defence ministries should have their own internal audit offices and the government's auditor-general should audit defence accounts on a regular basis. The results of the auditor-general's audits should be reported to the legislature in a timely fashion and irregularities addressed expeditiously. Cash flow and expenditures should be monitored closely. Methods of verifying the number of individuals employed in the armed forces and the defence ministry and of linking salary and wage payments to individual employees facilitate this monitoring process. Expenditure tracking studies can help determine whether resources are being spent as intended. Value-for-money audits by the auditor-general or other oversight bodies will help determine if resources are being spent efficiently. As in any other sector, the results of monitoring and evaluation work need to be fed back into strategic planning. Some of the specific issues that need particular attention in terms of strengthening the efficiency of resource use in the military sector are elaborated in box 2.6.

The case studies in this volume demonstrate that the capacity for financial management in the military sector is weak in Africa. In part this is because

Box 2.6. Components of the efficient use of resources

In order to strengthen the efficient use of financial resources in the military sector, it is important to give attention to the following four factors. These factors are not unique to the military sector. They are, however, of particular importance in that sector.

Sustainability

If the defence plan and programmes are not sustainable over time, this will lead to capabilities not being maintainable and becoming ineffective. Sustainability will only be achieved if government commits itself to the approved defence plan, all planning is done on the basis of a full life-cycle costing and the defence budget is spent in the most efficient manner possible. Care must also be taken in planning to accurately evaluate the effect of currency fluctuations on the life-cycle cost of capital equipment.

Funding of operations

It is not possible or desirable to budget for the execution of military operations other than routine operations that can be foreseen and accurately planned well ahead of time. Most military operations come at short notice and during a financial year for which the budget has been developed and approved many months previously. Examples of short-notice operations are peace-support missions, major disaster relief missions and even limited war. Trying to budget for the unforeseeable will result in a misappropriation of funds. The only way to handle this problem is through a central contingency fund managed by the finance ministry. For large-scale contingencies that exceed the capacity of such a contingency fund, the government will have to revise the total budget with regard to both departmental allocations and income.

Tooth-to-tail ratios

All possible effort must be made to ensure the optimal tooth-to-tail ratio of the defence force and the defence ministry; that is, to increase the proportion of deployable soldiers and reduce the number of soldiers undertaking staff work. Supporting structures are often bloated at the cost of operational capabilities. Determination of the size and capacity of support structures can only be done once the force design has been determined. Modern 'business process re-engineering' techniques can assist in the solution of this problem but will only be effective if top management is committed to this cause and ruthless in its application.

Direct client–supplier relationships

In many defence forces certain organizations and structures exist for historic reasons only. The client (e.g., a combat service) is forced by organizational culture or other interests to make use of the services of such an organization and is not allowed to shop around. This is bad practice and entrenches inefficiency. Accordingly, clients for services should be allowed freedom of choice and freedom to establish direct client–supplier relationships.

Other potential solutions for the improvement of efficiency are indicated in appendix 2C. These include: (*a*) outsourcing and public–private partnerships; (*b*) improved coordination between services; (*c*) improved management information through the use of better information technology; (*d*) use of reserves; (*e*) the better use of civilians in defence ministries; and (*f*) improved management and leadership through education, training and development. Of these, the improvement of management information through the use of better information technology might be the most crucial aspect of the improvement of efficiency in defence organizations.

overall financial management capacity is weak. At the same time, different standards are frequently applied to the military sector. The degree of transparency and accountability is often considerably lower in the military sector than in the government as a whole. Efforts are rarely made to identify deviations between approved and actual resource use; where such deviations are identified, problems are rarely corrected. If the defence forces are to be capable of fulfilling their mandated duties in a professional manner, however, it is important to use resources allocated to the military sector as effectively and efficiently as possible.

IV. Defence planning, programming and budgeting

No meaningful programming or budgeting can be done without the existence of a long-term or strategic defence plan, just as no meaningful plan can exist in the absence of a guiding policy. The development of both policies and plans in the military sector as part of the government-wide and sectoral budgetary processes was outlined above. This section discusses the planning and programming process in more detail and then links it back to the budgetary process.

The defence plan

Essentially, the defence plan is the document that specifies the measurable outputs that the military sector will produce in pursuit of the government's objectives, measured against the identified financial allocation within the medium-term expenditure framework of three to five years. The defence plan incorporates the strategic plan, the defence programmes and the budget. The plan should also cover longer periods (up to 30 years) for matters such as capital acquisition, infrastructure and personnel planning. The key elements of the defence plan are summarized in box 2.7.

The nature of the protective functions of government—which include intelligence, policing, justice and correctional services (or prisons) as well as defence—means that planning is always contingent. Requirements are driven by unpredictable factors such as internal crime levels and external instability. In the case of defence, planning must be done for a very uncertain future environment. This is complicated by the long period required to build and prepare defence capabilities, which implies the maintenance of certain capacities purely for possible future eventualities (i.e., defence contingencies).

The defence plan provides the framework for the performance agreement between the defence minister, the political leader of the ministry, and the permanent secretary, who heads the ministry and is its chief accounting officer. The performance agreement should be a written document that clearly specifies the outputs required from the ministry, the associated resource allocations and the performance measurements that will be employed. This serves as the con-

---

Box 2.7. Key elements of the defence plan

The defence plan, which should be a stable but flexible document over time, should include the following elements:

  • the strategic profile of the defence force, consisting of its mission, vision, critical success factors and value system;
  • the analysis and critical assumptions underlying the strategic plan;
  • a clear statement of the required defence capabilities (i.e., the force design and state of readiness) of the armed forces;
  • a clear statement of the required structure of the support force;
  • the supportive capital acquisition plan, the facilities plan and the personnel plan;
  • the administrative outputs required for the management of the defence function, including the provision of defence policy, strategy, plans, programmes and budgets; and
  • the identified short- to medium-term tasks of the armed forces that will require operational force employment.

---

tract between the minister and the permanent secretary. It must of necessity be a product of negotiation between these two individuals.

There are three primary outputs that must be specified in the defence plan.

1. *Defence administration.* This covers the top-level administrative outputs required for the management of the defence function. It includes the provision of defence policy, strategy, plans, programmes and budgets.

2. *Defence commitments.* These are the identified short- to medium-term operational force-employment tasks and objectives.

3. *Defence capabilities.* These include the force design, with the required readiness states as well as the supporting force structure. Defence capabilities are the main cost-drivers of defence.

The determination of the first two outputs is relatively simple, being based mostly on current and short- to medium-term future requirements. The determination of defence capabilities is, however, much more complex and long-term in nature.

Defence administration

Defence administration outputs are determined by an analysis of the legislative, policy and management framework within which the military must function. This analysis will be strongly influenced by the demands and requirements of government, specifically those emanating from the defence ministry and other national ministries such as the finance ministry and the public service and administration ministry. This programming function will identify specific objectives to be reached within a one- to three-year timescale. Examples of such objectives are listed in box 2.8.

These objectives are mostly determined, managed and coordinated by the policy and planning, finance and other staff divisions at the defence ministry or

---

Box 2.8. Examples of defence administration objectives

• Revise the defence act to be in line with the constitution for presentation to parliament by (date).
• Do a complete defence review for presentation to parliament by (date).
• Develop an updated personnel policy for the defence force for presentation to the defence minister by (date).
• Develop the defence plan for financial years (X) to (Y) for presentation to the defence minister by (date).
• Develop the defence budget for financial years (X) to (Y) for presentation to the finance ministry by (date).

---

defence headquarters. The resources allocated to these activities are relatively small and are mostly associated with the personnel costs of the associated staff divisions, administrative costs and the costs for professional services.

Defence commitments

Short- to medium-term defence commitments or operational outputs are determined through a military operational assessment. This process will rest heavily on the intelligence forecasts of the internal and external security environment for the short to medium term. It will also be strongly influenced by the objectives of the foreign affairs ministry and the internal safety and security ministry. This programming function will identify specific objectives to be reached within a one- to three-year timescale. Some examples of such objectives are given in box 2.9.

These activities are mostly determined and managed by the joint operations division at defence headquarters. The resources allocated to these activities are dependent on their scale, duration and intensity. These should include all employment costs, such as increased maintenance, fuel, ammunition, rations and operational allowances among others.

Defence capabilities

The determination of defence capabilities is discussed in detail in appendices 2B and 2C. The establishment, development and maintenance of defence capabilities constitute the main cost element of defence. The determination of the force design and structure is thus the prime area of debate between defence planners and political decision makers, including those responsible for financial management. In the defence plan the determined force design and the structure of the defence force must be clearly stated in terms of quantity (number of units) and quality (readiness states and preparedness). The development and maintenance of this force design and structure constitute a specific objective for the ministry. The staff work for the determination of this objective is primarily undertaken and coordinated by the policy and planning and joint operations divisions at the defence ministry or defence headquarters.

Box 2.9. Examples of defence commitments objectives

• Provide a force of battalion strength with tactical air transport and medical support to the peace mission in (X) from (date) to (date).
  • Support the police in crime prevention in (area) from (date) to (date).
  • Conduct border control operations in (area) in support of the police from (date) to (date).
  • Conduct maritime patrols to monitor infringements of territorial waters in (area) from (date) to (date).

The defence programmes

As defence ministries and forces are large organizations, the management of the top-level objectives is largely delegated to subordinates at the second level of management. These are typically service chiefs and chiefs of staff divisions at the ministry or defence headquarters. Each of these delegated managers will be responsible for a specific defence programme. These defence programmes essentially convert the strategic defence plan into a format where clear responsibility and accountability of the programme managers—who are also referred to as the principal budget holders—are established. Typical defence programmes are shown in box 2.10 and are discussed below.

Defence administration programme

The defence administration programme will identify those activities that are essential for the professional, efficient, transparent and accountable management of the defence function and will be coordinated at defence headquarters by the chief of staff responsible for the integrated functioning of all headquarters staff divisions. This programme should include, among others, sub-programmes for political direction (in the office of the defence minister), day-to-day running of the ministry (in the office of the permanent secretary), policy development, corporate departmental planning, strategic intelligence, defence foreign relations, financial management, corporate communication (public relations and internal communication), and internal auditing and inspection.

Objectives for this programme are derived from the top-level administration objectives in one of three ways. First, a top-level objective can be directly delegated to a programme manager at the second level. For example, the objective to 'develop the defence budget for financial years (X) to (Y) for presentation to the finance ministry by (date)' can be delegated to the chief of staff for finance.

Second, a top-level objective may lead to secondary objectives that can be divided among two or more programme managers at the second level while overall responsibility is maintained by the permanent secretary. For example, the objective to 'do a complete defence review for presentation to parliament by (date)' can be subdivided and delegated to the chief of staff for intelligence ('do a strategic intelligence assessment'), the chief of staff for policy and planning

---

Box 2.10. Examples of typical defence programmes

Programme	*Programme manager (principal budget holder)*
Defence administration programme	Chief of staff for policy, planning and finance
Force-employment programme	Chief of staff for joint operations
Force-provision programme (army)	Chief of staff for the army
Force-provision programme (air force)	Chief of staff for the air force
Force-provision programme (navy)	Chief of staff for the navy
Joint force-support programme	Chief of staff for joint support

---

('do a strategic defence assessment') and the chief of staff for joint operations ('do an operational assessment of short- to medium-term defence commitments').

Third, the permanent secretary should determine his or her own developmental objectives to ensure the continued improvement of the performance of the ministry. These could include objectives to improve the management processes of the ministry (delegated to the chief of staff for policy and planning), to improve information technology systems (delegated to the chief of staff for joint support), and to improve the command and leadership practices of the ministry (delegated to the chief of staff for joint support).

Force-employment programme

The force-employment programme will derive its objectives directly from the top-level defence commitments in the plan and will be coordinated at defence headquarters by the chief of staff for joint operations. This programme should also include sub-programmes for operational intelligence and counter-intelligence, joint force preparation, and command and control. Objectives for these sub-programmes are developed by the chief of staff for joint operations.

Other than those objectives derived directly from defence commitments in the top-level plan, typical force-employment objectives may include objectives to develop command-and-control skills through war gaming and exercises, objectives to prepare and exercise joint formations through military exercises, and objectives to ensure the intelligence for and security of operations.

The force-provision programmes

The force-provision programmes are the domain of the chiefs of the combat services (the army, the air force and the navy), who are responsible for the establishment, development and maintenance of combat-ready forces as agreed in the approved force design. These programmes derive their objectives directly from the approved force design and structure and will include sub-programmes for each of the capability areas as defined in the approved force design as well as for service-specific training and force preparation. Examples of these capability areas are: infantry, armour, artillery, anti-aircraft, engineering,

---

Box 2.11. Examples of typical joint force-support objectives

• Manage and execute the capital acquisition plan in support of the combat services.
• Manage and execute the departmental facilities plan.
• Provide and manage a personnel administration system for the department.
• Provide military health services in support of the combat services and defence commitments.

---

special forces, fighter aircraft, air reconnaissance, helicopters, air transport, submarines, surface combat ships and sea mine-warfare vessels.

Joint force-support programme

The joint force-support programme will identify those joint activities that are essential for the support of the defence administration, the force-employment programmes and, most importantly, the force-provision programmes of the services. The joint force-support programme will be coordinated at defence headquarters by the chief of staff responsible for the coordination of the supporting functions.

Most of the objectives for this programme will be derived through service agreements between the chief of staff for joint support and the other programme managers. This implies that, as certain functions can be executed more efficiently in a centralized manner, such functions should be identified and contracted to joint support by the service chiefs and other divisional chiefs by means of service agreements specifying the level and the cost of services required. This programme should include sub-programmes for personnel management, logistic services, including acquisition and procurement, and military health services. Some typical joint force-support objectives are shown in box 2.11.

Resource allocation to the defence programmes

The defence programmes provide the basis for performance agreements between the permanent secretary and the chiefs of staff of the combat services and headquarters staff divisions.

Performance agreements basically consist of the objectives to be achieved along with the time frame, the expected standards, the associated level of resource allocation and the required delegations of powers. In addition, these programmes include the service agreements negotiated directly between programme managers. These service agreements also consist of the objectives to be achieved with the time frame, the expected standards, the associated level of resource allocation and, where applicable, the required delegations of powers. As such, these programmes are the product of negotiations between the permanent secretary and subordinate chiefs as well as directly between programme managers.

This process of negotiation is iterative in that each objective must be evaluated for cost and then be either agreed or changed, as required. A change could be an increase in resources or a downscaling of an objective. In order to ensure efficiency, the permanent secretary (and other clients) must demand that programme managers accurately determine the cost of achieving set objectives and provide proof that all efficiency improvements have been considered. The cost of all activities should be regularly compared against a benchmark. The permanent secretary should consider increasing resources or downscaling the requirement only when convinced that the objective is being pursued in the most efficient way possible.

The defence programmes, in the final instance, provide the starting point for the detailed development of the defence budget down to unit level.

The budget

The strategic defence plan specifies the required outputs of the military sector at the highest level as well as the broad level of resource allocation envisaged over an extended period. The defence programmes, in turn, specify outputs in the form of objectives at the next lower level as well as planned allocations to the programme managers for producing these outputs. These must now be converted into business plans where specific activities for reaching these objectives are specified and accurately costed. These business plans are made at unit level (including directorates or sections at defence headquarters) and are in turn the basis for the performance agreements between the programme managers and unit commanders or section chiefs as well as for directly negotiated service agreements. The same considerations raised in the above discussion of performance and service agreements at the next higher level are valid for these agreements.

These business plans are written annually for the next financial year as well as for the subsequent years covered by the MTEF. The defence budget is the total of the business plans expressed in financial terms. It is the ministry's income and spending plan for a set period of time. It is a quantitative expression of the proposed plan of action for the reaching of defence objectives for that time period.

Budgeting is done at unit level, where all inputs that are required to execute the delegated activities must be accurately determined and costed. These input costs (budget items) will include: (a) personnel expenditure, such as salaries, allowances, bonuses and gratuities; (b) administrative expenses, such as subsistence and travel, transport, membership fees and registration, study expenses, and communications; (c) stores, including ammunition and explosives, spares and components for normal maintenance, construction and building material, office supplies, fuel and clothing, among many others; (d) equipment, such as vehicles, weapons, machinery and furniture; (e) rental of land and buildings;

Table 2.1. The typical annual budget cycle

Time period	Activity
Ongoing	Strategic planning and development of the defence plan (negotiations between the defence minister on behalf of the government and the permanent secretary, supported by strategic planners)
Month 1	Development of defence programmes (negotiations between the permanent secretary and programme managers and the drawing up of draft top-level performance agreements as well as direct client–supplier negotiations between programme managers for the determination of service agreements)
Months 2 to 4	Preparation of business plans (development of draft lower-level performance and service agreements through negotiation and the full costing from zero of all activities)
Month 5	Submission of draft business plans to programme managers for checking, evaluation and consolidation into a single budget for each programme; necessary amendments negotiated and agreed
Months 6 and 7	Consolidated budgets for each programme submitted to the ministerial budgeting committee (chaired by the ministry's permanent secretary) for evaluation, approval and consolidation of a single ministerial budget; necessary amendments identified, negotiated and agreed; on completion, the budget, signed by the minister and the permanent secretary, submitted to the finance ministry
Month 8	The government's medium-term expenditure committee evaluates ministerial budgets against government guidelines, priorities and available funds; required amendments are identified against governmental priorities
Month 9	The finance ministry provides final guidelines on the expected allocation to the defence ministry; the defence ministry amends plan, programmes and budget and prepares the defence minister's submission of the defence budget vote to parliament; the performance and service agreements are finalized
Month 10	The finance minister submits the national budget to parliament; parliament approves budget.
Ongoing	Expenditure according to budget; regular expenditure control exercised by the permanent secretary

and (*f*) professional and specialist services, such as consultation, outsourced services, and research and development.

Summary

It should be clear that the defence planning, programming and budgeting process is an iterative process involving negotiation between all levels of defence management. Planning is largely top-down, based on an analysis of requirements and environmental factors as well as an estimate of available resources.

As it moves down the organization, through performance agreements between superiors and their subordinates, more and more accurate costing is done until, at unit level, accurate zero-base budgeting can be done. These unit budgets, in turn, are added from the bottom up to constitute the total defence budget. This obviously entails many iterations to 'make ends meet resources'. The typical annual budget cycle is described in table 2.1.

V. Conclusions

The planning, programming and budgeting process is the central feature of defence management for providing resources to the defence force to ensure the defence and protection of the state, of its territorial integrity and of its people in alignment with national security and defence policy. The process rests on the rationale that defence budgets should be the result of good short-, medium- and long-term plans that are based on open and clear defence and national security policy. All plans, programmes and budgets should be driven by clearly defined and agreed outputs.

The defence planning, programming and budgeting process should clearly be aligned and integrated with the national public expenditure management process and, therefore, the principles applied to defence management should not differ markedly from those applicable to other activities of government.

The quality of these processes is crucial for ensuring national defence and security while not making the cost of defence too high relative to other social and developmental priorities. Inefficiency and imprudent use of scarce resources will undermine security and the broader national interest.

In the final instance, the process of defence planning, programming and budgeting must be based on modern management practices, principles and procedures and on accurate research, analysis and strategic assumptions. It must have a long-term focus and be the product of an inclusive process. It must be innovative and ensure permanent efficiency improvements in order to make defence affordable. While the nature of planning, programming and budgeting systems may vary widely internationally, the basic processes, techniques and principles advocated in this chapter should assist in ensuring the effectiveness and efficiency of defence as well as greater transparency and accountability in the allocation and management of defence resources.

Appendix 2A. Good practice in military procurement and acquisition

There should be little difference between public expenditure management in general and public expenditure management in the military sector. Defence procurement and acquisition should accordingly be carried out according to the same principles that guide public sector procurement in non-military areas: fairness, impartiality, transparency, cost-effectiveness and efficiency, and openness to competition.[1] In addition, it is essential that there be high-level consultation and evaluation of all major projects for all forms of public sector procurement and acquisition. Box 2A.1 presents a generic procurement process, applicable to all sectors of government.

At the same time, with the exception of procurement of works and commodities (such as construction, clothing, food, fuel, office equipment, general vehicles and consultancy services), defence procurement does exhibit some distinctive characteristics: (*a*) the relative importance of cost in determining which bid is accepted; (*b*) the confidentiality associated with national security considerations; (*c*) the time frame for major weapons procurement; (*d*) the complexity of defence procurement; and (*e*) the existence of international arms control treaty regimes and national legislation governing arms procurement. These distinctive characteristics are deviations in scale rather than principle. For example, as explained in chapter 2, adequate levels of confidentiality can be maintained without violating basic public expenditure management principles. There certainly should be scepticism about any claims that procurement of relatively standard works, services and commodities for the military should be subject to different rules.

These five distinctive characteristics are considered below.

Cost considerations in bidding

While standard procurement practice in non-military sectors is giving increasing emphasis to value for money, defence analysts argue that factors other than cost are more frequently the major factors in accepting a bid for weapon procurement projects in the military sector. They point out, however, that national legislation can play an important role in regulating the part that cost plays in weapon procurement processes in the military sector. In South Africa, for example, the 1998 Defence Review and the 1999 White Paper on defence-related industries spell out which technologies are considered 'strategically essential capabilities' and thus exempt from lowest-cost considerations.[2] The South African Parliament has approved both policy documents.

---

[1] Some countries distinguish between the 'procurement' of commercial goods and services and the 'acquisition' of armaments. Others use the term 'procurement' for both commercial goods and services and weapons or weapon systems. This appendix will follow the latter practice.

[2] South African Department of Defence, 'Defence in a democracy: South African Defence Review 1998', Pretoria, 1998, URL <http://www.mil.za/Articles&Papers/Frame/Frame.htm>; and South African

Confidentiality

Transparency in defence procurement must be limited by national security interests. Confidentiality clauses will be required in the arms procurement process. This, too, can be regulated by national legislation. The South African Defence Review lists a number of reasons for confidentiality in defence procurement. These include: the protection of third-party commercial information, the national security of South Africa, prevention of harm to South Africa's ability to conduct international relations, and the protection of South Africa's economic interests and the commercial activities of government bodies.[3]

The time frame for major weapons procurement

From inception to final acceptance of the product, procurement of major weapon systems may take as long as 15 years. Some flexibility needs to be built into the procurement process to take account of contingencies such as fluctuations in currency exchange rates. This long time frame also makes it essential that quality control takes place throughout the procurement process, rather than when the product is ready for delivery. Arms procurement projects should also take into account full life-cycle costs and support for the acquired systems. The long time frame also makes it essential to attempt to forecast spending farther into the future than in non-defence sectors. The UK, for example, has a 10-year 'long-term costing' system for defence.[4]

The complexity of arms procurement

Because of the complexity of arms procurement, sound management of the procurement process requires interdisciplinary project teams. Such teams should have expertise on engineering, resource management, contracting, quality assurance and design assurance.

In addition, because of the particular complexity of the procurement of major weapon systems, which can involve a substantial number of subcontractors, opportunities for corruption are great. These projects therefore require the highest level of management and scrutiny by governmental accountability mechanisms. For example, South Africa has three levels of approval for major arms procurement projects within its Department of Defence. For major projects, parliamentary approval may also be required.

International arms control treaty regimes and national legislation governing arms procurement

Procurement in the military sector is distinct from general government procurement in being subject to international treaties and specific national legislation. Some defence

National Conventional Arms Control Committee, 'White Paper on the South African defence related industries', Pretoria, Dec. 1999, URL <http://www.info.gov.za/documents/whitepapers/>.

[3] South African Department of Defence (note 2), paragraph 68.

[4] See, e.g., British Army, *Design for Military Operations: The British Military Doctrine* (Ministry of Defence: London, 1996), URL <http://www.army.mod.uk/doctrine/branches/doc.htm>, pp. 22–23.

Box 2A.1. A generic procurement process

A generic procurement process involves:

- a clear definition of the requirement;
- clear technical quality specifications and standards;
- an open request for proposals and tenders;
- tender adjudication according to set criteria;
- selection of a preferred bidder;
- drawing up of a contract;
- placing the contract or order;
- monitoring progress;
- reception of goods;
- quality assurance checks on goods received;
- acceptance of goods or rejection of goods not up to specifications;
- payment;
- distribution of goods.

---

budgeting specialists suggest that the oversight mechanisms associated with this national and international regulation increase transparency.

Appendix 2B. Strategic defence planning

Too often the defence debate is dominated by short-term perceptions of security, based on snapshot views of the world and the cost of defence. The argument is 'there is no threat, so why spend?'. As noted in chapter 2, strategic situations change rapidly, but the building of defence capabilities and expertise takes time. All strategic defence planning must therefore be done with a long-term view. To do so it is necessary to understand the major variables in defence planning: the ends, ways and means of defence. Government and defence planners share the responsibility for the determination of these ends, ways and means.

Figure 2B.1 presents these variables schematically. The scales show that what government requires from defence (the ends), taking into consideration the approved defence posture (the ways), must be balanced by defence capabilities (the means) and that this requires a determined amount of resources. The scales can be brought into balance by either reducing ends, adapting the defence posture (moving the pivot to the left) or increasing means and thus resources. If there is an imbalance or inconsistency between ends, ways and means, this will result in a strategic gap between what needs to be done and what can be done. This strategic gap must be managed as a risk by government. These three variables are discussed below.

The ends of defence

Defence ends are the required defence outputs in support of the government's goals and objectives, which include peace, security, stability and public safety. The primary responsibility for determining the ends of defence rests with the government (the parliament and cabinet).

Examples of defence outputs (ends) are: (*a*) provision of deterrence through the existence of mission-ready forces; (*b*) the meeting of international obligations such as search-and-rescue and disaster relief; (*c*) participation in peace missions; (*d*) peacetime border control and protection against non-military threats; (*e*) support to the police; and (*f*) support to civil authorities.

Ways of defence

The ways of defence are military strategic and operational concepts and are influenced by the government's national security and foreign policy as well as its strategic defence posture. The responsibility for determining the ways of defence is a dual responsibility of the government and the military, with the military primarily responsible for providing expert advice to the government.

Examples of strategic and operational defence postures (ways) are: (*a*) non-offensive defence or forward mobile defence postures; (*b*) a strategic defensive or offensive posture; (*c*) defence through regional defence cooperation and alliances or through self-defence.

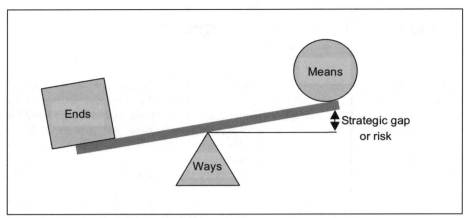

Figure 2B.1. Defence variables: the ends, ways and means of defence

Means of defence

The means of defence are essentially the operational capabilities of the defence force, as expressed in the force design. The determination of the force design is primarily the responsibility of defence planners and must be in alignment with the ends and ways as prescribed by policy.

Examples of force design elements are: infantry units, armour units, artillery units, naval surface combatants, naval sub-surface combatants, air force fighter squadrons, air force transport squadrons, air force helicopter squadrons, operational medical units and military attachés.

These defence means are the real cost-drivers of defence. The creation, maintenance and development of these capabilities are the primary consumers of defence resources.

Appendix 2C. A practical model for the determination of optimal defence capabilities

The determination of optimal defence capabilities to be developed and maintained,[1] along with the associated states of readiness, is the major challenge to the defence planner. This is because defence planning is premised on an uncertain future, is severely constrained by the availability of resources, will always be contested by sectional interests within the defence establishment and is extremely difficult to justify to a populace concerned with more immediate social and personal security issues. Furthermore, the potential consequences of being wrong are enormous in their implications for the future security and well-being of the state.

The development and maintenance of defence capabilities are also the main cost-drivers of defence. The solution of the defence capabilities equation, therefore, requires the major effort in the defence planning process. It is also the prime area of debate between the defence planner and political decision makers. Political decision makers cannot be expected to simply decide on the ends and ways of defence without major inputs regarding the implications of their decisions, especially the implications for the security of the state and the financial implications.

This poses the challenge to the defence planner of finding a rationale for the determination of defence capability requirements that will elicit the understanding and support of political decision makers and civil society. Obviously, such a rationale must be based on the need for efficiency in defence expenditure.

Defence value

If it is accepted that the primary objective of the defence force is to defend and protect the state, its territorial integrity and its people through the provision of contingency-ready military forces and that this is to be done within given financial restrictions, then, as stated in chapter 2, the most efficient solution must be sought. Efficiency implies the optimal output for any given input; that is, the best value for money. This raises the question of how to determine defence value. As defence is concerned with possible future events or threats (defence contingencies), each of which carries an implied risk to the state, *defence value is proportional to risk reduction*. Each defence contingency carries with it an associated risk. If the value of the relative risk of such contingencies can be determined, then this will allow for the development of a system for determining relative defence value.

---

[1] The word optimal in this context is intended to mean the greatest defence output for any given input or, simply put, the best defence value for money.

Box 2C.1. Optimizing force designs

Step 1. Determine the list of possible defence contingencies.

Step 2. Determine the defence value (risk reduction) of each contingency through probability and impact calculations.

Step 3. Determine the best operational concepts and the associated required mini-force design for each contingency.

Step 4. Determine the full sustainable cost for each mini-force design.

Step 5. Draw up a table or graph of all contingencies, indicating the defence value and associated cost for each.

Step 6. Evaluate the design and engage with decision makers.

Defence contingencies

The first step in the defence planning process is the determination of defence contingencies. This entails describing in some detail the possible future events that the defence force might have to deal with. In this process there are no limits and the more contingencies that are accurately described the better. This list should not be restricted to probable events, as these will be determined in the next step; instead, it should contain as many possible defence contingencies as can be imagined. Examples include: (*a*) invasion of the national territory by a foreign power; (*b*) punitive military action against the state; (*c*) coercive military action against the state; (*d*) disruption of national maritime lines of communication and trade; (*e*) military naval, air and land blockades; (*f*) border violations and cross-border crime; (*g*) natural and other disasters that defeat the means of civil society; and (*h*) peace missions in alignment with international and regional obligations.

Risk

Defence primarily concerns possible future events (defence contingencies) and the preparation to successfully counter them when they occur. For each such contingency a statistical probability of occurrence can be determined as well as the potential impact that the occurrence of such a contingency might have on the country. Obviously, contingencies of high probability and major impact carry more risk to the state than contingencies of low probability and minor impact: *risk is proportional to probability and impact*. High-risk contingencies have a high probability of occurrence and the potential for grave impact and vice versa.

The determination of probability

The determination of probability is the most difficult exercise in defence planning, as it is the most subjective and is somewhat like crystal ball gazing. It cannot be an exact science as it deals with an uncertain and ever-changing future. However, without considering probability it is extremely difficult to plan for the future and to determine priorities for defence capabilities to be maintained and developed. This appendix does not provide an exact formula for determining probability, but it does give guidance regarding some factors to be considered. In 'real life' the determination of the probability of occurrence of a contingency is mostly a task of the intelligence community, consisting of national intelligence, foreign affairs, and military intelligence and strategists. There are three guides to the determination of probability.

1. Evaluate the historic frequency of occurrence (both internationally and nationally) over a very long period.

2. Use a wide spread of probability over a range that is nearer 0.001 to 1 than 0.1 to 1. This ensures greater discrimination in the calculation of probability. As an example, the probability of an invasion could be nearer 0.001 than 0.1.

3. Since absolute probability is all but impossible to calculate, effort should concentrate on the determination of relative probabilities between various contingencies. The involvement of politicians, academics and civil society organizations in this exercise will greatly enhance the quality of the resulting product.

The determination of impact

The determination of impact is less subjective that that of probability. Nonetheless, this is not an easy exercise and the involvement of civil society and, in particular, academics in this endeavour is strongly recommended. The potential impact of a contingency that cannot be successfully countered can be calculated using the following parameters: (*a*) the potential loss of life; (*b*) the potential loss of infrastructure; (*c*) the potential loss of economic production and trade; (*d*) the relative loss of sovereignty; (*e*) the relative loss of national image and prestige; (*f*) the relative loss of international confidence; and (*g*) the effect on national morale.

Once the list of contingencies and their relative risk value (probability and impact) have been determined, the value part of the 'value for money' formula has been established. What remains to be done is to calculate the cost of dealing with these potential contingencies. This is another complex exercise.

Concepts of operations and force design

For each of the defined contingencies, the best operational concept to counter such an eventuality and the corresponding required capabilities (the 'mini-force design') must be determined. War gaming or simulation processes are the best tools for doing this. Once this has been done, each mini-force design must be costed accurately. This is a major exercise that requires the full and honest participation of the combat services and units down to the lowest level as well as of financial experts. If this is not accurately done, the basis for decision making is seriously undermined.

Costing

Each element of the mini-force design must be fully costed over its life cycle in order to be able to determine cost/benefit ratios for optimization. This cost consists of: (*a*) the annual personnel cost, (*b*) the annual operating cost and (*c*) the annualized capital cost.

The annual personnel cost is the full cost of all personnel-related expenses such as salaries, allowances, bonuses and gratuities. The annual operating cost is the full cost of the normal day-to-day running of the unit. This includes administrative expenses,

Table 2C.1. Selected practical challenges facing defence planning processes

Challenge	Potential solution
Accurate costing data	
The answers obtained will be accurate only if based on reliable costing data for each capability area for all personnel, operating and life-cycle capital costs.	This is a large, complex task and requires ongoing improvement and updating. The use of auditors within the defence ministry and from outside will enhance the accuracy of answers. The ultimate solution requires modern information technology systems.
Tooth-to-tail ratios	
The logic of the process provides a model for the optimization of the 'sharp end', or 'teeth', of the force. The process does not address the support structures, or 'tail', of the organization.	Determination of support structures can only be done once the force design has been determined. Modern business process re-engineering techniques can assist in the solution of this problem.
Service versus corporate interests	
One of the main challenges to the determination of real defence requirements remains inter-service rivalry. This leads to trade-offs and sub-optimal solutions.	This challenge requires dynamic leadership at the permanent secretary level and the use of professional staff in the joint planning and operations divisions. The use of modelling, simulation and war gaming will also help to alleviate this problem.
Efficiency improvements	
Money spent on defence must be spent in the most efficient and economical way possible. This means that innovative solutions must be found to reduce the cost of defence.	Some potential solutions for the improvement of efficiency are: (*a*) outsourcing and public–private partnerships; (*b*) improved coordination of services; (*c*) improved management of information through the use of better information technology; (*d*) use of reserves; (*e*) better use of civilians in defence ministries; (*f*) improved management and leadership through education, training and development.

transport, subsistence and travel, provisioning, day-to-day maintenance, fuel, and professional and specialist services. The annualized capital cost is calculated by adding the full procurement cost and the mid-life upgrade cost of capital equipment and dividing it by the expected number of years of operational life of the equipment.

The emphasis on full life-cycle cost is to ensure sustainability of the end result. If this factor is ignored, decisions will be taken that will prove to be unaffordable in the future. This is the cause of many militaries in the developing world having large inventories of unserviceable, unsupportable and unusable equipment.

Optimizing

Once the list of contingencies, the defence value calculations (relative risk-reduction values) and the cost of the elements of the force design are available, calculation of the best value for money can be done. The process for determining optimized force designs is shown in box 2C.1.

It must be emphasized that this process will not provide precise, scientifically accurate answers, but it will provide insight into the problems of defence planning and a good basis for discussion with decision makers. It removes the subjectivity of arguments by the individual combat services that their requirements be prioritized. It provides a menu for decision making in which the services that can be ordered can be compared against cost and from which the implications of decisions can be seen. It should be emphasized that the more inclusive the participation in this process is (by political decision makers, other government departments, academics and civil society organizations together with defence experts), the better and more credible the results will be.

Force design and supportive planning

The above process must culminate in the approval by government of the force design of the armed forces. This also implies a clear commitment by the government to provide funds to the defence ministry for the development, preparation and maintenance of such forces. Without this, no meaningful long-term planning or medium-term programming and budgeting can be done. The force design, together with the required support structures, will form the basis for the development of other long-term plans such as a capital acquisition plan, a facilities or infrastructure plan and the personnel plan. These are long-term plans providing for the procurement of weapon systems, facilities and personnel and the development, preparation, maintenance and eventual disposal of such assets. All of these plans should have a long-term horizon commensurate with the life cycles of these assets.

There are, of course, many practical challenges to this planning process. The most prominent of these are listed in table 2C.1.

3. Ethiopia

Said Adejumobi and Mesfin Binega

I. Introduction and background

Ethiopia is the only country in Africa that did not suffer colonial domination, apart from a brief period of Italian occupation (1936–41). It has a long history of self-rule: the country's emperors were repeatedly successful in repulsing foreign invaders and zealously preserved the country's independence. Indeed, Ethiopia established military culture in Africa: Emperor Haile Selassie laid the foundation for a modern standing army in Ethiopia in the run-up to the Italo-Ethiopian War in 1935–36. By 1969 Ethiopia had four army divisions with combat support services and logistical support units. Between 1974 and 1990, with the assistance of the Soviet Union, the Dirgue regime built a formidable armed force, nearly half a million strong.

The seemingly unending instability in the country's political life has undoubtedly affected how public services are ordered and how public finances are structured and managed. This includes the financing of state institutions such as the military. The different ideological orientations of the governments, from the monarchical regime of Emperor Haile Selassie via the Marxist-Leninist government of Mengistu Haile Miriam and the Dirgue to the current capitalist neo-liberal ideology of Meles Zenawi, suggests that there have been different conceptions of the military—its role, mission, size and strategic importance to the state. The size of the country's military budget has been determined by these changes in ideology as much as by the perceived external and internal threats.

This chapter analyses the nature of the budgetary process for the armed forces in Ethiopia, the focus being on the practice since the fall of the Dirgue regime in 1991. It highlights the roles of the various agencies and actors involved in the process, including the Ministry of National Defence (MOND), the Ministry of Finance and Economic Development (MOFED), Parliament and the Office of the Prime Minister. This section continues with an overview of the history, politics and economy of the country. Section II covers the political economy of military expenditure in Ethiopia, tracing the different phases in the development of the Ethiopian military, the factors and forces that affected it, and its implications for military expenditure. Section III described the federal budgetary process in Ethiopia, of which military budgeting is a major component, in order to facilitate an evaluation of underlying government policies (in relation to both structure and process) and the impact of that process on budgetary performance. In sections IV and V the formal budgetary process within the military estab-

lishment is outlined and then assessed. Section VI synthesizes the findings of
the research and points out lessons to be drawn from the exercise as well as
drawing attention to further areas of research. Section VII presents the conclusions of this chapter.

History, politics and economy

Ethiopia is an ancient country and is the largest nation in the Horn of Africa.
After the independence of Eritrea in 1993, Ethiopia became landlocked—the
only such country in the sub-region.

Ethiopia has a rich political history; its evolution as a country with independent political structures dates back to the middle of the fifth century BC. In the
20th century its political structure went through three distinct phases. First was
the period of monarchical rule, in particular the long reign of Emperor Haile
Selassie, which came to an end in 1974. During Haile Selassie's reign there was
an attempt to modernize the economic and political structures with a constitution and a burgeoning capitalist economy. However, political power remained
entirely concentrated in the hands of the emperor, and the economy continued
to be agrarian and feudal in nature.

The rise of the Dirgue regime in 1974 after the collapse of Haile Selassie's
rule saw the emergence of a socialist state in Ethiopia. Political power and the
economy were restructured in line with socialist ideology. Supreme power was
concentrated in the Workers' Party of Ethiopia, established in 1984, while a
centrally planned and controlled economy was instituted. A policy of collectiv-
ization was implemented, under which peasants were reorganized for com-
munal production. Public corporations and virtually every economic institution
were controlled by the state—this also had implications for how the military
was organized. The Dirgue regime faced serious resistance from both domestic
and external forces; it had to contend with ethnic-based rebellions and conflicts
with neighbouring countries, in particular Somalia and Sudan. In 1977 Somalia,
asserting a territorial claim, invaded Ethiopia. This was followed by a civil war
in Ethiopia, which sapped the strength of the armed forces. The Dirgue regime
fell in 1991 to the Ethiopian Peoples' Revolutionary Democratic Front
(EPRDF), a coalition of rebel groups in which the Tigrayan People's Liberation
Front (TPLF) was the dominant partner.

The new government, which is still in power, adopted a political ideology
that it describes as 'revolutionary democracy' and a neo-liberal capitalist economy. A federal constitution and system of government are in place, and there
is a high degree of decentralization of political power in the country. The main
features of Ethiopia's political system include the notion of ethnic federalism,
in which ethnicity and language form the basis of the federal units; considerable
regional autonomy; the right of secession granted to the federating regions;
political pluralism, which has allowed the formation of political parties; and the
granting of civil and political rights. There are nine regional states in the feder-

Table 3.1. The distribution of power between the central and regional governments of Ethiopia

Central government	Regional governments
Formulate overall economic, social, financial and development policies	Exercise powers not given expressly to the federal government alone, or given concurrently to the federal government and the regions
Approve and administer the federal budget	
Levy taxes and collect duties on revenue sources reserved to the federal government	Enact and execute a state constitution and other laws
Print and borrow money, mint coins, regulate foreign exchange and money in circulation networks, and so on	Formulate and execute economic, social and development policies
Formulate and implement foreign policy	Approve and administer the regional budget
Build and administer major constructions, communications networks, and so on	Levy taxes and collect duties on revenue sources reserved to the regions
Regulate inter-regional and foreign commerce	Administer land and other natural resources in accordance with federal laws
Establish and administer national defence and public security forces, including a federal police force	Establish and administer a regional police force, and maintain public order and peace within the region
Declare states of emergency	
Deploy the armed forces in emergencies beyond the capacity and control of regional government	

Source: Constitution of the Federal Democratic Republic of Ethiopia, Proclamation no. 1/1995, *Negarit Gazeta*, 8 Dec. 1994, URL <http://www.ethiopar.net/>.

ation; the distribution of power between the central and regional governments is detailed in table 3.1. Since the federal government collects most taxes, including import and export taxes, it wields tremendous power over regions through its control of the revenue-sharing scheme.[1]

The Federal Democratic Republic of Ethiopia has a parliamentary form of government. The legislature is bicameral, consisting of the House of Peoples' Representatives (lower house) and the House of the Federation (upper house). The House of Peoples' Representatives is the highest authority of the federal government. It has 12 standing committees, which include the Budget and Financial Affairs Standing Committee and the Foreign, Security and Defence Standing Committee. The President has a purely ceremonial role: the Prime Minister is the chief executive, the chairman of the Council of Ministers and the commander-in-chief of the armed forces.

In terms of the economy, a market-driven capitalist ideology has been adopted. A structural adjustment programme provides the framework for the government's economic liberalization policies. The Ethiopian economy pre-

[1] Kelly, J. E., 'Ethnic federalism, fiscal reform, development and democracy in Ethiopia', *Africa Journal of Political Science*, vol. 7, no. 1 (June 2002), pp. 34–35.

sents one of the paradoxes of economic development in Africa. In spite of the fact that the country is rich in natural resources, it has an underdeveloped, agriculture-based economy that relies on the primary products of coffee, hides, livestock, oil seeds and pulses, and recently khat (a mild intoxicant) as its main export products. The country is one of the least economically developed in the world, with 44 per cent of the population living below the poverty line. Between 1993 and 2003 the economy grew at an average annual rate of 4.7 per cent.[2] The national debt was $10.4 billion in 1998; the interest and principal arrears accumulated on the debt reached 84 per cent of gross national product (GNP) and 506 per cent of exports in 1997.[3] The huge debt burden of the country relative to its revenue base and productive capacity enabled the country to qualify for some debt relief under the Highly Indebted Poor Countries programme of the World Bank and the International Monetary Fund.[4] It also prompted the compassionate cancellation by Russia of $4.8 billion of debt incurred during the 17-year civil war, mostly to procure weapons and machinery in support of the Dirgue's military effort.[5]

The high level of militarization of Ethiopian society and the huge expenditure on the military sector have been major factors in the economic underdevelopment of Ethiopia. The cycle of conflicts and violence that has ravaged the country over the years did not provide a favourable investment climate; moreover, it led to the diversion of scarce resources to prosecute the civil war and the war with its neighbours. While the country currently enjoys relative peace, economic development and transformation are yet to follow from the adoption of the neo-liberal economic policies of the EPRDF, although some growth has been recorded. Levels of poverty, unemployment and social dislocation remain high in Ethiopia.

II. The military sector and the political economy of military expenditure in Ethiopia

While Ethiopia has a long military history, the emergence of a modern military force in Ethiopia, through centralization and professionalization, is a 20th century phenomenon. Beginning in the 1920s efforts were made to establish infantry battalions with some level of professional training. Russian military experts were first engaged in the 1920s, and in the 1930s Ethiopian soldiers were sent for training to the French military academy in Saint Cyr. In 1934 a military training school was established in the country, at Holata, with the assistance of a Swedish military mission. The soldiers trained at this local military institution

[2] World Bank, 'Ethiopia at a glance', Fact sheet, 15 Oct. 2004, URL <http://www.worldbank.org/eth/>.

[3] Economic Commission for Africa (ECA), *Economic Report on Africa 2002: Tracking Performance and Progress* (ECA: Addis Ababa, 2002), URL <http://www.uneca.org/era2002/>, p. 95.

[4] International Monetary Fund, 'Debt relief under the Heavily Indebted Poor Countries (HIPC) initiative', Fact sheet, Sep. 2004, URL <http://www.imf.org/external/np/exr/facts/hipc.htm>.

[5] 'Russia writes off US$4.8 bn debt', *Horn of Africa Bulletin*, vol. 13, no. 3 (May/June 2001), p. 12.

Table 3.2. Estimated strength of active military forces of countries in the Horn of Africa, 1997–2004[a]

Country	1997	1998	1999	2000	2001	2002	2003	2004
Djibouti	9 600	9 600	9 600	9 600	9 600	9 850	9 850	9 850
Eritrea	46 000	47 100	180 000–200 000	200 000–250 000	171 900	170 000	202 200	201 750
Ethiopia	120 000	120 000	325 500	352 500	252 500	250 000	162 500	182 500
Kenya	24 200	24 200	24 200	22 200	24 400	24 400	24 120	24 120
Sudan	79 700	94 700	94 700	104 500	117 000	117 000	104 500	104 800

[a] Somalia has lacked a centrally controlled military since 1991.

Sources: International Institute for Strategic Studies, *The Military Balance 1997/1998*; *1998/1999*; *1999/2000*; *2000/2001*; *2001/2002*; *2002/2003*; *2003/2004*; and *2004/2005* (Oxford University Press: Oxford, 1997–2004).

provided the leadership core of a group called the Black Lion Organization, which led the resistance to Italian occupation of the country.

The efforts to modernize the Ethiopian military received a boost after World War II. First, the air force and the navy were established with the help of Sweden and Norway, respectively. The British played a key role in the modernization of the army in terms of training and equipment, while a new military academy was established in Harar, modelled on the British Royal Military Academy, Sandhurst, and commanded by Indian officers.[6] In spite of these foreign connections and in contrast to other African countries, Ethiopia did not inherit its armed forces from a period of colonial rule; they were indigenous. The size of the military at the time of the collapse of Haile Selassie's rule in 1974 was estimated to be about 40 000, while the military budget was estimated to be $50 million in 1973.[7]

Dramatic shifts occurred in the nature and size, and consequent cost, of the Ethiopian military from the 1970s onwards, coinciding with the establishment of the socialist regime of Mengistu in 1974. Various factors accounted for this. The first was the political ideology of Marxism-Leninism adopted by the government in which the economy and polity were centrally controlled and public expenditure rose significantly. Public expenditure as a percentage of gross domestic product was 13 per cent in the 1960s but rose to 34 per cent by the 1980s.[8] The second factor was the culture of militarism that accompanied that ideology. In an effort to build a 'people's army', massive military recruitment was undertaken. As well as the usual channels of recruitment, such as the introduction of national military service from 1983, less orthodox methods were

---

[6] Zewde, B., 'The military and militarism in Africa: the case of Ethiopia', eds E. Hutchful and A. Bathily, *The Military and Militarism in Africa* (Codesria: Dakar, 1998), p. 262.

[7] Zewde (note 6), p. 275.

[8] Taye, H. K., 'Military expenditure and economic performance: the case of Ethiopia', *Ethiopian Journal of Economics*, vol. 5, no. 2 (Oct. 1996), p. 2.

also adopted, such as the recruitment of peasant militias. The third factor that inflated the size and cost of the military under the Dirgue regime was incessant conflict, domestic and external. Armed domestic opposition groups which waged war against the regime included the Eritrean Liberation Front and the Eritrean People's Liberation Front, both fighting for self-determination for Eritrea, the TPLF, the Oromo People's Liberation Front and the Ethiopian Democratic Union. On the external front, Ethiopia was confronted with a conflict with Somalia over the Ogaden region. Ethiopia's relationship with Sudan was also fraught with tension and conflict.

At the height of its strength, the Dirgue army was nearly 500 000 strong (including militia), consisting of infantry and mountain divisions, motorized divisions and a large number of tank battalions. It also had an air defence system, which deployed Russian anti-aircraft guns and surface-to-air missiles (SA-2, SA-3 and SA-7). The air force had 85 combat aircraft consisting of MiG-23 and MiG-21 fighters, bombers, and armed and transport helicopters. The navy had 32 craft in total, including 2 Russian-made frigates, 4 torpedo boats, 4 missile boats, 3 minesweepers (one of which was ocean-going) as well as 3 auxiliary ships for transport, 12 fast patrol boats and 2 minesweepers.[9]

The EPRDF, which took over power from the Dirgue in 1991, disbanded the old army and grounded the air force. With the independence of Eritrea, the Ethiopian navy ceased to exist. The EPRDF converted its own force into a new army and started to rehabilitate the air force. By 1998 Ethiopia found itself engaged in a massive war with Eritrea and was forced to hurriedly mobilize a large army and acquire new and sophisticated equipment. The size of the Ethiopian armed forces in 2001 was 252 500, the largest in sub-Saharan Africa at the time. Table 3.2 presents the estimated strength of the armed forces in Ethiopia and its neighbouring states. It shows that, before the demobilization that followed their border war, Ethiopia's military far outnumbered Eritrea's. These two countries continue to have the two largest armed forces in sub-Saharan Africa; indeed, in 2004 Ethiopia's military was 74 per cent larger than that of Sudan.

The inevitable result of the events of the past three decades was that military expenditure in Ethiopia skyrocketed. As table 3.3 shows, military expenditure increased from 1625 million birr ($413 million in constant dollars) in 1990 to peak at 5589 million birr ($719 million) in 1999 at the height of the war with Eritrea. As can be seen from the table, military expenditure fell for only a few years after the collapse of the Dirgue in 1991; it started to rise again from 1993. Two immediate factors account for this. The first was the border war with Eritrea. The war occasioned massive recruitment and deployment of troops and the diversion of resources for military purposes. The unstable nature of Ethiopia's relationship with Eritrea persists even after the signing of a peace agreement in

---

[9] Personal communication with the authors, Addis Ababa, June 2002.

Table 3.3. Military expenditure of Ethiopia, 1990–2004

Figures in US$ are in constant 2003 prices and exchange rates.

	Military expenditure		
Year[a]	$ m.	m. birr	as a % of GDP
1990	413	1 625	8.5
1991	205	1 095	5.3
1992	121	716	2.7
1993	134	819	2.9
1994	124	813	2.4
1995	104	754	2.0
1996	117	803	1.8
1997	215	1 512	3.4
1998	453	3 263	6.7
1999	719	5 589	10.7
2000	648	5 075	9.6
2001	438	3 154	6.1
2002	411	3 000	5.3
2003	349	3 000	4.3
2004	339	3 000	..

GDP = Gross domestic product.

[a] Years are calendar years, not financial years.

Source: SIPRI military expenditure database.

December 2000.[10] Second, in the post-Mengistu era the country still has to contend with internal civil strife in the south, the south-east and the south-west, where the Ogaden National Liberation Front and the Oromo Liberation Front are active. The military, therefore, still occupies a central position in the public profile and expenditure plans of the government, and so continues to consume enormous resources.

These two factors notwithstanding, the missions and roles of the armed forces have hardly changed under the last three regimes, except perhaps for some shifts in ideological emphasis. The army's role has always been to protect the territory of the country from external threat, to enforce security measures against internal insurgency, and to plan and organize civil defence, participate in civic construction projects and provide emergency relief during national disasters in peacetime. The air force's role has been to maintain air superiority within the country's airspace, defend the country from external aggression by air, provide air support for the army (and the navy before Eritrean independence) and during peacetime provide aviation services as required. During the imperial and Dirgue regimes, the armed forces had overtly or covertly assumed

---

[10] Agreement between the Government of the Federal Democratic Republic of Ethiopia and the Government of the State of Eritrea, Algiers, 12 Dec. 2000, available at URL <http://www.usip.org/library/pa/eritrea_ethiopia/pa_eritrea_ethiopia.html>.

the role of agents of social and political change. Partly as a result of Emperor Haile Selassie's belief in collective security (first through the League of Nations, then the United Nations), a belief shared by subsequent governments, Ethiopia participated in international missions in Korea, the Congo (Leopold-ville), Rwanda and Burundi.[11]

The past decade has been a period of transformation for the Ethiopian armed forces: one of its major tasks has been to build capacity.

III. The national budgetary process

Ethiopia has a dual budgeting system in which recurrent and capital expenditure are considered separately. Until recently these two budgets were prepared separately by the Ministry of Finance and the Ministry of Economic Development and Cooperation, respectively. In October 2001 these two ministries were merged to form the Ministry of Finance and Economic Development.[12] The new ministry determines budget ceilings for federal ministries and agencies and for the regions. In doing so, it takes stock of the performance of the economy for the previous year and makes economic projections for the following year in terms of growth, revenue, and so on. The MOFED does this in consultation with other state agencies, such as the National Bank of Ethiopia and the Central Statistical Authority. It is this macroeconomic framework that, when approved by the Council of Ministers and the Office of the Prime Minister, forms the background to the budgetary process in Ethiopia.

At the federal level the amount to be allocated to recurrent and capital expenditure is determined by government priorities, ongoing projects, non-discriminatory expenditure and institutional capacity.

The formulation phase

The MOFED is the major clearing house for the preparation of the federal budget in Ethiopia, although this is done in consultation with the various ministries that are the beneficiaries of the budget. The responsibilities of the Minister of Finance and Economic Development, as stipulated in the Council of Ministers Financial Regulations, consist of formulating and issuing directives that detail government financial policies in all areas of government finances; developing and maintaining appropriate standards of work and conduct for application throughout all public bodies; internal auditing functions; and pre-

[11] Ethiopia contributed troops to the United Nations (UN) Command in Korea, 1951–54; the UN Operation in the Congo, 1960–64; the UN Assistance Mission for Rwanda, 1993–96; and the African Union's African Mission in Burundi, 2003–2004. It currently contributes troops to the UN Mission in Liberia, since Sep. 2003, and the UN Operation in Burundi, since June 2004, URL <http://www.un.org/Depts/dpko/>.
[12] Federal Democratic Republic of Ethiopia, 'Reorganization of the executive organs of the Federal Democratic Republic of Ethiopia', Proclamation no. 256/2001, *Federal Negarit Gazeta*, 12 Oct. 2001, URL <http://www.ethiopar.net/>.

paring a financial plan for the country.[13] In addition, the minister now has the duty to initiate policy proposals that help to define the country's long-term development perspective; prepare and follow up implementation of long-, medium- and short-term development plans; and prepare the annual development programme.

The various steps involved in the process of budgeting in Ethiopia are described below.[14]

The first step in the process is the sending of Budget Calls and ceiling notifications to line ministries by the MOFED. The Recurrent Budget Call provides basic information such as the macroeconomic environment, aggregate recurrent budget ceiling and priorities for which the ministry must budget. The MOFED then prepares a proposed total recurrent budget, which is reviewed and vetted by the Office of the Prime Minister and on which the line ministries' budget proposals are based. For the capital budget, the process for a particular budget cycle begins with an assessment of the economic situation and by determining the financial balance. At this stage, the macroeconomic framework is reviewed, economic priorities in terms of capital expenditure are set and national goals are defined with respect to economic development. This is followed by the issuance of the Capital Budget Call, which provides detailed guidelines to line ministries regarding the capital budget ceiling and how to prepare their budget proposals.

The next step in the process is the submission of budgetary requests by the various ministries to the MOFED's Budget Department following established regulations and ensuring appropriate budget sub-heading classification. A line ministry may have formal pre-budget discussions with MOFED officials in order to clarify some issues or to justify certain budget claims that the line ministry may wish to make. Line ministries may overshoot their budget ceiling when they prepare their budgets; however, such an action has to be justified for it to be considered by the MOFED.

The budget hearing at the MOFED follows the submission of budgetary requests. This is the component of the process that reflects the democratic nature of the budgetary process. The minister or vice-minister of the line ministry or the head or director of a department or agency is called to defend its budget before the MOFED. The budgetary request of the line ministry is prepared in an issue paper, which is normally the subject of discussion at the budget hearing. The basic issues that are raised in the budget hearing include policies, programmes and cost issues. When necessary the budget request presented by a line ministry is discussed in detail. In addition, for the capital budget the MOFED, through its Capital Budget Steering Committee, holds budget hearings at which the line ministries defend their proposals. The key issues that form the core of the capital budget hearing and defence process include a focus on the status of projects; the implementation capacity of the

---

[13] Federal Democratic Republic of Ethiopia, 'Council of Ministers Financial Regulations', Proclamation no. 17/1997, *Federal Negarit Gazeta*, 1 July 1997, URL <http://www.ethiopar.net/>.

[14] For further details see Tizaau, T., *Budget Preparation and Finance Administration in Ethiopia* (Meskerem: Addis Ababa, 2001).

country's development strategy and the projects' compatibility with the strategy; the cost structure of the projects; and the regional distribution of the projects. In other words, the development potential and cost implications of the projects are put under scrutiny.

After the budgetary hearing, the MOFED's Budget Committee reviews the exercise and prepares its recommendations, including the proposed sources of finance. Funds are allocated from internally generated revenue, from foreign assistance and from the central Treasury. The total amount to be disbursed to the line ministry in the recurrent budget is the sum of these three sources of finance. Should the MOFED recommend a rise in the ceiling, this has to be approved by the Office of the Prime Minister first.

After the MOFED has reviewed the budget proposal, it is submitted to the Deputy Prime Minister for Economic Affairs. The Deputy Prime Minister then calls on line ministry representatives to further discuss the recommended budget before it is submitted to the Prime Minister. The Prime Minister may or may not authorize changes. From the Office of the Prime Minister, the draft recurrent budget is sent to the Council of Ministers for deliberations. The draft capital budget is also submitted to the Council of Ministers after a review and recommendations have been made by the Capital Budget Steering Committee.

The approval phase

Supreme authority for budget appropriation is vested in the House of Peoples' Representatives. The Prime Minister presents the budget recommended by the Council of Ministers to the House. After deliberation in a parliamentary session, it is sent to the Budget and Financial Affairs Standing Committee for review and recommendation. This committee reviews the budget in the presence of members of various other committees, receives written explanations from experts from the MOFED and makes its recommendation to the House. The entire House thereafter deliberates on the recommendations of the budget standing committee before the appropriation bill is approved. The House of Peoples' Representatives considers both the current and capital expenditure budgets as well as subsidies to the regions.

After the House of Peoples' Representatives approves the budget, it is signed by the President and is then made public through publication in the *Federal Negarit Gazeta*, the Ethiopian national gazette. Following this, the line ministries receive formal notification from the MOFED of their budget allocation for the next financial year. The MOFED then directs the Treasury to release the funds to the line ministries.

The implementation phase

The implementation phase of the budgetary process covers not only measures for disbursing funds already allocated but also the monitoring of how funds are spent to ensure that they are used judiciously and for the intended purposes.

Following the notification and publication of the budget the various ministries are required to prepare a fund disbursement chart that specifies salary allotment, a work plan and a cash flow and to submit the chart to the MOFED. These charts are verified by the MOFED, which then authorizes the Treasury to release the funds (both recurrent and capital) to the line ministries.

Funds are dispersed to ministries each month on the basis of the allotted budget. Every ministry is required to submit a 'monthly disbursement request' in which it reports the previous month's expenditure, detailing what was spent and how it was used, and makes a request for the next month's allocation through a work plan. The requests for fund disbursement by line ministries usually contain three main components: the payment of salaries, a request for operational expenditure (according to the cash flow plan) and a request for payment of capital grants. The MOFED's Fund Disbursement Department handles the process of fund disbursement for the ministries and keeps records of all transactions. The budget registrar in the Disbursement Authorization Department of the MOFED records the original budget, all transfers and supplementary budgets, the disbursements made and any undisbursed allocation.

Fund disbursement is cumulative and undisbursed funds for a particular month can be used in another month in the same financial year. Funds unused by ministries at the end of the financial year have to be transferred to the Treasury, although transfer to other activities is also allowed. With regard to capital projects, ministries are expected to prepare a schedule of advance payments compatible with the amount of work to be carried out on the various projects. This schedule is consolidated and approved by the MOFED and passed to the Disbursement Authorization Department for further action.

During implementation of the budget, new or unforeseen requirements may necessitate a request for a supplementary budget; this is permitted by regulations on the financial administration of the federal government. The Council of Ministers establishes a committee that includes representatives of the Office of the Prime Minister, the MOFED and the line ministry. This committee first assesses the new or unforeseen requirements, based on policy decisions at the highest executive level. Once approved at this level, it is submitted to the House of Peoples' Representatives for approval, after which it is passed back to the MOFED for authorization of disbursement.[15]

The MOFED coordinates the management and control of public funds in Ethiopia. It is this ministry that keeps the accounts of the federal budget and

---

[15] Federal Democratic Republic of Ethiopia, 'Financial administration proclamation of the Federal Government of Ethiopia', Proclamation no. 57/1996, *Federal Negarit Gazeta*, 19 Dec. 1996, URL <http://www.ethiopar.net/>.

prescribes regulations on financial management and control for ministries and government agencies. In addition, ministries are required to manage and control funds allotted to them following the central regulations and directives on financial management set out by the MOFED. The regulatory mechanisms of the budget include requirements that: (*a*) budgetary receipts be recorded in the appropriate budgetary account as prescribed in the financial regulations and in a timely manner; (*b*) collected revenue be recorded under the appropriate revenue account; (*c*) expenditure only be made in compliance with the financial regulations; (*d*) all books of accounts be closed each month and a monthly receipt and disbursement be prepared and submitted to the MOFED at the centre and regional finance bureaux in the regions; (*e*) periodic financial statements be prepared and submitted to the Council of Ministers and regional executive committees by the MOFED at the centre and regional finance bureaux in the regions; (*f*) a consolidated annual report be prepared and sent to the Council of Ministers and regional executive committees by the MOFED and regional finance bureaux.

The MOFED can be seen to play a central role in the budgetary process of the country. It controls the formulation and implementation of the budget of line ministries at various levels. During the writing of the Budget Calls it is instrumental in the setting of budget ceilings. It can make changes in the budget allocation of line ministries after review and analysis of the budget estimate submitted by the ministries. It decides the level of the budget to be recommended to the Council of Ministers. During implementation, it has the power to disburse funds. Through the monthly accounting reports, it scrutinizes the performance of the ministries in budget implementation, and it can decide on the level of funding to be authorized for disbursement. It can also approve transfers and recommend supplementary allocations.

Reporting and auditing

According to the proclamation establishing the post,[16] the Office of the Federal Auditor-General is tasked with the responsibility of undertaking financial and performance audits of the offices and organizations of the federal government. It does this by auditing the accounts of all federal ministries and agencies. The proclamation stipulates the penalties for anyone who obstructs the work of the Auditor-General through deliberate presentation of false documents or denial of access to required information. The annual report of the Auditor-General details his or her findings on the accounts audited. Unfortunately, the reports are usually late in arriving, sometimes by as many as three years. For instance, the report for financial year (FY) 1999/2000 was not presented to Parliament until June 2003. This delay diminishes the significance of the report since any

---

[16] Federal Democratic Republic of Ethiopia, 'A proclamation to establish the Office of Federal Auditor-General', Proclamation no. 68/1997, *Federal Negarit Gazeta*, 6 Mar. 1997, URL <http://www.ethiopar.net/>.

recommendation for remedial action to rectify an error arrives too late to avoid repetition of that error in intervening years. A lack of adequate staffing has been given as the main reason for this major lapse in the auditing process.

IV. The military budgetary process

The military budgetary process in Ethiopia is an integral part of the annual national budgetary system of the country. The line ministry for the military is the Ministry of National Defence.

According to the MOFED budget classification, the MOND is classified as a programme and the whole military budget is classified as recurrent expenditure, following the United Nations's classification. The MOND is divided into sub-programmes. In FY 1991/92 these sub-programmes were: (*a*) administrative and general services (MOND headquarters); (*b*) the ground force; (*c*) the air force; (*d*) the navy; and (*e*) defence construction. Essentially, this reflected the classification that existed during the Dirgue regime.

In FY 1992/93 a new sub-programme was introduced for the Political Organization Army Department, which was established to carry out the demobilization and resettlement of the EPRDF troops who left the army. When this department had accomplished its task, it ceased to be a component part of the military budget after FY 1995/96. In FY 1994/95 when the Navy Department had been closed and the navy disbanded, it also ceased to be part of the MOND budget. Defence construction was also withdrawn from the MOND and now operates independently, along business lines, under the supervision of a government department responsible for nationalized enterprises. However, a new sub-programme was added in FY 1994/95: Project 40720, a vast repair and maintenance complex for heavy armaments, tanks and military vehicles built by the Soviet Union during the Dirgue regime which also includes some other unfinished projects. In FY 2001/2002 three new sub-programmes were added: the Defence Engineering College, the Health College and the Dejen Defence Project Coordination Office. The last of these oversees the management of a number of factories established to provide the military sector with material and equipment, such as quartermaster items and mechanical tools. In FY 2002/2003 more radical changes were made in the programme classifications, leaving eight sub-programmes: (*a*) administration and general services; (*b*) the office of the minister; (*c*) defence procurement; (*d*) the ground force; (*e*) the air force; (*f*) the Defence University; (*g*) Project 40720; and (*h*) the Dejen Defence Project Coordination Office. The components of each sub-programme consist of item expenditures which include personnel services (emoluments, allowances and pension contributions), goods and services (materials and supplies, travel, maintenance and contracted services), fixed assets and construction, and other payments (subsidies, investments, grants and miscellaneous payments).

In terms of administration, the Minister of National Defence is the political head of the ministry, although in reality the Prime Minister exercises considerable influence. The federal constitution requires that the Minister of National Defence be a civilian.[17] At present the Budget Department, the Finance Department, the Procurement Agency, and the Administration and General Services Section of the MOND are all the responsibility of a minister of state, a civilian who is responsible directly to the Minister of National Defence. A civilian vice-minister heads the Defence Project Coordination Office. The head of the Budget Department, who is responsible for the formulation and administration of the budget, is also a civilian. In terms of the budgetary process, at least in the formal sense, civilian control appears to predominate.

Budget formulation

There is little or no difference between the budgetary process for the military and those of the other ministries. The military budget begins at zero every year; in other words, the sector undertakes only annual budgeting. There is no medium-term perspective to military budgeting. The budgetary procedure is described in this and the following subsections; a diagram of the process is presented in figure 3.1 and the calendar of the process is given in table 3.4.

The MOFED sends a Recurrent Budget Call, which includes a budget ceiling, to all ministries, including the MOND. The MOND headquarters, in turn, issues a Budget Call to the heads of the various sub-programmes, with a ceiling for each sub-programme, calling their attention to various directives. In the Budget Calls it is stressed that the budget preparation process should strictly follow existing budget preparation regulations, take account of policy decisions, meet budget standards, take account of the current price of goods and services, and so on. The budget proposals from sub-programmes include not only expenditure but also revenue. The Budget Calls also specify a deadline for the submission of budget proposals from sub-programmes. The prepared budget estimate is submitted for a budget hearing at the sub-programme level to determine the final estimate that will be sent to MOND headquarters.

Following the submission to MOND headquarters of the budget proposals by the sub-programmes, budget review and analysis are carried out by experts in the Budget Department of the MOND. This involves detailed analysis to establish that the budget estimates have been prepared in accordance with the Budget Calls. It also involves an assessment of whether the activities proposed in each sub-programme can be accomplished during the financial year, whether old and new projects have been clearly identified, and whether the budget estimate has been prepared by comparison with the previous year's performance and takes account of inventories. The objective of the exercise is also to enable the budget experts to prepare an accurate, realistic and credible consolidated budget estimate.

[17] Constitution of the Federal Democratic Republic of Ethiopia, Proclamation no. 1/1995, *Negarit Gazeta*, 8 Dec. 1994, URL <http://www.ethiopar.net/>, Article 87(2).

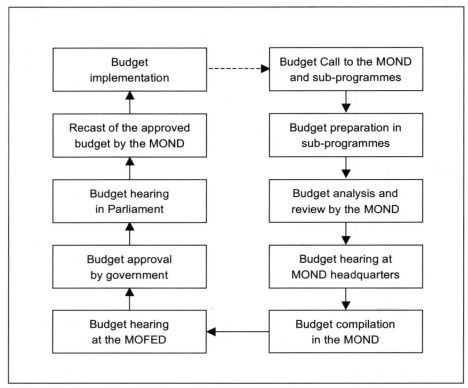

Figure 3.1. The military budgetary process in Ethiopia

MOFED = Ministry of Finance and Economic Development; MOND = Ministry of National Defence.

After review and analysis of the budget, a budget hearing is held at MOND headquarters, at which the sub-programmes are represented and the Minister of National Defence and the Chief of Staff are present, to decide on the budget level to be recommended for each sub-programme and for the military sector as a whole. Immediately after the budget hearing and on the basis of the decisions taken during that hearing, the MOND Budget Department prepares a consolidated military budget, which also includes revenue estimates—services may collect revenue from the sale of surplus property, medical services, aviation services and items from welfare stores or canteens.

Approval

The Foreign, Security and Defence Standing Committee of the House of Peoples' Representatives scrutinizes the defence component of the national budget submitted by the Prime Minister before passing it on to the whole House

Table 3.4. The financial calendar of the Ethiopian Ministry of National Defence

	Calendar	
Activity	Ethiopian	Gregorian
Budget Call from the MOND to sub-programmes	15 Meskerem–15 Tikimt	15 Sep.–15 Oct.
Budget preparation in sub-programmes	16 Tikimt–30 Tahsas	16 Oct.–8 Jan.
Budget analysis and review by the MOND	1 Tir–15 Tir	9 Jan.–23 Jan.
Budget hearing at MOND headquarters	20 Tir–30 Tir	28 Jan.–7 Feb.
Budget compilation in the MOND	1 Yekatit–30 Yekatit	8 Feb.–9 Mar.
Budget hearing at the MOFED	23 Megabit–29 Genbot	1 Apr.–6 June
Start of the financial year	1 Hamle	8 July
Budget approval by government	1 Hamle–8 Hamle	8 July–15 July
Recast of approved budget	1 Hamle–9 Nehassie	8 July–15 Aug.
Budget implementation	9 Hamle–30 Hamle	16 July–6 Aug.

Note: The Ethiopian financial year (which should be distinguished from the Ethiopian trade year) runs from 8 July to 7 July (1 Hamle to 30 Sene in the Ethiopian calendar).

MOFED = Ministry of Finance and Economic Development; MOND = Ministry of National Defence.

for approval. After the budget appropriated by the House of Peoples' Representatives has been passed on to the MOND by the MOFED, the final exercise in the budget formulation process is the budget distribution (or recast), which allows each sub-programme to adjust the approved budget according to their actual revised requirements.

Implementation

Once the budget recast is approved by the MOFED, the process of budget implementation starts with the monthly requisition by the MOND for its allotted funds. At this stage all the control mechanisms that apply to other ministries and agencies of the federal government also apply to the MOND. This includes the monitoring of the execution of the budget on a monthly basis. It is doubtful, however, whether this applies to the procurement of major military weapons.

Reporting and auditing

The role of the Office of the Federal Auditor-General in the budgetary process of the military sector is to audit its financial accounts annually and at other times when it deems it necessary. The auditing, as in other ministries, is performed at three levels: internal audit by the ministry, auditing by the MOFED and auditing at the federal level by the Auditor-General's office. By law, all persons appointed as auditors (including internal auditors) should be approved by the Federal Auditor-General.

V. Assessing the military budgetary process

The Ethiopian military budgetary system suffers from a number of deficiencies that hamper efficient allocation and use of resources. Among these are: a lack of continuity in the process; the lack of a well-articulated defence policy and strategic plan; inefficient implementation of the budget; emphasis on input rather than output; over-centralization of authority; and relatively strong yet opposing influences on the level of military spending.

The first thing to note about the Ethiopian armed forces is that, when the Dirgue regime collapsed, the army was not simply disbanded. The EPRDF also discarded well-established doctrine on military operations, logistics and training along with the organizational structure and all the rules, regulations and standing operating procedures, and it closed training and other facilities. It was as though Ethiopia had never had an armed force. Moreover, the replacement was not a modern armed force; it was a guerrilla force, with all that that implies in terms of doctrine, organization and weaponry. The EPRDF retained a handful of officers and men from the old force, but otherwise it had to start afresh, establishing a new organizational structure and operating procedures and re-establishing facilities that it had closed when it took over. The EPRDF army started out with principles and a value system that were the antitheses of those of a modern professional army. Over time all this has changed. Since 1991 the government has focused on the re-establishment of a professional army. During this process, the new armed forces had to engage Eritrea in a border war. It is against this background that the budgetary process should be evaluated.

One of the methods of modern budget administration is 'planning, programming and budgeting' (see chapter 2), although the Ethiopian military has not adopted it. A particular advantage of this method in the Ethiopia situation is the analysis of defence capability that it requires; such an analysis is important in a defence system in the process of transformation. However, the planning, programming and budgeting method assumes that there are already short-, medium- and long-term plans and that the major budget centres are structured in such a way that they functionally reflect national defence objectives. Ethiopia may have strategic plans but, since the planning, programming and budgeting method has not been implemented, if these plans exist, they do not play an important role in the budgetary process because there is no mechanism for coordinating the activities of those who plan and those who prepare the budget. Lack of transparency in the process does not allow for an understanding of the basis of defence allocations.

It is known that the level of budget allocation to ministries is determined through the prior setting of ceilings by the MOFED. This does not contribute to budget discipline or efficient management of the budget or the defence system in general. On the contrary, in the administrative environment described above it may encourage the padding and inflating of budgets. For this reason, and others to do with efficiency, the MOFED should study the pros and cons of the setting of budget ceilings as a budgetary tool in the absence of a defence policy and of overarching national priorities and policy goals.

Except for the past few years, actual expenditure on defence in Ethiopia has exceeded appropriations.[18] This may be largely owing to the fact that the MOND does not formulate its budget on the basis of medium- and long-term plans and may also be the result of the frequent external and internal conflicts. Long-term stability and the existence of medium- and long-term plans seem to be necessary conditions for budget ceilings to be an effective tool of the budgetary process.

In general, there are two possible approaches to budget formulation when attempting to achieve a goal. In the first approach, those responsible set budget ceilings and direct the implementing agencies to operate within the ceilings. There will of course be legal and administrative controls to ensure that implementing agencies with approved budgets adhere to the directives sent. This approach is usually less effective in maintaining budget discipline, as there is little basis for the ceilings.

The second and perhaps more useful approach is for the line ministries to first submit their spending estimates, without a ceiling being set beforehand. These estimates should give detailed justifications (usually on the basis of objectives or policy goals) for increases or decreases in budget, and should detail any new activities or programmes that are to be undertaken, such as fresh troop recruitment, the purchase of armaments or the construction of new facilities. Authorization may then be obtained from the government for the new or additional programmes and activities and for any cost increases after analysis of past budget performance. The emphasis is on justifying the new requirements, clearly indicating how they would enhance the readiness or capacity of the combat or support element concerned and, if the requirements arise during a period of conflict, how acquiring the new capability would contribute to the war effort.

This second method was used during the Dirgue regime, but it was still a 'line item expenditure' approach. It fell far short of enabling decision makers to be able to use the budget as a tool to achieve national defence goals. If the method were suitably refined (with a strategic plan and policy), it would allow for systematic analysis of defence requirements in terms of system costs and defence objectives. Since the method is iterative, it allows closer scrutiny of the objectives themselves, making it possible to consider alternative defence systems or postures. With the establishment of proper criteria it would be possible to select the optimum defence package. For these reasons, the Ethiopian Government should consider implementing the planning, programming and budgeting method, with the requisite analytical tools to ensure that the national defence goals are achieved and optimal use of resources is made.

Table 3.5, which presents military budget appropriations by sub-programme, shows that the Ethiopian armed forces have undergone a number of changes in

---

[18] See also table 11.7 in chapter 11 in this volume.

Table 3.5. Ethiopian military budget appropriation by sub-programme, 1991/92–2002/2003

Figures are in m. birr. Figures may not add up to totals due to the conventions of rounding.

Sub-programme	1991/92	1992/93	1993/94	1994/95	1995/96	1996/97	1997/98	1998/99	1999/2000	2000/01	2001/02	2002/03
Administration and general services	6.4	10.8	9.7	9.8	7.5	6.6	9.4	8.4	8.4	37.8	103.8	507.2
Ground force	568.7	599.3	586.8	579.3	638.1	704.3	789.0	895.4	2 412.4	3 537.9	2 149.3	1 122.4
Air force	10.6	28.0	37.7	47.7	46.0	30.4	36.3	74.4	74.4	531.6	404.0	32.4
Navy	2.9	7.4	9.3	10.4	6.8	4.2	..	..	..	..	..	..
Defence construction	4.4	5.1	4.2	..	..	..	..	..	..	..	..	..
Political Organization Army Department	..	9.7	9.9	9.9	0.4	..	..	..	..	..	..	..
Project 40720	..	..	..	6.0	6.0	9.4	12.1	4.9	4.9	8.1	70.4	14.3
Defence Engineering College/University	..	..	..	..	..	..	..	..	..	..	52.3	28.4
Dejen Defence Project Coordination Office	..	..	..	..	..	..	..	..	..	..	215.0	86.5
Health College	..	..	..	..	..	..	..	..	..	..	5.2	..
Office of the minister	..	..	..	..	..	..	..	..	..	..	..	6.4
Defence procurement	..	..	..	..	..	..	..	..	..	..	..	1 202.5
Total	**593.1**	**660.3**	**657.5**	**663.1**	**704.8**	**754.9**	**846.9**	**983.1**	**2 500.0**	**4 115.4**	**3 000.0**	**3 000.0**

.. = No such sub-programme in that year.

Sources: 'Budget proclamation', *Negarit Gazeta*, 1991/92–1994/95 and *Federal Negarit Gazeta*, 1995/96–2002/2003.

organizational structure since FY 1991/92. These were accompanied by a high turnover of personnel, resulting in a shortage of well-trained staff for budget administration. However, the size of the budget to be administered is huge for a low-income country. Under these circumstances and because of delays in policy formulation and in communicating policy decisions to implementing units, some delays in budget preparation and submission are to be expected. If the Budget Call is delayed, for example, this will shorten the time available for preparation of the budget. Those in the Budget Department of the MOND who analyse and review the process are also pressed to keep to the financial calendar of the MOFED. The cumulative result of all this is that the standard of the work throughout the budgetary process inevitably suffers.

A major activity of the budgetary process is the biannual taking of inventories of stocks of materials and supplies. This exercise is an integral part of budget preparation, as budget estimates take into account the balance of the stocks. Procurement plans are also reviewed on the basis of inventory results. Existing stocks are redistributed so as to avoid excessive concentration of stocks in one unit or shortages in another—this is done in order to reduce the size of the budget estimates, and it is accordingly regarded as a very important part of the budgetary process. However, if this aim is to be achieved effectively and a substantial budget reduction is to result from the exercise, then an efficient control system must be put in place with trained personnel to operate it. Owing to staff turnover and reorganization, this may not be practicable. Under these circumstances, it is to be expected that there will be a bias in favour of under-reporting stock levels, in the hope that budget ceilings will be increased or at least maintained.

In short, the overall picture is that conditions in Ethiopia are not conducive to the efficient implementation of the budgetary process in the MOND.

As far as the administration of the budget is concerned, apart from ensuring that salaries and benefits are paid and that materials and supplies are procured in accordance with organization and equipment tables, the overriding emphasis is on control: not enough attention is paid to efficiency. In fact, there does not even appear to be a mechanism that could contribute to achieving efficiency. The budget consists of line item expenditure calculated on the basis of budget standards, the established civil service salary scale and the lowest possible prices for goods and services. Such an exercise in itself and in isolation cannot ensure that the goals of the defence system or its sub-systems are cost-effective, nor can it assist in measuring mission effectiveness.

Furthermore, the recent changes in classification in the military budget with the introduction of the defence procurement sub-programme, which is centrally planned and administered, are leading to over-centralization of authority and a reduction in the powers of the service units, which can only have a negative effect on the optimal use of resources. Table 3.5 shows that this new sub-programme has been allocated over 40 per cent of the total military budget. While supplies of materials and equipment constitute a significant portion of the input to the military sector and there is a need to control costs (e.g., through taking advantage of bulk purchasing), this does not justify the classification of procurement as an independent category in the budget. Doing so is tantamount to taking from the service units (the ground and air forces) control over a significant portion of their resources: it deprives them of the opportunity to manage themselves efficiently and effectively. The service units are the best judges of their requirements and they should be allowed to make the necessary choices independently. Since some of the requirements of a service can be highly specialized, the right to manage its own financial resources is an integral part of a service's ability to manage itself efficiently. While central procurement need not mean that the budget for procurement is centrally planned and administered in the MOND, the recent change in budget classification is retrograde. It has come as a result of an overemphasis on cost reduction, to the exclusion of considerations of efficiency.

Ministry of National Defence expenditure increased by more than 180 per cent in real terms over the period 1992–2004. This partly reflects the strategic importance that the new regime attaches to the sector and the level of threat perceived by the state. However, allocations for defence remain high even after the reductions that followed the formal end of the Eritrea–Ethiopia War, in December 2000. There are two major factors that will affect Ethiopia's military expenditure in the future, aside from the actual performance of the economy itself. The level of foreign aid to Ethiopia, especially that from the World Bank and the International Monetary Fund, has in the past been contingent on reduction in the size of the armed forces. Consequently, the high level of expenditure may not continue. On the other hand, the Ethiopian military sector is in the process of transformation; this essentially means capacity building, with perhaps some change to the structure of the forces. Whatever the actual outcome of the opposing trends for capacity building and force reduction, there will be a need for a qualitative change in the management of the armed forces if undue burden on the economy is to be avoided and if the cost-effectiveness of the defence system is to be improved.

The role of the House of Peoples' Representatives in the budgetary process is minimal, even though the constitution grants the legislature a great deal of power. The President's role in the process is purely ceremonial; he has no constitutional power to influence the way in which the budget is formulated. While the House is the supreme body in terms of budget appropriation, the extent to which it exercises this authority is debatable. Although there is a standing committee for the budget, which is expected to study the budget proposals in detail and to submit its recommendations to the House, committee members lack the expertise to scrutinize the military budget properly and they do not have the services of experts at hand. In any case, the budget estimates are scrutinized as a whole, rather than by sector. The government announces through the media that budget hearings are going to be held and invites the general public to attend the hearings. Various interest groups have the opportunity to submit their views to the standing committee and many actually do so, but this is little more than a formality: the committee deals with the budget proposals in their entirety and, in general, the recommendations presented to the House are identical to those presented by the executive. The committee cannot therefore be said to be as accountable to the public as its constitutional role demands. In fact it is the Ministry of Finance and Economic Development and the Office of the Prime Minister that have the decisive role in the budgetary process. It is therefore important to devise means of enhancing the competence of the Budget and Financial Affairs Standing Committee.

VI. Issues arising from the study

There are several issues arising from this study that indicate the limitations of the research and of the policy issues arising from it.

Owing to the nature of the subject area (i.e., excessive confidentiality) and because of limited access, it has not been possible to unravel the informal processes and politics of the military budgetary process. Emphasis is placed more on the formal mechanisms and processes of the military budget and their critique.

Military budgeting starts at zero each year; there are no medium- or long-term strategic budget plans.[19] Equally, there is no evidence of the existence of mechanisms for coordinating the planning organs and the Budget Department of the MOND. In the process of issuing Budget Calls in the MOND, decisions on increases or decreases in manpower strength, variations in budget standards and capacity building are made. However, it is unlikely that decisions on major defence policy issues (which will be converted into specific goals and programmes) are communicated to the head of the Budget Department who will have to apply them in the budget. Extra- or off-budget spending for the military is often not disclosed by the state or the military sector.

Organizational changes in the armed forces as different regimes take power, either through coup or armed struggle, tend to be motivated by a desire for regime stability. This has an effect on the continuity and development of the armed forces and deprives the nation of an experienced and disciplined professional armed force.

External assistance in the form of loans and grants, both bilateral and multilateral, is detailed in the revenue side of the national budget by source, but it is not shown on the recurrent expenditure side for any sector, including the military. Budget allocations for demilitarization and demobilization after the EPRDF took power from the Dirgue regime are reflected in the government budget proclamations. They do include a foreign aid component, but this is not recorded in the recurrent budget.

---

[19] The MOFED does have 5-year strategic and 3-year rolling plans for the federal budget; these are not proclaimed by law but form the basis for the annual budgetary process.

The Civil Service Reform Budget Design Team—a body representing the former ministries of Finance and of Economic Development and Cooperation and the Decentralization Support Activity Project—was established in 1997 to recommend reforms in the budget processes and structure for the federal government. It made proposals on how best to coordinate the preparation of the recurrent and capital budgets.[20] Among the study's recommendations were changes in the format of the budget to promote consistency in the presentation of the recurrent and capital budgets and, most importantly, the preparation of the budget on a cost-centre basis. The latter proposal would bring together recurrent and capital expenditure so that budget managers could immediately see the total cost of a project or an administrative unit. Unit costs are used in the cost build-up of these cost centres. The team regards the use of these unit costs as a key technique for determining cost build-up and as a norm reference for costing the budget. The costs that the team have in mind are not the prices of items or services but ratios such as cost of transport per passenger or cost of education per pupil. Unit costs are developed for each major area of service and are calculated by dividing the total outlay by the output. Aside from the fact that the output of the military sector, in most cases, is not quantifiable, the necessary expertise for such an exercise does not exist in the MOND. In fact, the ministry has not yet set up a unit to undertake such a task. The measurement of costs and effectiveness in defence is very difficult, and the team's requirement for the calculation of unit costs would demand sophisticated cost-effectiveness analysis currently far beyond the capability of the MOND.

Reforms that have arisen from the recommendations of the Civil Service Reform Budget Design Team include organizational restructuring and a redistribution of duties and responsibilities in the MOND. Organizationally, a 'flatter' structure has been instituted, reflecting a move towards more decentralization. For example, budget and finance administration have been decentralized, as has local purchasing. Foreign purchasing remains centralized.

Redistribution of duties and responsibilities has meant that the Budget Department has been renamed the Plan and Budget Department and is now accountable directly to the Minister of National Defence, instead of the minister of state. The Material and Inventory Control Department has been separated from the Budget Department and made accountable to the minister of state. Inventory control will be undertaken once a year and will be computerized. Other reforms include: (*a*) the appointment of a new civilian vice-minister for policy and human resource development; (*b*) the initiation of the preparation of a strategic plan for the MOND; (*c*) in the future, annual and six-month performance reports will be presented to Parliament, and (*d*) the Hormat and Gafat engineering factories have been incorporated as sub-agencies of the MOND.

Significant as this reform is, it falls far short of a planning, programming and budgeting system. However, even with the existing system of budget prepar-

---

[20] Budget Design Team, *Budget Reform Design Manual*, version 2.1 (Ministry of Finance: Addis Ababa, Jan. 2000).

ation and implementation, the research indicates that, if the suggested reforms are to bring about the expected benefits, it will need to be complemented with training of personnel at all levels to upgrade the standard of budget administration in the MOND. Additionally, the ministry will need to establish a cost-evaluation unit staffed with highly educated and experienced professionals.

VII. Conclusions

There is a paradox in the military budgetary process in Ethiopia. While Ethiopia has an established military culture which should provide a basis for a well-structured, cumulative and entrenched tradition of military budgeting, the political instability that has plagued the country has tended to undermine this. Different regime types with different ideological orientations, governance models and world views impose different management patterns on the military. In the current liberal democratic dispensation, the military budgetary process is carried out by different organs of government spanning the executive, legislature and bureaucracy (specifically, the Ministry of Finance and Economic Development and the Ministry of National Defence). As well as the MOND, the MOFED plays a key role in the military budgetary process in preparation, implementation, monitoring and evaluation. A zero-sum budgetary system has been adopted in military budgeting in Ethiopia.

While the formal process of military budgeting in Ethiopia is well laid out, it is accompanied by an informal process. Yet a strictly formal process is important in determining who actually does what and how it is done, and who wields what power and how it is wielded. For instance, while the legislature is formally conferred with wide powers in budgetary matters, in practice little of it is exercised with regard to the military sector; instead, the Prime Minister plays a pivotal role in the military budgetary process.

Similarly, the input of civil society is still very limited in the military budgetary process. Although Parliament conducts public hearings on budgetary matters for the different sectors of governmental activity, including defence, this does not usually result in any significant public or civil society input into the military budgetary process. Military issues generally remain 'sensitive' and largely classified, so any participation by civil society organizations in necessarily limited and uninformed. Moreover, only a few civil society organizations have the competence and expertise to analyse the intricacies, mechanisms and processes of military budgeting. The perceived 'sensitive' nature of military budgeting also discourages the public disclosure of off-line or extra-budgetary expenditure by the state.

There is a need to further democratize the process of military budgeting in Ethiopia (and in most other African countries). The budgetary process should be open to public scrutiny and discourse in order to improve the techniques used, ensure greater efficiency and better resource allocation, and extend the accountability of the nation's military sector.

4. Ghana

Eboe Hutchful

I. Introduction and background

As one of the first African countries to gain freedom from colonial rule, great hopes were vested in Ghana. However, in spite of the euphoria that accompanied independence, economic difficulties and years of military rule stifled the promised development.

Since the restoration of democracy in 1993, Ghana has emerged as one of the more stable countries in West Africa and perhaps one of the few with any serious prospect of democratic consolidation. An important question, which this chapter addresses, is what this implies for civil–military relations in general and the modalities of military budgeting in particular.

This section continues with an overview of the history, politics and economy of Ghana, followed in section II by a description of the military sector. Section III outlines the national budgetary process in general, while section IV describes the military budgetary process in particular. Section V provides an assessment of the process and section VI presents the conclusions.

History, politics and economy

Ghana, previously the colony of the Gold Coast, gained independence from the United Kingdom in March 1957, one of the first British colonies in Africa to do so. On independence the country had a relatively well-formed economy and national institutions—at least compared to other former African colonies—including the armed forces. However, from the mid-1960s, largely as a result of financial overextension from ambitious but ill-conceived development plans and adverse external market conditions, Ghana began to slide into a deepening financial and economic crisis. The country did not begin to re-emerge from this until the mid-1980s, following the adoption of rigorous macroeconomic and public sector reforms, including privatization of state-owned enterprises. In spite of protracted adjustment efforts, macroeconomic stability has remained elusive, with a continuing struggle to contain the deficit, particularly as donor inflows have tailed off substantially in recent years.

Over the same period, the country suffered from a succession of military coups and periods of military rule, interspersed with short-lived returns to civil rule. Of the 36 years between independence and 1993, Ghana was under military rule for a total of 23 years.[1] Ghana's 1992 constitution established a multi-party political system, with a directly elected executive President,[2] and civilian rule was restored in January 1993. Presidential elections in November 1992 were won by Jerry Rawlings, who had led a military government since 1981. Successful elections were subsequently held in December 1996, when Rawlings was re-elected; in December 2000, resulting in the first change of government through the ballot box since independence; and in December 2004, when President John Kufour was re-elected for a second term. The legislature is the unicameral Parliament, which has 230 members representing single-seat constituencies.

Ghana is a predominantly youthful country, with some 47 per cent of the population aged 18 or under.[3] The five largest ethnic groups in Ghana are the Akan (49.1 per cent), Mole-Dagbanis (16.5 per cent), Ewes (12.7 per cent), Ga-Adangbes (8 per cent) and Guans (4.4 per cent).[4] English is the official language, but major indigenous languages include Twi and other Akan dialects, Dagbani, Ewe, Ga and Hausa. Some 69 per cent of Ghanaians are nominally Christian, with Muslims accounting for 15.6 per cent and animists for 8.5 per cent; but the syncretic nature of religion, with many Ghanaians combining Christianity and traditional religious practices, makes such classification problematic.

Ghana's main exports are gold, cocoa, timber, diamonds, bauxite and manganese, although tourism and foreign transfers (from the Ghanaian diaspora) have recently emerged as important sources of foreign exchange.[5] Agriculture accounted for 35.2 per cent of gross domestic product in 2003, down from 59.7 per cent in 1983, while industry and services accounted for 24.8 per cent and 40.1 per cent, respectively. Gross national income per capita amounted to $320.[6] Ghana currently stands 129th (out of 174) on the Human Development Index, which is at the low end of 'medium' human development.[7]

[1] The military regimes were the National Liberation Council (Feb. 1966–Sep. 1969), the National Redemption Council and the Supreme Military Council (Jan. 1972–June 1979), the Armed Forces Revolutionary Council (June 1979–Sep. 1979) and the Provisional National Defence Council (Dec. 1981–Jan. 1993).

[2] Constitution of the Republic of Ghana, *Ghana Gazette*, 15 May 1992, URL <http://www.ghana.gov.gh/living/constitution/>.

[3] Ghana Statistical Service, *Ghana Demographic and Health Survey, 2003* (Macro International: Calverton, Md., 2004), p. 1.

[4] Ghana Statistical Service, *Ghana Living Standards Survey 4* (Ghana Statistical Service: Accra, 2000), p. 5.

[5] University of Ghana, Institute for Statistical, Social and Economic Research (ISSER), *The State of the Ghana Economy in 1998*, various annual edns (ISSER: Accra, various years); and Centre for Policy Analysis (CEPA), *Ghana Macroeconomic Review and Programme*, various annual edns (CEPA: Accra, various years).

[6] World Bank, 'Ghana at a glance', Fact sheet, Sep. 2004, URL <http://www.worldbank.org/data/>.

[7] UNDP Ghana and Institute for Statistical, Social and Economic Research, *Ghana Human Development Report 2000: Science Technology and Human Development* (UNDP: Accra, 2001), p. xiii.

Table 4.1. Military expenditure of Ghana, 1990–2004

Figures in US$ are in constant 2003 prices and exchange rates.

| Year | Military expenditure | | |
	$ m.	m. cedis	as a % of GDP
1990	19.6	9 006	*0.4*
1991	28.1	15 230	*0.6*
1992	30.5	18 201	*0.6*
1993	35.7	26 600	*0.7*
1994	38.8	36 147	*0.7*
1995	39.6	58 823	*0.8*
1996	33.4	72 644	*0.6*
1997	33.5	93 148	*0.7*
1998	41.6	132 812	*0.8*
1999	44.1	158 060	*0.8*
2000	61.8	277 269	*1.0*
2001	38.8	231 740	*0.6*
2002	43.5	297 800	*0.6*
2003	50.6	439 200	*0.7*
2004	65.5	636 100	..

GDP = Gross domestic product.

Source: SIPRI military expenditure database.

II. The military sector

The Ghana Armed Forces (GAF) are descended from the Royal West African Frontier Force of the colonial period. The GAF consist of an army, a navy and an air force and have a total strength of approximately 7000.[8]

The Ghana Army has two infantry brigades, each with three battalions: the First Brigade, which constitutes the core of the Southern Command, with headquarters at Teshie near Accra; and the Second Brigade, which forms the core of the Northern Command, headquartered in Kumasi. In addition, there are two airborne companies, the Support Services Brigade, combat support units—the Reconnaissance Regiment, two engineering regiments, the Artillary Regiment and the Signals Regiment—and the Army Recruit Training School.[9]

The Ghana Navy has a total strength of approximately 1000, divided into two commands, Eastern and Western, based at Tema and Sekondi, respectively. Its equipment consists of six coastal patrol boats.[10] The Ghana Air Force also has a strength of approximately 1000. It consists of one combat unit, three transport

---

[8] International Institute for Strategic Studies (IISS), *The Military Balance 2004/2005* (Oxford University Press: Oxford, 2004), p. 235.

[9] The 64 Infantry Regiment, a commando rapid deployment force perceived to be the 'Praetorian Guard' of the Rawlings regime and often accused of human rights abuses, has been disbanded.

[10] IISS (note 8).

squadrons and one helicopter squadron.[11] In addition, Ghana has paramilitary forces in the form of the Customs and Excise Preventive Service and armed police units.

Organizational control over the armed forces is exercised by the Ministry of Defence (MOD), which is headed by a minister and a deputy minister. The MOD is divided into two wings: a civil wing headed by the Chief Director and a military wing administered by the Chief of Defence Staff (CDS). There is a joint General Headquarters (GHQ) for the three services, which was established in 1962 to enhance coordination and economize on administrative costs. General Headquarters is directly under the Office of the CDS and is headed by a Chief of Staff of major general rank. Below GHQ are the three service headquarters, with each service commander combining both command and administrative functions. General Headquarters is responsible for the formulation and implementation of policies relating to force levels (i.e., manpower, equipment and logistics) and the planning, training, development and use of the human resources of the GAF. General Headquarters is divided into five departments under directors-general, each with the rank of brigadier general, in addition to the Finance Department, headed by the Defence Financial Comptroller (DFC) who also has the rank of brigadier general, and the Office of the Military Secretary. General Headquarters also oversees a number of tri-service institutions, including the Defence Intelligence Agency, the Directorate of Legal Services, the GAF Command and Staff College, the Military Academy and Training School, and the Kofi Annan International Peacekeeping Training Centre.

The Ghana Armed Forces have not engaged in an external war since independence, but they have been extensively involved in peacekeeping. Ghana is a member of the Economic Community of West African States (ECOWAS), and the GAF actively participated in the ECOWAS Military Observer Group (ECOMOG) in Sierra Leone and the ECOWAS Mission in Liberia (ECOMIL).

The impact of the military regimes on the military sector was far from straightforward: during the 1960s spending went up substantially, in the 1970s there were modest increases, while formal military expenditure was slashed by the Rawlings regime in the 1980s. As a proportion of total government expenditure, military spending fell from 8–9 per cent in the mid-1970s to less than 4 per cent by the end of the 1980s and through most of the 1990s.[12] As a proportion of GDP, military expenditure declined from 1.9 per cent in 1976 to hit its lowest level of 0.4 per cent in 1983; as shown in table 4.1, during the 1990s, spending fluctuated between 0.6 and 0.8 per cent of GDP, with a temporary bump up to 1 per cent in 2000, well below military spending by most of Ghana's neighbours.[13] Thus, while overall government expenditure rose

[11] IISS (note 8).

[12] Republic of Ghana, *Budget Statement for Fiscal Year 1976–77*, and subsequent edns (Ghana Publishing Corporation: Accra, various years).

[13] See the comparative data in Ghana Armed Forces Review Board (Kpetoe Board), 'Report of the review of the roles and structure of the Ghana Armed Forces', Ministry of Defence, Accra, Sep. 1996, p. 36. Note that these figures *do not* include extra-budgetary expenditure, which is discussed below.

substantially after 1983 in response to structural adjustment, military expenditure stagnated or declined. This has had a significant impact on the military's infrastructure and operational capabilities. The civil war in neighbouring Côte d'Ivoire and the disturbances in Ghana's Northern Region pose significant challenges to the ability of the armed forces to cope with potential spillover from these conflicts, such as refugees and border incursions.

Political involvement led to deterioration in the standards of management of the armed forces (particularly during the 1970s) and reduced financial probity and accountability. This led to increasing corruption. A 1988 enquiry into the armed forces reported a 'spate of embezzlements, misapplication of funds and other criminal activities involving service personnel', observing that 'misappropriation of funds has spread from command to the ranks in certain places'.[14]

III. The national budgetary process

Since the 1960s, budgeting in Ghana has taken place in the context of macroeconomic crises and a resource-constrained environment, and so it has revolved around competition between ministries, departments and agencies to defend their share of declining resources. The process itself has been fundamentally input-driven—and consequently tightly controlled by the Ministry of Finance (MOF)—rather than results-oriented. The process shares with the civil service and the rest of the government machinery many technical weaknesses, such as weak planning and coordination.

Since the national budgetary process has changed with the introduction in 1999 of the Medium-Term Expenditure Framework (MTEF), a historical overview is necessary before describing the current process.

The pre-1999 budgetary process

Prior to the introduction of the MTEF in 1999, the budgetary process in Ghana operated within an annual cycle consisting of four main phases: formulation, approval, implementation and evaluation. During the formulation stage, a broad macroeconomic framework was prepared by the MOF. In the July or August prior to the start of the financial year in January, the framework was issued to the sectors of government as the Budget Guidelines. In addition to policies and priorities, the guidelines showed the national expenditure ceiling, on the basis of which expenditure levels were established for each sector. These 'indicative ceilings' were determined by the cabinet based on the resources and revenues available. The guidelines spelled out the macroeconomic targets for the year and the form in which estimates were to be presented, with the aim of encouraging the sectors to present realistic proposals.

---

[14] Erskine Commission, 'Report of the Commission of Enquiry on the Structure of the Ghana Armed Forces', Ministry of Defence, Accra, 1988, vol. 1, pp. 58, 62.

After receipt of the Budget Guidelines, a draft budget was prepared by each ministry and presented to the MOF. This was followed by a budget hearing in which the MOF reviewed the submissions of the individual ministries with a team from that ministry. The ministry teams were usually led by the minister and included the deputy minister and the Chief Director and accountant of the ministry. The budget hearings would normally be chaired by the Minister of Finance or, in his absence, the Deputy Minister of Finance or the Chief Director of the MOF. The MOF then reviewed the performance and outcomes of the previous year's budget and made a tentative decision on the allocations for the following year.

The preliminary budget figure from the budget hearing was then submitted to the cabinet for final determination. The MOF used this final figure to prepare the overall budget estimates, which were then presented for approval to Parliament (or, under military regimes, by the cabinet).[15] The approval stage in Parliament started with the examination of the estimates by the appropriate select committees and ended with the passing of the Appropriations Act. Thereafter, the budget entered the implementation stage when the Minister of Finance issued a warrant to the Controller and Accountant-General authorizing expenditure to the limit of the appropriation. The Controller and Accountant-General in turn instructed the Treasury to allow the expenditure of specific sums of monies by ministries, departments and agencies (MDAs).

Theoretically, the annual process ended with an evaluation of budgetary performance that noted any lapses that needed corrective action. This included the audit of the budget and the accounts. This aspect of the cycle was, however, poorly observed.

This was the theory of budgeting in Ghana. In reality, the annual allocation of resources in Ghana was simply based on the historical shares of the sectors, changed incrementally each year. This and the dominance of recurrent spending over capital investment meant that budgetary allocations were relatively invariant, and increases were usually marginal. In addition, even after the budget had been approved, substantial cuts could, and often did, ensue in the event of revenue shortfalls (this has continued, e.g., in 2001). To guard against this eventuality, and to protect their share of the budget, ministries typically inflated their estimates. Actual expenditure data show that very few sectors operated within the approved limits. Expenditure was rarely on target: MDAs were just as likely to operate beyond their budget as to be restrained by the MOF from spending specific line items of the approved budget.

Public expenditure reviews revealed serious weaknesses in budget preparation and expenditure controls. At the MDA level, the preparation and defence of the budget were often relegated to low-level staff, indicating a lack of commitment by those in authority. Very few MDAs had properly established budget or planning units to undertake the work of budget preparation. Crucial

---

[15] Thus, the budget estimate went through 3 stages: the draft figures from the ministries, the preliminary budget figure after the budget hearings and the final allocation decided by the Cabinet.

budgetary decisions that should have been made by MDAs were thus made by the Budget Division of the MOF, even though this unit was itself frequently criticized for its lack of professional staff and technical weaknesses. Not surprisingly, MDAs in turn demonstrated little commitment to programmes and targets imposed on them by the MOF; in many cases, 'MDAs felt that they were only spenders and not responsible or accountable for the formulation and execution of their budgets'.[16] In many ministries the implementation of the budget was managed by middle-level personnel and the staff assigned to the ministry by the Controller and Accountant-General's Department, rather than by the top official technically in control of the budget, the Chief Director of the ministry.[17] These staffing weaknesses were exacerbated by procedural problems. Notices for submission of annual budget proposals were frequently circulated by the MOF at the last minute, sometimes giving the MDAs as little as two weeks to prepare and submit budget proposals.

Weak financial controls and over-expenditure by MDAs were further encouraged by the fact that under the 1981–93 military regime of Jerry Rawlings there was virtually no oversight and no constitutional requirement for MDAs to answer for over-expenditure of their budgets. Both the Controller and Accountant-General's Department and the Auditor-General's Department, charged with overseeing the financial operations of MDAs, were severely short-staffed, with only a few of the professional accountants that they need to carry out their assigned mandates.[18]

An earlier effort was made to address some of these problems by the establishment in 1983 of the Public Administration Restructuring and Decentralization Implementation Committee. A Policy Planning, Budgeting, Monitoring and Evaluation Department was established in each ministry as the basis for the introduction of a 'policy, programming and budget' system. Once again, this initiative was undermined by severe shortages of skilled and professional manpower, and by poor linkages and coordination between these new units and other departments within the ministries.

The post-1999 budgetary process

The introduction in 1999 of the Medium-Term Expenditure Framework was supposed to address the shortcomings of the budgetary process noted in previous public expenditure reviews. In contrast to the previous annual budgeting

---

[16] Ministry of Finance (MOF), *Public Expenditure Review 1993* (MOF: Accra, Apr. 1994), p. 72; and MOF, *Public Expenditure Review 1994: Effective Planning and Execution of the Development Budget* (MOF: Accra, June 1995), Appendix 1, p. 5.

[17] 'Over expenditure of budgets by ministries, departments and agencies', *Ghana Civil Service Journal*, nos 1 and 2 (1995), p. 16.

[18] Hutchful, E., *Ghana's Adjustment Experience: The Paradox of Reform* (James Currey: Oxford, 2002), pp. 110–11.

cycle, the MTEF relies on a three-year rolling plan.[19] The MTEF has several objectives: (a) to facilitate better, and more transparent, relationships between policies and objectives, and between inputs (resources) and outputs (results); (b) to effect a shift from input controls—which had been at the core of the previous budgetary process—to 'outputs' and service delivery; (c) to give MDAs greater freedom to decide their budgetary priorities, thus encouraging 'ownership' by sector ministries, while also promoting greater coordination within sector MDAs—the 'sector' now becomes the basis of planning; and (d) to make monitoring of inputs and outputs more rigorous through quarterly expenditure reports, thus ensuring greater transparency and accountability in expenditure management.

The MTEF has also greatly simplified the budgetary process. Budget estimates are now arranged under four heads: (a) personal emoluments, (b) administration, (c) service activities (maintenance, spares, fuel, etc.) and (d) equipment or capital expenditure, thus simplifying the budgetary process by eliminating the many confusing heads of expenditure found in previous budgets. The MTEF also confers on the MDAs greater flexibility in budgetary matters. The MDAs now have the power to shift funds between the expenditure heads b, c and d (although head a remains fixed) and to break down the various line items into sub-items, as long as they remained within the budget ceilings.

Reviews of outputs (results) are supposed to be carried out by MDAs and submitted to the MOF. Reviews are based on the framework of Ghana's Poverty Reduction Strategy and are mandatory for all ministries, including the MOD.[20]

Under the MTEF, the circulation of the Budget Guidelines by the MOF is now followed by sector policy reviews. Five sectors have been identified: Governance and Public Safety, Administration, Economic, Infrastructure and Social. The introduction of a Governance and Public Safety Sector—roughly equivalent to the concept of a 'security sector'—is an innovation of the MTEF. This sector includes the MOD, the Police Service, the Bureau for National Investigation (an intelligence agency), the National Disaster Management Organization, and the Commission for Human Rights and Administrative Justice. Each sector articulates its own policies and the goals or objectives to be realized in the three-year period.

The policy review process begins with a series of meetings and seminars over macroeconomic and sectoral goals involving representatives of the sector and of the MOF and the National Development Planning Commission.[21] The first of these is a plenary session, attended by the political leadership and special minis-

---

[19] Under the MTEF, programmes which are not completed within a year are rolled over into the next year. Programmes are expected to be completed within 3 years. In theory, this contrasts with the previous 'envelope budget', in which a fixed amount was allocated for specific projects.

[20] Ministry of Finance (MOF), *Ghana Poverty Reduction Strategy 2003–2005: An Agenda for Growth and Prosperity* (MOF: Accra, Feb. 2003), URL <http://poverty.worldbank.org/prsp/>.

[21] In 2002, e.g., there were 4 such meetings for the Governance and Public Safety Sector, the first lasting 3 days and the others 2 days each.

Table 4.2. Timetable for the preparation of the Ghanaian budget for financial year 2003

Activity	Date
Policy review workshop	17–29 Sep. 2001
Submission of policy review reports	27 Sep. 2002
Strategic plan review and costing	10–12 Oct. 2002
Budget Guidelines issued with ceilings	12 Oct. 2002
Submission of draft estimates by MDAs to MOF	22 Oct. 2002
Policy and budget hearings for MDAs	29 Oct.–2 Nov. 2002
MDAs submit final draft estimates to MOF	12 Nov. 2002
MOF finalizes draft estimates	13–18 Nov. 2002
Submission of draft estimates to cabinet	19 Nov. 2002
Submission of final draft estimates to Parliament	30 Nov. 2002[a]

MDAs = Ministries, departments and agencies; MOF = Ministry of Finance.

[a] The deadline of 30 Nov. for the submission of estimates to Parliament is constitutionally mandated. Constitution of the Republic of Ghana, *Ghana Gazette*, 15 May 1992, URL <http://www.ghana.gov.gh/living/constitution/>, Article 179.

Source: Short, J., 'Country case study 4: Assessment of the MTEF in Ghana', Centre for Aid and Public Expenditure, Overseas Development Institute, London, May 2003, URL <http://www.odi.org.uk/PPPG/cape/>, table 1, p. 2.

terial advisers, where there is a discussion of national goals and a review of the previous year's policy and policy goals. Among sector issues discussed are matters of coordination and interoperability.

On the basis of the sector review, inputs are identified and cost projections made. For this purpose, each ministry is required to have a Budget Committee, headed by the Chief Director, with representatives from all the departments and units within the ministry. The Budget Committee is responsible for preparing the draft estimates. As a guideline for the submission of the draft estimates, the MOF issues a budget ceiling for each ministry and department within the sector, indicating what resources are available and inviting them to prioritize their activities.[22] The resulting estimates are then forwarded to the MOF by the MDAs. The estimates are prefaced by a mission statement and a set of objectives supposed to be realized by the particular ministry during the budget cycle.

The next stage is the budget hearings. After hearings with the various MDAs, and after the MDAs have been given the opportunity to revise their estimates, the MOF collates the estimates from each sector into a consolidated budget.

[22] Critics of these budgetary ceilings claim that, since they reflect the MOF's projections with regard to revenue and other receipts for the financial year, they often bear little or no relation to the anticipated budgetary needs of the MDAs, thus in effect rendering the whole review process and the identification of sectoral and national goals academic. Nevertheless, the MOF introduced seminars on costing techniques in 2002 to help MDAs undertake realistic costing under the MTEF, even though improved costing is unlikely to have much bearing on real budgetary allocations. Budget officials, Ministry of Finance and Ministry of Defence, Interviews with the author, Accra, July 2002 and Jan. 2003.

The final stage in the budget cycle is the MOF's presentation of the consolidated budget to Parliament for approval.

Table 4.2 presents the timetable for the preparation of the budget for financial year (FY) 2003, as set out in the MOF's Budget Guidelines. Timetables such as this allow an unrealistically short period for the development of an MTEF budget. The budget statement is generally made in the February of the financial year and the Appropriation Act approved in March or April.

IV. The military budgetary process

To a large extent the military budgetary process in Ghana has replicated the procedures and characteristics of the overall national budgetary process and has shared its technical weaknesses. However, in addition to the usual secrecy and lack of transparency which have come to be associated with the process in many other countries, the military budgetary process in Ghana has had several peculiarities of its own.

In the 1980s and 1990s structural adjustment programmes were undertaken to reform the public sector and its financial management structures. These programmes exacerbated the differences between the mainstream and military budgetary processes in two ways. First, these reforms were not directed at the security sector, other than in controlling the size of the military budget. Thus, attempts at reform of the budgetary process within the military lagged behind the rest of the public sector and so are a relatively recent development. Second, the structural adjustment programmes brought an inflow of donor funding to the public sector that was not replicated in the military sector; if anything, defence and security expenditure suffered greater retrenchment than other sectors, at least formally. The military sector responded to budgetary contraction by turning to extra-budgetary expenditure. This behaviour has to be taken into account when evaluating the allegedly 'exemplary' character of military expenditure management in Ghana.

Even so, the recent changes in the military budgetary process have been driven by, and largely reflected, changes in the overall national budgetary process; in other words, they have emanated from outside rather than from within the military.[23] These changes, such as the introduction of the MTEF, have increased convergence between the civil and military budgetary processes.

The pre-1999 military budgetary process

As in other government ministries, formal budgeting in the MOD began when the ministry received the Budget Guidelines from the MOF. The process was initiated by the Defence Financial Comptroller, who is the chief financial

---

[23] In the same way, the present structure of the MOD has reflected the provisions of the 1993 Civil Service Law (Provisional National Defence Council Law no. 327), rather than the peculiar needs of a defence ministry.

adviser to the Chief of Defence Staff. The DFC then issued letters to the three service commanders,[24] the Chief of Staff at GHQ, the Office of the Principal Secretary of the MOD (now the Office of the Chief Director) and other units, asking them to send in their requirements. These accounting units, whose expenditure formed the budget, were called 'allotment holders'. Once these individual estimates were collected the budget was compiled, with the DFC and the Office of the Chief of Staff coordinating the process. The estimates were then sent to the Office of the Principal Secretary and to the minister when they were ready for presentation to the MOF or Parliament. Once the budget had been approved the DFC was again in charge of allocating funds back to the allotment holders.

Several characteristics of the military budgetary process are worth comment.

Military domination of the process and weak ministerial control

As the account above suggests, the role of the civil wing of the ministry in the preparation of the budget was marginal; civilians entered the picture only when the internal budgetary process was virtually complete and the estimates were required to be forwarded to the MOF. The Office of the Principal Secretary (the civil wing of the MOD), far from being the budgetary authority, was considered merely another allotment holder and was invited by the DFC to submit its estimates like any other unit under the ministry. Once the ministry's budget had been approved and implemented, the DFC had effective authority over the allotments.

This process took control of the financial affairs of the armed forces out of the hands of the minister, as the chief accounting officer and final authority, and the civilians running the ministry, and placed it in the hands of the military itself. For all practical purposes ministerial control did not exist in the armed forces, a unique situation in the public sector.

The Ministry of Defence was (and continues to be) identified with the armed forces. Traditionally, the Minister of Defence was regarded as little more than a figurehead; the linchpin of the ministry was the Principal Secretary (now known as the Chief Director). The functions of the MOD were limited. In the main, it acted as a conduit or clearing house between the military and the political authorities. A primary responsibility of the MOD was to defend the military budget and other interests of the armed forces. The ministry had few planning, strategic, budgetary, accounting or procurement functions and many policy initiatives originated from GHQ. The MOD simply lacked the personnel and expertise; its staff complement was minimal and consisted mostly of junior civil servants and clerks. A survey of the ministry in 2000 observed that, owing to

---

[24] The service commanders had their own service financial controllers, who were posted from the Office of the DFC and were responsible for coordinating the preparation of the budgets of their units.

the history of coups, 'the Military seem to have usurped some of the functions and role of the MOD and made it more or less play second fiddle'.[25]

On the military side of the MOD, GHQ had a dominant role in budgeting and financial operations relative to the services. Armed Forces Regulations vested authority for the financial administration and accounting of the GAF primarily in GHQ and the DFC. These same regulations restricted the financial authority of the three service commanders, and then were entirely silent on the role and power of unit commanders in this area.[26] This high degree of centralization had negative consequences: as one report observed, with the growing squeeze on the military budget, 'securing approval for the procurement of even minor maintenance items has become so stringent and cumbersome that all Service HQs are finding it extremely difficult to administer their units, bases and stations'.[27]

Absence of strategic planning

The Ghana Armed Forces have traditionally operated without a defence policy, threat assessment, doctrine or force planning. Consequently, the military budgetary process was characterized by a lack of strategic planning, and there was no monitoring or evaluation mechanism to assess the pattern and quality of defence expenditure.

This problem went beyond the GAF. In theory, issues of strategy are the responsibility of the National Security Council. In reality, a strategic policy framework has never been developed in post-colonial Ghana.[28] Nevertheless, the armed forces could not escape blame entirely; within the institution, issues of strategy and doctrine received little attention, even among commanders.[29]

In the absence of policy and a strategic framework, the compilation of military estimates was dictated mostly by the ceilings imposed by the MOF. Thus, budgeting became a simple exercise, not markedly different from the process in the civilian ministries. Staff officers took the previous year's estimates and repackaged them for submission, noting what was actually approved and adding a large margin to protect against the risk of cuts.[30] In the course of each finan-

[25] Beneficiary Survey, 'Final report', Ministry of Defence, Accra, Apr. 2000, p. 21; see also Kpetoe Board (note 13), p. F-1.

[26] The pertinent regulations appear to be the 1970 Armed Forces Regulations (Finance), but articles 1.24 and 4.06 of the Armed Forces Regulations (Administration), vol. 1, also specify the roles of service and formation commanders.

[27] Erskine Commission (note 14).

[28] The post-independence government of Kwame Nkrumah (1957–66) came closest to developing such a framework.

[29] Dumashie, H. K. (Air Marshal), former Chief of Defence Staff, Interview with the author, Accra, Aug. 2002. Among the several reasons for this was the fact that most senior officers in the GAF had professional training up to Grade 2 Staff Course level only. As the 1996 Kpetoe Board's report suggested, 'The lack of . . . training at higher levels has made senior officers limited in their professional skills, outlook and education'. Kpetoe Board (note 13), p. F-20.

[30] Dumashie (note 29).

cial year the deficiencies of this form of 'budgeting' become apparent, with regular shortfalls.[31]

Inter-service rivalry

The fact that planning and coordination between the services played little or no role in the budgetary process exacerbated inter-service rivalry. Budgeting essentially took the form of independent exercises by the individual services, with the results collated by the MOD's Budget Committee and with little strategic coordination. Indeed, collaboration between the service commanders in the process was virtually non-existent. Except in a few cases, the CDS did not have the power—or perhaps the inclination—to force greater collaboration between the services; coming from a particular service, he tended to be seen as biased.

The budgetary process has traditionally been dominated by the army, by far the largest service.[32] Until the late 1980s, most of the foreign exchange allocation of the armed forces was appropriated by the army, leaving little to support the needs of the two smaller services. The army also dominated GHQ and the position of the CDS. The Support Services Brigade, established in 1969 to centralize and rationalize the logistics services of the armed forces, was also biased towards the army.

The army's appropriation of the bulk of defence spending contributed directly to the deterioration of the other two services noted by the Erskine Commission in 1988.[33] Responding to the findings of the commission, the government attempted to rectify this traditional bias by directing more resources to the air force and the navy, triggering a struggle between the services to enlarge or protect their turf and, for the first time, forcing service commanders to seek some coordination of the budget process.[34]

Role of the Ministry of Finance

Proceedings at the budget hearings were (and continue to be) a major means for the MOF to exercise control over the military budgetary process, particularly after the structural adjustment programmes.[35] However, these controls have tended to be fairly crude since, at least in the past, details of the budgetary

[31] Saaka, S. S., former Chief Director of the MOD, Interview with the author, Ministry of Defence, Burma Camp, Accra, July 1995.

[32] However, the centralization of control and disbursement of financial resources by GHQ and the lack of monitoring and dissemination of defence budget allocations and outcomes often make it difficult to determine the exact distribution of the budget between the services.

[33] Erskine Commission (note 14).

[34] This shift within the defence budget was particularly evident in 1995 and 1996 (see note 83 below). A former CDS observed that these 'budgetary swings' from the army to the air force and navy were the 'only times that we saw the Service Commanders relating'. Dumashie (note 29).

[35] It was not unusual for the Minister of Defence to complain that the restructuring plans of the MOD had been blocked by the refusal of the MOF to release the money required. Iddrissu, A. M., Minister of Defence, Interview with the author, Ministry of Defence, Burma Camp, Accra, Aug. 1995.

requests of the armed forces were not disclosed at the budget hearings. The MOF usually received a one-line statement specifying the amount required for the operations of MOD, with no breakdown of the figure. Questions were not invited or welcomed, for reasons of 'security'. The MOD budget hearings were little more than a ritual: to determine how much the military could spend, not how or why. It was not unusual for there to be two versions of the military budget, one highly confidential with accurate data and another designed for the public.[36]

Such devices are apparently no longer considered necessary: military estimates arriving at the MOF are now much more transparent, with a higher degree of detail and improved justification of proposed expenditure and acquisitions. What has not changed is the capacity problem within the MOF: the ministry still lacks officials with the requisite training or skill in defence analysis or procurement, and thus the ability to scrutinize defence proposals. An additional problem (discussed below) is that the MOF has had little control over the off-budget expenditure of the armed forces and, until recently, little information pertaining to this expenditure.

The post-1999 military budgetary process

Formulation and approval

The reformed budgetary process in the Ministry of Defence by and large follows the contours of the post-1999 national process. The MOD, like the other ministries, must preface its budget estimates with a mission statement and set of objectives. According to its mission statement, the MOD exists 'to proactively promote national defence interests' through: (*a*) 'Effective formulation, co-ordination, monitoring and evaluation of defence polices and programmes'; (*b*) 'Maintaining the Ghana Armed Forces (GAF) in a high state of preparedness for national and international engagements'; and (*c*) 'Active involvement in the promotion of peace and stability in the country and the sub-region'. The aims and objectives of the MOD are stated to be: (*a*) 'To enhance defence Policy and Control'; (*b*) 'To improve the state of combat readiness' of the GAF; (*c*) 'To support national effort aimed at transforming the nature of the economy to achieve growth and accelerating poverty reduction especially the vulnerable and excluded'; (*d*) 'To improve logistics and infrastructure facilities'; and (*e*) 'To improve civil–military relations'. [37]

The MOD budget process starts with the policy review organized by the MOF for all sector MDAs. The resulting review is presented to the Minister of

---

[36] MOF official, Personal communication, Accra, July 2005.

[37] Ministry of Defence, 'Vision and mission statement' and 'Aims and objectives', Republic of Ghana Internet site, URL <http://www.ghana.gov.gh/governing/ministries/governance/defence.php>.

Defence and the CDS for their input. Following their approval, the review is communicated to the 'cost centres' and 'allotment holders'.[38]

The Chief Director of the MOD then issues budget instructions to the Chief of Staff at GHQ. Thse are subsequently passed on to the various cost centres and allotment holders via the Department of Plans and Development, asking them to submit their draft estimates based on the reviewed policies and objectives, and on expectations regarding the availability of resources. The cost centres communicate these to their various commands, which in turn forward them to the units and departments under their jurisdiction. The budgeting sequence then flows back from the unit (battalion, station or base) to formation or command,[39] and then service levels.

At the unit level the budgeting exercise focuses on MTEF head b, 'administration'; head c, 'service activities' (maintenance, spares, fuel, etc.); and head d, 'equipment or capital expenditure'. It does not cover head a, 'emoluments', which is handled for the armed forces as a whole by the MOD's Department of Personnel Administration. During the exercise, units are expected to communicate any new threats identified within their area of operations. The units' submissions are also expected to address concerns regarding needs omitted or deferred as a result of lack of funding. The units usually have about two weeks in which to submit their proposals. There is no budget committee at this level.

The units then send their estimates to the next level, the formation or command, where they are collated and forwarded to the next level, the service headquarters. At this stage, the draft budgets list the anticipated needs of the units, formations and services; some preliminary costing is undertaken, in terms of identifying the resources and equipment required and their likely cost. These 'exhibits' (as these raw documents are called) are then sent to the Department of Plans and Development at GHQ. Here, coordination of the submissions from the various services is undertaken; duplication, overlaps and conflicts are identified; and costing is reviewed. The coordinating role of this department is a new element in the armed forces budgetary process since 1997.

The Department of Plans and Development forwards its preliminary figures to the MOD's Budget Committee, which then collates them in accordance with the four MTEF categories and design a three-year rolling plan. The MOD's Budget Committee has 10 members: the Chief Director (chairman), the Director-General of Plans and Development (deputy chairman), the Director of Plans, the Director of Finance and Administration, the MOD's accountant, the Deputy Director of Inspection and Monitoring, the Defence Financial Comptroller, the Deputy Director of Budget (from the Office of the DFC), the

---

[38] Budgeting terminology in the MOD now makes a distinction between so-called 'cost centres', which consist of the major departments (the civil wing of the MOD and GHQ); the 3 services and tri-service institutions such as the GAF Command and Staff College; and 'allotment holders', which are departments and units within the individual services.

[39] The formation is the brigade in the case of the army, the Eastern Naval Command in the case of the navy and the Takoradi and Tamale Stations in the case of the air force. The command is the army's Southern or Northern Command, the Western Naval Command or the Accra Air Force Base.

Officer-in-Charge (from the Office of the DFC) and the Deputy Director of Equipment (secretary).[40]

During this process the MOF communicates to the MOD its budgetary ceilings for the ministry. These ceilings are regarded as indicative rather than final; it is assumed that there is still room for negotiation with the MOF over the final budgetary figures. However, they are used as a basis for reprioritizing the needs of the armed forces and for allocating funds between the various cost centres and allotment holders. The Budget Committee follows this up with a series of meetings with these budgetary entities to review their requirements, including outstanding projects rolled over from previous budgets. These meetings are coordinated by the Department of Plans and Development.

The Budget Committee presents the resulting draft to the CDS. After this, the committee meets again for any amendments to the estimates. A final presentation is then made by the Budget Committee, led by the CDS, to the Minister of Defence.[41] Thereafter the approved draft estimates are submitted to the MOF.

The next stage is the budget hearing at the MOF. The MOD team, led by the minister, usually consists of the CDS and representatives of the Budget Committee, but not the service commanders. At the budget hearing, the Minister of Finance reviews the estimates with the MOD team and, after some negotiation, finalizes the ministry's ceilings for the year. The MOD team then returns to the ministry with this ceiling, re-examine the ministry's priorities and adjust the figures accordingly to arrive at the final estimates.

The final stage is when the MOD estimates are laid before Parliament. The team from the MOD that appears before the parliamentary hearing is led by the minister. At the meeting of the Parliamentary Committee on Defence and Interior, it is mandatory for the Minister of Finance to be present; this is not usually the case with other MDAs, where the presence of the Chief Director of the MOF is considered sufficient. The Parliamentary Committee in turn forwards its observations and recommendations to the floor of Parliament,[42] where the estimates are considered for final approval.

Procurement

The structure of military procurement in Ghana, and control over the procurement process, has had a chequered history, as a result of both weaknesses in the

---

[40] The Budget Committee includes no representatives from the 3 services. This may reflect the limited financial role of the services and the service commanders. Planning input from the services emanates primarily from the service directors within the Directorate of Plans and Development, who are of lieutenant colonel rank (wing commander in the case of the air force and commander in the case of the navy). Many of the meetings of the committee are actually chaired by the deputy chairman, who is a military officer.

[41] In spite of its formal constitutional mandate, the Armed Forces Council appears to have no role in the budgetary process, although on at least one occasion in the past it has intervened with the Minister of Finance when it considered the budgetary allocation for the military to be too low.

[42] Open discussion of the defence estimates on the floor of the House (rather than merely in committee) did not resume until 1994.

system and tussles between the civil and military wings of the MOD.[43] The current procurement system involves several committees at various levels within the MOD and the GAF.

The first is the Procurement Planning Committee, which is chaired by the deputy minister and has a regular membership of about 12 (although others may be co-opted), including the civilian Chief Director, the CDS, the GHQ Chief of Staff and representatives of the services. This committee starts its work, which in theory includes determining priority acquisitions in the light of the funding available, after Parliament approves the military budget.

The recommendations of the Procurement Planning Committee are forwarded to the Defence Contracts Committee, which is chaired by the minister with the Chief Director as secretary. This committee approves acquisitions and gives the authorization to tender.

Procurement decisions on behalf of individual services are actually initiated by Service Technical Committees, which are ad hoc committees put together by the respective service whenever major acquisitions are being considered.[44] Their recommendations are forwarded to the CDS and then on to the MOD and the Defence Contracts Committee. The MOD is expected to be represented on these service committees but the critical staffing situation in the ministry means that this does not often happen.

Tendering is undertaken by the MOD's Tender Board, chaired by the minister. There are also tender committees which carry out limited procurement for specialized units: these are the Ordnance and Stores Procurement Committee (chaired by the Director of Ordnance), the Defence Engineering Services Procurement Committee (chaired by the Director of Engineering Services) and the Food Tender Committee (chaired by the Director of Supply and Transport).

This is the MOD procurement structure on paper. However, the actual process appears to be much messier, as several allegations of corruption and impropriety in recent years would suggest.[45] The procurement process is allegedly often short-circuited by the military under claims of 'urgency', citing the need to fill immediate operational requirements. The military have their own preferred equipment types and established links to suppliers. It is not unknown for the military to place orders, and thus commit the MOD to a pur-

[43] The procurement system was criticized as 'hopelessly outdated' by a British training mission that studied the operations of the GAF at the invitation of the government of Hilla Limann (1979–81). During the 1980s the State Supply Commission was also requested to examine the GAF's procurement system and make recommendations for improvement. The fact that a senior civilian official of the MOD could still claim in 1995 that the GAF have 'no procurement system to speak of' suggests that nothing came out of these initiatives. Saaka (note 31). Unsuccessful efforts to reform the system under Limann are discussed in Hutchful, E., 'Restructuring civil–military relations and the collapse of democracy in Ghana, 1979–81', *African Affairs*, vol. 96, no. 385 (Oct. 1997), pp. 535–60.

[44] Service commanders can authorize minor purchases.

[45] For instance, the circumstances surrounding the procurement of 4 Russian Mi-17 helicopters from Wellfind, under a special loan intended to resupply Ghana's peacekeeping forces, attracted considerable adverse press comment. The MOD and the minister himself have gone to some trouble to rebut these allegations. Aning, K., *Military Imports and Sustainable Development: Ghana Case Study* (African Security Dialogue and Research: Accra, 2003).

chase, before requesting authorization from the ministry. 'Security' is also used as an excuse for limiting transparency.

The formal procurement process has been an area of considerable friction and competition at the highest levels of the MOD. This was certainly the case with minister E. K. T. Donkoh and his military chiefs; Donkoh complained that everyone in the MOD was 'running around trying to act as a procurement officer'.[46] Much of the current weakness in the system is blamed on the fact that the Procurement Planning Committee, which should coordinate procurement, is not functioning properly and has become virtually moribund.[47] This means that the individual services, rather than the MOD, are the driving force in procurement decisions, with adverse consequences for standardization and interoperability. The 1996 Kpetoe Board's review of the GAF noted that 'procurement within the MOD has generally been delegated to the GHQ directorates without adequate co-ordination and monitoring. Most major equipment acquisitions are done by individual services without any consultation with sister Services.'[48] This situation has not changed materially. Whether the 2003 Public Procurement Act, which seeks to regulate procurement practices across all public enterprises, makes a difference remains to be seen.[49]

V. Assessment of the military budgetary process

Impact of the Medium-Term Expenditure Framework

Even though the introduction of the MTEF has improved the military budgetary process, some problems have emerged. The principal problems are: revenue fluctuations and shortfalls, which have undermined predictability; and the late release of funds—and often no release at all—by the MOF, which means that many projects provided for under the approved budget frequently fail to materialize or fall far short of completion. In addition, actual expenditure bears little resemblance to approved budgetary allocations, with most ministries overshooting or, as is at least as often the case, underspending their allocations. In the armed forces, the shortfall areas are usually operational: fuel, rations, equipment, utilities and food. Finally, the lack of provision for contingencies means that unanticipated security operations—such as those in the Northern Region in 2001–2002[50]—and natural disasters can completely disrupt the military budget.

---

[46] Donkoh, E. K. T. (Lt Col.), Minister of Defence, Interview with the author, Burma Camp, Accra, 23 Aug. 2000.

[47] Interview with the author, Ministry of Defence, Accra, 30 Nov. 2004.

[48] Kpetoe Board (note 13).

[49] Public Procurement Act 2003, Act 663 (Government Printer: Accra, Dec. 2003), URL <http://www.parliament.gh/>.

[50] 'Ethnic clashes in northern Ghana', BBC News Online, 4 Dec. 2000, URL <http://news.bbc.co.uk/2/1690746.stm>.

On the whole, the budgetary allocations of MOD appear to be haphazard and unpredictable, although perhaps no more so than for other MDAs.[51] For FY 2003, the MOD proposed a total budget of 1.5 trillion cedis ($187.5 million) but received an allocation of only 439.17 billion cedis ($54.9 million). In FY 2004 the allocation was 636 billion cedis ($74.4 million).[52] In the negotiations for the 2004 budget, the Minister of Defence invited the Parliamentary Committee on Defence and Interior to meet with the MOD and the service commanders at Burma Camp, site of the MOD and GHQ. In presentations to the committee members, the three commanders pointed to the severe degradation in capability which had occurred in their service as a result of underfunding and the Chief of Staff outlined the state of peacekeeping capabilities. While the presentations certainly had the desired impact on the parliamentarians, the budgetary allocation for FY 2004 does not suggest that it made a difference where it really mattered. This is not surprising considering the limited power of Parliament in this respect.

Under the MTEF, as under previous budgetary systems, both head a, personal emoluments, and head b, administration, are protected, while heads c and d, service activities and equipment or capital expenditure, tend to bear the brunt of cuts. Emoluments are by far the largest category in the budgets of all ministries. This means that the ability to deliver service and sustain core functions—the goal of the MTEF—suffers, undermining the whole notion of 'results-oriented budgeting'.

Another feature is the large, and sometimes hidden, deficits carried by all ministries from year to year in the form of unpaid bills. For instance, by 2001 the MOD had outstanding utility bills of 26.8 billion cedis ($3.6 million), leading to threats to cut supply and an ongoing dispute between the MOD and the MOF as to who was going to settle these bills. There was also another 'off-budget' outstanding bill of 94.87 billion cedis ($12.9 million) made up of both local claims and foreign contractual obligations,[53] which the MOF had allegedly agreed to settle. The local claims included unpaid bills to food contractors and other suppliers; the MOD usually deals with this situation by simply moving on to new local suppliers. According to the MOD, total GAF indebtedness to the Tema Oil Refinery amounted to over 60 billion cedis ($6.7 million) in late 2004, attracting annual interest at a rate of 45 per cent.[54]

The MTEF's requirement for quarterly expenditure reports by MDAs is often not observed. Evaluations of 'outputs' are supposed to be carried out by the MDAs themselves, rather than by an independent agency. These reports have

---

[51] As the officer in charge of orchestrating the military budget complained, 'the MOF comes up with figures totally unrelated' to the budgetary needs and submissions of the GAF, even though the military deliberately 'aims at the barest minimum [required] to keep afloat'. Abdulai, A. K. (Brig.), Director-General for Plans and Development, Interview with the author, General Headquarters, Burma Camp, Accra, 10 Jan. 2003.

[52] Interview with the author, Ministry of Defence, Accra, 30 Nov. 2004.

[53] Parliamentary Committee on Defence and Interior, 'Report from the Select Committee on Defence on the 2001 draft annual estimates for the Ministry of Defence', Accra, Mar. 2001.

[54] Interview with the author, Ministry of Defence, Accra, 30 Nov. 2004.

tended to receive little attention and are in any case difficult in the current situation of unpredictable resource flows.

Interviews by the author with budget officials in the MOD and elsewhere suggest some disillusionment with the MTEF. There is a widely held opinion that the MTEF has failed to transform the financial environment for, and the basic approach to, budgeting. In particular, persistent revenue instabilities and budget cuts have undermined the predictability and 'strategic vision' supposedly associated with the MTEF. Budgetary allocations and adherence to the budget continue (as in the past) to hinge on resource availability. Thus, the budgetary process continues to be very much input-driven; in this sense, the power and intrusiveness of the MOF have in no way diminished.

All MDAs have responded by retreating into old and familiar budgetary habits, such as 'incremental budgeting'. According to the former Chief Director of the MOD who was responsible for implementing the MTEF in the ministry, the budgetary process in the MOD is 'no different from the past': 'we are still doing the [same] old thing'.[55] In his view, the MTEF is 'meaningless'. Figures are frequently arrived at by guesswork and are not based on any realistic projections. Budgeting has come to be seen as a 'mere academic exercise' and budget estimates thus have no sense of priorities. The MOF does not query this situation and fails to exercise appropriate controls because the MOF itself lacks commitment to the process.

The notion of 'strategic planning' has never been taken very seriously in the MOD. The MOD's statement of 'objectives' does not appear to be supported by any of the basic elements of strategic planning, such as a threat assessment; the identification of strategic options; and decisions regarding force structure, training and weaponry. This is not surprising given that there is still no defence policy on which to base the statement.

In the absence of a defence policy and strategic framework to guide the planning process, the CDS issues an OpTraLog (Operational, Training and Logistics) statement, which incorporates the GHQ's Policy Guidelines and Strategic Aims and addresses the roles of its departments. This has grown from the one- or two-page annual 'Strategic Letter' or 'Defence Directives' issued by previous CDSs to a 39-page document in its 2002–2003 version. However, the OpTraLog statement is still focused almost entirely on internal security threats; with the exception of peacekeeping and ECOWAS commitments, there is little discussion of an external role.

The output-oriented MTEF poses particular problems for the MOD. The type of outputs contemplated by the MTEF are not easily quantified in the case of an institution such as the MOD. How can 'security' be measured? When are people more, or less, secure? The problem is exacerbated by the marginal role played by the Governance and Public Safety Sector in the Poverty Reduction Strategy, which now forms the framework for evaluation of outputs.

---

[55] Saaka, S. S., former Chief Director of the MOD, Interview with the author, Accra, July 2002.

Extra-budgetary expenditure

Although its magnitude is hard to determine, there is no doubt that the use of extra-budgetary sources to offset the decline in military expenditure since the 1980s has become an important feature of military spending on new equipment and contingency expenses, particularly in meeting the needs of the air force and the navy. Indeed, a former CDS describes the military as 'notorious in extra-budgetary expenditures'.[56] This resort to off-budget spending, and the fact that for much of the 1980s defence expenditure was excluded from the official budget, presents a challenge to obtaining a true picture of Ghana's military spending.[57] This is particularly the case since the funds for most major acquisitions and refits do not necessarily come from the formal military budget approved by Parliament but are more likely to come from extra-budgetary sources: from Ghana's external peacekeeping accounts in particular and, in one recent instance, from a commercial loan. On the other hand, it is worth remembering that major military acquisitions of any kind have been few and far between.

There are several sources of extra-budgetary revenue. The first is the New York-based accounts of the Ghanaian United Nations peacekeeping forces. There are apparently several of these accounts; the exact number could not be established. The conduct of these accounts is characterized by lack of transparency. What seems clear is that the accounts have been a crucial, but not necessarily large, source of funding for military purchases. According to senior military and civilian officials in the MOD, most of the capital expenditure of the military is from these accounts.[58] However, these accounts cover not only capital spending: in one year the military withdrew about $500 000 to meet its food bill arrears.[59] Such expenditure appears to have been authorized directly by the President and is not reflected in the annual military budgets.[60] In addition to their use for military procurement, past governments have apparently also dipped into these accounts for a variety of undisclosed purposes, such as down-payment for the lease of a presidential jet.

---

[56] Dumashie, H. K. (Air Marshal), former Chief of Defence Staff, Written communication with the author, Aug. 2002.

[57] Both the International Monetary Fund and the Ghanaian MOF admitted in the mid-1990s that it was difficult to determine with any accuracy the actual levels of military expenditure. For this reason, this chapter refrains from alluding to any hard figures and from trying to reconcile the different data sources. For a relevant discussion see Omitoogun, W., 'Ghana', *Military Expenditure Data in Africa: A Survey of Cameroon, Ethiopia, Ghana, Kenya, Nigeria and Uganda*, SIPRI Research Report no. 17 (Oxford University Press: Oxford, 2003), pp. 49–62.

[58] Hence, purchases of new equipment do not appear in the published military budgets. Donkoh (note 46); and Dumashie (note 56).

[59] Donkoh (note 46).

[60] The accounts are controlled directly by the Office of the President and administered by the Controller and Accountant-General. Applications for withdrawals go directly to the Office of the President, which authorizes the Controller and Accountant-General, who in turn notifies the Chief Treasury Officer in New York. Since 1998, however, the MOF has been responsible for transfers into (and out of) the accounts. Parliament, which urged an audit of the accounts in 2001, does not appear to have any control.

The size of these offshore accounts directly reflects the scale of Ghana's peacekeeping activities, which, as one of the largest troop-contributing countries to the United Nations, are extensive. Such activities are increasingly regarded by the GAF, like many other countries' armed forces, as a form of 'commercial' investment.[61] In recognition of this, in 2002 the MOD proposed, and Parliament approved, a loan of $55 million from Barclays Bank to procure equipment (including four transport helicopters) to support Ghana's peacekeeping efforts. Similarly, after many years of almost uninterrupted degradation in force levels—currently less than a third of approved maximum force levels— the government has decided to recruit an additional 4000 troops specifically to boost peacekeeping capability. In addition to helping subsidize military spending at a time of severely contracted military budgets, peacekeeping missions have served as an important, and much prized, source of official patronage, allowing troops to supplement their meagre wages and to acquire a variety of goods not available to them in Ghana.[62]

A second source of 'under the table' expenditure is from contingency funds from elsewhere in the governmental machinery, provided to respond to crises such as natural disasters and the conflicts in the Northern Region.

A third source of extra-budgetary revenue is the military's own services and economic operations, such as the Military Hospital in Accra and the now-ceased Airlink domestic flight operations. Like the peacekeeping funds, this revenue is termed 'internally generated funds'; the Ministry of Finance allows MDAs to draw on a certain proportion of such funds to support their expenditure. Here again, the problem is that of transparency: the exact scale of the revenue from these internal sources is unknown—even to the civil wing of the MOD—and this information has been jealously protected by the military.[63] However, this lack of transparency is being gradually eroded. General Headquarters is now required by the MOD to submit monthly returns of revenue from its internal operations, although the returns are not yet monitored, and there is some scepticism within the ministry as to their comprehensiveness.

Parliamentary oversight of the budgetary process[64]

Parliamentary oversight of the military budget, such as it was, resumed in 1993 when the legislature reconvened after some 11 years of military rule. The frequent interruptions of constitutional rule by military coups since independence

---

[61] Adu-Amanfo, F. (Brig.), Director of Defence Intelligence (and an expert on peacekeeping), Presentation to Parliamentary seminar, GAF Command and Staff College, Accra, 24 July 2004.

[62] Erskine, E., *Mission with UNIFIL: An African Soldier's Reflections* (Hurst and Company: London, 1989), p. 156.

[63] Past and current Chief Directors of the MOD have spoken about the difficulty of obtaining data on this income from the armed forces. A long-serving Chief Director claims that he did manage to get such information from the Chief of Staff in GHQ, but purely as a 'personal favour'. Saaka (note 55).

[64] This section draws heavily on Hutchful, E., 'Parliamentary oversight of the security sector', Paper presented at a workshop on Security Sector Reform and Democratization in Africa: Comparative Perspectives organized by African Security Dialogue and Research, Accra, Feb. 2002.

had made it difficult for Parliament to build consistent traditions of reviewing military spending or to benefit from a learning curve.

The work of the Parliamentary Committee on Defence and Interior started in earnest in 1994 with visits to military installations. The 'awful conditions' encountered by the committee,[65] in barracks, hospitals and operational facilities, resulted in the committee becoming, in its own words, 'sympathetic to the cause of the military' and a cornerstone of support for increased military spending.[66] Since then, in its recommendations to the House, the committee has been consistent in its demands for greater budgetary support for the armed forces. For example, in 2000 the committee reported that 'over the years the Ministry of Defence has been under financed resulting in deterioration and in many cases total run-down of logistic facilities and welfare infrastructure. The Military has had to always employ her professional competence, discipline and loyalty to accomplish its mission in the face of acute deficiencies.'[67]

The committee has tried to make the MOF pick up the massive deficits which the MOD, like other ministries, has been forced to carry from year to year as a result of inadequate budgets. It has also tried to secure subsidies for the defence budget by advocating that the cost of certain expenditure and investment be borne by other government or public agencies, including local governments.

However, the committee's sympathy for the military should not disguise the difficulties that it has encountered in trying to execute its functions of evaluating spending proposals from the armed forces. The committee has no permanent or specialized staff and thus has limited expertise for analysing the budget. Its first chairman, retired Lieutenant Colonel Ebenezer Anku-Tsede, was dependent on the assistance of the military command when preparing reports to Parliament. Because the committee had no office of its own, instead of the military coming to Parliament, budget meetings have sometimes been held in military camps. This psychological atmosphere has not been conducive to the work of the committee.[68] The committee has often found that it lacks data critical for making a proper evaluation of the defence estimates. On the other hand, Parliament and the committee have not consistently pressed for expanded or independent access to data, on the assumption that this will not be forthcoming.[69] This relates to a broader problem: a tradition of self-censorship within Parliament. Parliament has never fully resolved the issue of how far it can or should go in considering the military budget, nor whether it has the right

[65] Anku-Tsede, E. (Lt Col. (rtd)), former chairman of the Parliamentary Committee on Defence and Interior, Interview with the author, Accra, July 1996.

[66] 'Report of the Committee on Defence and Interior on the Working Visit to the Air Force Stations in Takoradi and Tamale on 11th and 18th July 1994, Second Session of the First Parliament of the Fourth Republic', Parliament of Ghana, Accra.

[67] 'Report to the House on the Armed Forces Estimates for 2000', Parliament of Ghana, Accra, p. 8.

[68] Ackah, J., ranking member (and former Chair) of the Parliamentary Committee on Defence and Interior, Interview with the author, Accra, Feb. 2002.

[69] Ackah (note 68). According to Ackah, the intelligence estimates (presented to the Finance Committee as part of the budget of the Office of the President) represented an even greater challenge from the point of view of transparency.

to debate it openly or on the floor of the House.[70] Oversight of procurement has been equally limited: during the presidency of Jerry Rawlings, the committee seemed aware that arms and equipment (such as the G3 rifle and armoured vehicles) were being procured 'under the table', but took no action.[71] Equally, there has been no parliamentary oversight of the peacekeeping account held in New York, a source of extra-budgetary funds of some significance, even though the Auditor-General was asked to audit this account in 2001.

The lack of a formal defence policy means that there is no framework within which to discuss and evaluate issues of defence and defence budgeting. The work of the Parliamentary Committee in this area, and of Parliament generally, has thus been lacking in policy content and debate. As suggested above, the introduction of the MTEF has not resolved this problem. Like the Ministry of Defence itself, the committee has focused overwhelmingly on welfare issues as they affect soldiers, and these issues have formed the core of discussions of the budget with the minister and the MOD.

However, Parliament has begun to investigate this absence of a defence policy. For example, in a debate on the annual estimates of the MOD for 1997, J. H. Mensah, the parliamentary leader of the then-opposition New Patriotic Party (NPP), demanded that the MOD 'furnishes the House with a Defence White Paper against which we might be able to consider its budget in subsequent periods. . . . it certainly does not seem to me a very effective way of doing our job as a democratic Parliament to vote appropriations for a Ministry without any idea whatsoever about the policy that is to be implemented with those appropriations'.[72]

Two other controversial issues that Parliament has sought to tackle—although not particularly forcefully or successfully—are the auditing of military weaponry and the off-budget spending of the armed forces. In the first case, the refusal of the military to give the Auditor-General access to military stores was brought to the attention of the Public Accounts Committee and debated in Parliament.[73] The armed forces were urged to discuss the issue with the National Security Council and the government and to present Parliament with proposals as to how far auditing of military stores should go. However, it is not certain that even this permissive posture has produced any positive results.[74]

Regarding the issue of off-budget military revenue and expenditure, Parliament has complained about the secrecy surrounding the peacekeeping account. The response has been that, since every member of the armed forces knows how the peacekeeping funds are spent, there is no 'secrecy' about it within the

---

[70] *Parliamentary Debates* (Accra), 14 Aug. 1981, columns 1797–99.

[71] Anku-Tsede (note 65).

[72] Mensah, J. H., *Parliamentary Debates* (Accra), 19 Mar. 1997, column 2205.

[73] Mensah, J. H., *Parliamentary Debates* (Accra), 24 Mar. 2000, column 4189.

[74] See also the discussion on auditing below.

military itself.[75] This hardly addressed the question and again demonstrates the limited influence of the legislature when it comes to issues of defence spending.

Nevertheless, the Parliamentary Committee has enjoyed a good working relationship with the military high command. It is not always clear, however, that the positive sentiments expressed by Parliament are reciprocated. Senior MOD officials see the MOF, not Parliament, as the real powerhouse. It has become obvious to the MOD that Parliament and the Parliamentary Committee on Defence and Interior have no real impact on the defence estimates. A senior official of the MOD described discussions with the Parliamentary Committee as a 'sheer waste of time', complaining that it 'cannot add a pesewa' to the defence estimates.[76]

Parliament is not the only institution with an interest or role in the oversight of military expenditure. Non-governmental organizations (NGOs) and the Ghanaian media have shown increasing interest in the national budgetary process and increasing sophistication in engaging with it and with a range of public policy issues, particularly those connected with the Poverty Reduction Strategy. The opportunity for this increased engagement has been created by the growing transparency of the budgetary process, by the increasing receptiveness of parliamentarians themselves and by various projects—including one funded by the US Agency for International Development, USAID[77]—designed to build bridges between Parliament and NGOs. However, this interest has yet to extend to the military budgetary process itself, although both NGOs and the media maintain a sharp, but not always sympathetic or well-informed, vigilance on military expenditure and procurement,[78] and they thus play a potentially important oversight role.

A small number of NGOs—African Security Dialogue and Research, the Ghana Centre for Democratic Development, and the Foundation for Security and Democracy in Africa—have been working closely to broaden the capacity of the Parliamentary Committee to deal with military and security issues, as well as facilitating dialogue and interactions between the security and civil sectors, a situation unimaginable only a few years ago.

Auditing and financial control

Probably the most contentious issue to arise in recent years with regard to military expenditure is whether the Auditor-General's Department has the right to audit the accounts of the Ministry of Defence, as it does for other ministries and public agencies. In fact, the debate has been less about auditing the financial accounts—which has been done routinely—than the right to audit so-called

[75] Donkoh, E. K. T. (Lt Col.), responding to Mensah (note 73), *Parliamentary Debates* (Accra), 24 Mar. 2000, column 4189.

[76] Saaka (note 55). A 'pesewa' is figuratively a 'penny' or a 'cent'.

[77] This is USAID's Democratic Governance Program; see URL <http://www.usaid.gov/missions/gh/democracy/background/>.

[78] See Aning (note 45).

'warlike stores'. The 1999 Auditor-General's Report complained that the team that audited the MOD had been denied access to certain stores that included such items as arms, ammunition and aircraft on grounds of 'security'.[79] The military has reiterated this position in various forums.[80] Although this resistance to audit has officially been justified on the basis of 'national security', it could equally be related to the corruption that has sometimes characterized the procurement process. It is not clear whether this deadlock has been resolved.[81]

The issue of overall financial control also remains unclear. As indicated above, the Armed Forces Regulations, which date back to 1970, had made the Defence Financial Comptroller responsible for all matters relating to finance in the MOD as well as financial adviser to both the CDS and the Chief Director. The DFC was also responsible for internal auditing of the armed forces since the office responsible for this function, the Internal Audit Department, fell under his establishment. However, following the reorganizations introduced by the 1993 Civil Service Law, a new Division of Finance and Administration was created in the Office of the Chief Director, responsible for all financial matters relating to the MOD. The exact demarcation of power and responsibilities between the (civilian) Director of Finance and Administration and the DFC—who continues to be the chief disbursing and accounting officer for the armed forces and, to all intents and purposes, for the ministry as well—remains to be clarified. Underlying this issue is the deeper, and even more vexed, question of the relationship between the CDS and the Chief Director. Acknowledging the civilian Director of Finance and Administration as the ultimate financial authority in the ministry implies that the CDS would have to report the financial business of the armed forces to this officer, thus subordinating the CDS indirectly to the Chief Director. Hence, there have been suggestions that the civilian director should be responsible only for the civil branch of the ministry.

VI. Conclusions

Military budgeting in Ghana has many historical weaknesses, but there have also been some recent improvements, both in terms of the size of the budget and in terms of the budgetary process. The budgetary process has traditionally been driven by financial imperatives, and hence by the Ministry of Finance, rather than by strategy or doctrine. This is true for the public sector as a whole, the MTEF notwithstanding. While the extent to which the presence of a strategic policy framework would have alleviated these financial constraints is debatable, its absence has aggravated the problem and inhibited better management of scarce resources.

---

[79] *Parliamentary Debates* (Accra), 24 Mar. 2000, column 4041.

[80] For instance, the Director of Defence Intelligence, Brig. Adu-Amanfo, repeated this argument at the Ghana–South Africa Roundtable on Security Sector Reform and Democratization sponsored by African Security Dialogue and Research, Ministry of Defence, Accra, 8 June 2000.

[81] See the discussion on Parliament above.

There have been efforts to correct the most egregious shortcomings of the budgetary process. The most notable recent developments are the introduction of the MTEF and the reintroduction of parliamentary oversight—one the result of and the other incidental to democratization. However, within the armed forces there have also been modest changes. In place of a defence policy, the CDS issues an OpTraLog statement. The GAF have also adopted a long-term equipment rehabilitation and replacement programme, although it is not clear what this is based on, in the absence of threat analysis.

Another quiet but significant development is the key role assumed since 1997 by GHQ's Department of Plans and Development in coordinating the military budget, having orchestrated the introduction of the MTEF, and providing some semblance of a planning process

A more questionable development, given this context, is the extension of the armed forces' mission, both imposed and self-assigned. The 'mission creep' into civil and development areas is reflected in the rather vague and self-serving phrases in the MOD's recently revised mission statement, in particular, new references to the 'protection of the vulnerable and excluded'. The focus on poverty reduction has meant that the military has extended its objectives to include socio-economic goals, such as disaster management, extension of health services to civilians and the opening up of the Afram Plains to development, as core rather than secondary goals. However, lack of funding has not permitted even these modest developmental goals to be accomplished.[82]

The return to a parliamentary regime has also had a positive, if marginal, impact on the military budgetary process in several ways. For example, parliamentary oversight has resulted in somewhat greater transparency with regard to the armed forces. Having been unavailable for years, relatively detailed armed forces estimates are once again available to the public through the records of the parliamentary debates.[83] The need for ministers to respond to questions in Parliament on the budget has also helped to some degree to consolidate ministerial authority in the MOD. The introduction of the MTEF has facilitated this process in a variety of ways, one being to integrate military budgeting more closely into the overall public expenditure management system. Equally, the many problems in the execution of the MTEF have placed real limitations on the ability of the political authorities, and Parliament in particular, to carry out the policy and oversight functions associated with this new public expenditure management tool.

A major question remains the capacity of civilian policy, planning and oversight institutions in general and the MOD in particular to execute their assigned

---

[82] For instance, as its contribution to 'poverty alleviation' in 2002, the GAF were asked to pick 3 districts from the 3 most deprived regions for extension of health services. The selection was made, but the funding to execute the project never materialized.

[83] The defence estimates for 1995 and 1996 were formally published in separate documents, a practice that was not continued. Republic of Ghana, *Annual Estimates for 1995*, vol. 21, *Defence* (Ghana Statistical Service: Accra, 1995); and Republic of Ghana, *Annual Estimates for 1996*, vol. 21, *Defence* (Ghana Statistical Service: Accra, 1996).

roles. The MOD has still not been able to develop a defence policy framework, and thus exercises little policy direction over the military; 'policy initiatives' at the ministry continue to involve approving policies and programmes originating from GHQ, leading to a tendency to see the MOD as an appendage to the armed forces rather than the driving force.[84] Even though there is a Planning, Budgeting, Coordinating, Monitoring and Evaluation Division in the MOD, it does not have the capacity to function properly. A key problem is the unsatisfactory personnel situation in the MOD: the ministry has few senior or trained civilian cadres. Of the four directors mandated by the 1993 Civil Service Law, only one has so far been appointed. Until recently there was frequent rotation of senior personnel—essentially civil servants transferred, often unwillingly, from other ministries, in most cases moving on after only three or four years. There are no professional career lines and few of the training programmes and incentives that are available elsewhere in the civil service.

The Performance Improvement Programme (PIP), supported by the British Government and its Defence Advisory Team, aims to enhance the performance of the MOD by improving its organizational and management structure and human resource capability; establishing a management information system; and relocating the ministry from Burma Camp, the main military barracks in the capital. The PIP has moved very slowly, however, and appears to lack the necessary political commitment.[85]

The ultimate, but rarely stated, purpose of the PIP is to rebalance the relationship between the MOD on the one hand and GHQ and the GAF on the other by shifting powers and functions from the latter to the former. The MOD's Beneficiary Survey of April 2000 put the issue fairly bluntly, arguing that 'The supremacy of MOD over GAF would need to be put beyond any shadow of doubt particularly with the return of the country to Constitutional rule'.[86] Given the present level of complacency within the MOD, this is unlikely to happen soon.

[84] Beneficiary Survey (note 25), p. 21.
[85] The PIP commenced as part of the Civil Service Performance Improvement Programme, which ran from 1997 to 2001. However, the programme in the MOD showed little progress until an agreement was negotiated for British support in 2001. Support from the Defence Advisory Team runs until 2006.
[86] Beneficiary Survey (note 25), p. 3.

5. Kenya

Julius Karangi and Adedeji Ebo

I. Introduction and background

Kenya, like many other African nations, is a product of the contradictions of colonial rule; this is manifested in an ethnically fractured populace and a feeble economy. In the face of scarce and ever-shrinking resources, how those resources are distributed among the various competing priority areas and the factors which affect the process and determine the outcomes represent legitimate and fruitful areas of study.

This case study analyses the processes through which money is allocated to the Kenyan armed forces and the mechanisms for controlling such funds. The chapter begins with an overview of the history, politics and economy of the country. This is followed in section II by a description of the structure and composition of the military sector in Kenya. Section III describes the national budgetary process, highlighting the various actors and the underlying guidelines, especially the Medium-Term Expenditure Framework (MTEF). The military budgetary process is discussed in section IV, starting with a brief overview of the military budget, including its composition, and followed by an account of the mechanisms for controlling, monitoring and evaluating the military budgets. Section V presents an overall assessment of the military budgetary process by juxtaposing the formal mechanism with actual practices. In the concluding section VI recommendations for improving the military budgetary process are made.

History, politics and economy

Kenya gained independence from the United Kingdom in December 1963, following years of unrest caused by the Mau Mau armed rebellion. Shortly after independence, Kenya became a de facto one-party state ruled by the Kenya African National Union (KANU) of President Jomo Kenyatta. Kenyatta ruled until his death in August 1978, when he was succeeded by Daniel arap Moi. In 1982, amid growing political dissatisfaction and in order to silence the opposition, President Moi made Kenya a de jure one-party state. In 1992, however, Kenya caved in to Western and domestic pressure and permitted multiparty politics.

Other political parties were able to compete with KANU in the national elections of 1992 and 1997 and, for the first time since the early years of independence, members of opposition parties became Members of Parliament, introducing a system of checks and balances. A new parliamentary practice was established requiring that the official leader of the opposition in the House is also the chairman of the Public Accounts Committee, one of the most important committees of Parliament. The Public Accounts Committee examines the appropriation accounts and the report of the Controller and Auditor-General.

Kenya maintains a unitary constitution with a structure of government that has hardly changed since independence, despite some 29 piecemeal constitutional amendments.[1] Under pressure from the opposition parties (as well as international institutions and governments such as the International Monetary Fund, the World Bank, the USA and the UK), the Constitution of Kenya Review Commission was established in 1991 in order to reform the constitution through a process of constructive engagement with civil society. After much delay,[2] the new constitution, which reduces the powers of the President and creates a new office of Prime Minister to head government,[3] will be voted on in a referendum in October 2005.

According to the current constitution, executive power is in the hands of the President, who is also the head of state and commander-in-chief of the armed forces, and the Cabinet of 15 ministers, responsible for the day-to-day running of the country. The current President, Mwai Kibaki, was elected in December 2002, ending KANU's monopoly on power. The legislature is the unicameral Parliament or National Assembly. Of the 222 seats in Parliament, 210 are directly elected for a five-year term while the remaining 12 are filled by presidential appointees nominated by the parties in proportion to their electoral support. President Kibaki's National Rainbow Coalition holds 125 of the directly elected seats.

The Kenyan economy is basically agriculture-orientated, with that sector accounting for over 70 per cent of the total employed population.[4] The main cash crops are coffee, tea, pyrethrum and horticultural produce, especially flowers. Closely following agriculture are the manufacturing, tourism and general services sectors. Since independence, the Kenyan economy has had a chequered record of economic growth. It grew rapidly during the first decade after independence: between 1964 and 1971 the economy registered annual gross domestic product (GDP) growth averaging 6.5 per cent.[5] Throughout the 1970s and 1980s Kenya was showcased as a capitalist development success story in Africa. This economic development was, however, fuelled by massive

[1] Republic of Kenya, *Constitution of Kenya* (Government Printer: Nairobi, 1998), URL <http://www.kenyaconstitution.org/>.

[2] See, e.g., 'Kenyan constitution chief resigns', BBC News Online, 1 July 2004, URL <http://news.bbc.co.uk/2/3857457.stm>.

[3] National Constitutional Conference, 'Revised zero draft of a bill to alter the constitution', 27 Feb. 2004, URL <http://www.kenyaconstitution.org/>.

[4] Van Buren, L., 'Kenya: economy', *Africa South of the Sahara*, 30th edn (Europa Publications: London, 2000), p. 618.

[5] Van Buren (note 4).

Western aid,[6] and by the late 1980s the structural defects in the system became glaringly obvious. The defects were compounded by the short-term dislocation caused by a donor-inspired structural adjustment programme, inadequate macroeconomic management and political uncertainty.[7] A major deficiency in the system has been the absence of any noticeable link between budgets and policy goals owing to a combination of factors that are discussed in section VI.

II. The military sector

The military sector in Kenya consists of the army, the air force and the navy. However, for the purposes of this chapter, the General Services Unit (GSU), a paramilitary force, is also discussed briefly. The armed forces are managed by the Department of Defence (DOD), which, rather than constituting a separate ministry, is located in the Office of the President. There is a minister of state in the Office of the President who is in charge of matters pertaining to the DOD and also acts as the chairman of the Defence Council under powers delegated by the commander-in-chief (the President). Responsibility for the day-to-day running of the armed forces is assigned to the Chief of General Staff (CGS), who is in charge of command and control of the DOD. The position of CGS is established as the most senior in the military under the 1968 Armed Forces Act.[8] There is also a deputy secretary in the Office of the President who serves as the accounting officer of the DOD. Each of the three services has a commander who is responsible for command and control of the respective service and is answerable to the President through the CGS. The GSU is within the police force but is classified as a separate force. It plays a largely internal role in the country.

The army

The Kenya Army has a strength of some 20 000 personnel,[9] which remained essentially unchanged throughout the 1990s. The army is the oldest of the services in the Kenyan armed forces, with its origins in the 19th century when the Imperial British East Africa Company hired some *askaris* (the Swahili word for uniformed guards) to guard its investments on the coast. This small entity evolved over the years to become the King's African Rifles (KAR), the pre-independence predecessor of the Kenya Army.

---

[6] Between 1980 and 2001 Kenya received a total of $15 billion in development assistance. O'Brien, F. S. and Ryan, T. C. I., 'Kenya', eds S. Devarajan, D. Dollar and T. Holmgren, *Aid and Reform in Africa: Lessons from Ten Case Studie*s (World Bank: Washington, DC, 2001), p. 514.

[7] Economist Intelligence Unit (EIU), *Country Profile: Kenya* (EIU: London, 1998).

[8] Armed Forces Act, Chapter 199 of the Laws of Kenya, *Kenya Gazette Supplement*, 29 Nov. 1968.

[9] International Institute for Strategic Studies (IISS), *The Military Balance 2004/2005* (Oxford University Press: Oxford, 2004), pp. 236–37.

The army was formed to respond to external threats, but it was soon faced with internal problems such as the Shifta secessionist movement,[10] banditry and cattle rustling. In addition to its primary assignment of defending the nation against external land-based aggression, the army has acquired a secondary, largely internal, assignment—the provision of aid and support to civil authority in the maintenance of law and order during national disasters and emergencies. As well as the commitments of national defence and internal security, the Kenya Army has continuously participated in international peace-support initiatives of the United Nations (UN), and the Organization of African Unity (OAU) and its successor, the African Union (AU).

The air force

The Kenya Air Force (KAF) was established in June 1964 and currently has a strength of some 2500 personnel.[11] It is descended from the former British Royal Air Force station at Eastleigh in Nairobi, which was used as a staging post for the British Middle East Command during World War II. The primary roles of the KAF are to establish supremacy in the defence of Kenyan air space, provide aid to civil authority and support the army and the navy during operations. Like the Kenya Army, the air force participates in peace support operations worldwide.

Following the attempted military coup of August 1982, in which mainly KAF officers were implicated, the force was disbanded. The rump of the force was an appendage of the army until 1994, when it was restored as an independent service.[12]

The navy

As with the army and the air force, the Kenya Navy is an offshoot of colonial administration, being descended from the Royal East African Navy (REAN). The REAN served the four former British East African colonies—Kenya, Tanganyika, Uganda and Zanzibar—with its headquarters in Mombassa, Kenya.

The navy has two bases, in Mtongwe (Mombassa) and Manda (near Lamu). Like the other services, the navy contributes officers and men to UN peace-keeping missions in addition to its primary role of defending the country

[10] The Shifta separatist movement consisted of ethnic Somalis who wanted to be part of Somalia upon Kenya's independence. For a number of years the Kenyan security forces had to engage them in a low-intensity guerrilla war.

[11] IISS (note 9).

[12] Willis, D. (ed.), 'Kenya Air Force', *Aerospace Encyclopedia of World Air Forces* (Aerospace Publishing: London, 1999), p. 139.

against seaborne aggression. The current strength of the navy stands at some 1620 men.[13]

The General Service Unit

The General Service Unit is technically a unit of the police force, but for specific tactical, bureaucratic and, especially, historical reasons it is classified as a separate force. It was established in 1948 (before independence) as an emergency company, the Regular Police Reserve, to deal specifically with insurgency in the country and was re-designated in 1953 as an independent unit that was fully equipped to deal with the Mau Mau insurgency.

The GSU is still an independent unit headed by a commandant and with a strength of 5000 men.[14] It is a highly trained paramilitary force, reputed to be capable and firm in dealing with matters of internal security (such as anti-riot operations), and has been deployed mainly to deal with the Shifta insurgency (in joint operations with the other security forces) in the North-Eastern Province and other areas of the country in the recent past.

III. The national budgetary process

The Kenyan government budgetary process is a deliberate and systematic attempt to allocate public resources to various ministries and departments in order to finance activities and programmes within their respective mandates. The principal law on public finance is the constitution, with more specific provisions in the 1995 Exchequer and Audit Act.[15] This act specifies modalities for raising revenue for government (including the military) and managing expenditure. The act, together with the Paymaster-General Act,[16] also specifies procedures for releasing money from the consolidated fund to the accounts of operating ministries.[17]

The Minister of Finance has an obligation under the constitution to provide Parliament with draft estimates of revenue and expenditure for approval before the start of the financial year.[18] The constitution distinguishes between mandatory expenditure, the consolidated funds and public debt. In view of the fact that authority to withdraw from the consolidated fund is granted annually, the government must seek and obtain approval to raise revenues and incur expenditure before 30 June each year (i.e., before the start of the financial year), as

---

[13] IISS (note 9).

[14] IISS (note 9).

[15] Exchequer and Audit Act, Chapter 412 of the Laws of Kenya, *Kenya Gazette Supplement*, 1 June 1995, available at URL <http://www.cagindia.org/mandates/>.

[16] Paymaster-General Act, Chapter 413 of the Laws of Kenya, *Kenya Gazette Supplement*.

[17] Kirira, N., 'Kenya', ed. A. Fölscher, *Budget Transparency and Participation: Five African Case Studies* (Idasa: Cape Town, 2003), URL <http://www.idasa.org.za/>.

[18] Republic of Kenya (note 1), Section 100; and Kirira (note 17).

outlined in Parliamentary Standing Order Number 133. Parliament cannot, however, introduce any new expenditure or tax measures, nor can it increase those already approved. The government's request to Parliament is presented in a speech by the Minister of Finance in which proposed policy changes in the coming financial year are outlined; this is recognized as symbolizing the beginning of the legislative process.[19]

Organization

The national budgetary framework is composed of five levels and actors (see figure 5.1). At the apex is the Cabinet, which formulates national policies and objectives, followed by the Planning and Budgeting Steering Committee, which consists of permanent secretaries and coordinates policies and objectives. At the remaining levels are the Macroeconomic Working Group, which makes the economic forecasts and determines the resources available, and the sector working groups (SWGs), serving as coordination hubs for groups of ministries whose functions overlap; the MTEF Secretariat; and, lastly, the line ministries and departments.

The Medium-Term Expenditure Framework facilitates the full participation of line ministries and departments in the SWGs. In addition, the MTEF Secretariat within the Ministry of Finance (MOF) draws up the lists of ministries and departments that are to participate in each SWG, along with the terms of reference for each SWG. There are eight sector working groups: (*a*) agriculture and rural development; (*b*) physical infrastructure; (*c*) human resource development; (*d*) trade industry and tourism; (*e*) public administration; (*f*) public safety, law and order; (*g*) national security; and (*h*) information and technology.

A typical SWG consists of a chairman, a secretary (both of these from the MOF) and members drawn from line ministries or departments that have programmes and activities in the sector. However, a sector working group can incorporate other stakeholders from the sector when necessary. The main terms of reference of the SWGs include identifying sector objectives and core priorities; analysing the cost implications of the policies and strategies within the sector; identifying programmes and activities and their outcomes, along with output benchmarks within the sector; and streamlining the programmes' activities with the national spending limits and overall finance strategies.

While a ministry or department can participate in more than one SWG, the Department of Defence participates in only one—the National Security Sector Working Group (NSSWG). The DOD's Chief Finance Officer, its Chief of Finance and the 'Colonel, Budget' are members of the technical working team of the NSSWG, while the Senior Deputy Secretary and the Vice-Chief of General Staff are members of the NSSWG itself.

---

[19] Kirira (note 17), p. 117.

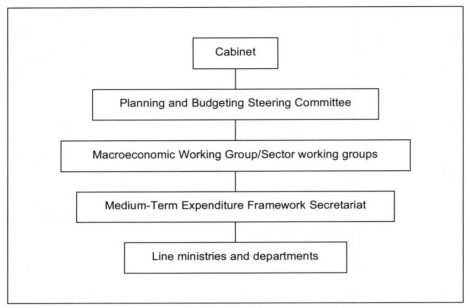

Figure 5.1. Actors in the Kenyan national budgetary framework

The Medium-Term Expenditure Framework

The current budgetary process is guided by the Medium-Term Expenditure Framework that was introduced in financial year 1999/2000 to replace the Forward Programme Review and Forward Budget System. The MTEF is defined as a deliberate strategic policy and expenditure framework within which the main organs of government are given greater autonomy in the selection and prioritization of their activities and the allocation of resources.[20] It is an effort to overcome the problems of the previous poor linkages between policy, planning and the budgetary process.

The overall aim of the MTEF is to impose discipline in the management of national resources by establishing an explicit link between the annual budgetary process, agreed national policies and long-term national development objectives. The MTEF was adopted to meet the need for sectoral planning with clearly articulated sectoral priorities; the need to link planning to budgeting; the need to improve the level of participation in the budgetary process; the need to

---

[20] Kirira, N., MOF Financial Secretary, 'Kenya's national economy, its capacity and performance and the implications of the MTEF budgetary process on military expenditure', Paper presented to the Senior Military Officers Seminar, Karen, Nairobi, 7 Aug. 2002.

plan ahead, say, for three years, with high predictability of resources; and the need for a method of monitoring and evaluation by linking input to output.[21]

The calendar of events for the MTEF activities of a financial year (1 July–30 June) starts early in the year, often in February, with the finalization of a revised budget for the outgoing year. This is followed in March with the submission of sectoral reports and the dispatch of Treasury Circulars and sectoral spending limits. The month of April is reserved for the bidding for resources by each sector, the submission of itemized budgets to the Treasury, the review and consolidation of MTEF budget estimates, and the submission of draft budget proposals to the Treasury for approval. The budget estimate is printed by mid-May. The MTEF calendar ends in June with the submission of estimates to Parliament for formal approval. This calendar applies to all line ministries, including the DOD. The main objectives of the MTEF are: (*a*) to improve the macroeconomic balance by developing a consistent and realistic resource framework; (*b*) to improve the allocation of resources to agreed strategic priorities both between and within sectors; (*c*) to secure the commitment of ministries and departments to increased predictability in resource allocations so that spending agencies can plan ahead; (*d*) to increase incentives for more effective (i.e., better targeted) and more efficient use of resources by ministries and departments by providing them with predicable funding levels and increased autonomy; (*e*) to link the annual budget to long-term development policies, objectives and plans; (*f*) to assess the actual cost of programmes, particularly new ones, and the likely financial implications in the long term; and (*g*) to review in detail all projects, particularly in the development vote and including those financed by external resources, vis-à-vis the benefits being generated and the consistency of project and sectoral objectives with national development objectives.[22]

IV. The military budgetary process

Any discussion of the military budgetary processes in Kenya should take into account the country's domestic and international security environment. Apart from the low-key insurgency operations in the North-Eastern Province, which have continued for over three decades, Kenya has never been involved in a conventional war; it has therefore never required heavy expenditure on war efforts, as have its neighbouring states. The military has, however, played a crucial role in ensuring the stability of the country since independence.

The most immediate potential security threats to any country are from its neighbours; therefore, based on the external threat analysis, a substantial

[21] Republic of Kenya, *National Development Plan 2002–2008: Effective Management for Sustainable Economic Growth and Poverty Reduction* (Government Printers: Nairobi, 2002), p. v.

[22] DOD Chief Finance Officer, 'DOD budget', Paper presented to the Senior Military Officers Seminar, Karen, Nairobi, 9 Aug. 2002.

Table 5.1. Military expenditure of Kenya, 1990–2004

Figures in US$ are in constant 2003 prices and exchange rates.

Year[a]	Military expenditure		
	$ m.	m. shillings	as a % of GDP
1990	390	5 684	2.9
1991	304	5 279	2.4
1992	224	5 027	1.9
1993	187	6 131	1.8
1994	156	6 577	1.6
1995	180	7 668	1.6
1996	210	9 756	1.8
1997	200	10 327	1.7
1998	188	10 381	1.5
1999	183	10 684	1.4
2000	197	12 614	1.6
2001	226	15 349	2.2
2002	244	16 844	2.0
2003	246	18 676	1.9
2004	237	20 158	..

GDP = Gross domestic product.

[a] Years are calendar years, not financial years.

Source: SIPRI military expenditure database.

amount of military expenditure has been related to these threats. The level of military spending, at an average over the period 1990–2003 of 1.9 per cent of GDP (see table 5.1), correlates with the rate of economic growth and can therefore be termed optimal.[23]

The most important determinant of peacetime military spending is the expenditure level of neighbouring states and the need to maintain spending on a par with them, or slightly higher depending on the perception of the threat (see table 5.2, which presents Kenyan Government figures). The situation in the eastern Africa region has, however, been stabilized by the reconciliation of the states through cooperative endeavours such as those of the Intergovernmental Authority on Development (IGAD) and the East African Community (EAC).[24]

Historically, Kenya's peace and tranquillity have been challenged by the many conflicts in East Africa, the Horn of Africa and the Great Lakes region. Protracted armed conflicts in Ethiopia and Uganda in the past have had a direct

---

[23] Kirira (note 20).

[24] The IGAD's mandate is to coordinate the efforts of the member states—Djibouti, Eritrea, Ethiopia, Kenya, Somalia, Sudan and Uganda—in the priority areas of economic cooperation, political and humanitarian affairs, and food security and environment protection. The EAC was re-formed in 1999 by Kenya, Tanzania and Uganda with the aim of widening and deepening coordination in political, economic and social fields.

negative impact on Kenya. The collapsed state of Somalia, which neighbours Kenya to the east, has had a significant impact on Kenya's internal security situation owing to a huge influx of refugees and the proliferation of small arms in the country.

As Kenya is a developing country, the level of technological advancement is still very low. The country does not develop or manufacture any military hardware and, hence, only insignificant funds are budgeted or spent on research and development. Each of the services operates a mix of systems. In the case of the KAF, for example, this means that maintenance of the front-line fighters, radar systems and missiles is scattered worldwide and the life span of this equipment is largely dependent on factors that are beyond the operator's or the country's control. Essentially, all the equipment in use by the military, such as tanks, aircraft, ships, communications systems and even vehicles, is purchased from developed countries and its maintenance alone takes over 20 per cent of the annual military budget. However, the bulk of DOD expenditure is on personal emolument, which takes about 45 per cent of the budget.[25]

Preparing the budget

The Department of Defence prepares its MTEF budget in line with guidelines given in Treasury Circulars issued by the Permanent Secretary of the Ministry of Finance. The exercise is carried out under the direction of the DOD's Departmental Budget Committee. The committee is chaired by the Chief of General Staff, with the Chief of Finance (usually a brigadier) as its secretary. The other members include the Vice-CGS, the Senior Deputy Secretary (the accounting officer), the service commanders (of the army, the air force and the navy), the assistant CGSs and the Chief Finance Officer (a civilian).

The Departmental Budget Committee reports to the National Security Sector Working Group, which is comprised of representatives of the Treasury, the DOD and the National Security Intelligence Service. The committee is serviced by the Budget Secretariat, which is a technical team that works on the details of the planning and preparation of the budget. The secretariat is headed by the Chief Finance Officer, assisted by the Chief of Finance, with the Colonel, Budget serving as the secretary. Other members of the Budget Secretariat are the chiefs of the DOD branches, directors of logistics (of the army, the air force and the navy), and the DOD's Administrative Under-secretary, Accounts Controller and Principal Personnel Officer.

---

[25] The exact percentage of the budget taken by personal emoluments is believed by experts to be more than the 45% suggested here; in fact, some believe it to be as much as 80%. Omitoogun, W., *Military Expenditure Data in Africa: A Survey of Cameroon, Ethiopia, Ghana, Kenya, Nigeria and Uganda*, SIPRI Research Report no. 17 (Oxford University Press: Oxford, 2003), p. 73; and MacDonald, B. S., *Military Spending in Developing Countries: How Much is Too Much?* (Carleton University Press: Ottawa, 1977), pp. 138–40.

Table 5.2. Military expenditure by Kenya and its neighbours as a share of gross domestic product, 1991–99

Figures are percentages.

Country[a]	1991	1992	1993	1994	1995	1996	1997	1998	1999
Eritrea[b]	..	..	21.4	13.0	19.9	22.8	13.5	29.0	22.9
Ethiopia	2.0	2.7	2.9	2.4	2.0	1.9	3.4	5.1	9.0
Kenya	2.4	1.9	1.8	1.6	1.6	1.8	1.8	1.9	1.9
Tanzania	2.0	1.9	1.2	1.2	1.5	1.4	1.3	1.3	1.3
Uganda	2.2	1.5	1.8	1.6	1.5	1.8	1.9	2.1	2.1

[a] Somalia does not appear in the table since it has not had a central government since 1991.
[b] Eritrea became an independent state in 1993.

Source: Kenyan Ministry of Finance, Nairobi.

The secretariat collects and analyses the proposals from the services' holders of authority to incur expenditure (AIE). It prepares and presents proposals to the Departmental Budget Committee, which in turn discusses and approves them, with or without amendments. The following subsections cover the strategic phases involved in preparing the military budget.

The formulation phase

In the preparation of the MTEF budget for the financial year, the Budget Secretariat considers submissions from the services and other units controlled by the DOD. The requirements are analysed and rationalized to produce an agreed figure that is presented to the Departmental Budget Committee and subsequently submitted to the NSSWG for further discussions.

As soon as the Treasury Circular, addressed to all accounting officers and giving guidelines for the preparation of the MTEF budget, is received, the DOD accounting officer writes to the chairman of the Departmental Budget Committee to instruct the services and the branches of the DOD to commence the exercise. The Vice-CGS in turn instructs the service commanders to commence the preparation of their inputs in the form of budget proposals. He also instructs the Budget Secretariat to coordinate the preparation exercise.

After several meetings, the NSSWG settles on a figure indicative of the DOD requirements for the year. However, the Treasury may finally fix a different ceiling after factoring in other sources of funding, such as appropriation in aid, during the bidding exercise, and this is what is eventually reflected in the printed estimates for the financial year. While preparing the itemized military budget, the components of the DOD budget are each considered. They include personal emoluments, pending bills carried over from the previous financial year and the contractual obligations that have to be met before the end of the financial year, and the operational requirements that must be met by the DOD. Other issues include increasing the tempo of infrastructure development,

modernization programmes and new projects to be undertaken by the department; and the regular support that the DOD continues to provide to its troops
deployed on UN and AU missions.

On the basis of the printed estimates, the Budget Secretariat prepares an
itemized budget and a proposed distribution of funds to the services and DOD
controlled units for approval by the Departmental Budget Committee and the
Treasury. In recent years, the Treasury has declined to include the pending bills
(most of which were accumulated over a number of years) in the approved
budgets, hence creating a problem for the budget holders: they are unable to
manage the allocations according to the financial year plans. The DOD receives
about 90 per cent of the exchequer issues (i.e., cash flow) from the Treasury as
well as some reimbursements from the UN. It has also managed to generate a
substantial amount of income in the form of appropriation in aid. However, the
latter two sources of revenue are required to be surrendered to the Treasury and
therefore cannot be used in reducing the pending bills, which are at times huge.

Over the past few financial years, the DOD has had carryover (pending) bills
amounting to about 13 per cent of the allocated budgets. Their payments are
spread over the next two or three financial years against each expenditure item,
and those that are uncleared because of a lack of provision or are time-barred
are paid as a first charge by the respective AIE holders. The bills are generally
categorized as: (*a*) bills undeclared prior to the end of the previous financial
year; (*b*) bills incurred because of a lack of exchequer issues; (*c*) bills incurred
because of a lack of provision; (*d*) bills that had provisions but are time-barred;
and (*e*) bills incurred due to unplanned emergencies or national operations.

Before the estimates are presented to Parliament for final approval, they are
presented to the Departmental Budget Committee. Upon approval of the proposed budget, the accounting officer forwards it to the Permanent Secretary of
the MOF. The DOD is usually invited to a series of meetings at the Treasury for
bidding and for final preparation of the printed estimates of revenue and
expenditure for all the government ministries, departments and state corporations. Budget ceilings for the DOD are therefore arrived at through sector bidding at the Treasury. The proposed budget, as amended during this process, is
then presented to Parliament by the Minister of Finance in mid-June.

The approval phase

The Kenyan military budget for each financial year is usually approved by
Parliament as a one-line budget item, under the following priority clusters:
morale and motivation; infrastructure and development; operations and
maintenance; modernization; and human resource development and training.
Occasionally, funds can be appropriated under the headings of aid to civil
authority and the poverty-reduction strategy.

The parliamentary Committee on Foreign Affairs and Defence is expected to
deliberate on the military budget, after which it passes on its recommendation.

Once Parliament grants approval, usually along with other portions of the national budget, the Treasury can start releasing the approved funds to the DOD.

The implementation phase

The preparation of the military budget for each financial year and the distribution of funds to the services and DOD controlled units are carried out by the Budget Secretariat and approved by the Departmental Budget Committee. The Treasury takes into consideration the requirements of all the stakeholders vis-à-vis the resources made available by the government to the DOD. However, it is important to note that the bulk of the DOD budget goes to meeting expenditure related to personal emoluments, utilities (water, electricity and telephone bills), contractual payments, unbudgeted UN peace operations and, importantly, pending bills. Central to the discussion on the implementation of the military budget is the procurement procedure, which is considered in detail below.

The funds appropriated are adequately monitored by both internal and external regulatory systems, managed by civilian government employees who are completely independent of the DOD's military administration set-up. Both of these systems are in addition to the DOD internal regulatory system, an in-house function performed, regulated and administered by uniformed personnel.

The internal system was established in accordance with powers bestowed upon the Treasury by the 1995 Exchequer and Audit Act.[26] Under the act, the Permanent Secretary of the Treasury, or any other officer in the Treasury authorized by the Permanent Secretary, is entitled to inspect all offices and to have unlimited access to 'all official books, documents and other records as may be necessary for the exercise of the powers and duties of the Treasury'. The internal auditors are deployed in the ministries and departments and they report directly to the Audit Inspector-General, who is based at the Treasury. Their main duties include: (*a*) evaluating the effectiveness of the internal control systems in relation to the government's financial objectives; (*b*) carrying out spot checks on revenue and appropriation in aid collection points, projects, pay parades, and supply and delivery sites to ensure compliance with government procedures and financial regulations; (*c*) periodically reviewing budgetary controls on the issue of AIEs, the collection of revenue and appropriation in aid, and accounting; (*d*) reviewing and evaluating the reliability and integrity of record keeping and reporting of financial and operating information; (*e*) reviewing the budgetary re-allocation process to ensure legislative and administrative compliance; (*f*) ensuring that revenue, appropriation in aid and other receipts due to the government are accounted for following proper procedure; (*g*) verifying and certifying periodical financial returns, such as pending bills returns,

[26] Exchequer and Audit Act (note 15), Section 4(2) and (3).

expenditure returns, and revenue and appropriation in aid returns among others; (*h*) reviewing and pre-auditing annual appropriation accounts, fund accounts and other statements prepared by accounting officers for submission to the Controller and Auditor-General, with a view to ensuring that accurate accounts are prepared to the required standards; and (*i*) carrying out investigations into irregularities identified or reported and reporting on any wastage of public funds resulting from general misuse or misappropriation of financial resources and government property.

The role of the internal auditors is complemented in the DOD by three internal control branches created to detect fraud, theft, wastage and other kinds of misuse. These branches, each headed by a brigadier, are directly answerable to the CGS as part of a conscious effort to manage the scarce resources allocated to the armed forces in a result-oriented way. The first of these branches is the Inspectorate, responsible for maintaining standards and the operational readiness of the armed forces through judicious use of resources. The Chief of Inspectorate also undertakes project inspection, monitors the institutional capacity of the armed forces and actively works to reconcile projects and standards with operational readiness. Second is the Chief of Audit and Inspection, empowered to audit public and non-public funds, stores, equipment and personnel in the armed forces. More importantly, the Chief of Audit and Inspection oversees adherence to accounting procedures; inspects account records, stores and personnel records; evaluates internal control systems to minimize fraud or loss of funds; inspects projects and contract documents in the interest of the armed forces; and investigates irregularities, either discovered or reported, in funds management. Third is the Provost Marshal, who is responsible for monitoring the operational needs and readiness of the military police.

Military procurement procedure[27]

In response to the numerous challenges that the Kenyan armed forces have experienced in the management of their affairs, a new approach to procurement was required. In early 1997 Defence Headquarters (DHQ) introduced the New Management Strategy (NMS), the main goal of which has been the prudent management of expenditure by enhancing value for money through delegation of financial authority to line managers. The core principles of the NMS include efficient accounting and transparency; specification of clear objectives where commanders are responsible for determining the means of delivery; a focus on output of activities as opposed to monitoring individual resource inputs; and the delivery of responsibility and authority to the lowest possible level.

---

[27] The procurement procedure outlined in this subsection are subject to changes made by the 2005 Public Procurement and Disposal Act, *Kenya Gazette Supplement*, 2005, URL <http://www.treasury.go. ke/ppd/>. In particular, Section 133 of the new act makes special provision for the classified audit of the procurement of certain items by the security sector.

In order that the NMS guiding principles could be fully embraced, DHQ established the Directorate of Systems and Procurement to procure the equipment and systems needed by the three services to the right specifications, within an agreed time-scale and cost, and in the most cost-effective manner within the overall military resources. The directorate is also involved in the preparation and monitoring of long-term plans and long-term costing associated with new defence acquisitions, refits and the management of long-term payments.

Two main committees are involved in the procurement process: the Equipment Committee, which is steered by the Directorate of Systems and Procurement; and the Equipment Approval Committee, whose chairman is the CGS. The task of the Equipment Committee is, having received the user requirements, to research, formulate and determine priorities on equipment policies and eventually forward its recommendations to the Equipment Approval Committee.

The Equipment Approval Committee is the final authority and has the ultimate responsibility for military equipment programmes, which include those for procurement, replacement or modification of defence systems, equipment and plants. The committee ensures that no major expenditure is committed without thorough and independent scrutiny to establish the military, technical, financial and managerial validity of projects both in their own right and in relation to other projects in the equipment programme. It also authorizes expenditure on major defence systems and plants. Defence policy, resources and manpower availability are also taken into account. The overall thrust of the current procurement arrangement is: (*a*) to procure the right quantity of the right equipment and systems at the right time, place and price by advocating bidding (selective tendering), both local and international, thereby attempting to obtain best value for money; (*b*) to expand domestic industry by giving priority to locally produced goods, thereby creating employment with a view to poverty alleviation; and (*c*) to advance the local technological base by insisting on technology transfer in line with the national objective of attaining new industrialized country status in the near future.

Five important factors influence the armed forces' procurement policy. First is the national defence policy. Although there seems to be no clearly articulated defence policy at the moment, there are related policy statements, presidential speeches and practices that constitute an 'informal' defence policy (see section V). Of importance here is the linking of defence policy, however informal and fragmented, to domestic and foreign policy and to government defence plans. Second is the operational environment, which determines the context, the force's mission and the equipment available to the military. Third is the technical advancement of the defence industry, especially in the form and sophistication of weapon systems appropriate for meeting the perceived threats; this is also shaped by the operational environment. Fourth is the considerable attention given to user requirements, as defined by operational experience and progressive improvements in design and materials. Finally, the life-cycle costing of weapons is taken into account; this covers trial and testing performance; production and introduction into service; industrial operation and maintenance; and disposal cost, as well as manpower needs.

Also central to the arms procurement process is the so-called 'Downey procedure' introduced as part of the NMS framework. It is essentially a stage-by-stage approach to procurement, with clear guidelines for each of the steps in a procurement cycle. Each stage is assessed after the project is re-endorsed and before further military expenditure is authorized. This is important for limiting technical risks that may lead to unnecessary costs and time overruns. It also limits the continuance of projects that have become obsolete or have been superseded by new technology.

The first stage of the arms-project life cycle is concept formulation and the feasibility study, which covers the period from the emergence of the idea for a project to the initial formal statement of an operational need. The concept-formulation stage is essentially a technical study to ensure that all new equipment is compatible with the principles of DHQ concept papers. Some of the factors that can contribute to the emergence of an idea include a need to modernize obsolete equipment or acquire advanced weapon systems, changes in defence policy requiring new capabilities or roles, intelligence relating to a new, actual or potential threat, and needs informed by participation in a foreign defence project. Other factors are the needs arising from new tactical concepts or a deficiency in existing inventory identified in operations, training, war gaming or operational research; a proposal by industry, possibly derived from commercial or export considerations; and work being done on the development of an existing project that stimulates the idea for its successor or some new use.

In theory, every equipment project should pass through each stage of development sequentially. In practice, however, the system is flexible and some stages may overlap or even be omitted, particularly in the case of small projects. Major equipment procurement is normally subjected to a rigorous application of the formal stages.

Auditing phase

The office of the Controller and Auditor-General, established by the constitution,[28] is empowered by the 1995 Exchequer and Audit Act to, first, authorize the issue of money from the exchequer account in the form of a 'grant of credit' within the overall sum appropriated by Parliament and, second, to audit public accounts as prescribed in the act to ensure that all appropriated monies are applied to the purposes for which they were appropriated and that the expenditure conforms with the authority that governs it.

The Controller and Auditor-General is answerable to Parliament through the Public Accounts Committee and has legal access to all documents (vouchers

[28] Republic of Kenya (note 1), Section 105.

and other accounting documents), stores, warehouses and cash which may be considered necessary to conduct the audit of the accounts presented to him or her by accounting officers. All queries concerning irregularities detected by the Controller and Auditor-General are directed to the relevant accounting officer. In the exercise of his or her functions and in accordance with the constitution, 'the Controller and Auditor-General shall not be subject to the direction or control of any other person or authority'.[29] The Controller and Auditor-General therefore has a secured tenure of office.

V. Assessment of the military budgetary process

The formal process of military budgeting is guided by a good legal framework for obtaining and accounting for funds. The formal process has also been improved by the introduction of the MTEF, which has made roles and responsibilities clearer. Moreover, openness seems to have been structurally enhanced by open parliamentary hearings, which by design are geared towards facilitating the participation of civil society—the press, individuals, companies and private institutions. However, it is still important to investigate the extent to which the actual process mirrors extant rules and regulations; that is, to investigate the extent of derogation from formal rules. In addition, it is imperative to look for missing links, even within the existing formal structures. This is the focus of this section.

Defence policy

Beyond the general recognition that the role of the Kenyan armed forces is the defence of the nation against external aggression and to assist the police in the maintenance of law and order, there is no documented articulation of the basis for military budgeting in Kenya: the country has no official defence policy. This renders the strategic assessment phase of the budgetary process rather elastic and fluid.

There have been official statements which give a general direction to Kenya's geo-strategic concerns and priorities. As far back as 1966, President Kenyatta stated that: 'Kenya wishes to live in harmony with her neighbours, we covet no inch of their territory. We will yield no inch of ours. We stand loyal to the OAU and its solemn decision that all African states shall adhere to the boundaries inherited at independence.' Speaking in 1978, President Moi affirmed that: 'The safety and security of our people and the integrity of our nation comprise the first responsibility of the government, but let me remind you that the defence of this country will depend on the loyalty and devotion of all our people just as much as the uniformed forces.' Moi's statement seems to indicate that Kenya

---

[29] Republic of Kenya (note 1), Section 105(5).

favours a broad-based defence policy, predicated on a human security perspective. However, a clear, documented codification of such a defence policy remains palpably absent. Empirically, it would appear that Kenya's grand strategy is to achieve peace and security through good neighbourliness, non-aggression, and internal peace and security.

Transparency

From 1969 to 1992, Kenya was a single-party state, with direct negative consequences for transparency in the budgetary process. Communication within government and between government and the larger society was highly dependent on the whims of the rulers. National security was seen as being synonymous with regime security. Despite the adoption of a multiparty political system in 1992, the single-party tradition and practice in government, including among technocrats, appear to be very resilient.[30] Specific oversight of military budgeting is constrained by the (mis)perception that military matters are 'state secrets'. Although a legal framework for transparency and accountability exists, in practice its applicability is suspect. For example, it has been noted that 'in some instances many of the officials who are required to follow these laws are unfamiliar with or unaware of their existence'.[31]

The ingrained negative attitude towards military matters, including budgeting, is compounded by the improper application or complete negation of formal rules on tendering and contract award, widespread corrupt practices and gross indiscipline in the public sector.[32] In 2004 the DOD was ranked as the second most corrupt organization in Kenya by Transparency International.[33]

Oversight

The exercise of an oversight function by the various agencies, actors and institutions, especially Parliament, is weak in practice. This weakness arises mainly from inadequate or absent information on budget and financial matters across government departments, including the DOD. In addition, material and information relating to budget matters are relatively expensive and are given in

[30] Kirira (note 17), p. 113.

[31] Kirira (note 17).

[32] Mwenda, A. K. and Gachocho, M. N., 'Budget transparency: Kenyan perspective', Institute for Economic Affairs (IEA) Research Paper Series no. 4, IEA, Nairobi, Oct. 2003, pp. 59–61; and Brzoska, M. et al., 'Einbeziehung von Verteidigungshaushalten in public expenditure management: Einschätzung der Situation in Äthiopien, Burundi, Kenia, Tansania und Uganda' [Incorporation of defence expenditure into public expenditure management: short assessment of the situation in Ethiopia, Burundi, Kenya, Tanzania and Uganda], Bonn International Center for Conversion (BICC) Paper no. 38, BICC, Bonn, May 2004, URL <http://www.bicc.de/publications/>, p. 18.

[33] Transparency International, The Kenya Bribery Index 2004 (Transparency International: Berlin, 2004), p. 8, URL <http://www.transparency.org/>. See also Brzoska et al. (note 32), p. 19; and 'Clay's feat', Africa Confidential, vol. 45, no. 15 (July 2004), p. 7.

formats that make their scrutiny difficult for parliamentarians, civil society and the press.[34] Publications on the budget are often sold only through the Nairobi-based Government Printer, effectively keeping it out of the reach of Kenyans living outside the capital city.

A 2004 report on military expenditure of countries in eastern Africa revealed serious oversight inadequacies in Kenya.[35] This report noted that the Controller and Auditor-General is seriously limited by inadequate power of prosecution and an acute institutional incapacity as evidenced by late submission of audit reports. Invariably, the formal deterrence function of audit reports to check budget mismanagement is severely compromised. The report also noted that the control measures in the Treasury are ineffective as a result of its structural link to the executive. Even the involvement of civil society and public debate on budget matters are limited, given that budget planning is restricted to a small group of high-ranking government officials and given the inadequacy of information about the planned distribution and use of resources.

The Medium-Term Expenditure Framework: defence planning and policy output

It is fair to conclude that Kenyan defence planning and practices hardly reflect overall operational needs or approved budget spending plans. First, the budgets are unrealistic, given the inadequate or ineffectual information available to oversight institutions. This is evidenced by the continued refusal of the Treasury to include 'pending bills' in the approved budget, thus creating serious implementation problems. Second, research by the Institute for Economic Affairs (IEA, a Nairobi-based think tank) has found that the military budget, as well as the overall national budget and the budgetary process, only marginally reflects national policy priorities.[36] Third, despite the euphoria that greeted the inauguration of the Kibaki Government, the age-old practice of diverting public funds for unbudgeted, covert political purposes continues unabated. According to the 2003 Public Expenditure Review (PER), even six years after the introduction of the Medium-Term Expenditure Framework there has been only minimal improvement in the administration of public finance. Moreover, the DOD, despite having received the third largest budget allocation, was both directly and indirectly exempted from the 2003 PER process.[37] Fourth, the DOD continues to overspend its budgetary quota, recording a large deficit of 6 per cent of its approved budget in 2003.[38]

---

[34] Kirira (note 17), p. 113.

[35] Brzoska *et al.* (note 32), p. 17.

[36] Mwenda and Gachocho (note 32), pp. 54–56.

[37] Ministry of Planning and National Development (MPND), *Public Expenditure Review 2003* (MPND: Nairobi, 2004), URL <http://www.planning.go.ke/pdf/per.pdf>, pp. 122–24.

[38] MPND (note 37).

Of the civil society groups surveyed by the IEA in 2003, a majority severely criticized the performance of the MTEF for the lack of public knowledge about its operational mechanisms and its intended purposes. Other criticisms include its poor coordination and linkages with complementary initiatives, such as poverty-reduction strategies; the lack of local ownership of, and the overbearing external influence on, the MTEF; and the relative lack of capacity building prior to and after its implementation.[39]

The introduction of new and apparently clearer rules for procurement has hardly stemmed the tide of procurement scandals; this is not unexpected, given the flagrant derogation from rules and procedures and the corrupt practices in the public sector, including the military. There have been various media reports on military expenditure in Kenya, such as the over-inflation of contracts for the procurement of four Russian military helicopters in 2001, the botched procurement of Czech military aircraft in 2003 and persistent rumours of corrupt practices in a $100 million purchase of military communication equipment.[40] Similarly, the October 2003 IEA report on budget transparency in Kenya concluded that the procurement procedure is ineffective because of a lack of transparency and openness, corruption, overpricing and outright theft. The process continues to be heavily influenced by informal, neo-patrimonial networks in which government officials routinely award contracts to certain favoured firms and individuals.[41] Indeed, some government officials have formed companies with their friends in order to apply for tenders.[42]

Finally, the MTEF has not stopped off-budget and extra-budgetary spending. Kenya is a major contributor to regional and UN missions, but the DOD does not provide a separate or special budget to meet this additional and quite expensive undertaking. The huge expenditure on these tasks is therefore met through the regular budget at the expense of planned projects that are often suspended. However, when these sums are repaid to the armed forces by the UN, it is difficult to determine whether they are actually returned to the Treasury.

VI. Conclusions and recommendations

Military budgeting in Kenya cannot be looked at in isolation from the country's economic and political frailty. The end of single-party rule and the adoption of multiparty democracy in 1992 did not lead to an immediate improvement in transparency and efficiency in the military budgetary process. In the absence of an officially articulated and recognized defence policy, the strategic evaluation

[39] Mwenda and Gachocho (note 32), p. 56.

[40] 'Opposition leader and minister clash over helicopter deal', *East African Standard*, 19 July 2001; and Muiruri, S. 'Military split on deal for Sh29b jet fighters', *Daily Nation* (Nairobi), 28 May 2003, URL <http://www.nationmedia.com/dailynation/>. For a more recent security-related corruption scandal see 'Clay's feat' (note 33).

[41] Mwenda and Gachocho (note 32), p. 58.

[42] Mwenda and Gachocho (note 32), p. 61.

phase has been vulnerable to a high degree of arbitrariness. The tendency has been to equate regime security with national security. The audit system is functional, although not at optimal levels of efficiency. Civil society and parliamentary oversight continues to be hampered by various factors.

The MTEF programme as contained in the national development plan for 2002–2008, however, promises to address some of these constraints.[43] The plan clearly indicates that with the new century may come opportunities in the form of increased regional (EAC and IGAD) and international cooperation and improved communication and information flow. The programme therefore inspires hope for greater progress. One of the advantages of the establishment of the EAC in 1999 by Kenya, Tanzania and Uganda is the anticipated scaling down of military expenditure in the region given that the organization's main objective is the development of policies and programmes aimed at widening and deepening cooperation among partner states in political, economic, social and cultural fields, research and technology, defence, security and legal affairs for the mutual benefits of the three countries.[44]

In the light of the preceding discussion, the following recommendations can be made.

1. There is an ever-present need for Kenya to adopt a well-articulated people-based defence policy. Efforts in this direction should be speeded up.

2. The DOD should embrace modern management techniques to enhance efficiency in the use of the department's allocated resources and budget. This could be achieved by the modernization of equipment and the maintenance of a small but highly effective and efficient force capable of maintaining the equipment and facilities but still able to fulfil its core primary and secondary roles.

3. The Kenyan economy is heavily dependent on agriculture because the manufacturing sector is still in its developing stages. There is, therefore, a need for the security forces to maintain an environment that is more conducive to the progressive development of tourism and an increased in-flow of foreign investment.

4. There is an urgent need for the Treasury to relieve the DOD of the heavy burden of pending bills, especially those incurred as a consequence of the Treasury not issuing funds, as they have a drastic negative effect on the plans for the financial year.

5. As the Treasury makes no separate financial provision for the DOD's peacekeeping missions, there is a need to channel UN reimbursements and other military-related revenue (appropriation in aid, for example) directly to the DOD account without surrendering it to the Treasury.

---

[43] Republic of Kenya (note 21).
[44] Treaty Establishing the East African Community, 30 Nov. 1999, URL <http://www.eac.int/>, preamble.

6. All personnel who handle the DOD budget at all levels should be professionally trained and retrained in order to minimize audit queries and wastage.

7. It is also important to improve the capacities of oversight institutions, strengthen internal and external control mechanisms, and enhance information dissemination and participation by civil society groups.

6. Mali

Anatole Ayissi and Nouhoum Sangaré*

I. Introduction and background

For the first three decades following Mali's independence from France in 1960, the military played a central role in the affairs of the state, even when the country was nominally a democracy. The role assigned to the armed forces ensured that they also received a relatively high share of the state's resources.

This chapter investigates the military budgetary process in Mali, focusing on the institutional capacity, structure and actors involved in the process. This section continues with an overview of the history, politics and economy of Mali. Section II explores the nature, structure and composition of the Malian defence and security sector. Sections III and IV address the specific object of this study by analyzing the national budgetary process and the four phases of the military budgetary process. Section V presents a critical assessment of the military budgetary process, juxtaposing the formal process and actual practice with a view to highlighting the differences. The concluding section VI summarizes the findings of this research and puts forward recommendations for improving accountability, transparency and efficiency in the military budgetary process in Mali.

History, politics and economy

Mali, formerly the colony of French Sudan, became fully independent on 22 September 1960 after periods of internal autonomy and federation with neighbouring Senegal. Since then Mali has had a relatively stable political history characterized by only two major political transitions: from (nominally) democratic government after independence to military rule in 1968, and back to democratic rule after 1991. On 19 November 1968 a growing economic crisis and bad governance prompted a military coup that overthrew Modibo Keita, the first President of Mali. A military committee, led by Colonel Moussa Traoré, was established to rule the country. The Traoré regime remained in power until 26 March 1991, when it in turn was ousted in another military coup following a popular uprising in which youths and students were key actors. The post-Traoré era was characterized by a gradual transition to democratic rule, the first such transition in West Africa. President Alpha Oumar Konaré, first elected in 1992

* The authors would like to thank David Beal, Junior Professional Consultant at the United Nations Institute for Disarmament Research (UNIDIR), Geneva, for commenting on this chapter and gathering data on Malian military expenditure.

and having completed the second of his permitted two terms in June 2002, successfully handed power to his elected successor, Amadou Toumani Touré, a retired general who had led the 1991 coup.

Under Modibo Keita's socialist regime of the First Republic (1960–68), the armed forces were used as a key pillar in a highly centralized and authoritarian political system. During this period, the army was used mainly for public works and protection of the environment. The military budget was essentially an operating budget, *budget de fonctionnement*, that consisted mostly of salaries. Communist regimes of Eastern Europe equipped the army with heavy armament and other military equipment. Under the military-led Second Republic (1968–91) the country was ruled by a military committee, which was transformed into a political party in 1974. During this period, in spite of the high military expenditure, the living conditions of military personnel remained poor. The armed forces were more independent of the Ministry of Economy and Finance (MOEF) and less accountable to other institutions of the state in those early years of independence. It was common to have military budget overruns, as well as flagrant violations of other fundamental budgeting principles and accounting rules. In addition, the armed forces followed a special code for public works contracts that differed from the national standard.[1] This situation changed after 1991, first under the transitional government and then under President Konaré. The new President aligned military budgeting with the rest of the public sector financial management system.

Economically, Mali is among the poorest countries in the world, with 65 per cent of its land area either arid desert or semi-desert. Economic activity is largely confined to the area irrigated by the River Niger. The chief economic activity is agriculture, with 80 per cent of the labour force directly engaged in farming and fishing; another 10 per cent are nomads.[2] The most important agricultural crops are cotton and peanuts. Other major food crops are rice, corn, sorghum, millet and cassava. Mali's limited industrial activity is concentrated on processing agricultural produce. The country is heavily dependent on foreign aid, including military assistance, from a variety of sources but especially France and, in the past, the countries of the former Eastern bloc.

II. The security sector

Mali's security sector consists of the armed forces (the army and the air force), the security forces (the National Gendarmerie, the National Police and the National Guard) and paramilitary forces. The paramilitary forces include the Forestry Service, the Customs Service and the Civil Protection Service. They qualify as part of the security sector because they go through basic military

---

[1] Prior to 1991, the armed and security forces implemented their public spending under a special regime which offered easier conditions, with soft internal procedures and fewer control mechanisms.

[2] Central Intelligence Agency (CIA), 'Mali', *World Factbook 2004* (CIA: Washington, DC, 2004), URL <http://www.cia.gov/cia/publications/factbook/>.

Table 6.1. Military expenditure of Mali, 1990–2004

Figures in US$ are in constant 2003 prices and exchange rates.

Year	Military expenditure		
	$ m.	b. franc CFA	as a % of GDP
1990	38.5	14.2	*2.1*
1991	..	..	..
1992	..	..	..
1993	47.8	16.8	*2.4*
1994	51.3	22.2	*2.3*
1995	54.8	26.9	*2.3*
1996	51.7	27.1	*2.1*
1997	59.9	31.3	*2.0*
1998	59.3	32.2	*1.9*
1999	67.0	36.0	*2.0*
2000	77.6	41.4	*2.2*
2001	78.1	43.8	*2.0*
2002	75.9	44.7	*1.9*
2003	81.4	47.3	*1.9*
2004	88.8	49.4	..

GDP = Gross domestic product.

Source: SIPRI military expenditure database.

training and take part in surveillance of the territory and the protection of persons and assets.

The total size of the armed forces is about 7350, including 400 personnel in the air force and 50 navy personnel.[3] The security forces total 4800, including 1800 gendarmes and 2000 republican guards.[4] Military expediture since 1990 is presented in table 6.1.

The role and duties of the security sector are defined in a code of conduct which came into effect in 1998.[5] In particular, the code states that the principal mission of the Malian armed forces is 'to prepare for and guarantee, if necessary by armed force, the defence of the homeland, the republican form of the state, its democratic heritage and the highest interests of the nation'.[6] As well as providing direction to Mali's defence policy, the code of conduct enumerates the three categories of mission that the armed and security forces can under-

---

[3] International Institute for Strategic Studies (IISS), *The Military Balance 2004/2005* (Oxford University Press: Oxford, 2004), pp. 238–239

[4] IISS (note 3).

[5] Ministry of Defence and Veterans (MODV), *Code de conduite des Forces Armées et de Sécurité du Mali* [Code of conduct of the armed and security forces of Mali] (Ministère des Forces Armées et des Anciens Combattants: Bamako, 1997), URL <http://www.hrea.org/erc/Library/armed_forces/>, Titles I and III.

[6] MODV (note 5), Title I, Article 1 (authors' translation).

take—in times of peace, internal turmoil and war—and specifies the role of the military in each.

The constitution of Mali specifies the actors and institutions involved in the management of the security sector and their respective powers in security and defence matters. The overall responsibilities of these actors and institutions and their relationships are further elaborated in an act adopted in November 2004.[7] While the constitution designates the President as the supreme commander of the armed forces, the Prime Minister is responsible for the implementation of the national defence policy.[8] The Minister of Defence directly implements the national defence policy and manages the armed forces, the National Gendarmerie and the National Guard. The Minister of Internal Security and Civil Protection is in charge of the non-military aspects of national security, but, when necessary, the National Gendarmerie, the National Police and the National Guard can be mobilized under the minister's authority. The ministers of Territorial Administration and of Economy and Finance also have specific roles in defence matters. The parliament, the National Assembly, is empowered by the constitution to determine the fundamental principles and general organization of the defence and security sector.[9]

III. The national budgetary framework and military expenditure

The national budgetary process in Mali is regulated by the 1996 financial law act.[10] The act includes general provisions related to the national budget, notably principles on income and spending, an implementation regime for Treasury operations and accounting, and voting procedures for the budget. The financial law act defines the general guidelines and principles according to which the national budget is elaborated and implemented.

There are four principal actors in the military budgetary process in Mali. First is the Prime Minister, who is constitutionally charged with the implementation of national policy, including defence. Second is the Minister of Defence, who implements national defence policy on behalf of the Prime Minister. Third is the Minister of Economy and Finance, who is responsible for the formulation and implementation of the annual finance act. In doing this, the Ministry of Economy and Finance exercises considerable control over other ministries and, when necessary, investigates breaches of budgetary discipline. The fourth actor is the National Assembly, which approves the annual finance bill.

---

[7] Loi no. 04-051 portant organisation générale de la défense nationale [National defence organization act], *Journal Officiel* (Bamako), 23 Nov. 2004. National defence was previously regulated by an ordinance issued on 1 Oct. 1999.

[8] Constitution de la République du Mali [Constitution of the Republic of Mali], *Journal Officiel* (Bamako), 25 Feb. 1992, URL <http://www.sgg.gov.ml/>, Articles 44 and 55, English translation available at URL <http://confinder.richmond.edu/>.

[9] Constitution de la République du Mali (note 8), Article 70.

[10] Loi no. 96-060 relative à la loi de finances [Financial law act], *Journal Officiel* (Bamako), 4 Nov. 1996, URL <http://www.sgg.gov.ml/>.

Table 6.2. Principal chapters in the budget of the Malian armed and security forces, 2002

Chapter	Item
11: Personnel	Salaries of the armed forces and of the other employees of the Ministry of Defence and Veterans
12: Office stationery	All spending related to the office stationery bureau; clothes and technical and special equipment; food
13: Travel allowances	Fees for travel within and outside Mali; training and lodgings
15: Administrative fees	Honoraria for lawyers and experts; payment of damages to victims of accidents
16: Fuel, transportation and upkeep	Everything related to ground transportation
18: Maintenance	Construction spending; maintenance of military barracks, administrative buildings and garrisons; rent
19: Other spending	Any spending which does not fall within another category; this chapter covers *dépenses à bon compte* and discretionary spending
26: Health and hospitals	Medical fees for treatment in Mali and abroad
27: Technical assistance	Spending related to technical assistance within the context of military cooperation
28: Contributions to international organizations	Spending related to Mali's participation in international military organizations
31: Investment	Building of barracks; acquisition of heavy *matériel*; insurance; etc.
37: Research and development	Spending related to research and analysis aimed at improving the structural and material conditions of the armed forces

Source: Loi no. 01-112 portant loi de finances pour l'exercice 2002 [2002 finance act], *Journal Officiel* (Bamako), 21 Dec. 2001,

The secondary actors in the budgetary process include the Director of Administration and Finance, who is responsible for preparing and implementing the budget of the armed forces and works under the authority of the Minister of Defence; the Director of National Financial Control, who monitors the legality of spending and formally authorizes payments; the Director of the National Budget, who makes money authorized for spending available to the end-users; and the Director of the Public Treasury, who pays the monies approved by the Finance Comptroller.

Since the armed and security forces are neither producers of goods nor, officially, providers of remunerated services, their budget is made up exclusively of charges (costs). In general, there are three categories of funds allocated to ministries: (*a*) evaluative funds, which cover spending beyond resources appearing in the annual finance act; (*b*) projected funds, which cover extra-budgetary spending required by changes in prices and inaccurate estimates in the finance act; and (*c*) limitative funds, which cover spending outside the other two categories. The armed forces benefit from neither evaluative funds nor projected funds, despite the appearance in the military budget of spending on items, such as legal fees and utilities, which are difficult to assess in advance: thus, the military budget is composed entirely of limitative funds and for this reason is exceptionally restrictive.

The national budget of Mali is structured around functional accounts. Each ministry, including the Ministry of Defence and Veterans (MODV), constitutes a functional account. Funds allocated to the MODV are assigned to different services within the ministry, termed functional units. The Government of Mali allocates spending to the security sector through two ministries: the MODV and the Ministry of Internal Security and Civil Protection. The share of these two ministries in the national budget for financial year (FY) 2002 was 6.49 per cent.[11] The budget of the armed and security forces does not include the intelligence service.

Military spending is divided into chapters and sub-chapters according to the nature of the planned expenditure. The budget of the armed forces for FY 2002 includes 29 chapters. Table 6.2 gives the main components of the budget of the armed and security forces in that year.

For a given financial year, in addition to funds allocated for recurrent spending, the finance act may allocate funds to the military sector to meet its enormous investment needs. These funds are either linked to a project authorized by a specific act or are authorized by the relevant authorities, in strict adherence to Mali's code for public works contracts.

IV. The military budgetary process

In May of each year, the Minister of Economy and Finance sends a budgetary planning letter (*lettre de cadrage du budget*) for the forthcoming financial year (which coincides with the calendar year) to all ministries, including the Ministry of Defence and Veterans. This initiates the budgetary process, which is divided into four phases: formulation, approval, implementation and auditing.

The formulation phase

The 1996 financial law act stipulates that, each year, the Minister of Defence should prepare a programme-based budget, made up of objectives, strategies for achieving the objectives and the expected outcomes. Each programme is budgeted for over a three-year budget cycle. In FY 2002 the programme-based budget of the MODV contained five programmes: general administration, management of military operations, army inspection, training and communications. In FY 2002 the budget of the Ministry of Internal Security and Civil

---

[11] Loi portant règlement général du budget d'État 2002 [2002 state budget auditing act], *Journal Officiel* (Bamako), 16 June 2004.

Protection contained three programmes: general administration, order and security, and disaster prevention.

Following the receipt of the budgetary planning letter, the Minister of Defence, taking into consideration the broad objectives of the government, gives instructions to the different units of the armed and security forces to commence budget planning. This is followed by a meeting between the minister and unit representatives in order to determine the overall departmental objectives and the expected policy outcomes for the following financial year. After this meeting, each unit of the military sector presents its draft budget and submits it to the MODV's Director of Administration and Finance, who in turn integrates the submissions into a draft budget. This draft, which must separate recurrent spending on the programmes from investment, is then submitted to the ministry's Department of Budget. The draft budget is subsequently reviewed and scrutinized within the MODV, before being forwarded to the MOEF by the July preceding the financial year.

Once the MOEF has received draft budget estimates from all ministries, the Director of the National Budget convenes a technical arbitration meeting for each ministry. The meeting with the MODV brings together high-level representatives from the various units of the MOEF, the MODV's Director of Administration and Finance, and other high-ranking military personnel. The technical arbitration meeting is followed by a larger budgetary arbitration meeting of officials of the MOEF and the MODV, this time convened by the Minister of Economy and Finance, which finalizes the national budget of the armed forces. These joint reviews, in which budget requests from each ministry are balanced against the resources available and the needs of the other ministries, are an important aspect of the formulation phase.

When agreement has been reached on the defence estimate, the Minister of Economy and Finance forwards it, as part of the annual finance bill, to the Council of Ministers. Following approval at this level, the draft budget is presented to the National Assembly for the approval phase.

The approval phase

In the National Assembly, the military budget is first examined by the Defence and Security Committee. The committee invites the directors of all the main divisions of the armed forces, the army chiefs of staff, the army joint chiefs of staff and the Minister of Defence for discussions on the mission, the annual objectives and the budgetary requirements of the armed and security forces. The committee can propose amendments to the budget or a reformulation of the objectives. Following the work in the committee, the draft budget is presented to a plenary session of the National Assembly for debate and voting. If approved, the budget estimates become the finance act and public dissemination of the act commences.

In the event that the National Assembly does not approve the budget before the beginning of the financial year, the government has 15 days to submit a new draft to parliamentarians in an extraordinary session, who have only eight days in which to approve it. During this period the government is authorized to grant credits on the basis of spending made during the previous financial year. If no decision is taken within these eight days, the budget comes into force without further consultations by the government.[12]

The implementation phase

The 1996 public accounting act determines the rules and principles governing the management of public funds.[13] Two categories of authority implement the national budget: officials with powers to authorize payments (*ordonnateurs* or directors) and those who monitor how money is spent (*comptables* or accountants). This principle of separation of these two functions is well respected in the armed forces.

The Minister of Defence (an *ordonnateur*) delegates powers for the implementation of financial operations to the Director of Administration and Finance, who supervises all budgetary and accounting operations in the MODV. Each unit of the armed and security forces has a director of administration and finance who is directly responsible for the implementation of the unit's budget. This role of the unit director is complemented by commanders of administrative centres in each military region, who are responsible for financial operations within their region.

The Malian military sector has some peculiar characteristics. One is that military accountants, unlike other public-sector accountants, are not appointed by or with the agreement of the Minister of Economy and Finance and do not take a professional oath (as is required by the 1996 public accounting act for all other public-sector accountants). They are thus not accountable to the Minister of Economy and Finance. Instead, the Minister of Defence, in his capacity as *ordonnateur*, is accountable for the authorizations made in the MODV by all other officials and also for the actions of the *comptables*. These other officials are nonetheless subject to disciplinary, penal or civil procedures, so they do have an impetus to control the financial operations of the units for which they are responsible.

These internal controls by the military hierarchy exist alongside external financial controls undertaken by the General Inspectorate of the armed forces, the Department of Public Accounts, the Department for the General Control of

---

[12] This practice, with slight modifications, is a common feature of the budgeting laws in nearly all francophone countries in Africa. Abdourhamane, B. I. and Crouzel, I., *A Comparison of the Budget Process in France and Francophone African Countries* (Idasa: Cape Town, 2004), URL <http://www.idasa. org.za/>.

[13] Loi no. 96-061 portant principes fondamentaux de la comptabilité publique [Basic principles of public accounting act], *Journal Officiel* (Bamako), 4 Nov. 1996, URL <http://www.sgg.gov.ml/>.

Public Service and the Department of Financial Control. This division is unique to the military sector.

Another characteristic of accounting practice in the military sector is the lack of a division of accounting positions into principal and secondary accountants, as is the case in all other ministries. Instead, commanders of administrative centres have a dual role with implementation (fund authorization) and accounting functions similar to those of principal accountants in civilian administration. Similarly, military accountants are not required to be accredited to an official with power to authorize payments. Thus, the principle of separation of authority between officials who authorize payment and those who oversee how money is spent is compromised, with the consequent implications for accountability.

The final peculiar characteristic is the frequent use of the system of *dépenses à bon compte* (literally, 'cheap' expediture) by the Malian armed forces. This includes spending for which prior authorization is not necessary. Money received in this way is considered to be a short-term loan and is given to those in need after the presentation of specific official papers. This practice is suitable for units that are far away from the big administrative centres and for issues that require a quick official reaction. On the basis of an agreement between the MOEF and the MODV, members of the armed forces can also benefit from loans from the Treasury's department responsible for investing and lending public money. These loans help to alleviate the harsh conditions of military life, such as the poor food in barracks.

The auditing phase

In order to deal with breaches of budgeting and accounting rules and principles, the state exercises control on aspects of public administration related to the management of public resources. There are three categories of control: administrative, judicial and parliamentary.

Administrative control

In addition to the internal control described above, the armed forces are subject to the authority of the Director for the General Control of Public Service, who ensures that expenditure is kept within approved limits.

Judicial control

According to rules of the Union Économique et Monétaire Ouest Africaine (UEMOA, West African economic and monetary union)[14] and national laws requiring good governance and transparency in the management of public administration, all public accounts must be collated by the Director of the National Budget and submitted to the Supreme Court for auditing. The account-

---

[14] The members of UEMOA are Benin, Burkina Faso, Côte d'Ivoire, Guinea Bissau, Mali, Niger, Senegal and Togo; see URL <http://www.uemoa.int/>.

ing division of the Supreme Court checks these accounts and gives its authorization for the annual auditing bill (*projet de loi de règlement*). The auditing
bill certifies the accounts of the financial year and approves any variation from
the original finance act. This bill forms the audited accounts of the government.
It is required to be submitted to the National Assembly no later than one year
after budget implementation.[15] However, it can take several years to prepare and
sometimes never gets to the National Assembly.

Parliamentary control

The National Assembly currently exercises control through its accounting division. When irregularities are noted in the report of the accounting division of
the Supreme Court, the National Assembly can establish a commission of
inquiry. When necessary, the National Assembly can invite witnesses, such as
ministers, for oral and written questioning.

V. Assessment of the military budgetary process: legal and de facto procedures

In Mali, as elsewhere, there is a gap between formal rules and procedures and
the actual conduct of public affairs. This gap is evidenced by the breaches in the
organization and implementation of the military budget. The official toleration
of these breaches represents the major weakness in the system.

'Tolerated derogations' and off-budget revenue

A key budgeting principle is comprehensiveness: all revenue and expenditure
must appear in the budget. This is not always the case in the Malian national
budget in general and the armed forces in particular, in spite of the clearly
defined legal framework and the procedures and principles analysed above.
Although these breaches in procedure are well known, they have often gone
unpunished and, as a consequence, have become institutionalized as 'tolerated
derogations'. An important example of tolerated derogation is the use of off-
budget income, notably from the public works and developmental missions of
the armed forces.

The armed and security forces have a statutory duty to participate in public
works as part of their contribution to the economic and social development of
the country. The armed forces undertake their developmental mission through
activities requested by the government, public administrations or territorial
collectives. These activities take place mainly in sectors that are not considered
to be cost-effective for profit-driven private companies; nonetheless, they serve
as revenue-generating ventures for the military.

[15] Abdourhamane and Crouzel (note 12).

Table 6.3. Deviation of actual military expenditure from budgeted expenditure in Mali, 1999–2003

Figures are in millions of francs CFA and in millions of US$ at constant 2003 prices and exchange rates.

Financial year	Approved budget		Actual expenditure		Deviation (%)
	m. francs CFA	$ m.	m. francs CFA	$ m.	
1999	33 276	62	37 749	70	*13*
2000	34 311	64	35 346	66	*3*
2001	34 139	61	33 967	61	*−1*
2002	35 449	60	36 759	62	*4*
2003	40 586	70	45 725	79	*13*

Sources: Lois de finances [Finance acts], *Journal Officiel* (Bamako), 1999–2003; and Lois de règlement [Auditing acts], *Journal Officiel* (Bamako), 2000–04.

One such activity is military engineering undertaken by the central military repair and assembly command. In the three financial years 2000, 2001 and 2002, the armed forces executed public works worth a total of 3.8 billion francs CFA ($5.5 million). This income did not appear in the national budget. In general, this income is used to cover the costs of the public works; if there is profit, it is invested in maintenance and new infrastructure for the army.

The military also provides an air service to isolated regions of Mali, notably cities in the north. This transportation system is used by the state and by civil servants working in these areas. There is generally no charge for these flights; exceptions include flights for private individuals or companies and use in the fight against locust invasion. When the armed forces are paid, the income, which is used for maintenance works, does not appear in the national budget.

Other sources of income include military assembly and repair shops equipped to build mechanical spare parts for public and private companies. These spare parts are sold but the income does not appear in the budget. Again, the income is used for maintaining old machines and investing in new equipment.

Another off-budget practice relates to private enterprises attached to military units. These privately managed firms include restaurants, leisure and sport centres, and officer's mess used by military personnel and their families and friends. Although these units are considered to be separate legal entities, they receive subsidies from the units to which they are attached and provide services exclusively to the army.

Derogation from strict formal accounting procedures also arises from the armed forces' participation in peacekeeping operations.[16] Although money

---

[16] As of 31 Dec. 2004, Malian troops were deployed in United Nations peacekeeping missions in Burundi, the Democratic Republic of the Congo, Liberia and Sierra Leone. Department of Peacekeeping Operations, 'UN mission's summary detailed by country', United Nations, New York, 31 Oct. 2004, URL <http://www.un.org/Depts/dpko/>.

received for these operations does not appear in the budget, the opportunities for misuse are limited. Nonetheless, this tolerated derogation applies specifically to the armed forces and confirms the relative flexibility enjoyed by the military sector in the observance of certain rules.

In spite of the availability to the military of these off-budget revenues, reported expenditure on approved items frequently exceeds the budgeted amount. This could be a result of the lack of comprehensiveness in the budget at the formulation stage or a lack of financial discipline in the armed forces. Table 6.3 shows that overspending occurred in four of the five years reported there.

External assistance

The official budget of the armed and security forces (as it appears in the annual finance act) is only a fraction of the economic resources dedicated to military activities in Mali. The bulk of the country's military equipment is supplied by external sources, especially France. Mali also receives military assistance from countries with which it has binding military assistance and cooperation protocols.[17] This assistance covers training, equipment, manoeuvres and peacekeeping operations.[18]

Limited transparency and accountability

From independence until 1991, the political history of Mali was largely the history of the relationship between the armed forces and the state's other institutions. This situation changed during the transition from military to civilian rule in 1991–92. Since then the armed forces have been progressively brought back into line with the general rules and principles guiding the national budgeting and accounting system, especially those concerning the implementation of the budget. Evidence of this normalization includes the abolition of the army's special code for public works contract and the imposition of a single national code.[19] In 1991 Mali adopted a single accounting system, a key feature of which was that it made the inventory and tracing of state holdings, notably furniture and real estate, easier and more reliable. In principle, this new system strengthened the management of military equipment, which should now follow the general guidelines defined by the Ministry of Economy and Finance.[20] This trend has been consolidated with a series of reforms of the public sector with a view to promoting transparency and accountability in the use of public resources.

[17] These countries include Algeria, China, Egypt, Germany, Russia, Tunisia and the USA.

[18] The armed forces do not benefit from Mali's national Special Investment Budget, which represents 95% of the investment capacity of the country. Eighty per cent of the fund is financed by external assistance. Lois de finances [Finance acts], *Journal Officiel* (Bamako), 1999–2003.

[19] See note 1.

[20] Presidential Decree no. 91-275/PM-RM, *Journal Officiel* (Bamako), 8 Sep. 1991.

However, in spite of these changes, there is little evidence that the process of budgeting is either transparent or consultative. State budgeting is still largely a private affair of the executive, with limited room for accountability. While this is a result of the powers conferred on the executive by the constitution, the existence of secrecy laws and the general reluctance to share public expenditure information with civil society, especially the media, prevent broader participation in the process. In addition, the special role of the military accountants contradicts the principle of separation of functions between officials who can authorize the release of funds and those who oversee how funds are used. The introduction of an anti-corruption agency by President Konaré in 1992 was meant to stem the rampant corruption in the public sector. The military sector, with all the secrecy surrounding its activities, is most susceptible to corruption, and the dual role of military accountants can only further erode the possibility of accountability.

In 1992 the MOEF established within the principal ministries—including the MODV—a delegation for financial control. The delegation's duty is to monitor and control all the financial operations in the ministry and to establish, jointly with the ministry's Director of Administration and Finance, a quarterly table of financial operations. The head of the delegation delivers authorizations for spending, public tenders and contracts and is accountable to the Director of National Financial Control, under the direct authority of the Minister of Economy and Finance. This new system aimed to increase transparency and accountability in the management of public spending, including the armed forces.

However, most accountants and many other actors in the military budgetary process only rarely report to the accounting section of the Supreme Court, as they are required by law to do. The military sector ought not be treated any differently from other parts of the public sector in terms of the level of resources granted and the application of sound public expenditure management principles.

Weak parliamentary oversight

The main reason for producing a comprehensive budget is that the National Assembly needs to have a complete picture of government income and expenditure in a single document in order to be able to exert control over spending. However, regular resort to extra-budgetary spending has left the National Assembly uninformed about true government financial operations. The various sources of off-budget income described above are beyond the reach of the legislators as they have little or no say in the management of the armed forces, including policy development. This is in part caused by a lack of expertise among legislators and by the absence of the resources needed to employ experts to support the National Assembly's oversight work. More importantly, it is a consequence of the powers granted by the constitution to the executive in state matters generally and for the security sector in particular. In many cases the

National Assembly acts simply to rubber stamp executive decisions on security issues.

While legislators are able to discuss the military budget, the executive can ignore their suggestions and is not bound by any amendments made. Even if the National Assembly refuses to approve the budget, the executive can simply continue to spend state funds without their consent after a pause of only a few days. Similarly, the audited accounts of the government, which should be presented to the National Assembly for approval within one year, are either late or do not arrive at all. The National Assembly has no power to sanction the executive for this failure.

Politicization of public service

Nepotism and political bias in public appointments in Mali, as elsewhere, breed mediocrity and encourage situations in which key technical decisions are informed by political interests that often contradict formal principles, planned budget objectives and accounting norms. Added to this is the fact that certain authorities and individuals appear to be untouchable by the law, even in the face of glaring mismanagement. This serves to dampen the morale of public sector workers, including those in the military sector, and encourages further derogation from formal rules. Counteracting impunity remains a key challenge of government reform in Mali.

VI. Conclusions and recommendations

While military budgeting and accounting in Mali obey the general guidelines set out in the 1996 financial law act and the 1996 public accounting act, there are still derogations from formal rules, as the above analysis shows. Although the fundamental principles of the financial law act are generally respected by the armed forces, the public accounting act is almost always violated. If the latter act is to be fully enforced in the military sector, profound adjustments and reforms will be needed.

Many of the weaknesses in the budgetary process of the armed and security forces are not specific to the sector but are common across the Malian political and administrative systems. The general accounting principles and budgeting guidelines are compromised by informal practices that persist mainly because of weak hierarchical control, an absence of effective judicial control and limited parliamentary control. Weak state authority, the lack of civic education for military and civilian officials, corruption, and financial delinquency are still widespread in the country despite the stated commitment of the political leadership to sanitize public life. The lack of capacity in several key areas of the system appears to be the major cause of these problems.

If implemented, the following recommendations would improve accountability and transparency in the military budgetary process.

1. Human and institutional capacity in budget administration should be strengthened.

2. The overall public administration structure, including the armed forces, should be depoliticized.

3. Rules related to accountability and transparency in the military sector should be progressively standardized. In addition, good governance in military budgeting is only likely to produce long-lasting benefits if ongoing efforts to reform budgetary processes in public administration are accompanied by a realistic redefinition of the optimal conditions of efficiency, accountability and transparency.

4. The progressive improvement in the management of public spending and resources will depend heavily on the outcome of ongoing structural adjustment programmes and poverty-alleviation initiatives. Hence, it is imperative to interlock national commitment with international engagement from the World Bank, the International Monetary Fund, the European Union and other bilateral partners. In essence, the Government of Mali, however well placed, cannot act alone.

7. Mozambique

Lázaro Macuácua

I. Introduction and background

A multiplicity of actors and a diversity of opinions in the military sector are acknowledged realities in Mozambique. Consequently, debates about national security have increasingly appeared in the public arena since the end of the civil war in 1992. An important contribution of the public debate on armed forces has been the progressive understanding that military issues are no longer restricted to military personnel and politicians but belong to the national agenda. However, public debate about such critical issues as military budgeting remains limited. Invariably, there is no public knowledge of, debate about or input into the military budget, nor is there any publicly accessible record of the exact military allocation.

This chapter analyses the budgetary process for the military sector in Mozambique with the aim of contributing to the ongoing debate about strengthening transparency, accountability and professionalism in the Mozambican military sector. This introductory section continues with a survey of the historical, political and economic context. Section II provides a description of the defence and security sector, including the components and structure of the armed forces, the governing doctrine (on missions and roles) and the nature of the security environment. Section III explores the formal national budgetary process, which in turn leads to an exploration of the military component in section IV. Section V undertakes a critical assessment of the formal process of military budgeting, focusing on its strengths and weaknesses, both perceived and real. Issues of institutional capacity, off-budget military spending, and lack of accountability and transparency are highlighted. The last section provides conclusions and offers recommendations for improving the process.

History, politics and economy

Mozambique is an ethnically and linguistically diverse country, with 13 national languages and numerous other dialects spoken by 11 ethnic groups, most of which transcend national boundaries. The official language is Portuguese, which is spoken mainly in the cities. English and French are taught in secondary schools and are spoken by many young professionals as well as senior government officials and political leaders.

Mozambique gained its political independence from Portugal on 25 June 1975, after a 10-year liberation struggle led by the Frente de Libertação de

Moçambique (FRELIMO, liberation front of Mozambique). On independence, FRELIMO established a one-party, socialist state.

Mozambique's solidarity with liberation fighters elsewhere in the sub-region provoked serious threats to its national security, with direct military aggression and the raising, training and funding of a clandestine dissident military intelligence group, the Resistência Nacional Moçambicana (RENAMO, Mozambican national resistance), by the Rhodesian minority rule regime of Ian Smith. When Rhodesia became independent in 1980, as Zimbabwe, RENAMO moved its base to South Africa; its subsequent military activities were to prolong the civil war between the rebel movement and the FRELIMO-led government into the 1990s. Following informal peace efforts initiated by the Catholic Church and after two years of protracted negotiations, a general peace agreement was signed in Rome in October 1992.[1] The ensuing United Nations-sponsored peace process paved the way for Mozambique's first ever multiparty elections, in October 1994, which were mainly a contest between the two warring factions, then transformed into political parties.

The presidency is held by Armando Guebuza of FRELIMO, who took office in February 2005.The parliament is unicameral, with 250 members elected for a term of five years through a system of proportional representation.

A new constitution was adopted in December 2004 which defines the objectives of Mozambique's defence and security policy to be the defence of national independence; the preservation of the sovereignty and the integrity of the country; the guaranteeing of the normal functioning of institutions; and the safeguarding of citizens against any kind of armed aggression.[2] The authority of the constitution over the defence and security forces is symbolized by the oath to be taken by all members of the forces.[3]

Since 1988 the Mozambican Government has pursued a wide-ranging programme of economic stabilization and structural reform, which has reaped impressive results. Market liberalization, completion of an ambitious privatization programme, fiscal reform and progress on public sector reform have contributed to strong economic growth; for example, gross domestic product (GDP) grew by 7 per cent in real terms in 2003.[4]

Additional investment projects in titanium extraction and processing and in garment manufacturing are expected to improve the country's balance of trade. However, the scale of foreign investment should not be overestimated; there have been some setbacks. Indeed, 2002 was a bad year in terms of foreign investments, and the elections in 2003 and 2004 may have discouraged investment in those years.

---

[1] General Peace Agreement for Mozambique, Rome, 4 Oct. 1992, available at URL <http://www.usip. org/library/pa/mozambique/pa_mozambique.html>.

[2] Constituição da República [Constitution of the Republic], *Boletim da República* (Maputo), 22 Dec. 2004, Article 265.

[3] Constituição da República (note 2), Article 266.

[4] International Monetary Fund (IMF), 'Republic of Mozambique: request for a new three-year arrangement under the poverty reduction and growth facility', IMF Country Report no. 04/342, Washington, DC, June 2004, URL <http://www.imf.org/external/country/moz/>, p. 5.

In spite of the overall progress, Mozambique continues to depend heavily on foreign assistance for much of its annual budget, and a majority of the workforce is engaged in subsistence agriculture and is thus firmly rooted below the poverty line. A substantial trade imbalance persists, although it has diminished with the opening of some large-scale projects such as the Mozal aluminium smelter, the country's largest foreign investment project, and the Pande natural gas project in Inhambane.

II. The defence and security sector

Mozambique's defence and security sector consists of the police, the Serviço de Informação e Segurança do Estado (SISE, state information and security service) and the military establishment. The three services of the Forças Armadas de Defesa de Moçambique (FADM, armed defence forces of Mozambique), the army, the air force and the navy, form the core of the military sector. Mozambique does not have a paramilitary force. To ensure the progressive development of the FADM, the military establishment is currently undertaking a legal review of the statutes governing the FADM. One of the achievements of this review was the approval in December 2004 of a new structure for the military establishment.[5]

Although the end of both the cold war and apartheid have fundamentally altered Mozambique's security environment by reducing high-level threats to national security, other threats abound, both military and non-military. The needs for sub-regional security cooperation, internal consensus and national cohesion have become imperative security issues. It has been argued that, although these threats to security seem distinct, they are in fact connected, as each exhibits serious multiplier effects.[6] Accordingly, a feasible solution is to join with partners in Southern Africa in their attempts to adapt themselves to the new philosophy of interdependence. On the basis of that philosophy, Mozambique has been playing an important role among member states of the Southern African Development Community (SADC) in speeding up the establishment of a regional security architecture. This is evidenced by its accession to the 2001 SADC protocol that created the Organ on Politics, Defence and Security Cooperation.[7] There are also concurrent efforts for the implementation of the strategic plan for establishing the Organ and the drafting of an SADC mutual defence pact.[8] However, the signing of these agreements and protocols

---

[5] Decree 48/2003, *Boletim da República* (Maputo), 24 Dec. 2004.

[6] Macaringue, P. J., 'Mozambique defence in the post-war era', MA dissertation, Department of Politics and International Relations, Lancaster University, 1998, pp. 30–31.

[7] SADC, Protocol on Politics, Defence and Security Cooperation, Blantyre, 14 Aug. 2001, URL <http://www.sadc.int/>.

[8] SADC, 'Strategic indicative plan for the Organ on Politics, Defence and Security Cooperation', Aug. 2004, URL <http://www.sadc.int/>.

Table 7.1. Directorates of the Mozambican Ministry of National Defence and their functions

Directorate	Functions
Defence Policy	Undertake strategic studies on defence; suggest measures and guidelines in order to promote civil–military relations; promote research and issue studies on national defence; ensure the development of the Ministry of National Defence, and coordinate the external activities of the ministry
Human Resources	Coordinate the technical assistance necessary for developing human resources in the military sector
Defence Equipment	Ensure the attainment of stated defence goals by coordinating the equipment and operational needs of the armed forces
Finance and Logistics	Plan, acquire, allocate and control the logistic and financial means of the military sector; design policy on management of the national defence facilities and infrastructure
Military Health	Provide health services and assistance to members of the armed forces
Defence Intelligence	Gather the intelligence necessary for attaining defence goals
General Inspectorate	Ensure proper management of the human, material and financial resources at the disposal of the defence establishment

Source: Ministerial Diploma 81/95, *Boletim da República* (Maputo), 7 June 1995.

has meant very little in practical terms since SADC member states tend not to adhere to commonly agreed rules and protocols.[9]

Finally, the relatively stable security environment also permits the FADM's involvement in civilian activities designed to improve the level of human security, especially in rural Mozambique. Such activities include humanitarian search-and-rescue operations, the clearing of minefields, the collection and destruction of weapons and explosives, and the rehabilitation of some basic socio-economic infrastructure. Externally, the FADM has been involved in peacekeeping operations in Burundi, Comoros, the Democratic Republic of the Congo, East Timor and Sudan,[10] and has actively participated in joint military exercises, such as Blue Hungwe in Zimbabwe in 1997 and Blue Crane in South Africa in 1999, all of which have been confidence- and security-building measures for Southern Africa.

---

[9] Nathan, L., 'The absence of common values and failure of common security in Southern Africa, 1992–2003', Working Paper no. 50, Crisis States Research Centre, London School of Economics, July 2004, URL <http://www.crisisstates.com/>.

[10] See, e.g., Dwan, R. and Wiharta, S., 'Multilateral peace missions: challenges of peace-building', *SIPRI Yearbook 2005: Armaments, Disarmament And International Security* (Oxford University Press: Oxford, 2005), pp. 139–98.

The Ministry of National Defence

Just after independence, the Ministry of National Defence (MOND) was estab-lished by presidential decree.[11] This decree defines the role and functions of the ministry, placing emphasis on the military component of the national defence policy. The decree also underscores the fundamental responsibility of consoli-dating independence and national unity and sets the parameters for structuring the armed forces.

In the relatively new, multiparty democratic environment the MOND is polit-ically responsible for the management of the military component of defence policy, the administration of the armed forces, providing logistic support, and overseeing and controlling the resources provided by the government.[12] These tasks are the responsibility of the MOND directorates for Defence Policy, Human Resources, Defence Equipment, and Finance and Logistics. There are also directorates for Military Health and Defence Intelligence and the General Inspectorate.[13] The functions of these directorates are enumerated in table 7.1. Figure 7.1 presents the structure of the MOND.

The Minister of National Defence is the political head of the MOND and is designated as the executive authority for the defence establishment. As such, the minister has the primary responsibility for political oversight, for implemen-tation of the national defence policy and for ensuring that political and oper-ational priorities are taken into account in the plans of the ministry. The Minis-ter of National Defence also directs the budgetary process in the ministry through the annual formulation of the institutional framework of activities and guidelines necessary for defining the rules of management of financial resources allocated to the MOND and the FADM. In addition, the minister maintains transparency and efficiency in the budget implementation process.

The Forças Armadas de Defesa de Moçambique

The process of creating new armed forces was regulated by a protocol of the 1992 peace agreement.[14] The protocol provided for the formation of a new, 30 000-strong defence force, composed of equal numbers of volunteers from the two warring factions. The new-look force was to consist of 24 000 person-nel for the army, 4000 for the air force and 2000 for the navy. A joint commis-sion for the formation of the FADM was created to oversee the administration of the armed forces prior to the inauguration of the new, post-war government. The joint commission was also expected to formulate the rules governing the FADM, including the criteria for selecting members of the Forças Armadas de Moçambique (FAM, armed forces of Mozambique) and of RENAMO for the

---

[11] Presidential Decree 01/75, *Boletim da República* (Maputo), 27 July 1975.
[12] Presidential Decree 04/2003, *Boletim da República* (Maputo), 27 Nov. 2003.
[13] Ministerial Diploma 81/95, *Boletim da República* (Maputo), 7 June 1995.
[14] General Peace Agreement for Mozambique (note 1), Protocol IV.

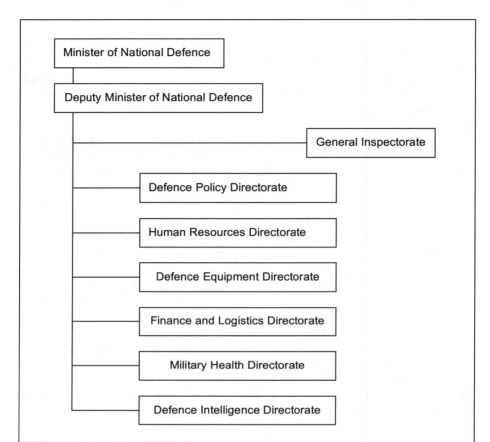

Figure 7.1. The structure of the Mozambican Ministry of National Defence

formation of the FADM and the naming of the commanding officers of the main commands.

The formation of the FADM did not, however, go as smoothly as anticipated, since the expected number of volunteers proved to be unattainable. Several hundred RENAMO and FAM troops were unwilling to join the FADM, as they did not want to repeat their previous experiences of long periods of service in generally poor conditions. As a consequence, of the targeted 30 000 men, only 12 195 joined the FADM: 8533 from the FAM and 3662 from RENAMO.[15]

In the post-war period the FADM has been managed by the reconstituted MOND.[16] The 1990 constitution defined the objective of Mozambique's defence and security policy to be to guarantee the normal functioning of state

[15] Macaringue (note 6), p. 60.
[16] Macaringue (note 6), p. 60.

institutions and to secure citizens against any armed aggression.[17] The 1997 defence and security policy act subordinates the defence and security forces to the law when in pursuit of their missions,[18] while the 1997 national defence act prescribes the fundamental principles and norms for the national defence policy and the armed forces.[19] Mozambique has a conscription law making military service mandatory.[20]

The missions of the armed forces in a war situation, especially their engagement in war, are directly under the command of the commander-in-chief of the defence and security forces (i.e., the President). In peacetime and in accordance with the national defence act, the commander-in-chief is empowered to direct the participation of the armed forces in missions of the United Nations or regional security organizations and in humanitarian missions and missions for development assistance.[21] There has also been a progressive development of civil–military relations in post-war Mozambique, especially in relation to the respect and obedience shown by the armed forces to democratically constituted authorities and their non-partisan posture in a multiparty environment.

The national defence policy

Since the late 1980s Mozambique has experienced multiple transitions: from a centralized to a market economy, from one-party to multiparty politics and from war to peace. The formation of the national defence policy has consequently been influenced by these complex processes and transitions. According to Henrique Banze, Mozambican defence and security policy reflects the political stalemate between political representatives of the former rebel movement, RENAMO, and of the ruling party, FRELIMO; the low level of confidence and the mutual distrust between the two parties; and the domination of parliament by FRELIMO.[22] The policy has also been influenced by external pressure to implement radical political and economic reforms and by the extremely weakened defence capabilities that resulted from the amalgamation of elements with completely different combat standards, with military personnel drawn from the former rebel movement and government regular forces.

The actual formulation of the defence policy was spearheaded by the National Directorate for Defence Policy, which set up a working group consisting of

---

[17] Constituição da República de Moçambique [Constitution of the Republic of Mozambique], *Boletim da República* (Maputo), 2 Nov. 1990, Article 59, English translation at URL <http://confinder.richmond.edu/>.

[18] Lei do Política de Defesa e Segurança [Defence and security policy act], Act 17/97, *Boletim da República* (Maputo), 7 Oct. 1997.

[19] Lei da Defesa Nacional [National defence act], Act 18/97, *Boletim da República* (Maputo), 7 Oct. 1997.

[20] Lei do Servico Militar [Military service act], Act 24/97, *Boletim da República* (Maputo), 23 Dec. 1997.

[21] Lei da Defesa Nacional (note 19), Article 25.

[22] Banze, H., 'Mozambican security agenda: from liberation to development', MSc dissertation, Department of Peace and Development Research, Gothenburg University, 2001, pp. 68–70.

skilled military and civilian personnel. This working group was responsible for drafting the concept paper that formed the basis for subsequent discussion. The discussion included important contributions from security experts from research centres such as the the the Centro de Estudos Estratégicos e Internacionais of the Instituto Superior de Relaçoes Internacionais in Maputo. The draft defence policy was thereafter sent to parliament for approval as official public policy.[23] In general terms, the 1997 defence and security policy act enumerates the main responsibilities of the FADM—to act as the military component of national defence—and states its mission.[24]

The basic principles underlining the defence policy include: (a) the collective responsibility of citizens for national defence, promotion of state security and public order; (b) the strengthening of national unity and the safeguarding of national interests; (c) the prohibition of compulsory conscription and voluntary enlistment into the defence and security services of citizens under 18 years of age; (d) the political neutrality of the defence and security establishments and their obligation to abstain from participating in actions or activities that could jeopardize the internal cohesion and unity of the nation; (e) the exclusive fidelity of the military to the constitution and other binding legal texts, and obedience to the commander-in-chief; (f) respect for the use of legitimate force where necessary to accomplish peace and security, the emphasis being on conflict prevention or the negotiated settlement of conflicts; (g) the creation of a peaceful and secure climate at national, regional and international level; and (h) contributing to the construction and maintenance of a stable and peaceful international order.

The overall objectives of the defence policy are to guarantee the independence, sovereignty, integrity and inviolability of the national territory; to guarantee the defence and normal functioning of Mozambique's institutions; and to defend state property and the country's strategic interests. In addition, the policy aims to prevent or combat drug trafficking, organized crime and terrorism. Finally, it seeks to promote respect for the law, to maintain public order and security, and to protect the state by guaranteeing its economic and social development.

III. The national budgetary process

From independence in 1975 until 1992 the national budgetary process, especially the military budget, was neither open nor participatory, given the poor security environment prevailing during the civil war. The volatile military situation also prompted the government's provision of huge financial resources to the security sector. However, accountability and transparency became core principles in the public sector and in the military budgetary process following the post-war reforms and the intrusive demands of major international donors

---

[23] Banze (note 22), p. 69.
[24] Lei do Política de Defesa e Segurança (note 18).

and development agencies, including the International Monetary Fund (IMF) and the World Bank. Yet internal commitment remains critical to transforming the process, as demonstrated by the 1997 budget framework act, which contains regulations for the preparation and implementation of the state budget.[25] Another internal factor is the desire to reduce the huge debt burden, which has also inspired greater attention to budget performance and the use of financial resources.

The budget framework act establishes the principles, rules and norms relating to the budget and general accounting procedures. Its key objective is to modernize the procedures for state budget management, enabling improved public sector management, accountability, the timely provision of quality information and the reduction of waste in the use of the allocated resources. The act represents a fundamental change in the management of public finances, given that it holds the executive authorities of state institutions (including ministries) accountable for the use of resources allocated to their institution. The act requires that the state budget itemizes all the revenue to be raised and all the expenditure planned in a specific financial year. Moreover, the act makes the budget an annual document that must be made public and provides for public entities responsible for the management and execution of the state budget to face disciplinary, civil and criminal sanctions for errors or omissions in budget execution. Finally, the Administrative Court is empowered to exercise jurisdictional control of public expenditures—that is, to act as the auditor-general of the state—and to prepare a report on state financial matters for parliament.

In conformity with the legal provisions set by parliament in addition to the budget framework act, the government is expected to present the state budget to a plenary session of parliament. Every three months parliament also receives account updates from the government, covering both revenue and expenditure outlays. The act also empowers the government to take the measures necessary to enable the timely execution of the state budget by the end of the financial year, on 31 December.

The Ministry of Planning and Finance and military funding

Given the volatile security environment in the post-independence era, for a considerable period of time the major share of the state budget was channelled to the defence and security sector. Inevitably, the war economy was characterized by a high level of secrecy and an acute lack of transparency. In addition, the military budget was presented in an aggregated form. It was argued that 'this budget is permanently exposed to frequent variations, which are sometimes abrupt, as this is the outcome of the development of military activity rather than the nature of the expenditure'.[26]

[25] Lei do Enquadramento do Orçamento e da Conta Geral do Estado [State budget and general account framework act], Act 15/97, *Boletim da República* (Maputo), 10 July 1997.
[26] Antunes, M. de Azevedo, *Lições de finanças públicas* [Lessons of public finances] (Instituto Comercial de Maputo: Maputo, 1979), p. 108 (author's translation).

Table 7.2. Military expenditure of Mozambique, 1990–2004

Figures in US$ are in constant 2003 prices and exchange rates.

Year	Military expenditure		
	$ m.	b. meticais	as a % of GDP
1990	107	136	*10.1*
1991	106	178	*4.5*
1992	106	259	*5.1*
1993	115	399	*5.0*
1994	134	762	*5.7*
1995	59	522	*2.5*
1996	54	704	*2.2*
1997	60	840	*2.1*
1998	71	1 013	*2.2*
1999	86	1 250	*2.4*
2000	85	1 400	*2.5*
2001	95	1 700	*2.4*
2002	95	2 000	*2.4*
2003	105	2 500	..
2004	59	1 585	..

GDP = Gross domestic product.
Source: SIPRI military expenditure database.

However, Mozambique's joining of the IMF and the World Bank in 1984, the end of the armed conflict in 1992, and the subsequent commitment to a 'peace dividend' approach affected economic planning, resource allocation and budget practices.[27] In 1995, for instance, the government pledged to reduce military expenditure to 2.4 per cent of GDP (see table 7.2, which presents Mozambique's military expenditure since 1990).[28] A significant feature of the new budgeting framework is the oversight role of the Administrative Court.

The year 1997 marked the actual turning point in the development of the budgetary process with parliament's approval of the budget framework act. This was augmented in 1998 by the approval by the Council of Ministers of a decree that empowers the Ministry of Planning and Finance (MOPF) to analyse and review the budget proposals from all state institutions, especially the ministries.[29] Accordingly, the MOPF compiles and harmonizes the draft budgets of all government departments, forwards the consolidated budget to the Council of Ministers for debate, and controls the use of resources by all government ministries by undertaking monthly and annual accounting and auditing. When

[27] A 'peace dividend' approach indicates a government's intention to divert resources used for war to social development, especially health and education.

[28] United Nations Development Programme (UNDP), *Moçambique, paz e crescimento económico: oportunidades para o desenvolvimento humano* [Mozambique, peace and economic growth: opportunities for human development] (UNDP: Maputo, 1998), p. 35.

[29] Decree 07/98, *Boletim da República* (Maputo), 10 Mar. 1998.

Table 7.3. Military assistance received by Mozambique from select donors, 1999–2002

Year	Donor	Value ($)	Assistance
1999	Portugal	. .	Rehabilitation and equipping of the Laboratory for Clinical Analyses, Military Hospital, Maputo
2000	USA	. .	Language laboratory for training in English at the Logistics Training Centre, Maputo
2002	USA	600 000	Rehabilitation of the Engineering School, Boquisso
2002	China	1 800 000	Non-lethal military equipment: 8 trucks, health equipment, diving equipment, boots and uniforms
2002	China	700 000	Surgical equipment and de-mining equipment
2002	China	7 000 000	New military premises and training facilities

. . = Not known.

Source: Ministry of National Defence, Maputo.

appropriate, the MOPF can request the intervention of the Finance Inspectorate and take other necessary measures.

It is assumed that the FADM is not eligible for foreign funding or aid, given that it is not at the top of the government's list of priorities. However, the FADM benefits from other, non-financial contributions from donor countries in the form of training programmes, regional courses in defence and disaster management, and through its participation in peacekeeping operations. The MOND's major partners for military and technical cooperation are China, Portugal, the UK and the USA, although these partnerships are not based on any formal agreement. The areas of cooperation are training, technical assistance, health and the supply of non-lethal equipment. Table 7.3 details some of the assistance from donors to the Mozambican Government.

IV. The military planning and budgetary process

The decree defining the military budgetary process divided the process into four phases: planning and formulation, approval, implementation and audit.[30]

The planning and formulation phase

The planning stage takes place between March and May of each year, with the Ministry of National Defence drafting a budget concept paper in accordance with guidelines provided by the Ministry of Planning and Finance.[31] This

[30] Decree 07/98 (note 29).

[31] When initiating the state budgetary process for the forthcoming financial year, the MOPF is expected to send to all state institutions preliminary or definitive budget limits, the methodology for collecting information and any other instructions to be taken into consideration in the preparation of the budget proposals. Decree 07/98 (note 29), Article 2.

internal process involves senior officers attached to the Finance and Logistics Directorate of the MOND. As the military establishment lacks a strategic development plan, this process is not preceded by any open internal discussion on what should be reflected in the paper.

The head of the MOND Finance and Logistics Directorate sends the resulting concept paper to the Minister of National Defence, who formally approves the draft budget in a process that runs from May to the end of June. Following ministerial approval, the MOND, like any other ministry, is expected to send its draft budget to the MOPF by 31 July.[32] The MOPF then reviews all the ministerial budget proposals and integrates them into the government's overall socio-economic macroeconomic policy. Once this is done, the Minister of Planning and Finance submits the draft finance bill to the Council of Ministers, where it is discussed and approved before being sent to parliament for its approval.

The approval phase

In parliament, the finance bill is first reviewed by the portfolio budget committees, including the Defence Portfolio Committee, and thereafter at a plenary session. The plenary debate is followed by the mandatory vote of approval or disapproval, which is required to take place by 31 December of each year.[33] It is during the parliamentary debate that the opportunity for civil society involvement exists. However, there is currently minimal participation of civil society groups, except for campaigns for debt forgiveness. Upon approval of the bill, the President is expected to formally announce the state budget and subsequently make it public for implementation.

Parliament exercises oversight of the military budget through the periodic reports from the executive on the revenue and expenditure of all ministries (including the MOND), in accordance with the 1997 budget framework act.

The implementation phase

Once the state budget is made public, the government, in accordance with existing legal provisions, takes the necessary measures to achieve budget goals over the course of the financial year. In the implementation process, the government is expected to take into account the principles of cost-effectiveness and prudent management of approved finances.[34]

The important issue of defence acquisition and procurement follows the sub-contracting format used by all government departments and overseen by the MOPF. This formal process involves open bidding by interested private commercial firms. In case of acquisition through an existing agreement with a company or technical partner, the military establishment must seek prior author-

---

[32] Decree 07/98 (note 29), Article 3.

[33] Lei do Enquadramento do Orçamento e da Conta Geral do Estado (note 25), Article 18.

[34] Lei do Enquadramento do Orçamento e da Conta Geral do Estado (note 25), Article 20.

ization from the Minister of Planning and Finance.[35] Legally, each government body or ministry is empowered to oversee the implementation of the budget, according to its internal hierarchy.[36] Hence, each month the Finance and Logistics Directorate of the MOND provides an updated account of the implementation of the resources allocated to the MOPF following a prescribed format.

The extent to which the formal procedure is followed remains unclear. Gaps remain between the process established by legislation and day-to-day practice.

The audit phase

The MOND has internal auditors who report to the Inspector-General, who in turn reports to the Minister of National Defence on financial and accounting processes connected with the implementation of the budget. The Administrative Court undertakes external auditing functions in an independent and impartial manner and reports directly to parliament under the general state account process. For this purpose, at the end of each financial year (31 December) the MOND initiates an accounting process that presents the ministry's use of allocated resources to the Administrative Court (acting as auditor-general). Usually, this process ends by June, when a dossier is delivered to the court.

V. Assessment of the military budgetary process

Institutional capacity and derogation from formal rules

To qualitatively evaluate Mozambique's military budgetary process, it is important to highlight the facts that: (*a*) the state budget for the defence and security sector cannot exceed the donor-imposed ceiling of 2 per cent of GDP and the sector must be funded only by the state budget; (*b*) knowledge about the detail of the military budget remains limited to a small group of people, and the process of drafting is not as open and transparent as it could be; and (*c*) the existing legal basis for military budgeting does not give sufficient support for budgeting on a long-term, strategic basis.

A critical overview reveals huge gaps between the established formal rules provided by the 1997 budget framework act and the actual budgetary practices. Two limitations particularly apply to the military sector. First, the presentation of military estimates in aggregated form compromises reliability and obscures the basis for budgetary allocation to the defence and security sector as a whole and within the sector.

The second limitation is not peculiar to the defence and security sector: there is a serious shortfall in the capacity, especially skilled manpower, required to

---

[35] The signing of contracts or agreements with any entity requires prior authorization of the Minister of Planning and Finance if it imposes any responsibility on the state treasury, even if the expenditure is already covered by the state budget. Lei do Enquadramento do Orçamento e da Conta Geral do Estado (note 25), Article 23.

[36] Lei do Enquadramento do Orçamento e da Conta Geral do Estado (note 25), Article 18.

achieve the established goals of prudent financial management and the observance of existing legal provisions in budget implementation across the public sector. This problem is further accentuated by acute structural weaknesses related to the lack of institutional coordination to ensure maximal use of the available skilled people; a lack of morale among the civil servants who perform these tasks; and the relative lack of sanctions for civil servants who do not follow formal processes. All this demonstrates that, in spite of the existence of a formal, legal framework and an apparent political will for continuous reform, the institutional context cannot be overlooked.

Lack of a strategic plan

The defence policy of 1997 urgently requires a review in order for it to meet current exigencies. The need for a review was harshly brought home to government during the floods of 2000 and 2001 when, despite the huge patriotic and professional zeal of the FADM in undertaking search-and-rescue operations, they were severely handicapped by the lack of operational readiness and capacity for such a role.

In addition, although it has a defence policy, the country lacks a strategic defence plan which would allow for medium- to long-term planning for the armed forces. In particular, there is no Lei de Programação Militar (military planning act), a legal instrument that commits the government to supply equipment to the military. Yet, given the imposed spending limit, the government needs to prioritize and make long-term plans more than ever, so that the needs of the forces can be spread over several annual budgets.

Off-budget expenditure and revenue

Off-budget spending arises when 'There is a large, autonomous military sector; The military are directly represented in political institutions; . . . There are significant security problems, including armed conflict; [and] A period of protracted war is coming to an end'.[37] It is not an established practice in Mozambique.

Three factors account for the low incidence of off-budget spending in Mozambique. First, the country is not facing problems of political governance that require the direct intervention of the military establishment. Second, there have been progressive economic and security reforms in the post-war era. Third, the country's monetary and fiscal policy was designed and is closely scrutinized by the IMF and the World Bank, whose anti-military spending posture ostensibly reduces the potential for off-budget activity. In addition, the government's preoccupation with increasing its credibility in donor circles has

---

[37] Hendrickson, D. and Ball, N., 'Off-budget military expenditure and revenue: issues and policy perspectives for donors', Conflict, Security and Development Group Occasional Papers no. 1, Department for International Development and King's College London, Jan. 2002, URL <http://csdg.kcl.ac.uk/>, p. i.

translated into a commitment to tackle off-budget spending and the lack of accountability and transparency.

However, despite legal provisions,[38] the official budget does not always include all revenue, the figures related to aggregated borrowing, the provisional endowment for expenditure and investments or the provisional endowment under the management of the MOPF intended to cover unexpected expenditure. Moreover, given the country's vulnerabilities and the perceived threats to its security, it is difficult to imagine that Mozambique will strictly adhere to the imposed spending limit. The general lack of transparency in the defence and security sector makes an objective assessment difficult.

A corollary of off-budget spending is the appearance of non-military expenditure in the military budget estimate. This is partly owing to the improved political and security environment, which has increasingly diverted the FADM towards humanitarian search-and-rescue operations and the rehabilitation of some economic infrastructure, as demonstrated in the aftermath of the floods of 2000 and 2001. Disturbingly, the defence establishment does not provide for any contingency funds in its budget; thus, during emergencies the FADM either diverts resources from other pre-planned activities or resorts to extra-budgetary allocation from the MOPF's national contingency fund. Finally, given Mozambique's peace dividend approach to defence funding—which limits military activities to basic training and the minimum capacity building required for undertaking external missions arising from international and sub-regional obligations—it is unclear how reimbursements and revenue accruing from the FADM's involvement in peacekeeping operations are managed.

The role of the political system

The decision by each country on whether to have a particular military institution is not just a matter of convenience but is mainly the outcome of a number of perceptions influenced by history, the security environment, geopolitical position, and strategic, economic and political factors.

However, in a country such as Mozambique, where the government's priority is fighting absolute poverty, amortizing public debt and laying the foundation for sustainable economic growth, the existence of the military and the associated military expenditure is sometimes seen to be antithetical to broader socio-economic goals. This viewpoint is often backed by donors, expressed in the stringent conditions that accompany development assistance packages. The huge foreign aid component of Mozambique's national budget leaves it susceptible to this tendency. Not surprisingly, the absence of a strategic military plan only serves to confirm this tendency. There does seem to be a superficial commitment by political elites to this viewpoint, especially in parliament as

---

[38] The government is expected to make public the resources necessary to cover all expenditure and ought to give details of the expected minimum revenues and the maximum limits on expenditure. Lei do Enquadramento do Orçamento e da Conta Geral do Estado (note 25), Articles 9 and 10.

demonstrated by the existence of the specialized Defence Portfolio Committee and by the debate over the ceiling on military expenditure of 2 per cent of GDP. This ceiling, admittedly an imposition, favours the current priority of the Mozambican Government as approved by the donors: to concentrate efforts on fighting absolute poverty. It also favours the national political elite's argument concerning the defence and security sector: that reliance on external financing should be avoided in order to prevent Mozambique's geopolitical, economic and military interests from being compromised.

The challenge lies in balancing the government's neo-liberal orientation with sustaining a secure environment, which has proved central to developmental aspirations in much of the developing world. There is little doubt that a professional, well-equipped, adequately funded, less-politicized, accountable and transparent military is central to the environment needed for economic growth.

Parliamentary oversight

Parliamentary oversight of the budget is weak, as FADM personnel are, in general, members of one or other of the two main political parties. In addition, the part of the state budget allocated to the military sector is only for basic military training and the minimum requirements of external humanitarian and peacekeeping missions. The nature of defence planning and budgeting predisposes parliament to symbolic, elementary oversight of the military sector. Further factors are the absence of a strategic plan and of a policy for the development and acquisition of major weapon systems, which could empower the military sector to request funds in excess of the spending ceiling.

The lack of parliamentary oversight is also connected to the lack of technical knowledge and expertise on the part of members of the Defence Portfolio Committee. Even parliament recognizes that accountability and transparency in military establishments are a long-term project requiring allocation of funds for capacity building. Yet, the same parliament is remarkably reluctant to acknowledge, let alone discuss dealing with, its own institutional limitations.

VI. Conclusions and recommendations

Over the past decade there have been some improvements in the availability to the public of budget information. There has also been a conscious effort to build a framework for accountability and greater transparency in the use of public resources and the delivery of public goods. However, the overall budgetary process for the military, as for much of the wider public sector, is hampered by serious institutional weakness and an acute shortage of skilled personnel, factors that increasingly make the process weak and less formalized. Moreover, the relative lack of information and the restricted participation by the public in the military budgetary process are compounded by the absence of an effective legal framework and weak civil society involvement. Recently, however, there has been increased publilc engagement with the legislature. The greatest limitation facing military planning, budgeting and financing lies in the absence of a long-term, strategic defence plan.

Overall, military planning and budgeting face challenges in introducing modern management practices and accurate research, analysis and strategic assumptions. It will be an enormous challenge to use the existing structures to satisfy future requirements for effective and efficient budgetary processes. To effect all the necessary changes in the budgetary process, and still remain cost-effective and efficient, will require careful planning and decision making based on reliable information. In addition, further reform initiatives are required in the conduct of the budgetary process itself, especially in the areas of capacity building for budget personnel and inter-institutional linkages and collaboration. For this purpose, the training and retraining of civil servants need to be addressed.

Other crucial recommendations include: (*a*) the improvement of budget documentation to better explain the policy basis for budgetary allocation to all sectors, including defence; (*b*) the strengthening of the process of drafting the state budget and all the documents that contribute to it, in order to be in accordance with the provisions of the 1997 budget framework act; and (*c*) the promotion of greater openness and transparency concerning military expenditure in order to strengthen domestic civil–military relations and improve mutual trust among the countries of the region. Moreover, it is imperative for military leaders to be educated in the principles of budget management, transparency and accountability, including administrative practices. Finally, there is a need to support the efforts of civil society groups to improve their capacity to contribute meaningfully to public debates on military matters.

8. Nigeria

Wuyi Omitoogun and Tunde Oduntan

I. Introduction and background

In 1999, elections in Nigeria produced a civilian administration, raising new hopes after 15 years of military dictatorship. The new government announced programmes to reform the military, pursue economic recovery, fight corruption and mismanagement, and institutionalize democracy. Six years on, a critical citizenry is asking what real changes have taken place as violent inter-ethnic rivalries, a weak economy and a poor social base still pose profound challenges to national security. Added to these are Nigeria's international responsibilities, regional image and territorial controversies. These factors have defined the concept of national security and the organization of state and national defence.

This chapter examines the process of budgeting for the Nigerian Armed Forces against this background. This section continues with an overview of the country's history, politics and economy while section II describes the Nigerian military sector. Section III discusses the formal national budgetary process and presents a critique of the process. The military budgetary process and its weaknesses are examined in sections IV and V. Section VI presents the conclusions and recommendations.

History, politics and economy

The West African state of Nigeria was built up by the gradual, expansionist colonialism of the United Kingdom, starting with the colony of Lagos in 1861. By 1914 the various protectorates and colonies had merged to form a unified Nigeria, but administration remained largely decentralized. At independence in 1960 Nigeria inherited a federal structure that continues to exist today, albeit in greatly changed form. There are over 350 ethnic groups in Nigeria, the three largest of which represent about 71 per cent of the population. Colonial policies that aggravated divisions meant that at independence it was obvious that ethnic rivalry was going to hinder nation building.[1] The greatest crisis that Nigerian unity has had to face is the attempted secession in 1967 of the Eastern Region. The consequent civil war of 1967–70, also known as the Biafran War, resulted in more than 1 million deaths.[2] Divisions still persist along several lines:

---

[1] Coleman, J. S., *Nigeria: Background to Nationalism* (University of California Press: Berkeley, Calif., 1971).

[2] See, e.g., Akpan, N. U., *The Struggle for Secession, 1967–1970* (Frank Cass: London, 1972).

religion, North versus South and ethnicity. The ethnic basis of many political parties means that contests for political power are often inter-ethnic contests.

Between independence in 1960 and the end of military rule in 1999, the military ruled Nigeria for a total of 29 years, compared with only 9 years of civilian democracy. Presidential elections were held in February 1999, following the death in 1998 of the military dictator General Sani Abacha. The winner was Olusegun Obasanjo, a retired general who himself had led a military regime in the 1970s. President Obasanjo was re-elected in April 2003, defeating yet another former military ruler.

According to the 1999 constitution, the President is head of government as well as head of state.[3] The President appoints ministers and heads the Federal Executive Council, which consists of the President, the ministers and the 36 state governors. The legislature, the National Assembly, consists of the House of Representatives, with 360 elected constituency members, and the Senate, with 109 members elected to represent the federal states.

Nigeria's economy is dominated by the oil industry, which provides 95 per cent of export revenue, more than three-quarters of government revenue and about a third of gross domestic product.[4] In spite of its oil wealth, Nigeria remains a poor country, but its human and natural resources mean that it has the potential for great prosperity.

The factors of population, size and potential wealth have generally defined Nigeria's national self-image. Successive Nigerian governments have maintained the idea that Nigeria is destined to play a leadership role in Africa and in championing the cause of the African people. This image has shaped Nigeria's external policy since independence. At the same time, Nigeria has had to contend with territorial disputes with its immediate neighbours. Political instability and economic weakness in these neighbouring states are also of concern to Nigeria. However, the greater challenge to Nigeria's security is internal.

II. The military sector

The character and orientation of the Nigerian military reflect its colonial background. The colonial army, which was transformed into the Nigerian Army at independence, was created for use in the wars of conquest and pacification of Nigerian peoples and the entrenchment of foreign rule, including the collection of taxes and policing functions. The public image of the military is as an instrument of enforcement and control. In the environment of internal divisions, which have always limited governmental legitimacy, the military sees itself as the single institution upon which the unity and cohesion of the country depends. Military officers have justified coups and the takeover of government as being necessary to prevent the fragmentation of the fragile nation. In government,

---

[3] Constitution of the Federal Republic of Nigeria 1999, promulgated by Decree no. 24 of 1999, Abuja, 5 May 1999, available at URL <http://www.nigeria-law.org/>.

[4] World Bank, 'Nigeria: country brief', Sep. 2004, URL <http://www.worldbank.org/ng/>.

Table 8.1. Military expenditure of Nigeria, 1990–2004

Figures in US$ are in constant 2003 prices and exchange rates.

| Year | Military expenditure | | |
	$ m.	m. naira	as a % of GDP
1990	324	2 229	0.9
1991	310	2 415	0.7
1992	267	3 004	0.5
1993	361	6 382	0.9
1994	253	7 032	0.8
1995	292	14 000	0.7
1996	247	15 350	0.5
1997	267	17 920	0.6
1998	340	25 162	0.9
1999	585	45 400	1.4
2000	422	37 490	0.8
2001	632	63 472	1.1
2002	573	64 908	1.1
2003	595	76 890	1.2
2004	518	76 100	..

GDP = Gross domestic product.

Source: SIPRI military expenditure database.

however, the military has proved to be less immune to the vagaries of national politics.

Over the years the missions and roles of the armed forces have reflected the security concerns of the nation and the perceived responsibilities of the country to the continent. The core role of Nigeria's armed forces has remained the defence of the sovereignty and territorial integrity of the nation and of its interests and values. At various times the armed forces have provided support and reinforcement to immigration policy, the customs departments and the Nigerian Police; they have provided 'economic defence' (to protect oil installations); and they have participated in disaster management and humanitarian relief operations. The mission statements of the armed forces have shown a consciousness of the domestic and external security challenges to the nation. However, the extent and application of Nigeria's defence policies have been the subject of critical domestic debate. Analysts have argued, for instance, that the country's national defence objectives are over-ambitious and unrealistic in the light of the resources required for their achievement.[5] The nexus between effective, concise

[5] Vogt, M. A., 'Nigeria's defence policy: an overview', eds A. E. Ekoko and M. A. Vogt, *Nigerian Defence Policy: Issues and Problems* (Malthouse: Lagos, 1990), p. 102; and Adejo, A., 'The question of Nigeria's defence policy: a critical assessment', *African Journal of International Affairs and Development*, vol. 4, no. 1 (1999), p. 38.

policy and the material resources needed to achieve the set policy goals is conspicuously absent in the Nigerian case.[6]

The Nigerian Armed Forces consist of the army, the navy and the air force. The Nigerian Army is the biggest of the three services[7] and is organized in five divisions: two mechanized, two motorized and one armoured. The Nigerian Navy has three commands: the Western and Eastern commands and the Naval Training Command. The Nigerian Air Force is organized in three commands: Tactical Air Command, Training Command and Logistics Command. In addition to each service's headquarters, there is a joint Defence Headquarters, headed by the Chief of Defence Staff. The size of the military grew astronomically during the civil war, from about 10 000 in 1967 to over 250 000 in January 1970.[8] Personnel costs continue to account for approximately three-quarters of recurrent military expenditure.[9] Table 8.1 presents military expenditure in Nigeria since 1990.

The political leadership of the Nigerian military is provided by the Ministry of Defence (MOD), led by the Minister of Defence. The minister has generally been a military officer; however, in 2003 the retired military officer who had held the post since 1999 was succeeded by a civilian. The ministry is headed by a Permanent Secretary. This post has always been held by a civil servant, who reports to the minister.[10] The Permanent Secretary heads the civilian employees of the ministry and acts as the chief accounting officer. The Chief of Defence Staff is responsible for the armed forces and is the chief military adviser to the President as commander-in-chief.

The MOD's major function is the formulation and execution of the national defence policy and the planning of military expenditure. The ministry provides administrative and support services for the training, equipping and combat readiness of the armed forces, allowing them to perform their missions and functions, both actual and potential.[11] The National Assembly exercises oversight of the Nigerian military through its broad powers to regulate the establishment and composition of the armed forces granted by the constitution.[12] In

---

[6] Vogt (note 5).

[7] There are conflicting figures on the strength of the Nigerian armed forces. This issue is discussed below.

[8] Wushishi, M. I., 'The Nigerian Army: growth and development of combat readiness', ed. T. A. Imobighe, *Nigerian Defence and Security: Issues and Options for Policy* (Macmillan Nigeria: Lagos, 1987), p. 54.

[9] Omitoogun, W., *Military Expenditure Data in Africa: A Survey of Cameroon, Ethiopia, Ghana, Kenya, Nigeria and Uganda*, SIPRI Research Report no. 17 (Oxford University Press: Oxford, 2003), p. 90.

[10] In the 1970s permanent secretaries were the most senior civil servants of their ministries. The so-called 'super Perm-Secs' were permanent secretaries with the highest political connections and had the ear of the head of state. Some of them were more powerful than their ministers and were even members of the ruling military councils.

[11] Danjuma, T. Y. (Gen.), Minister of Defence, 'Mission statement of the Ministry of Defence', Ministry of Defence, Abuja, 1999, URL <http://www.nopa.net/Defence/messages/1.shtml>. See also Federal Government of Nigeria, 'National Defence Policy' (draft), Lagos, 2001.

[12] Constitution of the Federal Republic of Nigeria 1999 (note 3), Sections 4(2), 5(5), 217(1) and (2), 218 and 219.

addition, the National Assembly exercises control over all defence matters, including internal security matters and declarations of war.

III. The national budgetary process

The budgetary process in Nigeria has evolved alongside the vicissitudes of national politics, especially the progressive militarization of Nigerian politics and society since independence. In 1966 Nigeria's first military regime, under Major General Johnson Aguiyi-Ironsi, abolished the federal system, ostensibly to counter the effect of ethnic divisions on national politics. By this move to unitary government, Aguiyi-Ironsi effectively undermined the formal structures of national government that had been established prior to independence, destroyed regional structures and introduced a centralization for which there was neither precedent practice nor, indeed, structure and personnel. A new order for government business, including budgeting, had to be created, but it was never formalized, creating confusion for public servants. The impracticality of this new system, among other factors, led to the collapse of the government later in 1966. However, Aguiyi-Ironsi's regime laid the basis for the style of government of future military regimes and initiated the expansion of the Nigerian military in terms of size, prestige and indulgences. The pace was speeded by the civil war of 1967–70.

Left without a formal framework, the bureaucrat's role was transformed from implementation of government policy to policy improvisation. Budgeting, like all aspects of governance under the military, was driven by the personality of each succeeding head of state rather than by any established institutional mechanism. No sustained effort was made by any of the military governments to systematically formulate a process, except for a short-lived attempt by the regimes of Murtala Mohammed and Obasanjo between 1975 and 1979. In effect, the general budgetary process has not significantly changed since 1960, but each government, especially military regimes, merely used the process when it suited it. The implications of non-adherence to due budgetary processes are obvious in Nigeria's highly corrupt public sector.

The formal process

The formal budgetary process in Nigeria consists of four broadly defined phases: formulation, approval, implementation, and auditing and reporting. These formal phases are described below, along with the de facto process.

The formulation phase

The process of budgeting in Nigeria begins with the determination of the macroeconomic framework in which expenditure estimates for the following financial year (which coincides with the calendar year) are formulated by the

Federal Ministry of Finance (FMF), the National Planning Commission (NPC) and the Central Bank of Nigeria. This usually takes place in or around March each year. Simultaneously, the Nigerian National Petroleum Corporation, the Office of the Accountant-General for the Federation (OAcGF) and the Federal Inland Revenue Service draw up revenue estimates.

The second stage involves the invitation of budget officers in the various ministries to seminars organized by the federal government's Budget Office. These seminars cover the budget guidelines and describe how the ministries should make proposals.

The third stage involves the issuance of what is known as the Budget Call Circular (BCC) by the Budget Office to ministries and agencies.[13] This document requests estimates of expenditure and revenue for the year within the set framework and guidelines. In practice, the BCC is central to the budgetary process and is considered by many to mark the beginning of the annual budget preparation. The BCC is usually issued in July but sometimes later. As recently as 2003 it was issued in November.[14]

The BCC stipulates the guidelines for the submission of programme proposals by ministries and extra-ministerial departments and agencies. The guidelines are based on the government's economic programme. The macroeconomic framework is usually determined by a joint pre-budget review by the Budget Office and the NPC. The framework attempts to make an accurate aggregation of revenue projections, the government's economic policy, developmental targets, and sectoral capital and recurrent spending proposals for that financial year. In other words, the BCC represents an annual programme in a wider framework of economic planning.

Each year the FMF sets budget ceilings for ministries. Annex 1 of the BCC stipulates that the Budget Office must complete a 'ceiling to expenditure projections' form before the BCC is dispatched to any ministry or agency. Whether this happens regularly is unclear. However, ministries and agencies generally have an understanding of a spending limit, whether the FMF specifies such ceilings or not. This understanding is derived from the involvement of the ministries in the formulation of economic policy through the NPC. In addition, the planning board of each ministry or agency is expected to be knowledgeable about the macroeconomic developments and the revenue profiles of the federal government. Since each year's capital budget is extracted from the National Rolling Plan (described below), ministries have a clear understanding of the ceilings that apply to such spending.

Upon receiving the BCC, the Permanent Secretary of each ministry, in consultation with the Director of Finance and Supplies and the Director of Research, Planning and Statistics, is expected to constitute a Budget Commit-

---

[13] See, e.g., Okonjo-Tweala, N., Minister of Finance, 'Call circular for the 2005 federal budget', Budget Office, Abuja, 10 Aug. 2004, URL <http://www.budgetoffice.gov.ng/bcc.html>.

[14] Federal Government of Nigeria, 'Federal Government of Nigeria 2004 budget preparation and submission call circular', Budget Office, Lagos, 17 Nov. 2003, URL <http://www.budgetoffice.gov.ng/bcc.html>.

tee, comprising the Deputy Director of the Budget Division and one deputy director from each of the departments in the ministry. This committee prepares the ministry's budget estimates, which are then forwarded to the ministry's Committee of Directors, headed by the Permanent Secretary, for consideration and adoption. The minister gives the final approval within the ministry. Copies of the approved draft estimates are thereafter forwarded to the Budget Office.

The Budget Office then invites the ministries to defend their budget estimates in line with the government's policy and the approved ceiling. The estimates arrived at after these discussions are forwarded to the Cabinet Budget Committee in the Presidency (the President's office) and the Federal Executive Council for discussion, adoption and transmission to the National Assembly for approval.

The National Rolling Plan

An important aspect of the formulation stage of the national budgetary process is the role played by the National Rolling Plan in the allocation of resources to capital projects. The rolling plan is Nigeria's equivalent of the medium-term expenditure framework, with which it shares basic characteristics.[15] After independence in 1960, national economic planning was based on the National Development Plans, a five-year medium-term planning system. In 1990 these were replaced by the National Rolling Plan. The rolling plan offers the advantage of a longer-term strategy, with annual reviews. It avoids the abrupt cessation of each five-year plan in a politically unstable environment and, being more flexible, allows for more participation by the private sector.

The first year of the three-year rolling plan always coincides with the annual capital budget when resources are allocated to projects and programmes. This allows for annual reviews of economic plans in the light of changing economic realities. The rolling plan was expected to help stabilize planning for capital projects spanning several years so that their cost could be spread over a number of annual budgets. The National Rolling Plan is more comprehensive and forward-looking than the annual budgets, especially in relation to the full project cycle (including construction and maintenance) and new capital projects. It represents a conceptual framework for national planning that extends beyond the annual operational and governmental budgets.

However, financial allocations are made to projects only through the annual budgets. The allocations for other years within the rolling plan are mere projections that ease planning and ensure resource availability. Since 2001 any capital project that is to be included in the annual budget must have been included in the rolling plan.

---

[15] Personnel of the Federal Ministry of Finance, Interview with the authors, Abuja, June 2002. Nigeria formally adopted the Medium-Term Expenditure Framework in June 2004, when a 3-year (2005–2007) medium-term budget framework was announced by the Minister of Finance. 'Govt plans three-year budget', *The Guardian* (Lagos), 12 Aug. 2004.

The institutional framework for the National Rolling Plan is coordinated by the National Planning Commission and involves the FMF, the Budget Office, many government departments and the National Assembly. The FMF controls the first year of the rolling plan since it also constitutes the annual budget. The general form of each subsequent annual budget is determined by the rolling plan. In turn, the rolling plan is defined by the economic environment and the government's economic policies. The government's economic policy includes a statement of the guiding principles of the policy, the type of economy envisaged, the objectives of the policy, the instruments for achieving those objectives and the annual targets to be met.[16] The key parts of the economic policy are aggregated by the Budget Office and are used to form the budgetary framework from which the Budget Call Circular is prepared.

The approval phase

During the military era, it was simply the ruling military councils, usually made up of the leading military officers, that approved the budget. In the current democratic dispensation, the draft budget estimates are sent to the National Assembly as the Appropriation Bill to begin the process of approval by both houses. The National Assembly can make modifications to the bill before passing it into law.[17]

The budget is distributed to various committees of the Senate and House of Representatives for detailed discussion. The committees often invite ministries and agencies to explain their estimates. The recommendations of the committees are then sent to the Finance and Appropriation Committee of each house for collation. The two committees meet several times to reconcile any differences that may exist. They may also conduct their own public hearings. A final reading of the bill takes place in each house of the National Assembly, after which the bill is passed and becomes the Appropriation Act once the President has signed it. If the President refuses to sign the bill as approved, a two-thirds majority vote in each house can pass the bill directly into law.

No timetable for the approval process is specified in the constitution. However, the National Assembly has requested that the executive submit the draft budget estimates no later than three months before the financial year begins.[18]

The implementation phase

Once the budget has been approved by the National Assembly the process of implementation begins with the Minister of Finance issuing the appropriate

---

[16] National Planning Commission, 'The rolling plan and its relationship to the budget', Paper presented at the Workshop on Budget Preparation for Officers of Federal Ministries and Parastatals, Abuja, 10–11 Sep. 1997.

[17] Constitution of the Federal Republic of Nigeria 1999 (note 3), Sections 80 and 81. See also Agbese, P., 'Legislative oversights: principles, mechanism and rationales', Paper presented at the International Conference on Legislative Oversight of the Nigerian Military, Abuja, June 2002.

[18] Nigerian Senate, Appropriation Act 2002, National Assembly, Abuja, Mar. 2002.

quarterly warrant to the Accountant-General for the Federation to release funds to the Treasury in line with the approved estimates. The funds are then made available to each ministry or agency on request by the responsible officer, usually the minister or the Permanent Secretary.

If there is an urgent need, funds may be released early to a line ministry or agency through a special request to the Minister of Finance by the accounting officer of the ministry (usually the Permanent Secretary). Such an advance payment is charged against the ministry's or agency's next quarterly allocation.

The auditing and reporting phase

Auditing actually begins during the implementation stage, during which the accounting officers in the ministries are expected to monitor expenditure and make monthly returns to the OAcGF detailing how their ministry's allocations were spent. External bodies are also empowered to monitor the budget to ensure accountability and proper feedback in the system. These bodies include the National Assembly;[19] the National Planning Commission, which reviews the effectiveness of capital projects on a quarterly basis in association with the Planning, Research and Statistics departments of the various ministries;[20] the National Economic Intelligence Commission, which enforces the implementation of tax regulations and considers other issues concerning revenue collection;[21] and the Office of the Auditor-General for the Federation (OAuGF), which is responsible for enquiring into and reporting on public expenditure and which submits its reports directly to the Public Accounts Committees of the National Assembly.[22]

The Auditor-General for the Federation is independent and has a secured tenure guaranteed by the constitution. However, the laws relating to the audit of public accounts are outdated, being based on the 1958 Audit Act. While sections of the 1999 constitution touch on the audit of public accounts,[23] these are of a general nature and application. The lack of an updated audit act prevents the proper functioning of the Auditor-General.

The de facto process

What is described above is the formal process, as established by the constitution and other legal frameworks, which allows for checks and balances and the efficient use of resources. The de facto process, however, is very different. Until the institution of the current democratic dispensation in 1999, no seriousness was attached to pursuing due process in budget formulation and implemen-

---

[19] Constitution of the Federal Republic of Nigeria 1999 (note 3), Section 88.

[20] National Planning Commission Decree, Decree no. 71 of 1993, 23 Aug. 1993.

[21] National Economic Intelligence Committee (Establishment, etc.) Decree, Decree no. 17 of 1994, 15 Feb. 1994.

[22] Constitution of the Federal Republic of Nigeria 1999 (note 3), Section 85.

[23] Constitution of the Federal Republic of Nigeria 1999 (note 3), Sections 85–87.

tation. While military regimes were renowned for paying little regard to due process in state administration in Nigeria, until 1985 they acted with some sense of modesty. From 1985 until 1999 the process of budgeting seems to have been completely abandoned and funds were allocated with little regard for need.[24]

Although the new, democratic government of President Obasanjo is trying to revive due process in budget making, the rampant corruption common in the past military regimes is still evident in the budget process. In 2001, on the eve of the second anniversary of the present administration, the President asked the various ministries and extra-ministerial departments to provide a list of the projects promised since 1999 and a list of those projects that had been executed. Few had anything to show. In addition, over 70 billion naira (c. $600 million) that had been allocated to federal ministries and agencies were found to be held in bank accounts whose interest would eventually go into private pockets.[25] In order to discover this, the government had to employ the services of private audit firms, bypassing its own agencies, including the OAuGF, the OAcGF and the NPC. The implication of the approach is that the government has little faith in its own agencies and that those agencies are themselves in need of reform to perform their tasks in the budget process. Political influences also continue to impinge on the budgetary oversight functions of the National Assembly. There are allegations that parliamentary committee members demand bribes from ministries before approving budget estimates.[26]

The Obasanjo Government is demonstrably committed to restoring order in government business, including budgeting. As a first step, the Budget Office was separated from the FMF and made directly answerable to the President. In early 2000 the government established a Budget Review Committee, headed by Professor Dotun Philips, to examine among other things the budgetary processes of ministries and agencies from conceptualization and formulation to implementation, with a view to identifying bottlenecks and structures and practices that militate against transparent and realistic budgeting, especially on capital projects. As a result of the report of the committee and of a study conducted for the government by the World Bank,[27] a new procurement policy,

[24] Ukwu, I. U., 'Public expenditure and financial accountability in Nigeria: an overview', Paper presented at the Training Workshop organized by the Federal Ministry of Finance in collaboration with the World Bank, Kaduna, 24–26 Apr. 2002.

[25] 'Bogus budget figures', *The Guardian* (Lagos), 26 June 2001; and 'Report indicts ministries, agencies over budget claims', *The Guardian* (Lagos), 23 June 2001. Another investigation by the Public Accounts Committee of the House of Representatives in 2004 found the same level of corruption in the ministries. 'Ministries, parastatals stink, says Reps panel', *The Guardian* (Lagos), 22 June 2004.

[26] 'Na'abba refutes Mbang bribery charge on impeachment bid', *The Guardian* (Lagos), 2 Sep. 2002, p. 1. In Mar. 2005 the President of the Senate and some members of the National Assembly's Education Committee were accused of demanding and receiving a bribe of over $400 000 from the Minister of Education in return for favourable consideration of his ministry's budget estimates during budget defence. The Senate President was forced to resign after the allegations were announced by President Obasanjo in a special national television broadcast.

[27] Federal Government of Nigeria, 'Strengthening the federal budget system in year 2000 and beyond', Report of the Budget Review Committee, Lagos, Mar. 2000.

called the 'due process', was introduced in 2001.[28] In addition, a new Budget
Monitoring and Price Intelligence Unit was created in the Presidency to monitor
the budgetary process, especially the implementation and supervision of capital
budgets and projects. Similarly, budget control departments were re-established
in each of the ministries to monitor the budgetary process.

A major feature of the budgetary process during the military era that is being
tackled by the current government is the lack of proper coordination between
the two main government agencies in charge of the budgetary process, the Federal Ministry of Finance and the National Planning Commission. The functions
of the FMF and the NPC overlap in several ways, and until recently they issued
different Budget Call Circulars. Within the ministries, too, evidence of lack of
coordination still persists. There is no agreement on the effective date for the
commencement of the annual budgetary process. The different actors become
involved in the process at different times, and there does not seem to be any
regularity in the dates of such participation. In the Budget Office the annual
budgetary process begins in January. The BCCs are generally issued in July.[29]
In the Ministry of Defence, the staff consider August to mark the start of budget
preparation;[30] however, there is a statutory requirement that budget preparation
must start six months before the commencement of the budget, that is, in July.[31]
The ministries' responses to the BCC are expected to reach the Budget Office
three months before the budget's commencement, but rarely do. The irregular-
ity in the process is reflected in the late arrival of annual budgets. The 1999
budget was not approved and operational until August of that year. The 2002
budget was a matter of lengthy controversy between the President and the
National Assembly before it was eventually approved, months into the financial
year.

Transparency has been enhanced by the regular monthly television interviews
with the President. All ministers and their permanent secretaries conduct open
press events and phone-in television interviews. However, despite all these
efforts, it is not clear how much the government has succeeded in establishing
order in state business. While the government claims that it has made much
progress, critics insist that business is still conducted 'as usual'.[32]

Fears have been expressed about the effectiveness and sustainability of the
reforms since they are manifestly personality-driven rather than systematic or

---

[28] For background to the institution of 'due process' in the budget process see Ezekwelsili, O., Special
Assistant on Budget Matters to the President, 'Integrating the due process principle into the budget
process', Paper presented at the National Seminar on Implementing the 2002 Budget, Enugu, 3–5 Apr.
2002.

[29] The dates on the FMF's 'Discussion schedules for ministries' fall in June or July.

[30] Personnel of the Ministry of Defence, Interview with the authors, Abuja, June 2002.

[31] Galadanchi, C. B., 'Budgetary process in Nigeria', Paper presented at the Two-Day Conference on
Defence Budgeting, National War College, Abuja, Nov. 1999.

[32] See, e.g., 'Nigeria's budgets fraudulent, wasteful—lawmaker', ThisDay, 3 July 2005; and Ogbodo,
J. A., 'Obasanjo v reps: one nation, two budgets and looming threat to democracy', The Guardian (Lagos),
15 May 2005.

rules-based.[33] The stature and commitment of the President seem to be the only strengths that the reforms have. Reforms whose success depends on the personality of the President are particularly vulnerable in a complex society such as Nigeria's, all the more so since presidential powers are not overwhelming but require continuous consideration of geopolitical and ethnic considerations. This is in addition to the obvious limitations of personal control over a wide variety of budgetary factors. Nevertheless, the budgetary process in the current regime is markedly different from those of the military regimes.

IV. The military budgetary process

The formal process of budgeting for the Ministry of Defence is not very different from those of the other ministries. Like other ministries, the MOD has to respond to the BCC, and its long-term programmes must be included in the National Rolling Plan before they can appear in the annual budget. The only difference from the other ministries is in decision making on strategic procurement, which is left to the military hierarchy. The Chief of Defence Staff leads the decision-making process, which is organized in Defence Headquarters.

As a result of the long years of military rule, and the pervasive corruption that it engendered, the military budget has been of great interest to civil society, especially the media and academia. The military budget is one yardstick by which civil society and the critical citizenry measure the seriousness of the government's commitment to social and economic development; it is continually compared with the budgets of other sectors in the ongoing 'gari versus gun' debate.[34] In addition, defence contracts have been some of the most attractive for businessmen and corrupt officials alike.[35] Military governments focused on the military budget for security reasons. Indeed, the last three military heads of state held the defence portfolio personally. As a consequence of these factors, the military budgetary process has been subject to multiple sources of control: from the three services, from the MOD and from the government.

Since the end of the civil war in 1970, the MOD has consistently received one of the highest budgetary allocations. This is perhaps because the MOD is one of the few ministries to be funded solely by the federal government, whereas most other federal ministries have analogues in the states.

The formal process

Like the national process, the military budgetary process consists of four broadly defined phases: formulation, approval, implementation (including stra-

---

[33] See, e.g., Olumense, S., 'Under Obasanjo's bed', *The Guardian* (Lagos), 24 July 2005.

[34] Gari is a staple food in Nigeria. Adekson, J. B., 'On the theory of modernizing soldier: a critique', *Current Research on Peace and Violence*, vol. 8, no. 1 (1978), p. 18.

[35] Adekanye, J. 'B., *The Retired Military as Emergent Power Factor in Nigeria* (Heinemann Educational Books: Ibadan, 1999), pp. 36–38.

tegic procurement), and auditing and reporting. The process is organized by the ministry's Budget Planning and Implementation Committee. This committee is headed by the Permanent Secretary and includes the directors of the three service departments, who are usually civilians, the ministry's Director of Finance, the heads of finance of the three services and a representative of Defence Headquarters.

The formulation phase

Budgeting in the Ministry of Defence is a year-round occupation. In the absence of a government White Paper on defence,[36] each arm of the military produces its budget proposal based on perceived needs, in line with the Budget Call Circular. These are then coordinated through the office of the Chief of Defence Staff in Defence Headquarters.

Each service has a Planning Board, the membership of which includes the MOD's service director. The Planning Board aggregates submissions from the units to make the service's budgetary estimates. Since the National Planning Commission involves the services in the formulation of the National Rolling Plan, much of the military capital budget is simply extracted from the rolling plan. This covers mainly construction work and the refurbishing of equipment, not the more strategic acquisitions. At every point in the budgetary process the ceilings provided by the FMF and the government's revenue forecasts guide staff. Each unit and level in the service has to defend its budgetary proposals before the next higher level.

In addition to the three services, agencies to be budgeted for include the MOD itself and its Joint Services Department, the Command and Staff College, the National War College and its Centre for Peace Research, the National Armed Forces Rehabilitation Centre, the Directorate of Military Pensions, the Defence Intelligence Agency, defence missions and the Defence Industries Corporation of Nigeria (DICN). The proposals from the services and agencies are submitted to the Joint Services Department in the MOD for harmonization. The estimates from the services are then combined with those of civilians at the ministry and forwarded to the FMF as the military budget estimates.

At the FMF, the MOD team, usually led by the Permanent Secretary, has to defend the ministry's budget estimates, especially when the budget ceiling is exceeded, as is usually the case. After leaving the FMF, the budget passes through the Presidency and the Federal Executive Council, usually with no alteration, before it is sent to the National Assembly.

---

[36] The government is in the process of formulating policy guidelines for the armed forces. The first draft was issued in 2001 but the White Paper has not been released. Federal Government of Nigeria (note 11). In Jan. 2005 it was reported that the government had approved a new policy, based largely on the 2001 draft; this policy document was not made public as of Aug. 2005. 'Govt okays news defence policy', *The Guardian* (Lagos), 20 Jan. 2005.

The authorization phase

After the Appropriation Bill is presented to the National Assembly, it is considered in committee. For budget purposes, all committees become subcommittees of, and function according to the rules of, the Finance and Appropriation Committee of the House of Representatives or the Senate.

Since 1999 the Defence Committee of the Senate has been further divided into three subcommittees to oversee the three services of the Nigerian Armed Forces. Each of these service subcommittees discusses and approves the budgetary estimates of its service. The same process takes place in the House of Representatives. The Defence Committees' aggregated draft is then forwarded to the Senate's Finance and Appropriation Committee. In the course of examining the details of the budget, the Defence Committee can call the Minister of Defence and officials of the MOD to defend the ministry's estimates.[37]

The implementation phase

Once the budget is approved, funds are disbursed in the manner indicated in the Appropriation Act. Allocations are normally released quarterly. The FMF produces the breakdown of the budget as approved by the National Assembly for each ministry and agency. Upon receipt of the approved budget, the Funds Allocation and Budget Committee of the MOD reappraises the budget against the ministry's proposals and, where funding falls short of expectation, recommends a reordering of priorities within the budgetary limits. Similarly, the services appraise and reorder their priorities.

The implementation of the MOD's budget is as in other ministries, the only significant difference being that the MOD keeps only the capital budget (including funds for the procurement of strategic military weapons), passing the recurrent budget to the services. However, in practice, the ministry merely controls the money while the services execute the capital projects themselves. This practice has been common for several years with a concerted effort to change the situation and for the ministry to assert itself in the process only being made since 2003.

The Accountant-General sends internal auditors to the MOD whose task is to ensure that financial regulations are followed in the disbursement of funds and that proper records are kept.

Strategic procurement

The Services Chiefs Committee, consisting of the Chief of Defence Staff and the three service chiefs, is responsible for joint strategic and logistic planning and makes the major decisions involving strategic acquisitions. The strategic procurement process begins within the services when they define their respective equipment requirements. Generally, the need for equipment can be said to

---

[37] Constitution of the Federal Republic of Nigeria 1999 (note 3), Section 67(2).

result from 'technical advances, Combat Development concepts, enemy capabilities, obsolescence of an existing equipment, experience gained during operation or training and information from friendly user countries'.[38]

Once equipment requirements have been identified, the Equipment Committee is requested to undertake a preliminary study of how the need can be satisfied in terms of technical possibilities and cost. If this study is favourable, the next stage in the process involves requesting the relevant service's Department of Staff Duties to prepare in conjunction with the potential user what is called the General Staff Target (GST). The GST usually reflects the end users' requirements for the equipment to be purchased. The GST is passed on to the service chief for examination and approval. If approved, it is then passed on to the Equipment Committee for a feasibility study based on the GST and on a comparative analysis of the available technologies, cost and time, problem areas and production cost estimates.

The Equipment Committee decides whether to proceed with the equipment purchase or not. If the decision is to proceed, user requirements are prepared with details of the expected characteristics and performances, which also serve to justify the need for and choice of equipment. Estimated cost, technical details and other factors are included in the user requirements. Once the choice of equipment is approved, a trial is carried out in the presence of the MOD representative in charge of projects for the service, since the ministry will finance the project. The final decision lies with the Procurement Committee of the MOD, which includes representatives of the services, relevant parastatals and the National Assembly. Once a weapon system has been decided upon and approved, its cost is included in the MOD budget estimates.

The auditing and reporting phase

Spending in the military sector is monitored in various ways. Internal auditing in undertaken by the Audit, Monitoring and Evaluation units of the Ministry of Defence, which monitor the finances and projects of the armed forces. The Auditor-General conducts an annual general audit.

The National Assembly also has a role in supervising military spending. This involves regular debates as well as visits to and monitoring of defence projects by the Defence Committees of the two houses.

A major feature of the audit process in Nigeria is delay. Before the audit process began again in 1999, the last audit of the accounts of the federal government was in 1991.[39] The MOD, which has been one of the biggest spending ministries, has one of the highest numbers of abandoned projects. Most of the infrastructure of the armed forces is in a deplorable condition. In addition, a 2001 report showed that the armed forces owe over 1.7 billion naira (*c.* $12 mil-

---

[38] Innih, G. A., 'The procurement process', ed. Imobighe (note 8), p. 46.

[39] Ajiboye, J. O., acting Auditor-General for the Federation, 'Auditing and financial monitoring', Paper presented at the National Seminar on Implementing the 2002 Budget, Enugu, 3–5 Apr. 2002.

lion) in utility bills accumulated over the years.[40] It is clear that, despite annual budgetary provisions and fund releases, responsibilities such as these have not been fulfilled. Corruption is rampant and there are few processes to ensure accountability. The many years of military rule have led to impatience with due process and the tendency is to bypass or ignore vital institutional arrangements in order to achieve usually selfish ends.

The formal system described above is based on legal and procedural regulations that apply internally and at all levels. Apart from the many articles of the constitution that regulate national planning and budgeting, other regulations include the FMF's Guide to Budget Procedures and the National Assembly's parliamentary procedures and practices. It is clear that since the return to democratic rule the process is at least nominally followed. However, there are obvious bureaucratic and political influences that impinge on the budgetary process.

V. The major weaknesses of the military budgetary process

The process of budgeting for the military sector in Nigeria is bedevilled by problems, although there have been marked overall improvements since 1999. The main weaknesses in the process are: (*a*) the lack of a defence policy; (*b*) weak control by the MOD; (*c*) inefficient disbursement of funds; (*d*) the lack of transparency; (*e*) weak parliamentary control; (*f*) extra-budgetary revenue and expenditure; and (*g*) the limited involvement of civil society. Individual corruption remains an all-pervading problem.

The lack of a defence policy

A significant absence from the military budgetary process in Nigeria is that of a defence policy and, by implication, of a coherent strategy to guide the process.[41] The ideal starting point for military budgeting is policy development or review. This should begin with a broad assessment of the country's security environment and threats, followed by choices of the methods to be employed to address each major threat and its causes. The methods should include, but not be limited to, the deployment of armed forces. From this process flows the defence policy, which should be reviewed annually based on the results of the previous year.

Although military authorities in Nigeria claim that there has always been a defence policy, none has ever been published, let alone reviewed.[42] Similarly,

---

[40] Ministry of Defence, In-house investigation into abandonded projects, Abuja, 2001.

[41] See, e.g., Imobighe, T. A., 'The defence budget: analysis of content and process', ed. Imobighe (note 8); Aderinto, A. A., 'Defence budgeting and management', eds Ekoko and Vogt (note 5); and Vogt (note 5).

[42] The 2001 draft defence policy makes a veiled reference to this unpublished policy but also admits that 'Nigeria has never had a crystallised national security strategy that forms the basis for the development of other policies. However, there exists in the country's constitution and certain statutes, principles and doctrines, which constitute the nation's articulated goals and aspirations and the means to achieve them.' Federal Government of Nigeria (note 11), vol. 2, chapter 1, p. 3.

Box 8.1. Extracts from Nigeria's draft National Defence Policy, 2001

National defence objectives

• Protect Nigeria against external threat and aggression
• Provide defence as well as strategic advice and information to the government
• Promote security consciousness among Nigerians
• Respond to requests to aid civil authorities
• Participate in disaster management and humanitarian relief operations at home and abroad
• Assist other government agencies and levels of government in achieving national goals
• Protect Nigerians wherever they may reside
• Evacuate non-combatant Nigerians from crisis-hit countries in collaboration with the Ministry of Foreign Affairs
• Ensure stability in the West African sub-region, which constitutes Nigeria's primary zone of strategic interest
• Participate in bilateral and multilateral operations
• Contribute to international peace and security

Specific tasks for the armed forces within the national defence objectives

• Provide advice and information to government on developments in defence worldwide
• Protect the sovereignty of Nigeria through surveillance and control of Nigeria's territory, airspace and maritime areas of jurisdiction
• Protect Nigeria's onshore and offshore strategic assets
• Provide a national search-and-rescue programme
• Provide military aid to civil authorities in conjunction with the National Emergency Management Authority
• Evacuate non-combatant Nigerians from crisis-hit countries in collaboration with the Ministry of Foreign Affairs
• Initiate bilateral and multilateral contacts and exchanges with select countries
• Initiate multinational operations to stabilize any state or group of states in the West African sub-region
• Participating in peace-support missions sponsored by the African Union and the United Nations
• Attain the capabilities to carry out other functions as may be prescribed by an act of the National Assembly

To achieve the above objectives, the military will be guided by selected strategies, which include 'prevention, protection, deterrence, rapid mobilization, force projection and cooperation with allies'. To achieve these objectives through the strategies proposed and given the neglect the military has suffered over the years, it is proposed that 'Nigeria's defence budget shall not be less than 2.5% of GDP for the next 10 years'.

Source: Federal Government of Nigeria, 'National Defence Policy' (draft), vol. 2, Lagos, 2001.

---

there is no evidence of there ever having been a coordinated policy to guide strategic acquisitions. The MOD has never produced a White Paper that explains the government's programme for defence. It has been argued that, 'while periodic reviews of Nigeria's foreign policy were undertaken and results implemented by government, one can confidently assert that officially and for several years Nigeria operated without an obvious defence policy'.[43] This lack of policy has affected strategic planning and the programming that should turn policy and doctrine into operational capability. In the absence of a policy each service of the armed forces has made its own interpretation of the country's foreign policy and core values and on that basis proceeded to make acquisitions to satisfy its needs. In the 1980s, for instance, the Nigerian Navy had an intense equipping programme: it acquired several modern warships that were inappropriate for Nigeria's immediate needs. This sent the wrong signals to the country's immediate neighbours, especially the francophone countries, which consequently formed a security organization outside the framework of the Economic Community of West African States (ECOWAS).[44] This was at a time when Nigeria was campaigning intensely for closer sub-regional unity and integration.[45]

The lack of policy coordination between the three services is echoed in the lack of coordination in operations. Each arm of the military plans separately and independently, with little consultation or harmonization of needs. Inter-service rivalry further aggravates this problem. While the problem of coordination was meant to be solved through the creation of the post of Chief of Defence Staff and the Services Chiefs Committee, there is little evidence to suggest that the intended result has been achieved.

Budgeting for defence has until recently been conducted in a policy vacuum with little or no strategic vision. The 2001 draft National Defence Policy was circulated among defence experts for comments at the time with a view to publishing a government White Paper on defence for the first time (extracts from the draft policy are given in box 8.1).

Weak control by the Ministry of Defence

One consequence of the lack of a defence policy is the inability of the MOD to perform the functions assigned to it. While there appears to be significant civilian input into the formal budgetary process, and civilians theoretically control the ministry, including the funds allocated to it, the reality is quite different. The service commanders control the recurrent expenditure of their respective services, leaving the ministry in control of the allocation for capital projects and the recurrent expenditure for other units of the MOD. Any impression that the ministry is in charge of this most critical part of military expenditure is false: in reality, the services control all the funds but leave them in the hands of the ministry simply for safe keeping. There are two reasons for this: long years of

---

[43] Vogt (note 5).

[44] The Accord de Non-agression et d'Assistance en matière de Défense (ANAD, Agreement on non-aggression and on assistance in defence matters) was signed on 7 June 1977 by Burkina Faso, Côte d'Ivoire, Mali, Mauritania, Niger, Senegal and Togo, with Benin and Guinea as observers and supported by France.

[45] Vogt (note 5), p. 102.

Table 8.2. A comparison of the Nigerian Ministry of Defence's proposed budget, government-announced estimates and actual releases from the government, 1999–2002

Figures are in million naira and current prices.

Year	Proposal by the MOD	Approved estimate	Actual release to the MOD
1999	95 094	45 400	30 662
2000	71 202	37 490	43 687
2001	86 617	63 472	75 910
2002	117 848	64 908	38 807

MOD = Ministry of Defence

Sources: **Proposals and actual releases**: Nigerian Ministry of Defence, Budget Office, personal communication, May 2003; **Approved estimates 1999, 2000 and 2001**: Central Bank of Nigeria, *Annual Report and Statement of Accounts* (Central Bank of Nigeria: Abuja, 2001 and 2002); and supplementary allocations for 1999 as reported in the media; **Approved estimates 2002**: Nigerian Senate, Appropriation Act 2002, National Assembly, Abuja, Mar. 2002.

military rule and the lack of expertise on defence matters among the senior civilian members of the MOD.

Military rule ensured that for several years Defence Headquarters, rather than the MOD, was the real centre of decision making. Decisions were made by the commander-in-chief and the service chiefs, and instructions were merely passed on to the MOD for implementation. This tradition took root over the years as military rule became almost entrenched in Nigeria. As the ministry has taken proper control of the decision-making process since 1999 the practice has changed, but it is difficult to assess the extent to which the change has been institutionalized. Between 1999 and 2003 the Minister of Defence was a former military officer and an influential member of the ruling party who had access to the President. The minister and the President were largely responsible for negotiating most of the country's external military aid, leaving the service chiefs feeling marginalized given the considerable influence that they had wielded in the past.[46]

The lack of expertise on defence matters among top-level civilians at the MOD has, over the years, ensured that the military can dismiss as uninformed any input from the ministry on strategic matters. These two problems eroded whatever control the law envisaged for the MOD, especially on policy and the control of funds.

---

[46] For details of how, in order to maintain the independence of their services, the service chiefs prevented certain proposed constitutional changes that would have affected the running of the armed forces see Imobighe, T. A., 'The organizational structure of Nigeria's defence establishment', ed. Imobighe (note 8), pp. 4–9.

Inefficient disbursement of funds

The manner in which funds are disbursed after spending has been authorized is another weakness. The three Service Headquarters that control funds for recurrent expenditure often hold on to funds for too long, thereby affecting the proper functioning of the units under them.[47] Similarly, the capital funds controlled by the MOD are not released by the ministry when they are due to be released. Instead, the funds are held until the last quarter of the financial year; all funds are then disbursed so that unspent monies are not returned to the Treasury but are shared by influential members of the ministry.[48]

Lack of a proper system of evaluation, auditing and monitoring has allowed these bad practices to continue. This breeds corruption and does not allow for the proper execution of projects. However, since 2000, rather than money being held up at the ministry, the FMF has been withholding the capital funds of the MOD (and other ministries) and merely releasing small portions of it, all in the name of controlling graft. In 2001 and 2002 only about 20 per cent of the appropriated capital vote was released to the MOD.[49]

The reconciliation of accounts is also a problem, caused by the separation of the control of funds between the services and the MOD.

The effect of all this is the existence of different versions of the 'official' military expenditure of Nigeria.[50] There are great discrepancies between the approved budget (in the annual Appropriation Act), the funds disbursed by the FMF and the actual expenditure of the MOD. This problem has become acute since 2001 (see table 8.2).

The lack of transparency

The lack of meaningful disaggregation of the Nigerian military budget means that there is only a limited degree of transparency in the funding of the armed forces. The budget is divided into two major parts: recurrent and capital expenditure. Recurrent expenditure, which includes personnel costs (including pensions) and overhead costs (mainly travel, office maintenance and training), has taken an average of 82 per cent of the entire defence allocation in the past seven years (see table 8.3). This has been a source of concern for successive governments since accurately calculating the number of military and allied personnel and pensioners has proved a major challenge to the Ministry of Defence. The most time-consuming function of the MOD's Personnel Department is the seemingly endless review and updating of the Nominal Roll and the calculation of personnel emolument. The ministry has often had to use personnel audits and staff pay-appearances to check for 'ghost' workers. The Nigerian

[47] Aderinto (note 41).

[48] Aderinto (note 41).

[49] Ministry of Defence, Budget Office, Personal communication with the authors, Abuja, June 2003.

[50] For a detailed discussion of the problems associated with military expenditure data in Nigeria see Omitoogun (note 9), in particular chapter 7 on Nigeria.

Table 8.3. The composition of Nigeria's military expenditure, 1999–2005

Figures are approved budgets, in million naira and current prices.

Year	Recurrent expenditure	Capital expenditure	Total expenditure	Recurrent expenditure as a proportion of total expenditure (%)
1999	28 091	4 856	32 947	85
2000	33 119	6 955	40 074	83
2001	47 072	16 400	63 472	74
2002	86 054	22 094	108 148	80
2003	51 044	8 573	59 617	86
2004	65 400	10 657	76 057	86
2005	90 334	21 535	111 869	81

Sources: **Years 1999–2003**: Central Bank of Nigeria, 'Public finance statistics 2003', *Statistical Bulletin*, vol. 14, part B (31 Dec. 2003), URL <http://www.cenbank.org/documents/data.asp>, tables B.1.5 and B.1.6; **Years 2004–2005**: Appropriation Act 2004 and 2005, Budget Office, Lagos, 2004 and 2005, URL <http://www.budgetoffice.gov.ng/>.

Army is currently engaged in verifying the retirement claims of military pensioners (well over 70 per cent of pension applications were found to be unverifiable), although an accurate census of serving officers and men has not been undertaken. The armed forces are estimated to number about 80 000 men.[51] The documentation system in the military reflects the poor state of record keeping in the nation as a whole.

The components of the MOD's capital budget include *inter alia* building and renovation work on barracks, hospitals and training institutions; furniture and equipment for laboratories, libraries, and so on; computerization and information technology; purchase of vehicles; refurbishment and modernization of existing strategic systems; procurement of spares for military equipment; the re-kitting of personnel; and the construction of ammunition dumps.

There is a lack of long-term planning for military acquisitions, primarily because of the lack of a defence policy. Moreover, very little detail is provided on even the minimal programme that exists. The lack of information on the way in which many well-known military activities are funded is a major source of concern to those who deal with the military, not least the National Assembly and civil society. The National Assembly's major criticism of the budget is the absence of the kind of detail that would facilitate the process of authorization and monitoring.[52]

---

[51] This estmiate was given by Gen. Theophilous Danjuma, former Chief of Army Staff (1976–79) and Minister of Defence (1999–2003). See Onuorah, M., 'Na'abba backs downsizing of military', *The Guardian* (Lagos), 16 May 2000; and Oloja, M., Eluemnour, T. and Onuroah, M., 'Govts drop plan to trim military', *The Guardian* (Lagos), 24 Dec. 2000.

[52] Members of the National Assembly have complained that they could not obtain copies of the breakdown of the 2005 budget several weeks after the President presented the bill to a joint session of the assembly. Ogbodo (note 32).

Weak parliamentary control

Despite the powers granted to the parliament on budgetary matters and spending, the National Assembly has not been able to perform its oversight functions properly since 1999 (the same weakness was evident during the period of democratic rule in 1979–83).[53] This is a result of both the general lack of experience of the members of the National Assembly[54] and their specific lack of understanding of basic defence issues. The lack of stability in the committee system in both houses of the National Assembly is also a major weakness. It is generally thought that a seat on a Defence Committee is one of the most sought-after positions in the National Assembly since there are few public hearings and because of the perceived benefits of membership. During the first term of the new National Assembly, 1999–2003, the membership of the Defence Committees changed almost completely three times. This has not permitted capacity building through learning from experience.

As a result of the apparent dearth of expertise among the legislators on military budgetary matters the Defence Committees depend largely on the expertise of the retired military personnel among their members. However, they rarely work against the interest of the military. It is instructive that the National Assembly only rarely reduces the military budget estimates presented to it, while it has approved funds for personnel costs without knowing the real strength of the armed forces.[55]

It is also significant that the National Assembly has not discussed defence matters as openly as the democratic dispensation demands. Sessions of the Defence Committees are not public. In both 2000 and 2001 the budgets announced to the public did not contain appropriations for the military. In both of these years supplementary allocations were made for the MOD. In acting in this way, the National Assembly colludes with the executive to hide information on the defence sector from the general public. This adds to the need for a value-for-money audit as well as a 'value expenditure' tracking system.

Respondents in the National Assembly have complained that the parliament is not well equipped to deal effectively with military budgetary matters. Since the library of the National Assembly is poorly stocked, its research capacity is as limited as the public knowledge on defence matters. The National Assembly has also failed to maintain useful linkages with non-governmental organizations.

In addition to these shortcomings, the National Assembly has been the subject of public concern because of its performance and actions. Much infighting among parliamentarians, allegations of corruption and huge emoluments earned

[53] Aderinto (note 41); and Imobighe (note 41).

[54] Senator Tokunbo Afikuyomi made this point in a recent article. Afikuyomi, T., 'Legislative issues: a critique', *The Guardian* (Lagos), 16 May 2005.

[55] This point was made by Dr Haruna Yerima, a member of the House of Representatives and of the Defence Committee, at a seminar on Security Sector Governance, Abuja, 19–20 Apr. 2004.

by senators and members of the House of Representative have demeaned the institution in the public eye.

Extra-budgetary spending and revenues

The weak parliamentary control and the lack of transparency have allowed the large extra-budgetary spending and revenue that are a common feature of the Nigerian budgetary process. This abuse includes use of funds from federal government extra-budgetary accounts on military activities, income from MOD agencies, and revenue from peacekeeping and foreign aid.

The government has several accounts that are outside the purview of the law, which it uses to augment its spending. These include the Petroleum Savings Trust Fund (PTF, now defunct), the Nigeria Trust Fund, the Stabilization Account, dedicated accounts, the Oil Windfall and Special Debt Accounts, and External Loan Savings. Of these, only the first three were established by law or decree; the rest were created for administrative convenience by successive regimes with no clear rules for deposits and withdrawals. Auditing of these off-budget accounts is outside the constitutionally assigned role of the OAuGF. In 1988–94 these accounts were believed to contain up to $12.4 billion.[56] Most of the government's extra-budgetary activities are funded from these accounts.

In addition to the funds in the military budget, the federal government provides funds for 'policy matters'. Such military operations as Nigeria's involvement in the Liberian and Sierra Leonean crises and internal security operations are considered policy matters, and the government bears full financial responsibility for them. Policy matters are not reflected in the MOD's budget: they may be funded from any of these off-budget accounts or the national security budget. The total extent to which the funds are committed to military activity is difficult to determine, but, for example, it is believed that the activities of ECOMOG (the ECOWAS Military Observer Group) in Sierra Leone and Liberia in the 1990s were funded through these accounts.[57] Nigeria's involvement in ECOMOG is believed to have cost the country about $12 billion.[58]

Several military construction projects were funded by the PTF during its lifetime (1994–2000) but were not reflected in the military budgets. While the PTF activities in other sectors were made open to public scrutiny, those in the defence sector were not. A recent government investigation of the activities of the PTF found contract inflation to be its major problem.[59]

Similarly, while it is not clear whether military spending is hidden in the budgets of other sectors, unplanned and extra-budgetary projects of the armed forces and their involvement in non-military functions suggest that other sectors

---

[56] Apampa, S. and Oni, T., 'Nigeria', ed. A. Fölscher, *Budget Transparency and Participation: Five African Case Studies* (Idasa: Cape Town, 2002), URL <http://www.idasa.org.za/>, p. 193.

[57] Apampa and Oni (note 56).

[58] Dawkins, W. and Holman, M., 'Obasanjo, leader on a mission for a nation in debt', *Financial Times*, 15 Sep. 2000, p. 6.

[59] 'How Buhari managed PTF', *The Guardian* (Lagos), 3 Nov. 2002.

may bear some of the costs of military activities. It is not known if the Nigerian Police pays for the involvement of the armed forces in anti-robbery operations or if the Presidency pays for major internal operations such as those in the town of Odi in 1999 and Benue State in 2001.[60] However, the government has proposed a special budgetary allocation specifically for military operations. Each budget contains a number of contingency votes, security votes, 'service-wide' votes and margins for variation for which spending breakdowns are not provided and under which unbudgeted military projects can be financed. It is clear, therefore, that funding for internal defence operations, national intelligence and the presidential guards is provided directly by the federal government, just as the hit squads of the military era were funded by the Office of the Head of State.

The lack of detail in the budgets presented to the National Assembly means that there is no proper scrutiny of allocations to the various ministries and government departments. This allows the executive much room for manoeuvring once the money is appropriated.

Extra-budgetary revenue

Since military personnel do not pay taxes, the most important source of government income from the defence establishment is interest on loans. The Nigerian MOD and the armed forces also obtain independent income in the form of rent on service infrastructure, interest on cash deposits, proceeds from in-service businesses, such as the officers' messes, and proceeds from the sale of scrap. Such earnings are supposed to be remitted to the federal Treasury. During the era of military rule, ministries and agencies failed to remit such earnings. It is not known how large the income from these sources is today, as it is not reported.

Following the insistence since 1999 on 'due process', the Budget Call Circular asks that information on income be provided by the ministries and agencies. Given the government's focus on revenue generation, officials are expected to justify their performance through reports of their earnings and so the BCC requests that any failures to meet revenue targets be explained. Respondents from the FMF believe that since 1999 there has been an improvement in the returns from ministries and agencies, although they remain meagre.[61] Nonetheless, owing to its new policy of holding people directly responsible for specific tasks, the government is reaping some return from its agencies.

---

[60] 'Nigeria inquiry into Odi deaths', BBC News Online, 31 Dec. 1999, URL <http://news.bbc.co.uk/2/581730.stm>; and 'Army clampdown after Nigeria killings', BBC News Online, 26 Oct. 2001, URL <http://news.bbc.co.uk/2/1621651.stm>

[61] Personnel of the Federal Ministry of Finance, Interviews with the authors, Abuja, June 2002.

Income from Ministry of Defence agencies

Of the many government agencies under the Ministry of Defence, two are supposed to be profit yielding: the Defence Industries Corporation of Nigeria,
based in Kaduna; and the Naval Dockyard, in Lagos. Neither makes a profit;
instead, the MOD continues to budget for them.

The DICN is supposed to manufacture and sell light military hardware, but it
has never been successful in doing so. The MOD still budgets for the capital
expenditure of the DICN and the Naval Dockyard, while the two agencies are
expected to provide for recurrent expenditure. It is clear, however, that they
both still depend on the MOD.

Revenue from foreign aid

The federal government conducts all negotiations with foreign states and itself
receives any aid. The foreign assistance is then normally channelled to the
particular projects for which the funding is provided. The Ministry of Defence
makes provisions for any required counterpart funding.

The Nigerian Government provides military assistance to a number of African states in the form of training at the Nigerian Defence Academy and other
military training institutions and supplies used military hardware. However, this
is regarded as a policy matter and is not factored into the MOD's budget.

The limited involvement of civil society

Prior to the restoration of democracy in 1999, civil society involvement in the
budgetary process generally and the military budgetary process in particular
was very limited. However, a small but vocal segment of acdemia and the
media engaged the military hierarchy in an open debate on the level of military
expenditure in the early to mid-1980s. The debate was healthy but it did not
result in any change in the level of military spending. Nevertheless, it showed
the willingness of the military to engage in an open debate on important issues.
That culture did not grow as subsequent military regimes stifled debate.

Since 1999 there appears to have been a renewed interest in the military
budget by civil society. The lack of a properly articulated defence policy document that could serve as a basis for engaging the military, however, is limiting
the extent of civil society participation in the military budgetary process.

VI. Conclusions and recommendations

The problems in the process of budgeting for the military in Nigeria include the
absence of a clear and concise policy, articulating military requirements and
projects, to guide the budgetary process. This absence hinders any long-term
commitment to apply due process in military budgeting. The existence of extra-
budgetary funds, which are accessible to many sectors, including the military,

also limits the degree of adherence to due process and obstructs proper planning. In addition, participation in the budgetary process is restricted both within and outside government. Many crucial actors, including members of civil society, are excluded. The limited participation underscores the public perception of the actors as grossly corrupt. Regular reports seem to confirm this.

What links these problems is clearly the nature of Nigerian politics. The legacy of the many years of military rule, and the consequent social and political evolution, has produced a political system defined as much by its uncertainties as by its rules. There is an apparent lack of political consensus about the form of the Nigerian state and, concomitantly, on whether and why there should be a due process. This is especially symbolized by the failure of the National Assembly to provide the stringent oversight that is required before any change in the military budgetary process can take place, leaving it much as it was under military rule. This failure is compounded by the National Assembly's lack of capacity and expertise in military matters.

The solutions are obvious: it is necessary to continue with reform of the defence sector until a culture of adherence to due process is embedded. It is hoped that, as democracy continues, governance will cease to be as improvized as it has been and there will greater trust in the long-term survival of the system. The following specific recommendations for an improved system flow from the observed weaknesses in the system.

1. A new defence policy should take into account both the national economic policy framework and the security environment.

2. The Ministry of Defence should be further strengthened in order to be able to perform its role as the centre of policy direction for the armed forces

3. Clear rules and procedures should be established for the deposit, release and use of funds in the extra-budgetary accounts. All the accounts should be subject to audit by the Auditor-General.

4. The rules and procedures guiding the military budgetary process should be adhered to.

5. Conscious effort should be made to broaden the defence policy debate and the military budgetary process in order to allow contributions from members of civil society, many of whom have knowledge of the defence sector.

6. The capacity of members of the National Assembly and its Defence Committees should be improved. The leadership of the assembly should ensure continuity in the membership of the committees to allow for the members to learn through experience.

7. There should be more transparency in the actions of the executive, including the timely provision of information and improvement in the quality of information provided.

8. The Office of the Auditor-General for the Federation should be strengthened by reducing the authority of the executive to appoint and dismiss the Auditor-General.

9. Sierra Leone

Osman Gbla

I. Introduction and background

Sierra Leone offers an interesting case study for critical reflections on the military budgetary processes in Africa. The country was for a long time subject to single-party and military regimes that were noted for sidestepping budgetary rules and regulations. The reintroduction of multiparty democracy in 1996 changed the situation for the better, particularly after the adoption in 2001 of the Medium-Term Expenditure Framework (MTEF) for budget formulation.

As a country in transition from war to peace, Sierra Leone is also confronted with the arduous task of ensuring a transparent and accountable military budgetary process, which this chapter examines. This section continues with background information on the history, politics and economy of the country. Section II describes the country's security forces. Section III outlines the national budgetary framework in general while section IV discusses the military budgetary process in particular. Section V assesses the extent of adherence to formal rules in military budgeting in Sierra Leone, and section VI gives conclusions and recommendations.

History, politics and economy

Sierra Leone is a West African country, bordered by Guinea and Liberia. Its capital, Freetown, was founded in 1787 as a haven for freed slaves. The United Kingdom claimed the coastal region as a colony in 1808 and the hinterland as a protectorate in 1896. Sierra Leone gained independence on 27 April 1961, and become a republic in April 1971.

After periods of democratic, military and one-party rule, a further military coup in January 1996 paved the way for elections in February and March of that year. However, the new, democratic government of President Ahmed Tejan Kabbah was deposed in May 1997 by junior military officers led by Major Johnny Paul Koroma. The Revolutionary United Front (RUF), led by Foday Sankoh, which had started a civil war in 1991 during the period of one-party rule, was invited by Koroma to join his government.

The democratically elected government was restored in March 1998 following a Nigerian-led intervention by the Economic Community of West African States (ECOWAS), but the RUF continued to fight. In Lomé in July 1999 the government of President Kabbah and the RUF reached an agreement to end the conflict,[1] with the peace to be monitored by the United Nations Observer Mission in Sierra Leone (UNOMSIL), later replaced by the United Nations Mission in Sierra Leone (UNAMSIL).[2] In early 2000, however, civil war erupted again. After the capture of Sankoh in May 2000 and the reinforcement of UNAMSIL by British forces,[3] the RUF formally recognized the democratic government in July 2001 and agreed to the implementation of the Lomé Agreement. In January 2002 President Kabbah declared the civil war to be finally over. The Special Court for Sierra Leone, established jointly by the UN and the Sierra Leone Government, is responsible for the trial of those accused of breaching international humanitarian law and Sierra Leonean law since 30 November 1996.[4]

The government of President Kabbah is now in its second term, having been re-elected in May 2002. The restored 1991 constitution provides for a unicameral Parliament of 124 members—112 directly elected and 12 paramount chiefs—and an executive consisting of the directly elected President and the Cabinet.[5]

The country's economy is dominated by subsistence agriculture, which accounts for over half of Sierra Leone's gross domestic product and about two-thirds of employment.[6] Sierra Leone is also endowed with rich mineral resources: diamonds, gold, rutile, iron ore and bauxite. Thus, mining is the second most important economic activity with (registered) diamond exports accounting for 85 per cent of all exports in 2002.[7] The country is highly dependent on external assistance and, since the end of the civil war in 2002, international donors have become principal actors in the country's budgetary processes.

II. The security sector

The key security actors in the country are: the Republic of Sierra Leone Armed Forces (RSLAF), the Sierra Leone Police, the Prisons Department, the National Fire Authority, the Immigration Department, the Central Security Unit, the National Security Coordinating Group and the National Security Council.

---

[1] Peace Agreement between the Government of Sierra Leone and the Revolutionary United Front of Sierra Leone, Lomé, 7 July 1999, URL <http://www.sierra-leone.org/lomeaccord.html>.

[2] UN Security Council Resolution 1181, 13 July 1998; and UN Security Council Resolution 1270, 22 Oct. 1999, URL <http://www.un.org/Docs/sc/>.

[3] UN Security Council Resolution 1289, 7 Feb. 2000.

[4] Agreement between the United Nations and the Government of Sierra Leone on the Establishment of the Special Court for Sierra Leone, Freetown, 16 Jan. 2002, URL <http://www.sc-sl.org/scsl-agreement. html>; and Wiharta, S., 'Post-conflict justice: developments in international courts', *SIPRI Yearbook 2004: Armaments, Disarmament and International Security* (Oxford University Press: Oxford, 2004), pp. 191–206.

[5] The Constitution of Sierra Leone (Act no. 6 of 1991), *Sierra Leone Gazette* (Supplement), vol. 122, no. 59 (25 Sep. 1991), URL <http://www.statehouse-sl.org/constitution/>, Chapters 5–7.

[6] World Bank, 'Sierra Leone at a glance', 15 Sep. 2004, URL <http://www.worldbank.org/data/country data/aag/sle_aag.pdf>.

[7] World Bank, 'Sierra Leone: country brief', Sep. 2004, URL <http://www.worldbank.org/sl/>.

The military was established in 1829 as the Sierra Leone Police Corps; following reorganization as part of the 1999 Lomé Agreement, it is now known as the RSLAF. The force, which includes ex-combatants of the former Sierra Leone army, the RUF and the 'civil defence forces',[8] has a strength of 12 000–13 000, including approximately 200 navy personnel.[9] Over a 10-year period the strength is planned to be reduced to around 10 000. The RSLAF's principal function, as stated in the 1991 constitution, is to 'preserve the safety and territorial integrity of the State, to participate in its development, to safeguard the people's achievements and to protect [the] constitution'.[10]

A police force was first established in 1808 under the colonial system. The 1998 Sierra Leone Policing Charter defines the role of the police in relation to the needs of the people, emphasizing professionalism, equal opportunity and local-needs policing.[11] There is a uniformed branch, a Criminal Investigation Department, a Special Branch and a paramilitary force, the Operational Support Division. The Operational Support Division, in conjunction with other units, is charged with maintaining law and order, preventing crime and maintaining the security of property. The police forces operate under the Ministry of Internal Affairs.

The final component of the security sector is the intelligence service. This service cuts across all security units but is coordinated by the Military Intelligence Branch and the Central Intelligence Security Unit.

The Ministry of Defence (MOD) is the major government body responsible for coordinating the activities of the country's armed forces. The ministry's mission is to formulate, implement, monitor and evaluate strategic defence policies for the RSLAF within a democratic framework.[12] The MOD is also responsible for long-term operational planning, deployment of the armed forces and the transformation of the RSLAF into an accountable and incorruptible organization.

President Kabbah holds the office of Minister of Defence. The MOD is headed by a deputy minister, assisted by a civilian Director-General and the Chief of Defence Staff (CDS). The Director-General is the ministry's principal accounting officer (accountable to the executive and Parliament) and the government's principal civilian adviser on defence and is responsible for policy formulation, finance, procurement and administration. The CDS is the professional head of the RSLAF and the principal military adviser to the Minister

---

[8] The civil defence forces were irregular forces, largely dominated by local hunting groups, that were formed in 1994 to protect local communities from the RUF, prompted by a lack of confidence in the armed forces. In the south and the east the main CDF group were known as the Kamajohs, a Mende word meaning hunter. In the north the main groups were the Kapras, a Temne word for hunter, and the Gbethis.

[9] International Institute for Strategic Studies, *The Military Balance 2004/2005* (Oxford University Press: Oxford, 2004), p. 243.

[10] The Constitution of Sierra Leone (note 5), Section 165(2).

[11] Kabbah, A. T., 'Policing charter', National broadcast, 2 Sep. 1998, text available at URL <http://www.sierra-leone.org/kabbah090298.html>.

[12] Ministry of Defence (MOD), *Defence Management Plan* (MOD: Freetown, Dec. 2001), p. 8.

of Defence and the government.[13] The functions of the posts of Director-General and CDS reflect the importance of both military and civilian advice on political, financial, administrative and operational matters.

III. The national budgetary process

Sierra Leone's national budgetary process has undergone significant trans-formations over the years. Under single-party and military rule, adherence to budgetary rules and regulations was rare. The return of multiparty democracy in 1996 introduced a sense of commitment to the application of budgetary rules, particularly after the adoption of the Medium-Term Expenditure Framework in 2001.

The budgetary process has four major stages—formulation, enactment (or approval), implementation and auditing—that require input from a wide range of individuals and institutions. The major actors involved include the Cabinet, the Ministry of Finance (MOF), in particular the MOF's Budget Bureau, the Accountant-General's Office, the Auditor-General's Office, Parliament, and various government ministries, departments and agencies.

Since the national budget is largely donor-funded, there is also involvement in the budgetary process by the International Monetary Fund, the World Bank, the UK, through its Department for International Development (DFID), and other donor countries, such as the USA. Donors participate in the determining of budget ceilings for all government ministries, departments and agencies. They also participate in Consultative Group meetings, in which the funding of various aspects of the government budget is discussed. Naturally, donors also play a role in tracking the use of funds.

The formulation stage

The final annual budget is the product of a long process supervised by the Budget Bureau of the MOF. The bureau is headed by a Director, who works under the general supervision of the Financial Secretary of the MOF and acts as the principal adviser to the Minister of Finance on all matters relating to the preparation and monitoring of the budget.[14] The budget-formulation process for a financial year (which corresponds to the calendar year) starts in the preceding July with the issuing of a Budget Circular Call (BCC) by the Budget Bureau to all vote controllers (i.e., those who control the spending in the various divisions of the budget). The BCC requires the submission to the bureau of all budget proposals, which must include estimates of revenue and expenditure, at least three months before the beginning of the financial year. The bureau also sets

---

[13] MOD (note 12), p. 3.

[14] Public Budgeting and Accounting Act (Act no. 1 of 1992), *Sierra Leone Gazette* (Supplement), vol. 123 (1992).

indicative ceilings for all ministries; these ceilings are not usually firm, as there is room for negotiation and adjustment.

Upon the Budget Bureau's receipt of budget proposals, all vote controllers and their representatives are invited to defend their estimates, and civil society groups are invited to make comments. This process is important for enhancing the participation of major stakeholders in budget formulation. Since financial year (FY) 2002 the budgetary process has become more inclusive as it now includes a series of national consultative workshops and seminars on expenditure priorities and resource allocation. These consultations include input made by various representatives of Parliament, the paramount chiefs and line ministries. Following the consultations, the Budget Bureau compiles all the estimates in a 'Bound Volume', which is sent to Parliament for approval: the 1992 Public Budgeting and Accounting Act requires the Minister of Finance to present the budget to Parliament one month before the beginning of the financial year.

A significant development in the formulation process was the adoption in 2001 of the Medium-Term Expenditure Framework. The MTEF involves the preparation of a strategic plan that defines the objectives, activities and expected outcome for each government ministry, department and agency over a three-year period.[15] The aim of the framework is not only to promote sectoral planning and an efficient system of public expenditure, but also to develop a participatory outcome-monitoring process.[16]

The enactment stage

The enactment stage involves the submission of the budget proposal by the Minister of Finance to Parliament and the subsequent debate and enactment into law. The 1991 constitution gives Parliament the authority to impose taxes, to appropriate funds for government services (i.e., approve the budget) and to authorize the withdrawal of money from the Consolidated Fund account.[17] In discharging these functions, the parliamentary Finance Committee sends out questionnaires to all vote controllers and government accounts personnel requesting information on the budget allocation for the previous year, the actual amount received, the current estimates and critical areas that would be affected by any budget cuts. Parliament usually invites the Minister of Finance, the vote controllers and the relevant accounting staff to offer explanations on unclear points or outstanding financial matters before new funds are approved.

The Bound Volume is examined by Parliament through its Finance Committee and the nine appropriations committees. These committees, established in 1996, screen the estimates of the various ministries, departments and agencies.

---

[15] Ministry of Finance (MOF), *Report of the Public Expenditure Tracking Survey (PETS), January–June 2001*, vol. 1, *Main Report* (MOF: Freetown, Nov. 2001), p. 8.

[16] Ministry of Development and Economic Planning (MODEP), 'Interim poverty reduction strategy paper for Sierra Leone (IPRSP)', Freetown, June 2001, URL <http://www.daco-sl.org/encyclopedia2004/3_strat/3_1prsp.htm>, p. 45.

[17] The Constitution of Sierra Leone (note 5), Sections 110, 111(3), 111(4) and 112.

This enables parliamentarians to develop a critical understanding of the structure of the budget before passing it into law, expedites the passage of the Appropriations Bill and, ultimately, enhances transparency in the budgetary process.

This approval process contrasts sharply with the procedure under military rule, when the budget was authorized by only the top echelons of the military hierarchy. There was no thorough scrutiny of the bill by any parliamentary committee, and the Bound Volume was approved after a simple reading on the floor of the House and a brief review by the Committee of Supply, a committee of the whole House. Following the reintroduction of democracy, the right to parliamentary scrutiny was established during the 1997 budget debate when the Minister of Finance was questioned on alleged financial impropriety at the Treasury. A full account of the monies appropriated by Parliament in the preceding year was demanded as a precondition for approving the new Bound Volume. [18]

The implementation stage

After approval of the budget by Parliament, the various ministries, departments and agencies are expected to distribute and use their funds as authorized. This stage has two parts: spending of appropriated money and monitoring by a variety of agencies to ensure that monies appropriated are used as intended.

Budget implementation starts with the Minister of Finance issuing a general warranty to the Accountant-General requesting the release of approved funds to the Treasury. The authority for expenditure communicated through the Accountant-General to the Minister of Finance gives authorization to all vote controllers to distribute and use funds as approved. However, if there is sufficient justification for claiming that an appropriated sum is insufficient or if there is a legitimate need for expenditure not covered by the budget, a supplementary estimate may be presented to Parliament for approval as a supplementary budget.[19]

Budget implementation is monitored to ascertain whether the money appropriated is spent as stipulated and to evaluate the extent to which policy goals have been met. The various ministries play a crucial role in this regard by putting in place internal mechanisms for the monitoring of budget implementation. For example, vote controllers are required to submit monthly spending reports to the Accountant-General. In addition, Parliament, the Accountant-General's Office, the Auditor-General's Office and the National Revenue Authority (established in September 2002) also exercise budget-oversight functions.

Another development with a positive impact on budget monitoring is the adoption of a participatory outcome-monitoring system, the Public Expenditure

---

[18] Parliamentary clerk, interview with the author, Sierra Leone Parliament, Freetown, 6 Sep. 2002.

[19] Public Budgeting and Accounting Act (note 14), Section 2(i).

Tracking Survey, first commissioned in August 2001.[20] The survey tracks the expenditure of the central ministries and measures improvements in the quality of services delivered by government facilities and in the community. The government has also introduced, through the MTEF, a new budget and accounting code that details the allocation of public resources by activity and by region. This facilitates the tracking of resources and matching them with activities in rural areas. The information given to civil society groups and the beneficiaries of the nation's budget by members of the MTEF Technical Committee also enhances budget monitoring. Moreover, the establishment of the National Revenue Authority complements the monitoring process by merging the functions of the income tax and customs departments with a view to enhancing coordination and efficient revenue collection.

Lastly, the government, with the support of the United Nations Development Programme, has established the Integrated Approach to Aid Coordination database to keep a comprehensive record of aid flows to Sierra Leone and track the use of donor funds.[21]

The auditing stage

The Auditor-General's Office plays a pivotal role in monitoring budget implementation by examining accounting practices in all ministries. However, there is a general lack of capacity for external auditing in Sierra Leone. Prior to 1996 there was little auditing of government accounts. Since 1996 and especially since the end of the civil war the challenge has been to train the staff of the Auditor-General's Office to become more professional and effective auditors.

The 1992 Public Budgeting and Accounting Act confers numerous powers on the Auditor-General regarding the judicious use of public funds. The act tasks the Auditor-General to ensure *inter alia*: (*a*) that accounts have been properly kept, (*b*) that all public monies have been fully accounted for and (*c*) that monies have been expended for intended purposes.[22] The Auditor-General's Office therefore has the principal responsibility for monitoring the implementation of the budget, although it shares this function with other monitoring institutions and civil society groups. The Auditor-General's report must be presented to Parliament within six months of the end of each financial year,[23] drawing attention not only to irregularities in the accounts but also to any other matter which in the auditor's opinion should be brought to Parliament's attention. Unfortunately, the Auditor-General has no power to prosecute in case of financial improprieties or the misappropriation of public funds; this is the prerogative of the Public Accounts Committee of Parliament.

[20] MOF (note 15).
[21] MODEP (note 16).
[22] Public Budgeting and Accounting Act (note 14), Section 65.
[23] This has been increased to 12 months by the Government Budgeting and Accountability Act (Act no. 3 of 2005), *Sierra Leone Gazette* (Supplement), vol. 136 (2005), Section 66.

The World Bank's Country Financial and Accountability Assessment for Sierra Leone, conducted in 2001, showed among other things that a number of the provisions of the 1992 act did not adequately reflect the important oversight roles of both Parliament and the Auditor-General's Office in the execution and monitoring of the national budget.[24] In an effort to address this anomaly, the 2005 Government Budgeting and Accountability Act was passed 'to ensure transparency, accountability and sound management of the budget, assets and liabilities of the Government of Sierra Leone'.[25]

IV. The military budgetary process

In Sierra Leone's national budgetary process, the MOD must compete with other ministries for allocations, which are, of course, contingent on the funds available to the country. However, considering the crucial role of the military in ensuring peace and stability in the country, especially in the context of the civil war and the peace-building process, the government gives high priority to the military when making budgetary allocations. For example, the budget for FY 2003 allocated 11.6 per cent of total recurrent expenditure to the security sector (including the police force).[26] Table 9.1 shows the budget allocation for the military for the three-year MTEF cycle from 2002 to 2004. Table 9.2 shows military expenditure in Sierra Leone since 1990.

In spite of the fact that defence is a major focus of the government, this does not result in unduly preferential treatment of the military sector. On the contrary, like those of all other government ministries, the MOD's budget allocations each year are far less than its original estimate. In 2002, although the security sector obtained the third largest share of the budget, after health and education, it received over 30 per cent less than the requested amount.

The MOD's current budget is composed of four items: (*a*) defence administration, for the offices of the Director-General and the Chief of Defence Staff; (*b*) the Joint Forces Command, for the land, air and maritime forces; (*c*) the Joint Support Command, for support units such as the Joint Medical Unit, the Joint Logistics Unit, the Joint Provost Unit, the Engineering Regiment, the Joint Communications Unit, the Armed Forces Training Centre and the Armed Forces Personnel Centre; and (*d*) the Territorial Defence Force, which become operational in 2005. Expenditure is divided into recurrent and capital expenditure. Recurrent expenditure covers personnel costs and consumable items that are routine in nature, such as stationery, food, fuel, ammunition and lubricants.

[24] World Bank, 'Republic of Sierra Leone Country Financial and Accountability Assessment', Washington, DC, 2001.

[25] Dauda, J. B., Minister of Finance, 'Government budget and statement of economic and financial policies for the financial year 2005', Speech delivered to the Sierra Leone Parliament, Freetown, 10 Dec. 2004.

[26] Dauda, J. B., Minister of Finance, 'Government budget and statement of economic and financial policies for the financial year, 2003', Speech delivered to the Sierra Leone Parliament, Freetown, 29 Nov. 2002, text available at URL <http://www.statehouse-sl.org/gov-budget-2003.html>.

Table 9.1. Sierra Leone military expenditure for financial years 2002–2004

Figures in US$ are in constant 2003 prices and exchange rates. Figures may not add up to totals due to the conventions of rounding.

Budget item	2002[a] m. leones	2002[a] $ m.	2003[b] m. leones	2003[b] $ m.	2004[b] m. leones	2004[b] $ m.
Personnel pay	24 271	11.1	23 000	9.8	25 762	9.6
Recurrent	31 095	14.3	38 850	16.5	42 379	15.8
Capital	2 350	1.1	250	0.1	7 507	2.8
Development	3 369	1.5	3 500	1.5	7 151	2.7
Total	**61 085**	**28.0**	**65 600**	**27.9**	**82 799**	**30.8**
Total excluding pay	**36 814**	**16.9**	**42 600**	**18.1**	**57 037**	**21.2**

[a] Figures for 2002 are actual expenditure.
[b] Figures for 2003 and 2004 are estimated expenditure.

Source: Woodman, T. G. W., 'Finance and budget', Presentation, Ministry of Defence, Freetown, 21 Oct. 2003.

Capital expenditure is for those items that provide repeated or continuous service over the long term, that tend to be more expensive and that have residual value after use. Capital expenditure can be for 'classified' or 'unclassified' items: classified items include weapons, helicopter gunships, armoured vehicles and communications equipment; unclassified items include furniture, office equipment, boots and uniforms.[27]

The process of budgeting for the military is not very different from that of any other government ministry. Like all other ministries, the MOD budget operates under the formal process of the MTEF, divided into four stages: formulation, authorization, implementation and auditing.

The formulation stage

Sierra Leone's MTEF budget-formulation process requires all government ministries, including the MOD, to prepare strategic plans that clearly define objectives, activities and performance benchmarks. These plans form the basis of the budget estimates. For the MOD, these plans must clearly spell out the military sector's mission, vision and objectives. The defence White Paper has provided reference points for drawing up strategic defence plans.[28] It describes the country's defence mission, objectives, tasks and management priorities and sets out key performance indicators against which the military sector will be judged.

---

[27] Ministry of Defence (MOD), Directorate of Defence Policy, *Defence White Paper: Informing the People* (MOD: Freetown, 2002), URL <http://www.statehouse-sl.org/policies/defence-white-paper.html>.
[28] MOD (note 27), Chapter 5.

The MOD's Office of Plans and Programmes makes extensive use of the White Paper when formulating the defence planning assumptions that are used in budget formulation. The MTEF involves the issuing of detailed defence planning assumption by the MODs to all programme managers, who in turn provide detailed plans for costing. The assumptions, plans and costing are then scrutinized to ensure that they are affordable and realistic. This is usually done in the presence of the MOF's Financial Secretary in order to ensure transparency.

The formal military budget-formulation process follows the overall national format: it starts in July of the preceding year with the receipt of the Budget Circular Call from the MOF. The BCC requires the Director-General of the MOD to submit a budget proposal, including estimates of revenue and expenditure, to the Budget Bureau three months before the beginning of the financial year. The estimates are supposed to be realistic, accurate and in accordance with guidelines, such as the indicative ceilings, issued by the Minister of Finance.[29] The Director-General sends the BCC to the MOD's Budget Office for circulation to all unit and programme managers and division heads, who are required to prepare and submit their respective estimates. Upon receipt of unit estimates, the MOD's Budget Office undertakes a centralized costing exercise with inputs from, and screening of, line managers' estimates. The budget estimates are thereafter submitted to the MOF.[30] As part of the defence of the overall budget of the MOD before the Appropriations Bill is approved, the MOD's vote controllers, other accounts personnel and, occasionally, unit managers are required to defend their individual budgets.

The authorization stage

During the authorization stage Parliament scrutinizes the recurrent and development estimates of the MOD which have been submitted to Parliament as part of the overall Bound Volume.[31] This integrated approach gives Members of Parliament time to reflect on the estimates and to raise questions during the debates leading to approval.

The crucial phase during authorization takes place in the various appropriations committees, with the Defence, Internal and Presidential Affairs Committee overseeing the defence component of the Bound Volume. The committee may send out questionnaires to the Director-General of the MOD soliciting information on any areas of the budget that raise interest, particularly concerning previous allocations.

---

[29] Financial Administration Regulations 1998, *Sierra Leone Gazette*, vol. 129, no. 70 (10 Dec. 1998).

[30] Official of the Budget Office, Interview with the author, Ministry of Defence, Freetown, 22 Aug. 2002.

[31] Public Budgeting and Accounting Act (note 14).

Table 9.2. Military expenditure of Sierra Leone, 1990–2004

Figures in US$ are in constant 2003 prices and exchange rates.

| Year | Military expenditure | | |
	$ m.	m. leones	as a % of GDP
1990	10.1	1 369	*1.4*
1991	17.5	4 792	*2.1*
1992	22.3	10 081	*3.0*
1993	23.9	13 244	*3.0*
1994	22.6	15 546	*2.9*
1995	21.8	18 898	*2.9*
1996	16.0	17 119	*2.0*
1997	7.6	9 315	*1.1*
1998	..	..	..
1999	..	..	..
2000	24.9	55 000	*4.1*
2001	16.8	37 868	*2.2*
2002	15.3	33 371	*1.5*
2003	18.1	42 600	*1.7*
2004	17.0	45 503	..

GDP = Gross domestic product.

Source: SIPRI military expenditure database.

The implementation stage

The overall responsibility for implementing the military budget is entrusted to the Director-General of the MOD acting as chief accounting officer.[32] The Director-General can then delegate implementation to programme managers and division heads. Such delegation ensures that each officer can be held personally accountable for the aspect of the budget assigned to him or her. As well as helping to end the bureaucratic preoccupation of the previous, centralist administration, it also helps managers to defend their programmes.

Various individuals and institutions monitor the spending of the military budget. The MOD's Directorate of Organization, Management and Audit is responsible for evaluating and reviewing internal audit systems. The Ministry of Finance prepares quarterly monitoring reports on all ministries, including the MOD, highlighting inadequacies and making recommendations for improvements to the process. In addition, the Accountant-General's representative in the MOD is required to discharge monitoring functions on behalf of the government and to develop an efficient accounting system. Parliament also exercises oversight functions through its authority to scrutinize and approve budget estimates. Reforms in the MOD have improved budget monitoring, as any requi-

---

[32] Financial Administration Regulations 1998 (note 29).

sition for military expenditure must be made at commander level (in the Joint Support Command). The commander prepares the requisition and sends it to the Director-General in order to ascertain whether it agrees with the expenditure guidelines of the MOD.[33]

Arms procurement

An important component of the implementation phase is procurement, including arms procurement, which is very capital intensive. Procurement procedure is outlined in the new 2004 Public Procurement Act,[34] a principal result of which was the establishment in February 2005 of the National Public Procurement Authority. The act requires that all public procurement must be subject to one of the following: (*a*) 'international competitive bidding', for goods or services worth more than 600 million leones ($255 000) and for works (e.g., construction) worth more than 900 million leones ($383 000); (*b*) 'national competitive bidding', for goods and services worth less than 600 million leones ($255 000) and for works worth less than 900 million leones ($383 000); (*c*) 'limited international bidding', for goods or works of any value, but not for services; or—the most frequently used option—(*d*) 'request for quotation shopping' for goods or services worth less than 60 million leones ($25 500) and for works worth less than 150 million leones ($63 800).

The Public Procurement Act limits its application to the military sector by permitting the Minister of Defence to classify a procurement as being related to national defence or national security and allowing the National Public Procurement Authority to modify the rules and procedures of the act for such a procurement, but this modification 'shall be governed only defence considerations'.[35] This does not extend to the procurement of such items as general stores, uniforms, stationery, office equipment and standard vehicles.

Within the MOD, procurement is dealt with by the Equipment Approvals and Procurement Committee, which is chaired by the Director-General. This committee is responsible for the overall policy and management of military acquisition. The committee is authorized to endorse all acquisitions and must scrutinize and agree to the operational requirements. It is also responsible for the approval of procurement and support strategies for individual programmes and pieces of equipment.

The auditing stage

External auditing of the MOD is done by the Auditor-General's Office under the terms of the 1992 Public Budgeting and Accounting Act. A representative of the Auditor-General in the MOD is responsible for ensuring that the ministry's accounting system meets the standards set by law.

[33] Official of the Budget Office (note 30).
[34] Public Procurement Act (Act no. 14 of 2004), *Sierra Leone Gazette* (Supplement), vol. 135 (2004).
[35] Public Procurement Act (note 34), Section 1.

There is also an Audit Directorate in the MOD, an independent body headed by a civilian which is answerable only to the Auditor-General and the Accountant-General. This directorate is tasked with: (*a*) the production of a consolidated annual audit report, (*b*) liaising with the Auditor-General's Office and (*c*) drawing up defence audit policy.[36] Some of the achievements of this directorate include the establishment—with some difficulty—of an internal control system and the introduction of on-the-spot verification of goods supplied to the MOD. It is noteworthy that constraints such as the lack of trained and qualified personnel and the late presentation of audit reports to Parliament are greatly hampering the auditing of the MOD's budget.

V. Assessment of the military budgetary process

Since the reintroduction of multiparty democratic rule in 1996, Sierra Leone has witnessed a great improvement in the budgetary process, especially following the adoption of the MTEF in 2001. The process has become more consultative, more open and, above all, more goal driven.

Under single-party and military rule, proper accounting and audit practices were sidestepped by the government, which siphoned off state resources from the military. Sierra Leone's protracted civil war, which lasted for more than a decade, meant that both the country's resources and its armed forces were mismanaged. Some of the weaknesses in the military budgetary process and recent developments are discussed below.

Past and present weaknesses

Prior to 2001 the budgetary provisions of Sierra Leone's constitution were generally ignored and the executive used the military budget as a channel for corrupt practices. Similarly, under military rule, the ruling juntas made major decisions regarding the military budget with very little involvement of the MOD: the military rulers found it easy to ignore input from civilian personnel in the MOD. Directly or indirectly, the MOD was subordinated to the military establishment in budget matters. The MOD was made up of only a few civil servants, who were divorced from the military. This resulted in the ministry being frequently bypassed by the military, who preferred to deal directly with the President. The restructuring of the MOD since 2001 has changed both its internal structure and the relationship between the civilian civil servants and military officers, who now work together in the ministry under the leadership of a civilian Director-General.

Under military rule, the executive, rather than Parliament, authorized budgets for all ministries, including the MOD. As a result, requirements such as the tabling of estimates in Parliament one month before the beginning of the finan-

---

[36] Ministry of Defence, 'Report on the activities of the MOD for the financial year 2002', Freetown, 2003, p. 23.

cial year were never followed. This sometimes led to bloated and unrealistic budget estimates, and key actors in the budgetary process had little opportunity to make input. Indeed, during the reign of Major Koroma (1997–98), the military head of state often directly instructed the Governor of the Central Bank to release funds from the Consolidated Fund without following any formal budgetary procedure. In addition, during the civil war the military sector was greatly favoured in financial allocation, as its funding was categorized as war expenditure. It is doubtful whether the money allocated actually served the stated objectives.

Off-budget income and expenditure in the military sector were also a major feature of the military budgetary process in Sierra Leone. Off-budget income included revenue from mining concessions given to senior military officers for military services rendered to other governments. The proceeds from these ventures never appeared in the budget.

The ongoing reform of the MOD and the direct involvement of external actors in the budgetary process have greatly reduced off-budget expenditure since 2001. One exception arises from the participation of the RSLAF's maritime wing in joint surveillance operations to capture poachers in the country's waters. The memorandum of understanding between the RSLAF and the Ministry of Marine Resources requires that the revenue from the operations go to the Consolidated Fund and that a certain percentage should be paid to the military. It remains unclear if the portion due to the military has ever been paid, as it does not appear in the maritime section of the military budget.

A principal weakness in the current military budgetary process is the absence of a well-articulated strategic plan for the military sector. In the absence of such a vital guiding document, it is not surprising that military budgets have sometimes been bloated and unrelated to the actual needs of the military. The MOD's recent Defence Management Plan and White Paper have been designed by the MOD to overcome this major problem.[37] It is important to highlight that the process of drafting the White Paper has led to improved inter-ministry consultation between the MOD and the ministries of Foreign Affairs and International Co-operation, Internal Affairs, and Development and Economic Planning.

The MTEF requires the Ministry of Defence and all other government ministries to prepare budgets based on guidelines set by the Ministry of Finance. These guidelines require the preparation of strategic plans that clearly define objectives, activities and expected outcomes. The military budget is now formulated and implemented with the participation of both military and civilian personnel and, together with the budgets of other ministries, is tabled before Parliament for enactment into law. However, practices pre-dating multiparty democracy continue unabated, even with the post-civil war institutional reforms.

[37] MOD (note 12); and MOD (note 27).

The most significant of these practices is the President's continued role as the Minister of Defence. Admittedly, as head of state and commander-in-chief of the armed forces, the President is chairman of the Defence Council, the highest decision-making body on defence matters. However, the constitution does not specifically make the President the Minister of Defence. The practice of merging the two posts, which originated in the 1970s when the then head of state wanted to have a direct influence on the military, shows that old habits die hard. It would benefit reform if the President were to appoint another person to be directly in charge of the defence portfolio. The Minister of Defence would still have to report to the President for major decisions, as in any other sector. This separation of presidential and ministerial functions is important in moving away from the centralist form of administration to which Sierra Leone has been accustomed.

Oversight

While Parliament is empowered to scrutinize and authorize the budget, and also to monitor its implementation, the Defence, Internal and Presidential Affairs Committee is constrained in its discharge of oversight functions by delays or the outright unavailability of necessary information on the budget and the late submission of audit reports. Parliament also faces serious institutional capacity challenges, underscored by an acute shortage of the administrative and technical staff required to support its work. There are only four parliamentary clerks attached to the 31 committees of the House, for instance.[38] In addition, parliamentarians lack the requisite expertise on defence matters generally and the military budget in particular. This limits the extent to which they can contribute to executive proposals for defence management. Furthermore, the Defence, Internal and Presidential Affairs Committee is so overburdened with other responsibilities that it has very little time for effective monitoring. In spite of these obstacles, since the introduction of the MTEF Parliament has been able to improve the overall budgetary process, including that in the military sector.

The reformed MOD's internal audit unit, the Directorate of Organization, Management and Audit, maintains effective audit procedures which hold individuals accountable for funds entrusted to them and constantly reviews and improves budget rules and procedures. However, both tasks are very difficult to perfect overnight in a country where military budgeting has long been exposed to centralist informal procedures. In addition, the Budget Bureau of the MOF monitors the implementation of the military budget through its quarterly monitoring reports. These reports are supposed to be made available to the public, but a majority of Sierra Leoneans do not have access to them owing to the cul-

---

[38] Lahai, B., 'Parliamentary oversight: the Sierra Leone experience and constraints', Paper presented at the Workshop to Strengthen Legislatures in Commonwealth West Africa, Freetown, 22–25 Feb. 2005, URL <http://www.cpahq.org/activities/RegionalandLocalSemina/WAPP/wapppresentations/>, p. 6.

ture of secrecy in military matters and in public expenditure management generally.

The country's budget still receives substantial support from the World Bank and the International Monetary Fund and from other countries, including the UK (through its DFID) and the USA. By sponsoring and participating in consultative meetings with members of the MOF and other relevant ministries on budget formulation, foreign and international institutions play a crucial role in Sierra Leone's overall budgetary process. In addition, they offer support in setting budget ceilings and in mid-term reviews. The British DFID, for example, provides advisers to the MOD, including a civilian adviser to the Director-General, a civilian adviser to the Finance Department and two military advisers in the areas of logistics and procurement, all to ensure the judicious use of donor funds.[39] While this system seems to work, the sooner Sierra Leoneans are trained to take over key functions, the better ongoing reforms will take root.

The role of civil society in monitoring the military budget is still relatively weak and underdeveloped owing to the absence of well-organized civil society groups with technical competence on military budget matters. Furthermore, the culture of secrecy in the military still minimizes open and frank debate on defence matters, including its budget.

A positive aspect is the MOD's reconstitution as both a department of state and a military headquarters. This serves to enhance civil–military dialogue and relations. For the first time in Sierra Leone the military and civilians are working together as a fully integrated team.

VI. Conclusions and recommendations

Sierra Leone's military budgetary process is not entirely different from that of other sectors. The budgetary process for the military sector continues to undergo significant transformation owing to the more open nature of the political system since 1996, as well as the effect of post-civil war reforms and reconstruction. While progress has been made in the level of parliamentary involvement and oversight, considerable effort is still required to improve the institutional capacity of Parliament and to institutionalize the audit system. Civil society groups also need to be able to increase their participation in the military budgetary process.

The following recommendations for improving Sierra Leone's military budgetary process can be made.

1. The institutional capacity of Parliament should be enhanced.

2. The Auditor-General's Office should be reformed and fully resourced by the government, with more professional staff. This would help the Auditor-

---

[39] For more on the British DFID's support for the Sierra Leone MOD see Sköns, E. *et al.*, 'Military expenditure', *SIPRI Yearbook 2005: Armaments, Disarmament and International Security* (Oxford University Press: Oxford, 2005), pp. 337–42.

General to deply staff throughout the country and facilitate the proper auditing of government accounts and the preparation of the report to Parliament.

3. The Auditor-General, in close consultation with the Public Accounts Committee of Parliament, should be mandated by law to refer financial irregularities contained in the audit report to the Anti-Corruption Commission for investigation.

4. Financial delegation should be stressed in the ongoing reform process in order to improve accountability in the military budgetary process.

5. Timely access to information should be facilitated to enable stakeholders to study that information and to make constructive input into the budgetary process

6. Training on budgetary procedures and related issues should be arranged for civil society groups to enable them to understand and to engage in the budgetary process.

10. South Africa

*Len le Roux**

I. Introduction and background

South Africa joined the community of democratic nations as recently as 1994. Since then it has undergone fundamental transformation from a closed and isolated apartheid regime to a democratic state that is playing an increasing role in international affairs. Internally, government has been transformed to ensure transparency and accountability in governance and to focus all spheres of government on service delivery.

Defence management in South Africa has also been vastly transformed. This transformation has focused on making the military sector accountable to civil authority, improving transparency in defence management, making the Department of Defence (DOD) representative of the people of South Africa, ensuring greater efficiency, and aligning the norms and standards of defence with the constitution, international law and national culture.

This chapter presents the challenges that faced the South African DOD in the early post-apartheid years and the way in which these challenges were met. It stresses the importance of placing the defence planning and budgetary process within the broader national financial process and of subjecting all departmental and sectoral budgetary processes to national legislation and control.

The chapter starts with a survey of the historical background of the political and economic development of South Africa and then, in section II, describes the structure of the DOD. Section III discusses the South African national financial, legislative and budgetary framework. Section IV examines the military planning and budgetary process, with particular attention to the details of the military budget. This is followed in section V by an assessment of the military budgetary process. Section VI provides conclusions and recommendations for improvement.

* The author wishes to acknowledge the invaluable support of the South African Department of Defence. Much of this chapter is based on information provided by Jack Gründling (Chief Financial Officer of the department), Rear Admiral Rolf Hauter (Chief Director of Strategy and Planning at South African National Defence Force Headquarters) and Nick Sendall (Chief Director of Defence Policy of the Defence Secretariat). The professional assistance given by Cor Haak (Defence Programme Officer of the National Treasury) in commenting on a draft is also acknowledged with gratitude.

History, politics and economy

After decades of ever-increasing unrest and the fully fledged armed freedom struggle of the 1970s and 1980s, in February 1990 President F. W. de Klerk lifted the ban on the liberation movements and released political prisoners, notably Nelson Mandela of the African National Congress (ANC). This was followed by a long, bumpy negotiation process to dismantle the system of apartheid. In April 1994 South Africa held its first democratic election under an interim constitution.[1]

The new ANC-led coalition government under President Mandela embarked on a programme to promote the reconstruction and development of the country and its institutions. This called for the simultaneous pursuit of democratization and socio-economic change, as well as reconciliation and consensus building founded on a commitment to improving the lives of all South Africans, in particular the poor. Converting democratic ideals into practice required a radical overhaul of the machinery of government at every level, oriented towards service delivery, openness and human rights. A significant milestone of democratization during the Mandela presidency was the delivery in 1996 of a new constitution that is regarded highly in the democratic world.[2]

South Africa entered the post-Mandela era under the presidency of Thabo Mbeki after the second democratic elections, held in June 1999. Among other aims, President Mbeki's administration is committed to the development of Africa based on democracy, good governance and a cooperative approach to resolving political and economic challenges common to African countries. This is clearly demonstrated by the leading role that South Africa has taken in the establishment and functioning of the African Union and in the New Partnership for Africa's Development (NEPAD). NEPAD forms the basis of South African foreign policy.

The 1996 constitution of South Africa entrenches the separation of powers, offers appropriate checks and balances, and includes a far-reaching bill of rights. Socio-economic rights such as housing, health care, access to food and water, social security and basic education are recognized. South Africa is a federal state, governed by a democratically elected government based on universal adult suffrage. The South African Government is composed of national, provincial and local spheres, which are distinct but interdependent and interrelated.

The Parliament of South Africa consists of the National Assembly and the National Council of Provinces. The National Assembly has 350–400 members elected through a system of proportional representation for a term of five years. The National Council of Provinces consists of 10 representatives from each of the nine provinces. The role of the council is to represent provincial interests in the national sphere of government: the members receive mandates from the provinces before making certain decisions. The council cannot, however, initi-

---

[1] Constitution of the Republic of South Africa (Act 200 of 1993), 31 Dec. 1993. Many of the acts referred to in this chapter are available at URL <http://www.info.gov.za/documents/acts/index.htm>.

[2] Constitution of the Republic of South Africa (Act 108 of 1996), 8 May 1996.

ate a bill concerning money; this is the prerogative of the Minister of Finance in the National Assembly.

South Africa has a wealth of natural resources and the largest and most advanced economy on the continent. However, like other developing economies, South Africa's economy is highly susceptible to trends in its major trading partners. Regional political instabilities sometimes negatively affect investor perceptions. South Africa has, however, been highly commended for its successful macroeconomic policies. South Africa is a leader among emerging markets worldwide and is a competitive producer of not just raw commodity exports but also value-added goods.

The challenge is to translate these positive factors into levels of investment that are high enough to promote sufficient economic growth to reduce the substantial unemployment and poverty in the country. At present there are still wide disparities of wealth, with obvious implications for broader socio-political policy directions. Given its history of inequality and its position as an African country whose fate is bound up with those of its neighbours and the continent, South Africa shares a large set of interests with the developing economies of the world.

II. The Department of Defence

The 1996 constitution provides for the establishment of a defence force and states that the 'primary object of the defence force is to defend and protect the Republic, its territorial integrity and its people in accordance with the Constitution and the principles of international law regulating the use of force'.[3] It requires that a member of Cabinet be responsible for defence and determines the rules for the deployment of the defence force. The constitution also provides for the establishment of a civilian defence secretariat.

The Minister of Defence is the political head of the Department of Defence. The minister is designated as the 'executive authority' for the military budget by the 1999 Public Finance Management Act and, as such, has the primary responsibility for political oversight of the military budget.[4] The minister is responsible for ensuring that political priorities are linked to departmental spending plans and the delivery of service and for determining departmental priorities. As the executive authority, the minister is responsible for ensuring that the department performs its statutory functions within the limits of the allocated funds.

The DOD, consisting of the Defence Secretariat and the South African National Defence Force (SANDF), came into being on 27 April 1994 with the establishment of the new, democratic South Africa. The SANDF was formed by integrating the former South African Defence Force; the defence forces of the former, nominally independent homelands of Bophuthatswana, Ciskei, Transkei

---

[3] Constitution of the Republic of South Africa (note 2), Chapter 11, Security services, Section 200(2).

[4] Public Finance Management Act (Act 1 of 1999 as amended by Act 29 of 1999), 2 Mar. 1999.

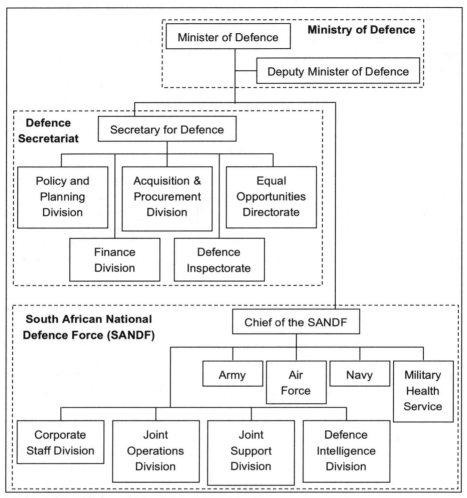

Figure 10.1. Structure of the South African Department of Defence

and Venda; the guerrilla armies of the ANC and the Pan Africanist Congress, respectively Umkonto We Sizwe and the Azanian People's Liberation Army; and the KwaZulu Self-Protection Forces of the Inkatha Freedom Party.

This integration of forces into a new defence force was preceded by negotiations for the interim constitution. The formulation of South Africa's future defence policy was a crucial issue during the transition. The 1993 interim constitution established the SANDF as the only defence force for the republic and required that it be 'a balanced, modern and technologically advanced military force'.[5] The interim constitution provided for the integration of forces into the

[5] Constitution of the Republic of South Africa (note 1), Chapter 14, Police and defence, Section 226.

Table 10.1. Military expenditure of South Africa, 1990–2004

Figures in US$ are in constant 2003 prices and exchange rates.

Year[a]	Military expenditure		
	$ m.	m. rand	as a % of GDP
1990	4 177	10 982	*3.8*
1991	3 528	10 699	*3.2*
1992	3 105	10 724	*2.9*
1993	2 827	10 713	*2.5*
1994	2 992	12 352	*2.6*
1995	2 662	11 942	*2.2*
1996	2 314	11 143	*1.8*
1997	2 128	11 131	*1.6*
1998	1 917	10 716	*1.5*
1999	1 816	10 678	*1.3*
2000	2 120	13 128	*1.5*
2001	2 371	15 516	*1.6*
2002	2 538	18 138	*1.6*
2003	2 596	19 638	*1.6*
2004	2 645	20 169	. .

GDP = Gross domestic product.

[a] Years are calendar years, not financial years.

Source: SIPRI military expenditure database.

SANDF and determined the fundamental policy framework on which further developments were to be based.

In order to enhance the professionalism of the military and allow it to focus on the core business of the provision, development and deployment of military forces, the civilian Defence Secretariat was created. A Secretary for Defence was appointed as head of the department and as the DOD's accounting officer.[6] The Secretary for Defence is the principal adviser to the Minister of Defence on defence policy.

The other component of the DOD, the SANDF, is headed by the Chief of the SANDF, who executes military policy, directs the work of Defence Head-quarters and manages the overall functioning and operations of the SANDF. The Chief of the SANDF is also the principal adviser to the Minister of Defence on military, operational and administrative matters within his or her competence.

The SANDF consists of four services—the South African Army, the South African Air Force, the South African Navy and the Military Health Service—as well as four staff divisions that report primarily to the Chief of the SANDF— the Corporate Staff Division, the Joint Operations Division, the Joint Support Division and the Defence Intelligence Division. Four divisions and one

[6] Defence Act (Act 42 of 2002), 31 Dec. 2002, Section 8(a).

directorate report primarily to the Secretary for Defence—the Policy and Planning Division, the Finance Division, the Acquisition and Procurement Division, the Defence Inspectorate and the Equal Opportunities Directorate. The structure of the DOD is illustrated in figure 10.1.

In 2004 the total personnel strength of the DOD (including all supporting services) was approximately 72 750, with an additional 60 000 in reserve. The personnel strength of the army was approximately 36 000, of the air force 9250, of the navy 4500 (plus 2000 civilians) and of the Military Health Service 6000.[7] There are no paramilitary forces in the DOD. Table 10.1 presents South African military expenditure for the period 1990–2004.

III. The national financial framework

The 1996 constitution of South Africa lays down the framework for the division of responsibilities between national, provincial and local governments. It prescribes an equitable division of revenue between the spheres of government, taking into account their respective functions. The constitution also provides for a national treasury, an independent auditor-general and an independent central bank, and it sets out the principles governing financial accountability to Parliament and the annual budgetary process. The constitution establishes the following standards.

1. 'National, provincial and municipal budgets and budgetary processes must promote transparency, accountability and the effective financial management of the economy, debt and the public sector.'

2. 'National legislation must prescribe the form of national, provincial and municipal budgets; when national and provincial budgets must be tabled; and that budgets in each sphere of government must show the sources of revenue and the way in which proposed expenditure will comply with national legislation.'

3. 'National legislation must establish a national treasury and prescribe measures to ensure both transparency and expenditure control in each sphere of government by introducing generally recognised accounting practice; uniform expenditure classifications; and uniform treasury norms and standards.'

4. 'When an organ of state in the national, provincial or local sphere of government, or any other institution identified in national legislation, contracts for goods or services, it must do so in accordance with a system which is fair, equitable, transparent, competitive and cost-effective.'[8]

With these constitutional provisions, financial management in the South African Government has been substantially transformed since 1996. The changes in

---

[7] International Institute for Strategic Studies, *The Military Balance 2004/2005* (Oxford University Press: Oxford, 2004), pp. 244–45.

[8] Constitution of the Republic of South Africa (note 2), Chapter 13, Finance, Sections 215(1), 215(2), 216(1) and 217(1), respectively.

financial management include budget management. The new approach to financial management culminated in the 1999 Public Finance Management Act and related regulations and instructions, which came into operation on 1 April 2000.

The Public Finance Management Act represents a fundamental change in the government's approach to the handling of public finances, as it moves the emphasis away from a highly centralized system of expenditure control by the National Treasury. It holds the heads of departments accountable for the use of resources to deliver services to communities. The act emphasizes: (*a*) regular financial reporting, (*b*) independent audit and supervision of internal control systems, (*c*) improved accounting standards, (*d*) greater emphasis on output and performance, and (*e*) increasing accountability at all levels.

The act represents a fundamental break with the past regime of opaqueness, hierarchical management and weak accountability. The key objectives of the act are to modernize the system of financial management, to enable public sector managers to manage but at the same time be more accountable for the services delivered to the public, to ensure the timely provision of reliable information, and to eliminate waste and corruption in the use of public assets.[9]

The act empowers the National Treasury to develop the overall macroeconomic and financial framework; coordinate financial relations and the budget preparation process with the provincial governments; manage the implementation of a budget; and promote and enforce revenue, asset and liability management. The act empowers the National Treasury to issue regulations and instructions. It also requires the appointment and specifies the composition of audit committees. It defines financial misconduct and deals with the procedure for disciplining public officials who are found guilty of such an offence, providing for criminal prosecution in extreme cases.

The Public Finance Management Act therefore empowers the National Treasury not only to implement the budget of the national government, but also to play a role in the financial oversight of other organs of state in all spheres of government. The act confers responsibilities on accounting officers to report on a monthly and an annual basis, including the submission of annual financial statements two months after the end of a financial year and to publish annual reports in the prescribed format, which includes reporting on output performance. It requires Parliament to vote by programme (the main division of government spending), rather than by department. This requires further information on outputs per programme and limits the powers of departmental accounting officers to move funds between programmes. Such movement is restricted to 8 per cent of the total allocation for a programme without the authorization of the National Treasury.

---

[9] Manuel, T. A., South African Minister of Finance, Foreword to the Explanatory Memorandum on the 1999 Public Finance Management Act (note 4).

The Medium-Term Expenditure Framework

An outcome of these economic reforms and the new financial policy has been the implementation of medium-term planning and budgeting in South Africa. Medium-term spending plans of national departments are prepared annually within the context of the government's macroeconomic and financial framework as set out in the previous year's budget. This framework, the Medium-Term Expenditure Framework (MTEF), sets the limits within which national departments have to compile their business and spending plans. The Medium-Term Expenditure Allocation (MTEA) is an indication of the expenditure that can be afforded within the MTEF and that will be voted for a department for the following three financial years. It also gives an indication of how expenditure is to be allocated within the department.

The introduction of the MTEF has brought greater transparency, certainty and stability to the budgetary process, and has strengthened the links between policy priorities and the government's long-term spending plans. It is intended to provide a tool with which to assess priorities and to confront any trade-offs that must be made between affordability and the constitutional requirement for equitable division of revenue between the spheres of government.

The MTEA represents an important political choice. The budgetary process is therefore designed to empower government to make informed choices about spending priorities and to assess the trade-off between spending options. At the same time, the process aims to give national departments a degree of certainty about their future allocations, so that they can more securely plan for ways to deliver the maximum possible output at the lowest cost. In compiling their Budget Planning Submissions (also referred to as an estimate of expenditure), national departments are obliged to plan their programmes, objectives and activities within their MTEA, and policy proposals must always be measured in terms of what can be afforded. Changed policies, circumstances and priorities are to be accommodated within the MTEA.

Since the MTEAs are based on affordability, there is a risk that objectives will not be reached on schedule or that service provision will be inadequate. To enable government to make informed choices about allocation of funds and to cover risks, departments are allowed to submit options to indicate how a change in the proposed allocation of funds may minimize or avoid risk to service provision. The options chosen by departments must be linked to the budget priorities and other policy considerations approved by the Cabinet.

Annually, the National Treasury issues guidelines to all departments for the preparation of their budgets for the next MTEF cycle.[10] These guidelines detail the process, timescales and format that departments are to follow when preparing their budgets and include information on budget reform and best practice

---

[10] 'Budget 2002, Medium term expenditure framework treasury guidelines: preparing budget submissions', National Treasury, Pretoria, 2002, URL <http://www.finance.gov.za/documents/budget/2002/guidelines_02/>.

to enhance the management of public finances. These Treasury instructions and guidelines drive departmental budgetary processes.

To illustate current practice, the budgetary process for financial year (FY) 2003/2004 (1 April 2003–31 March 2004) is shown in figure 10.2 and can be briefly summarized as follows.

1. *Prioritization stage.* The process commenced with the Ministers' Committee on the Budget (MinComBud), the Budget Council and the Cabinet giving consideration to policy priorities for the new medium-term expenditure period.[11] This stage ensures political oversight of the budgetary process by allowing government to manage the tensions between competing policy priorities and budget realities.

2. *Preparation of new MTEF submissions.* Departments reviewed their strategic plans for 2002–2004 and prepared their new MTEF submissions. The submissions include the departmental accounting officer's covering letter, details of reprioritization (within existing resources), policy options, departmental receipts and expenditure schedules.

3. *Macroeconomic and financial framework and division of revenue.* A review of the macroeconomic and financial framework and the division of revenue took place in the National Treasury, the MinComBud, the Budget Council and the Budget Forum for final decision by the Extended Cabinet.[12] This led to the preparation of the medium-term budget policy statement.

4. *Medium-term allocation process: recommendation stage.* During this first stage of the medium-term allocation process, discussions between departments and the National Treasury took place in hearings of the Medium-Term Expenditure Committee (MTEC). These discussions were guided by the outcomes of the prioritization stage, the review of the macroeconomic and financial framework, and the division of revenue.

5. *Medium-term budget policy statement.* The Minister of Finance tabled the medium-term budget policy statement before Parliament. This statement promotes transparency and accountability as it sets out the government's medium-term macroeconomic and financial position and its broad policy and spending priorities for the next three-year period three months before the detailed budget is presented to Parliament. Parliament and the public are therefore able to actively engage with the government's medium-term priorities and spending plans.

6. *Medium-term allocation process: decision stage.* The Minister of Finance reviewed the recommendations of the MTEC and tabled these before the MinComBud, the Budget Council and the Budget Forum. The recommendations of

---

[11] The MinComBud is a formal Cabinet committee of ministers that evaluates MTEA recommendations. The Budget Council consists of the Minister of Finance and the finance members of the 9 provincial executive committees. The council is consulted on any financial matter affecting the provincial governments.

[12] The Budget Forum consists of the members of the Budget Council plus 5 members nominated by the South African Local Government Association and 1 member from each of the provincial local government associations. The Extended Cabinet consists of the national Cabinet and the 9 provincial premiers.

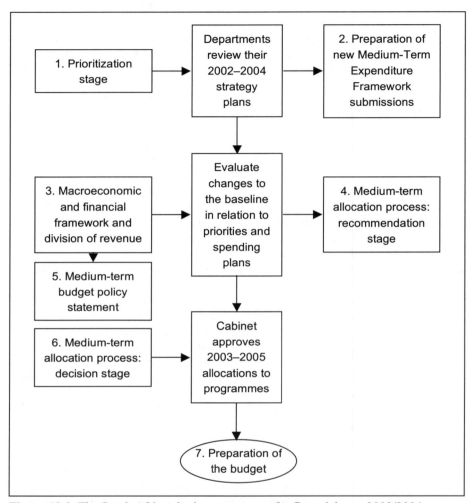

Figure 10.2. The South African budgetary process for financial year 2003/2004

these bodies were submitted to the Cabinet. The decisions of the Cabinet were set out in Treasury allocation letters sent to departments, which detailed the final allocation, the underlying rationale and any conditions.

7. *Preparation of the budget.* Following Cabinet approval, the final stage was the preparation of the budget documentation tabled before Parliament by the Minister of Finance on budget day. The details of this process within the Department of Defence are discussed in the next section.

IV. The military planning and budgetary process

Before discussing the military planning and budgetary process, it is important to describe the composition of the budget itself.

The military budget

The Department of Defence annually produces a strategic plan, which forms the basis of its budgetary process.[13] At the end of the process the budget is included in the strategic plan and is also published by the National Treasury as the Defence Vote.[14]

The DOD strategic plan for FYs 2002/2003–2004/2005 defines the core objectives of the DOD as: the preparation of the SANDF to enable it to respond to contingencies, the command and control of SANDF forces during deployments, and administration and support.[15] The programme structure of the Defence Vote, through which the DOD pursues these objectives, provides for nine defence programmes: (*a*) defence administration ('To conduct the overall management of the Department by formulating policy, providing strategic direction and organising the department in terms of its force design and structure'), (*b*) landward defence, (*c*) air defence, (*d*) maritime defence, (*e*) the Military Health Service, (*f*) defence intelligence, (*g*) joint support, (*h*) command and control, and (*i*) the Special Defence Account ('for financing special defence activities and purchases').[16] The Defence Vote for FYs 2002/2003–2004/2005 provides detailed financial figures for all programmes as well as the required outputs, performance indicators and targets.[17]

The expenditure estimates for the MTEF period 2003/2004–2005/2006 for each programme are presented in table 10.2. Table 10.3 presents the estimates for the same period in terms of standard items of expenditure.

The programme and item structures of the budget and the extensive amount of detail provided in the Defence Vote show that the South African DOD budget is both comprehensive and transparent. Nearly all expenditure on the military is reflected in the budget; the only exception is expenditure on rent and maintenance of state property used by the military, which is instead detailed in the budget of the Department of Public Works. This arises from an arrangement whereby the Department of Public Works is the 'owner' of all state property.

The South African military is funded largely through the national budget. However, in recent years the SANDF has received foreign financial aid for the rescue work done in Mozambique during the floods of 2000 and 2001, the

[13] Department of Defence (DOD), *Defence in a Democracy: Strategic Business Plan FY2004/05 to FY2006/07* (DOD: Pretoria, 2004).

[14] National Treasury, 'Vote 22: defence', *Medium Term Budget Policy Statement 2004* (National Treasury: Pretoria, Oct. 2004), URL <http://www.finance.gov.za/documents/mtbps/>, pp. 159–66.

[15] Department of Defence (DOD), *Strategic Plan for Financial Years 2002/03 to 2004/05* (DOD: Pretoria, 2002), p. 7.

[16] DOD (note 15), pp. 7–8.

[17] National Treasury (note 14).

Table 10.2. Estimated South African military expenditure by programme for the Medium-Term Expenditure Framework period of financial years 2003/2004–2005/2006

Figures are in millions of rand. Figures may not add up to totals due to the conventions of rounding.

Programme	2003/2004	2004/2005	2005/2006
Defence administration	660.3	688.5	723.3
Landward defence	3 188.4	3 300.7	3 548.0
Air defence	2 138.0	2 204.6	2 303.9
Maritime defence	1 050.9	1 084.1	1 091.6
Military Health Service	1 254.2	1 304.4	1 376.9
Defence intelligence	153.5	165.1	176.2
Joint support	2 039.2	2 089.1	2 203.5
Command and control	722.0	716.9	722.4
Special Defence Account	8 843.7	8 935.8	10 386.6
Total	**20 050.1**	**20 489.3**	**22 532.4**

Source: National Treasury, 'Vote 22: defence', *Estimates of National Expenditure 2003* (National Treasury: Pretoria, Feb. 2003), URL <http://www.finance.gov.za/documents/budget/>, pp. 488–518.

deployment of protection forces in Burundi, an AIDS awareness programme, the destruction of small arms, the retraining of soldiers for demobilization and peacekeeping exercises. Foreign aid has also been received in the form of direct donations of medical equipment and aircraft.[18]

Clear procedures exist for the receipt of such aid. Any offer of aid from a donor country must be made to the Secretary for Defence acting as head of department and accounting officer. Once the Secretary has accepted such an offer in principle, an agreement is drafted and the National Treasury is consulted. Once the agreement is signed, the donor deposits the funds in the Reconstruction and Development Programme Fund in the South African Reserve Bank. The DOD requests the funds when required and deposits them in its Paymaster-General Account. The funds then appear in the Financial Management System, permitting the relevant agency to spend the funds for the purpose for which they were intended. Income and expenditure statements are prepared for all foreign aid received and are forwarded to the particular donor. Donations are also disclosed in annual financial statements and annual reports of the DOD as prescribed by the National Treasury.[19]

The DOD also benefits from other non-financial contributions from donors, such as the US International Military Education and Training programme and the Ashridge courses on defence management held in the United Kingdom. The

---

[18] Gründling, J., DOD Chief Financial Officer, Interview with the author, Defence Secretariat, DOD, Pretoria, 20 June 2002.

[19] Gründling (note 18).

Table 10.3. Estimated South African military expenditure by standard expenditure item for the Medium-Term Expenditure Framework period of financial years 2003/2004–2005/2006

Figures are in millions of rand. Figures may not add up to totals due to the conventions of rounding.

Expenditure item	2003/2004	2004/2005	2005/2006
Personnel	7 093.4	7 251.9	7 556.8
Administrative	576.2	618.5	627.3
Inventories	959.4	985.0	1 041.0
Equipment	407.8	435.7	489.9
Land and buildings	12.3	11.2	11.7
Professional and special services	1 915.1	2 003.9	2 161.6
Transfer payments	9 075.3	9 172.7	10 633.6
Miscellaneous	10.5	10.5	10.5
Total	**20 050.1**	**20 489.3**	**22 532.4**

Source: National Treasury, 'Vote 22: defence', *Estimates of National Expenditure 2003* (National Treasury: Pretoria, Feb. 2003), URL <http://www.finance.gov.za/documents/budget/>, pp. 485–518.

DOD is not charged for these courses and costs do not appear in financial statements.

The DOD has recently become involved in United Nations (UN) peace-support operations. It has been partially reimbursed for South African forces deployed with MONUC, the UN Mission in the Democratic Republic of Congo.

South Africa does not provide direct military aid to any other country.

Other departmental receipts include the sale of old and surplus equipment (other than major armaments managed through the Special Defence Account, as described below), the rental of state quarters to married personnel, and the board and lodging of single personnel. The principle involved is that the DOD retains all income related to items for which the DOD originally budgeted. Other income is paid over to the National Revenue Fund.

The DOD does not hold any contingency funds in its budget; instead, a contingency fund is managed by the Minister of Finance. Should unforeseen events arise that require the deployment of the SANDF, the DOD can make representations to the National Treasury for extra funds. This money is transferred to the DOD budget at the end of the financial year, but only if the DOD has been unable to fund other approved activities as a consequence of the extra expense.

For a number of years, the SANDF has been deployed in support of the South African Police Service for the maintenance of internal law and order. Such deployments consist principally of infantry companies on border patrols and in direct support of other police operations; air support in the form of surveillance and tactical transport by light aircraft and helicopters; and maritime anti-crime coastal patrols. Although such support to the police uses forces from the

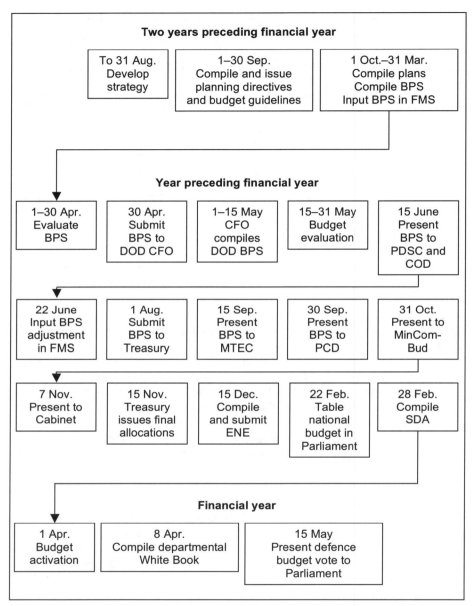

Figure 10.3. The South African Department of Defence budgetary process for a financial year (1 April–31 March)

BPS = Budget Planning Submissions; CFO = Chief Financial Officer; COD = Council on Defence; DOD = Department of Defence; ENE = Estimate of national expenditure; FMS = Financial Management System; MinComBud = Ministers' Committee on the Budget; MTEC = Medium-Term Expenditure Committee; PCD = (National Assembly's) Portfolio Committee on Defence; PDSC = Plenary Defence Staff Council; SDA = Special Defence Account.

SANDF, the marginal cost is around 2 per cent of the annual military budget.[20] This is the principal element of military expenditure that is not for military purposes. Examples of smaller and less regular military expenditure for non-military purposes are support to civil authorities in emergency situations, the maintenance of essential services and search-and-rescue operations. Where possible, such expenses are reimbursed to the DOD, but often they are funded from the military budget.

The budgetary process

The military budgetary process in the South African Department of Defence is formalized and governed by a departmental policy jointly promulgated by the Secretary for Defence and the Chief of the SANDF in 2000.[21] This new policy is based on the 1999 Public Finance Management Act, Treasury regulations and Treasury guidelines on preparing budget submissions.

The DOD budgeting policy aims to ensure that the procedures, principles and techniques prescribed by government are properly followed and applied within the department in order to ensure an effective, efficient, transparent and affordable military budget. The principles underpinning this policy strive to ensure that: (a) the budget is based on a strategic plan which specifies objectives, activities, outputs and measurable performance indicators for each objective; (b) the budget is based on output rather than input; (c) the budget is based on the activities to be executed; (d) the budget is based on the costing and prioritization of activities that need to be executed; (e) the budget is within the bounds of affordability; and (f) there is a consistent link between the budget, the strategic plan, the output to be delivered and the outcome to be achieved.

The different phases in the process which transforms the departmental strategy into an approved and implemented military budget are discussed below. Figure 10.3 gives a schematic representation of this process.

The strategic phase

The strategic phase is a continuous process in which departmental and military policies and strategies are developed, formalized and approved by the Military Command Council, chaired by the Chief of the SANDF, and the Plenary Defence Staff Council (PDSC), chaired by the Secretary for Defence. During this phase future opportunities and threats are identified and evaluated, and internal strengths and weaknesses are assessed in order to define defence strategies and requirements as well as implementation plans. To ensure that planning is realistic, account is taken of the Medium-Term Expenditure Allocation to the military sector. One of the major results of this phase is a clear indication

[20] Hauter, R. (Rear Admiral), Chief Director of Strategy and Planning, Interview with the author, SANDF Headquarters, DOD, Pretoria, 18 June 2002.

[21] Department of Defence, 'Budgeting policy within the Department of Defence', DOD Instruction FIN/00011/2000, DOD, Pretoria, 2000.

of the future size and shape of the DOD, as this defines force development and force preparation activities.[22]

During this phase the strategic profile of the department (its vision, mission and main functions), departmental policy and strategy, defence objectives and outputs, and the service delivery improvement programme for the next three years are formulated and approved by the Minister of Defence. This is published as the DOD strategic plan, which is printed and distributed internally and externally.[23]

In September of each year the detailed annual DOD planning and budgetary process is initiated by the distribution of planning directives and budget guidelines. These instructions set the schedule for developing the plan and budget. The details are refined when the Treasury guidelines on the preparing of budget submissions are issued in May of the following year. The process started in September 2002 therefore developed the plan, programmes and budget for the MTEF period 2004/2005–2006/2007; that is, for the period that commenced 19 months in the future.

The detailed planning and budgetary process continues with a planning conference at which the Minister of Defence and the Secretary for Defence provide guidelines and identify priorities. The Joint Operations Division of the SANDF provides anticipated requirements for joint force preparation and employment within the planning period. The financial guidelines are taken from the previous MTEF.

After this conference, planning directives and budgeting guidelines are compiled and issued to the top-level budget holders (TLBHs). These TLBHs are the chiefs of the four services and certain chiefs of staff, such as the chiefs of the Policy and Planning, Joint Operations, Joint Support, Defence Intelligence, and Acquisition and Procurement divisions.

Top-level budget holders and their subordinate budget holders undertake planning for about six months. Budget holders at all organizational levels compile their respective operational and business plans and submit these to their next higher authority for evaluation and approval.

The formulation phase

During the formulation phase (which overlaps with the strategic phase) all budget holders compile Budget Planning Submissions according to the prescribed format. Care is taken to ensure that the Budget Planning Submissions are based on reliable information in order to support informed decision making. All activities (outputs) and items (inputs) which can be afforded are costed and balanced according to the chosen strategy, policies, priorities and guidelines, and the Medium-Term Expenditure Allocation. The risks arising from activities that cannot be executed owing to an insufficient MTEA are clearly indicated.

[22] Hauter (note 20).
[23] DOD (note 13).

The Budget Planning Submissions are included in the Financial Management System by the end of March of the following year. Each budget manager coordinates the opening and closing of the applicable budget cycle on the Financial Management System for his or her area of responsibility.

During April TLBHs evaluate the Budget Planning Submissions of their lower-level budget holders and approve the submissions, adapt them or refer them back for revision. Top-level budget holders decide on the formats and dates of evaluations within their own areas of responsibility. At the end of April the TLBHs submit their consolidated Budget Planning Submissions to the Chief Financial Officer of the DOD according to a prescribed format.

The Chief Financial Officer compiles a departmental Budget Planning Submission for the DOD based on the Budget Planning Submissions of the TLBHs, the information captured on the Financial Management System and the operational plans of the TLBH. This is normally completed by the middle of May.

From the middle to the end of May the Budget Planning Submissions of the TLBHs are evaluated by the Departmental Planning and Budgeting Evaluation Committee (DPBEC). This committee is co-chaired by the Chief Financial Officer and the Chief of Corporate Staff and consists of members from the policy and planning, strategy, budgeting, joint operations, personnel planning and logistical planning environments. The chairpersons may co-opt others to serve on the DPBEC for a specific purpose or period from the National Treasury or the National Assembly's Portfolio Committee on Defence. Plans are interrogated, risks determined and options developed. Based on its evaluation, the committee prepares recommendations for the approval or adjustment of the Budget Planning Submissions of the TLBHs.

The next phase in the process is the departmental approval phase, which involves the formal approval of the draft budget by the Secretary for Defence and the Minister of Defence; this runs from May to the end of June. The evaluation of the submissions and the recommendations on the budget by the DPBEC are presented to the PDSC and the Council on Defence, chaired by the Minister of Defence. This presentation includes the recommended allocation to each TLBH, risks that need to be managed because of insufficient funds, unfunded mandates and any other recommendations that the committee feels it needs to make. Based on the recommendations from the evaluation committee and the instructions of the PDSC and the Council on Defence, final adjustments are made to the Budget Planning Submission on the Financial Management System and the system is closed. Finally, the DOD presents its Budget Planning Submission to the National Treasury's Defence Programme Officer in the prescribed format by the beginning of August. The prescribed format includes a comparison of expenditure during the previous three financial years, projected expenditure during the current financial year and the estimates for the following three financial years for each programme and sub-programme.

The last stage within the executive arm of government is governmental approval, which is an interdepartmental process of revision followed by formal approval of the budget by the Cabinet. In September the accounting officer (the

Secretary for Defence) and the Chief Financial Officer present the DOD Budget Planning Submission to the Medium-Term Expenditure Committee for detailed discussion. The Budget Planning Submission is also presented to the Portfolio Committee on Defence for approval and to give it the opportunity to formulate resolutions for presentation to the MinComBud or the Cabinet.

By the end of October the recommendations of the MTEC are presented to the MinComBud, which then formulates its own recommendations and submits them to the Cabinet in November. The Cabinet then approves the MTEA. Final adjustments are then made on the Financial Management System, based on the approved main programmes, sub-programmes and main items. These data are input in the form in which they will be presented to Parliament and are then submitted to the National Treasury.

The approval phase

After approval by the Cabinet, the Minister of Finance tables the national budget before the National Assembly in February. Cabinet ministers also present their respective budget votes for approval by Parliament. In addition to approving the respective budgets, Parliament also has the opportunity to compare the budget objectives with the policies and priorities of government. The Portfolio Committee on Defence undertakes parliamentary oversight of the military budget. This committee is currently the only parliamentary committee on defence and is responsible for: (*a*) evaluating and confirming the programmes and sub-programmes of the department, (*b*) evaluating and confirming the policy choices and priorities of the department, (*c*) evaluating the department's chapter in the estimate of national expenditure, (*d*) confirming the explanatory memorandum of the department, and (*e*) making resolutions on the military budget allocation for submission to the MinComBud or the Cabinet.

Once Parliament has approved the budget, it is ready for implementation by the various ministries and departments.

The implementation phase

One of the first actions of the implementation phase is the compilation of the Special Defence Account for submission to the ministers of Defence and Finance for approval. On 1 April of each financial year the Director of Budgeting, in conjunction with a representative of the State Information Technology Agency, activates the budget as contained in the Financial Management System. The departmental estimate of expenditure, the departmental 'White Book', is then printed and issued to all TLBHs. Finally, the Minister of Defence presents the military budget vote to Parliament in May.

The approved budget serves as a plan of action by which expenditure can be controlled. Managing expenditure in order to deliver the planned and approved results is the responsibility of all actors in the process, from the unit commanders and commodity managers up to programme managers, the Chief Financial Officer and the accounting officer. In this process, the programme managers, the Chief Financial Officer and the accounting officer exercise control and supervision in order to evaluate the effectiveness and efficiency with which objectives are being met. The DPBEC and the PDSC play important roles in the control of expenditure according to the plans.

Internal auditing of the military budget and expenditure is undertaken by internal auditors who report to the Inspector-General of the Defence Inspectorate, who in turn reports to the Secretary for Defence. In order to increase objectivity and impartiality, in March 2000 the Secretary for Defence appointed an independent audit committee, consisting mostly of people from outside the DOD, which is empowered to direct the work of the internal auditors.

The South African DOD makes a distinction between 'procurement' and 'acquisition' processes. The procurement process is the means by which commercial goods and services are obtained using the General Defence Account and involves contracting for a requirement on the basis of an existing commercial specification.[24] Procurement of goods and services is done through the State Tender Board and by delegation of duties from the board to departments. This process is sufficiently transparent.

The acquisition process is the means by which major armaments are obtained using funds from the Special Defence Account, described more fully below. This process may involve requirement planning, operational research, technology acquisition, design and development, operational qualification, quality assurance, industrialization, production, commissioning, maintenance and disposal.

The budgetary process for armament acquisition, although subject to different authorization levels and bodies, is not an independent activity. It is executed within the same framework, process and timescales as the DOD operating budget. Budgeting for capital projects begins with force development planning, which is controlled by the Director of Planning. The primary input for the budgeting cycle is the SANDF capital acquisition master plan.

Money from the Special Defence Account is spent according to a schedule (spending plan) recommended by the Secretary for Defence and approved on an annual basis by the ministers of Defence and Finance. These requirements must be in accordance with the DOD strategic plan and the defence budget as voted in Parliament.

The Special Defence Account

Currently, the largest programme in the military budget is the Special Defence Account. This account was created by the 1974 Defence Special Account Act to cover costs incurred for any special defence activities approved by the ministers of Defence and Finance.[25] The programme is intended to provide for the acqui-

---

[24] The General Defence Account is used for defraying expenditure needed for operating purposes limited to a single financial year. Flexibility in its use is provided by the ability to pre-commit 50% of current budget allocation to the 3 following financial years.

[25] Defence Special Account Act (Act 6 of 1974), Section 1.

sition of military equipment and strategic armaments, the maintenance of required military capabilities and the financing of sensitive military activities.

The Defence Special Account Act recognizes that the DOD has certain responsibilities that need to be dealt with in a special way. The act is not unique: similar acts for the police and intelligence services are identified in the 1995 Auditor-General Act.[26] Parliament appropriates funds for the Special Defence Account during the debate on the Defence Vote on the recommendation of the ministers of Defence and Finance. An additional source of income for the account is proceeds from the sale of armaments that were purchased with funds from the account and that are no longer required.

The Special Defence Account is divided into four sub-programmes: 'procurement services', 'strategic defence procurement', 'operating' and 'intelligence related'. In FY 2003/2004, 91 per cent of the funds in the Special Defence Account went to the procurement services and strategic defence procurement sub-programmes, which are for the procurement of military equipment over the long term.[27] The operating sub-programme covers the maintenance of equipment. No outputs or targets are indicated for the intelligence-related sub-programme, which amounts to about 0.6 per cent of the Special Defence Account or 0.3 per cent of the defence budget.

The second of these sub-programmes accounts for the Strategic Defence Procurement Package, which was approved by the South African Government in 1998 and initiated in 1999 after much publicity and debate. This package involves the acquisition of 3 submarines and 4 corvettes from Germany, 30 light utility helicopters from Italy, 28 fighter aircraft from Sweden and 24 fighter-trainer aircraft from the UK. These systems were acquired to replace obsolete SANDF equipment and were all provided for in the Defence Review.[28] It also aims to increase industrial participation by South African companies in the military and other sectors. The total value of the package amounted to $4.8 billion in 1999 (30.3 billion rand at the time), to be paid over a period of 12 years.

The scale of this procurement programme means that it is overseen by a ministerial committee consisting of the ministers of Defence, Finance, and Trade and Industry. The ministerial committee in turn reports to the Cabinet.

The auditing phase

External auditing of the Department of Defence is done by the Auditor-General. The 1996 constitution designates the Auditor-General as one of the state institutions that support constitutional democracy and it guarantees the independence and impartiality of the office holder. The Auditor-General is appointed by the President as the statutory independent auditor of the executive authority.

---

[26] Auditor-General Act (Act 12 of 1995), 14 June 1995, Section 4.

[27] Department of Defence (DOD), *Annual Report 2003/2004* (DOD: Pretoria, 2004), URL <http://www.dod.mil.za/documents/annualreports/annualreports.htm>, p. 173.

[28] Department of Defence (DOD), 'Defence in a democracy: South African Defence Review 1998', Pretoria, 1998, URL <http://www.info.gov.za/documents/subjectdocs/subject/defence.htm>.

This appointment and the conditions of service, powers, duties and related matters are covered by the constitution and the 1995 Auditor-General Act. The Auditor-General reports to the National Assembly's Standing Committee on Public Accounts.

Government auditing involves the investigation and evaluation of financial management practices, financial statements, performance and compliance with requirements by government and related institutions. The aim of an audit is to form an opinion on whether the institution under review has fairly presented its operations in the financial statements and whether it has complied with all relevant laws and regulations. The audit also investigates the control mechanisms of the institution in order to ensure that public funds and assets are safeguarded, accounting systems function properly and public funds are spent effectively.

The annual DOD budget for external auditors appointed by the Auditor-General is approximately 25 million rand ($4 million). All DOD financial statements are audited and the auditor's reports are included in the DOD's annual report.[29]

V. Assessment of the military budgetary process

The South African national and military budgetary processes are formalized and structured. The major strengths of the military budgetary process are the legislative framework, which governs all national departments; the degree of political control and oversight; and the high degree of transparency. The formal departmental processes, structures and procedures are also positive characteristics of the process.

Perhaps the greatest strength of the budgetary processes in South Africa is the strict adherence to the legislative framework. The adherence to rules and the willingness of the political authorities to permit the system to function as designed ensures the institutionalization of the processes and, ultimately, the realization of policy goals through the efficient application of allocated resources. The willingness of the executive to apply the necessary control mechanisms in order to check abuse is an important factor in the process.

The robust oversight of the process by the legislature is also a strength of the process. Cooperation between the government and the legislature through regular consultations in the budget formulation process ensures the early participation of Parliament in the budgetary process and thus facilitates scrutiny when a detailed budget is later submitted to Parliament.

The subsequent parliamentary oversight is extensive, as the Portfolio Committee on Defence consists of capable people who are well informed about military issues in general and the military budget in particular. In spite of the fact that the majority of the committee members come from the ruling ANC, they still scrutinize the budget with the utmost seriousness and objectivity.[30]

---

[29] Gründling (note 18); and DOD (note 27).

[30] E.g., when in 1994 President Mandela attempted to influence the committee's decision on the choice of language to be used for command and control by the SANDF, the members resisted, insisting that

The committee's active involvement in the development of South Africa's defence policy has also increased members' understanding of the issues at stake and made them active participants in the management of the SANDF, but without their interfering in the micromanagement of the DOD. The approval granted in 1998 for the multi-billion dollar Strategic Defence Procurement Package was facilitated by the knowledge of most committee members of the basis for such arms acquisition, since they participated actively in both the making of the defence policy and the Defence Review, in which the need for such extensive arms procurement was articulated.

There is also a high level of transparency in legislative activities. Parliamentary sittings are open to the public and, since 1994, a number of steps have been taken to make Parliament more accessible. The aim has been to make it more accountable, as well as to motivate and facilitate public participation in the legislative processes. Two such steps are the establishment of an Internet site, which encourages comments and feedback from the public,[31] and the parliamentary television channel, which broadcasts live coverage of sittings of Parliament and committees.

Transparency

There is substantial transparency in the South African DOD policy, planning and budgeting processes. This has been assured primarily by the clear constitutional commitment to transparency, by the national financial legislative framework and by the unequivocal role that was played by the parliamentary defence committees during the development of military policy after 1994. Transparency in military and financial management is demonstrated by the manner in which the 1996–98 Defence Review and the 1996 White Paper on defence were developed and approved.

Defence policy

Great effort was put into the establishment of the new defence policy through the elaboration of a White Paper on defence and the Defence Review.[32] This policy includes a redefinition of South Africa's defence posture and strategy, the roles and tasks of the SANDF, the required military capabilities, human resources policies, the management of military land and the environment, the military acquisition process, and the military legal system. During the development of policy governing the tasks, operational concepts and required capabil-

English be chosen. Modise, T., 'Parliamentary oversight of the South African Department of Defence: 1994 to 2003', eds L. le Roux, M. Rupiya and N. Ngoma, *Guarding the Guardians, Parliamentary Oversight and Civil–Military Relations: The Challenges for SADC* (Institute for Security Studies: Pretoria, 2004), pp. 45–53.

[31] Parliament of South Africa, URL <http://www.parliament.gov.za/>.

[32] Department of Defence (DOD), 'White Paper on National Defence for the Republic of South Africa: Defence in a Democracy', Pretoria, May 1996, URL <http://www.info.gov.za/documents/whitepapers/index.htm>; and DOD (note 28).

ities of the SANDF, a needs-driven but cost-constrained approach was used. This entailed an analysis of the present and future security environments relevant to South Africa, the identification of probable future defence contingencies and associated risks, and an evaluation of the capabilities required to confront these contingencies. This was then accurately costed and debated within the parliamentary defence committees and by civil society. After nine regional and three national consultative conferences, Parliament decided on what was considered to be an affordable core force: a balanced and sustainable nucleus maintaining capabilities and expertise for immediate requirements and the ability to expand if required. Parliament also accepted the risks that this entails. Defence policy is therefore based on an appreciation of the security environment and the consequent risks as well as the economic realities and priorities of South Africa. The processes used in the development of the new defence policy were open and consultative and have been internationally acclaimed for the manner in which they were conducted. Unfortunately, the development of defence policy occurred in the absence of a broader national security policy and this remains a shortcoming of the process to the present day.

According to Gavin Cawthra, Director of the Centre for Defence and Security Management at the University of the Witwatersrand, non-governmental organizations 'played a crucial role in drawing [up] the White Paper, but . . . although public consultations took place, the process was in fact the preserve of a small elite of defence experts. The parliamentary defence committees . . . drove this process, while the role of civil servants in the Ministry of Defence was minimal.'[33] Cawthra goes on to say that the Defence Review 'was largely driven by civil servants in the newly established Secretariat for Defence. However, this process was more consultative than that of the White Paper and a far wider spectrum of role-players [was] involved. The Secretariat consulted very widely with government and non-government stakeholders and interest groups and a series of well-attended meetings, workshops and conferences [was] held around the country.'[34]

Since the completion of the Defence Review in 1998, it has become clear that other social and developmental priorities of government as well as developments in the exchange rate of the South African rand will continue to place restrictions on the attainment of the envisaged force design and that some adaptation will be required. A revision of the Defence Review is currently in progress and the Portfolio Committee on Defence called for submissions and held public hearings in October 2004. The DOD is currently in consultation with the committee, but no final report has yet been produced or opened for consultation with civil society.

Following the writing of the White Paper and the completion of the Defence Review, parliamentary defence committees have continued to be involved in

[33] Cawthra, G., 'From "total strategy" to "human security": the making of South Africa's defence policy, 1990–99', *Journal of Peace, Conflict and Military Studies*, vol. 1, no. 1 (Mar. 2000), URL <http://www.uz.ac.zw/units/cds/archive.html>, pp. 51–67.
[34] Cawthra (note 33), p. 53.

further defence policy development and the drafting of defence legislation. They have contributed to the development of the 2002 National Conventional Arms Control Act, the 2002 Defence Act, the 2003 Anti-Personnel Mines Prohibition Act, the 2003 Armaments Corporation of South Africa Limited Act and the DOD's Human Resource Strategy 2010.[35]

Policy development and approval processes are currently well coordinated both within the DOD and between departments. Before the PDSC can approve a policy it must be satisfied that all stakeholders have been consulted and that the policy complies with other policies. Before the Cabinet approves policy it must have been approved by the appropriate sectoral clusters at director-general and ministerial levels in order to ensure coordination.[36]

Since 1994 real advances have also been made in ensuring democratic control over the military and good civil–military relations. This is evident in: (a) the clear constitutional principles governing the security services and the SANDF,[37] (b) the constitutional provisions regarding the authority of the President as commander-in-chief of the SANDF and his authority to order the SANDF into service,[38] (c) the constitutional provision that a member of the Cabinet must be responsible for defence,[39] (d) the constitutional provision for multiparty parliamentary committees on defence with oversight powers,[40] and (e) the constitutionally determined functions of the SANDF.[41]

The DOD strategic plan and budget

The DOD strategic plan and the detailed budget are developed within the DOD as described above. These processes are based on approved defence policy and guidelines received from the Cabinet and the sectoral clusters at ministerial level. During these processes there is considerable interaction with the National Treasury, the Minister of Defence and the other state mechanisms designed to ensure the alignment of departmental budgets with national objectives and priorities. There is, however, no direct involvement of or consultation with

[35] National Conventional Arms Control Act (Act 41 of 2002), 31 Dec. 2002; Defence Act (Act 42 of 2002), 31 Dec. 2002; Anti-Personnel Mines Prohibition Act (Act 36 of 2003), 2 Dec. 2003; Armaments Corporation of South Africa Limited Act (Act 51 of 2003), 31 Dec. 2003; and DOD (note 13), p. 7.

[36] Sendall, N., DOD Chief Director of Defence Policy, Interview with the author, Defence Secretariat, DOD, Pretoria, 20 June 2002. The South African Government operates in so-called sectoral clusters. Both Cabinet members and department heads meet in these clusters in order to coordinate plans and actions. These clusters are: the Economy, Investment and Employment Cluster; the Government and Administration Cluster; the Social Cluster; the Justice, Crime Prevention and Security Cluster; and the International Relations, Peace and Security Cluster. All matters that are referred to Cabinet must first pass through the relevant cluster.

[37] Constitution of the Republic of South Africa (note 2), Chapter 11, Security services.

[38] Constitution of the Republic of South Africa (note 2), Chapter 11, Security services, Sections 201(2) and 202(1).

[39] Constitution of the Republic of South Africa (note 2), Chapter 11, Security services, Section 201(1).

[40] Constitution of the Republic of South Africa (note 2), Chapter 11, Security services, Section 199(8).

[41] Constitution of the Republic of South Africa (note 1), Chapter 14, Police and defence, Section 224. Section 24(1) of Schedule 6 of the 1996 constitution (note 2) states that inter alis Sections 224–28 of the 1993 interim constitution continue in force.

broader civil society. Annually, on the completion of the DOD strategic plan and the military budget, these are published and openly distributed.[42]

The South African DOD does not report its defence budget to the UN Department for Disarmament Affairs using the standardized Instrument for Reporting Military Expenditures.[43] This appears to contradict the defence White Paper, which states that South Africa should pursue the implementation of confidence- and security-building measures such as the 'Annual consultation and exchange of information on defence budgets, force structure, modernisation plans and troop deployment'.[44]

Accuracy of the military budget

The positive factors of political oversight, control measures and transparency as well as strict internal control mean that the military budget and expenditure data can be assessed as being valid and reliable. The military budget covers nearly all military expenditure, excluding the rent and maintenance of state property used by the military, which appears instead in the budget of the Department of Public Works. The programme and item structures of the budget, as well as the detail contained in the DOD strategic plan and the Defence Vote, ensure that figures are reliable and accurately reflect the real cost of military activities.

Tables 10.4 and 10.5 provide figures for budgeted and actual military expenditure for FY 2003/2004 by programme and by standard expenditure item. These tables indicate that, although there is some significant deviation from the budget, in particular under the 'administrative' expenditure item, deviation within the main programmes is negligible. This gives a good indication of the large degree to which military funds are in fact spent on the outputs and objectives approved in the budget vote.[45]

Weaknesses

There are few weaknesses to be found in the South African military budgetary process. At present there is some misalignment between the approved force design and structure and the funds made available in the MTEF. This leads to difficulties in prioritizing military activities and in long-term planning. This problem is being addressed by a strategy that is being debated by the Portfolio

[42] DOD (note 13); and National Treasury (note 14).

[43] The Instrument was established in 1981. United Nations, *Transparency in Armaments: United Nations Instrument for Reporting Military Expenditures, Global and Regional Participation 1981–2002* (United Nations: New York, 2003), table 3; this book and information on more recent reporting are available from the Internet site of the UN Department for Disarmament Affairs, 'Transparency in armaments', URL <http://disarmament2.un.org/cab/milex.html>.

[44] DOD (note 32), chapter 3, p. 14.

[45] This is further demonstrated by the fact that the Auditor-General approved the DOD's accounts for 2000/01 and 2001/02 without qualification, although certain qualifications were attached to the audit opinion in 2002/03 and 2003/04. Department of Defence (DOD), *Annual Report 2000/2001*; *2001/2002*; *2002/2003*; and *2003/2004* (DOD: Pretoria, 2001, 2002, 2003 and 2004), URL <http://www.dod.mil.za/documents/annualreports/annualreports.htm>.

Table 10.4. Budgeted and actual South African military expenditure by programme for financial year 2003/2004

Figures are in millions of rand. Figures may not add up to totals due to the conventions of rounding.

Programme	Revised allocation	Actual expenditure	Under- or overspend (%)
Defence administration	658.1	658.1	–
Landward defence	3 111.9	3 111.9	–
Air defence	2 151.2	2 151.2	–
Maritime defence	1 013.6	1 013.6	–
Military Health Service	1 337.6	1 337.6	–
Defence intelligence	134.3	132.9	*-1.05*
Joint support	2 105.9	2 091.6	*-0.68*
Command and control	1 246.4	1 288.1	*3.35*
Special Defence Account	8 015.8	8 015.8	–
Special functions	25.1	25.2	–
Total	**19 800.0**	**19 826.0**	*0.13*

Source: Department of Defence, *Annual Report 2003/2004* (Department of Defence: Pretoria, 2004), URL <http://www.dod.mil.za/documents/annualreports/annualreports.htm>, p. 155.

Committee on Defence and the Cabinet. In terms of classification, the only expenditure directly in support of the military which is not reflected in the military budget is that spent on military property by the Department of Public Works.

The other major weakness is the extent of oversight of the Special Defence Account, as allegations of irregularities and corruption have dogged the Strategic Defence Procurement Package. First, in 2000 the Auditor-General revealed that, because of hidden costs, the programme was going to cost much more than the amount approved by Parliament, which shows that the legislators did not consider the overall cost (including the likely effect of inflation) of the programme to the country.[46] Second, corruption charges have been levelled against high-ranking officials of the state involved in the negotiation of the arms deals. A senior parliamentarian and an advisor to the Deputy President have been found guilty of corruption.[47] Deputy President Jacob Zuma himself is now facing charges of corruption and has been 'release[d] ... from his

---

[46] Engelbrecht, L., 'South African MPs left cold by arms deal', Defence Systems Daily, 16 Oct. 2000, URL <http://defence-data.com/>, also available at URL <http://www.armsdeal-vpo.co.za/articles00/mps_left_cold.html>.

[47] Tony Yengeni, chairman of the parliamentary defence committee during the negotiation of the Strategic Defence Procurement Package, was sentenced in Mar. 2003 to 4 years in jail for receiving a bribe—a substantial discount on a luxury Mercedes-Benz car—from one of the companies involved. Phillips, B., 'Jail term for ANC man', BBC News Online, 19 Mar. 2003, URL <http://news.bbc.co.uk/2/2863531.stm>. Schabir Shaik, the former financial adviser to Deputy President Jacob Zuma, was sentenced to 15 years in jail for soliciting bribes from a French arms firm between 1995 and 2002. 'Guilty verdict in SA graft case', BBC News Online, 2 June 2005, URL <http://news.bbc.co.uk/2/4603009.stm>. Shaik's conviction is currently awaiting appeal.

Table 10.5. Budgeted and actual South African military expenditure by standard expenditure item for financial year 2003/2004

Figures are in millions of rand. Figures may not add up to totals due to the conventions of rounding.

Expenditure item	Revised allocation	Actual expenditure	Under- or overspend (%)
Personnel	7 209.3	7 209.3	–
Administrative	764.3	804.6	*5.27*
Inventories	983.1	983.1	–
Equipment	413.9	413.9	–
Land and buildings	11.9	11.9	–
Professional and special services	2 112.5	2 098.6	*–0.66*
Transfer payments	8 277.4	8 277.0	*–0.00*
Miscellaneous	2.3	2.3	–
Special functions	25.1	25.1	–
Total	**19 800.0**	**19 826.0**	*0.13*

Source: Department of Defence, *Annual Report 2003/2004* (Department of Defence: Pretoria, 2004), URL <http://www.dod.mil.za/documents/annualreports/annualreports.htm>, p. 156.

responsibilities as Deputy President of the Republic and Member of the Cabinet'.[48] However, a government investigation team, consisting of the Auditor-General, the Public Protector and the National Director of Public Prosecutions, looked into the allegations surrounding the Strategic Defence Procurement Package. The investigation team reported to Parliament in November 2001 that, although there had been irregularities and improprieties in the conduct of certain officials in government departments, they had found no evidence of improper or unlawful conduct by the government itself.[49]

A potential weakness arises from the increasing power of the ANC over its members in Parliament. Since any ANC legislator who bucks the party line may be expelled from the party, there is reason to suspect the extent of Parliament's independence in matters that are of importance to both the executive and the party.[50]

---

[48] South African Government, 'Statement of the President of South Africa, Thabo Mbeki, at the joint sitting of Parliament on the release of Hon Jacob Zuma from his responsibilities as Deputy President, National Assembly', Cape Town, 14 June 2005, URL <http://www.info.gov.za/speeches/year/>; 'SA's Zuma welcomes day in court', BBC News Online, 21 June 2005, URL <http://news.bbc.co.uk/2/4114008.stm>.

[49] Baqwa, S., Fakie, S. A. and Ngcuka, B. T., 'Joint investigation report into the Strategic Defence Procurement Packages', Cape Town, 15 Nov. 2001, URL <http://www.info.gov.za/projects/procurement/>; and Engelbrecht, L., 'Arms report clears South African government', Defence Systems Daily, 16 Sep. 2001, URL <http://defence-data.com/>, also available at URL <http://www.armsdeal-vpo.co.za/articles02/clear_government.html>.

[50] Johnson, R. W., *South Africa: The First Man, The Last Nation* (Weidenfeld and Nicolson: London, 2004).

VI. Conclusions and recommendations

It can be stated that the South African defence policy, planning and budgeting processes are substantially transparent and in line with the principles of democratic civil–military relations. Good executive and parliamentary approval and oversight procedures exist and ensure the alignment of defence policy with political priorities. This alignment is also ensured by the good interdepartmental cooperation that exists in the national budgetary process. Oversight and control of military expenditure ensure that resources are spent on the activities for which they were planned. The South African DOD is therefore clearly accountable to the Minister of Defence, Parliament and the public. The military budget fairly reflects the true economic resources devoted to military activities in South Africa. It is, however, unfortunate that the DOD does not report its annual budget to the UN Department for Disarmament Affairs according to the standardized Instrument for Reporting Military Expenditures.

Financial policy and economic reform in South Africa have led to the introduction and implementation of medium-term planning and budgeting in the form of a three-year Medium-Term Expenditure Framework. The MTEF has brought greater transparency, certainty and stability to the budgetary process, and has strengthened the links between policy priorities and government's medium-term spending plans. Military planning, programming and budgeting take place within these financial and defence policy frameworks: there is a clear formal planning and budgeting process in the South African DOD and this process is aligned with the national MTEF.

Implementation of the following five recommendations would improve the military budgetary process in South Africa.

1. South Africa should develop a comprehensive national security policy to guide defence policy. The South African DOD, in conjunction with the Portfolio Committee on Defence, should then revisit the assumptions on which the force design described in the Defence Review is based. The main assumptions that need to be reconsidered are the internal role of the SANDF, the future role of the SANDF in peace missions and the sustainable level of the military budget. This will assist in aligning military planning and the MTEF.

2. Expenditure on the rent and maintenance of state property used by the military, which currently appears in the budget of the Department of Public Works, should appear in the military budget. This would ensure the full visibility of military expenditure and the full costing of all military activities.

3. The process for reimbursing the DOD for non-military expenditure, such as support for the South African Police Service in maintaining internal law and order, should be streamlined in order to ensure that these expenses are clearly identifiable.

4. The DOD should continue to develop its relationship with civil society through direct interaction and develop its Internet site in order to further enhance transparency and increase public understanding of the role of the mili-

tary. Furthermore, to maintain the consultative approach that the DOD adopted during the development of the defence White Paper and the Defence Review, the DOD should proactively involve civil society in the development of the annual strategic plan. This could be done by *inter alia* the provision of a public discussion forum on the DOD Internet site.

5. In the interest of improved confidence- and security-building measures, both regional and international, the DOD should report its annual budget to the UN Department for Disarmament Affairs using the standardized Instrument for Reporting Military Expenditures.

11. A synthesis of the country studies

Wuyi Omitoogun

I. Introduction

This study examines the processes of budgeting for the military sector in eight African countries—Ethiopia, Ghana, Kenya, Mali, Mozambique, Nigeria, Sierra Leone and South Africa—using an analytical framework that consists of principles of public expenditure management and integrated defence planning, programming and budgeting. The essence of the analytical framework is two-fold: (*a*) to enable the measurement of good practice in military budgetary processes in the selected countries; and (*b*) to serve as a conceptual foundation on which to base the analyses in the case studies and, by implication, provide the basis for a comparative analysis. In assessing the processes in the countries within the good practice framework, it must be kept in mind that these are high standards to which even advanced democracies do not fully measure up. The objective is to identify the gap between good practice in military budgeting and the existing practices depicted in the case studies, with a view to suggesting and promoting ways of raising standards in these countries.

In section II of this chapter the budgetary processes in the eight African countries are discussed in the context of the good practice framework adopted for this study (see chapter 2). The countries are categorized in section III on the basis of their adherence to the good practice principles, while section IV provides explanations for the countries' level of adherence to the principles. Section V summarizes the findings of the study and presents the conclusions.

It is important to note that, while all the countries have long histories of military budgeting, and this history is reflected in the case studies (although the South Africa case study covers only the post-apartheid period), for consistency and comparability the assessment in this chapter is based only on the period in which all eight countries were under democratic rule, that is, since 1999.

II. The country studies in the context of the good practices framework

All the countries in this study have established procedures for budgeting generally, including budgeting for the military sector. These procedures are no different from the standard procedures for budgeting elsewhere, with recognizable and defined stages. The process is guided by norms, rules and laws which are intended to ensure a predictable pattern in the process and, presumably, positive outcomes. However, as seen in the country studies (chapters 3–10), the practices of the countries, and therefore the outcomes of their processes, differ. This section assesses and compares the state of established legal military budgetary processes in the eight countries within the framework of the good practice principles: principles of defence planning and programming and of public expenditure management. The assessment spans the four distinct but interrelated phases which any budgetary process must comprise: formulation, approval, implementation (including arms procurement) and auditing.

Defence planning and programming

Defence planning and programming are fundamental to the making of a meaningful military budget whose output can be easily measured.[1] However, with the exceptions of South Africa and, since 2003, Sierra Leone, the countries in this study lack strategic defence plans developed from well-articulated risk assessments and detailed analysis of the security and economic environments in which they operate. These countries, including nations with relatively high levels of military spending, such as Ethiopia and Nigeria, also lack clearly defined defence policies from which well-developed strategic defence plans can develop.[2] Most of the states do not make adequate threat assessments. For instance, while internal security threats and peacekeeping operations are becoming a preoccupation of most of their militaries, the countries continue to plan and budget mainly for external defence.[3]

The absence of a well-articulated defence policy in five of the countries studied—Ethiopia, Ghana, Kenya, Mali and Nigeria—makes defence planning no more than a mechanical reaction to circumstances, with dire consequences for planning and budgeting. While it is often argued that 'policy is what government does and not what it says it wants to do', the lack of a formal defence policy prevents broad participation in any debate and review process, causing decision making in defence policy to be a narrow and exclusive business. This has a negative impact on the military budgetary process because it reinforces the myth of the military as a special part of the public sector. In addition, the challenges facing the military, and against which the budget will be targeted, are not clearly articulated or, if articulated, are known only to the small circle of people involved in the military decision-making process. The lack of a clearly articulated defence policy that spells out the tasks and functions of the armed forces also affects the scope of the military budget. This is a major problem in

---

[1] It should be noted that the existence of a formal plan does not guarantee that it will be followed. Nigeria has several development plans that were judged to be excellent on paper but were never used by the country's various governments. The same applies to Kenya. Mwenda, A. K. and Gachocho, M. N., 'Budget transparency: Kenyan perspective', Institute for Economic Affairs (IEA) Research Paper Series no. 4, IEA, Nairobi, Oct. 2003.

[2] Mozambique is an exception to this; see chapter 7 in this volume.

[3] For an elaboration of the changing nature of tasks for African armed forces see Williams, R., 'Defence and development: some thematic issues', *Development Southern Africa*, vol. 18, no. 1 (Mar. 2001), pp. 57–77; and Williams, R., 'African armed forces and the challenges of security sector reform', *Journal of Security Sector Management*, vol. 3, no. 2 (Mar. 2005).

Table 11.1. Defence planning, programming and budgeting in Ethiopia, Ghana, Kenya, Mali, Mozambique, Nigeria, Sierra Leone and South Africa, 2003

Country	Strategic defence plan	Defence programmes	Defence budget
Ethiopia	No	No	Yes
Ghana	No	No	Yes
Kenya	No	No	Yes
Mali	No	No	Yes
Mozambique	No	No	Yes
Nigeria	No	No	Yes
Sierra Leone	Yes	No	Yes
South Africa	Yes	Yes	Yes

these five countries since the military are requested to undertake tasks that are unrelated to their traditional role, without there being any formal provision for such tasks in the budget. On the other hand, some military-related tasks that are becoming a regular feature of their activities, such as peacekeeping, are not considered as part of the military budget in countries such as Nigeria.[4]

The absence of strategic planning and a sectoral policy in countries such as Ghana, Kenya and Nigeria also affects how resources are allocated within the military sector itself. Thus, inter-service rivalry and the level of influence that each service can exert, rather than the strategic significance of their requirements, determine the resource-sharing formula in most of the countries. Examples of services exerting their influence include the Nigerian Navy in the 1980s (see chapter 8), the Ghanaian Army prior to the late 1980s (see chapter 4), and the army and navy in Kenya after the air force's abortive coup of August 1982 (see chapter 5).

Without formal policies and a strategy to carry them out it is also difficult to efficiently manage the resources of the military. Given the arbitrariness that has characterized the budgetary processes across Africa over time, formal policies should at least provide a guide as to what to budget for and how this should be done. This will also enable the general public to know the justification for the size and structure of the armed forces. Although Nigeria now has a draft defence policy, this has been a draft since 2001 and its contents are not widely known.[5] While Mali has a code of conduct for its armed forces in view of their history of repression and *coups d'état*, the aim of government policy in the sector is not defined. This also means that programming—the link between a defence plan and the budget—is lacking, thereby creating a missing link in the military budgetary process chain.

---

[4] It should be noted that, since peacekeeping operations are contingent by nature and unpredictable in terms of occurrence, length and intensity, budgeting for them is not straightforward. However, when operations are carried out over a fairly long period of time, as in the case of ECOMOG operations, then they should be budgeted for as part of the military budget.

[5] Extracts from Nigeria's draft defence policy are given in chapter 8 in this volume.

As shown in table 11.1, while all the countries studied except South Africa lack a strategic defence plan and defence programme, they all engage in the annual ritual of military budgeting. The absence of a strategic plan that should provide the basis for all military activities means that the budget does not reflect perceptions of threats to the state and may contain much overlap as the services make independent and often similar requests for equipment, resulting in duplication and waste.[6] One major advantage of defence planning and programming is that it encourages coordination among the services and eliminates waste resulting from duplication in addition to spreading the cost of major equipment over several annual budgets.

As mentioned above, the absence of a link between military budgets and military activities in most of these countries is traceable to a lack of definitive policies, plans and programmes to guide activities in the sector. The absence of this essential guide, which should provide direction for all activities, including budgeting, constitutes a fundamental weakness in the budgetary processes in all the countries in the study with the single exception of South Africa. Table 11.2 shows the current practices in the eight countries with regard to basic steps involved in managing military expenditure from the defence planning stage through budget formulation to the evaluation phase. These steps are a breakdown of the four crucial interrelated components of managing expenditure outlined in chapter 2.

The military budgetary process and the principles of public expenditure management

All the sample countries possess or claim to possess a legal framework and a hierarchy of military and civilian authorities that make decisions on the country's external defence. However, when assessed against the good practice principles, the processes in all the countries, except South Africa, display many gaps, not only in adherence to basic principles but also in the institutional arrangements meant to facilitate the process. There is little noticeable planning in the military budgetary processes of any of the countries and in many there is a particular absence of a link between defence policy (where one exists) and the military budget. It does not appear that the macroeconomic framework has much bearing on the military budgetary process.

What follows below is an assessment of the military budgetary processes in the eight countries on the basis of seven of the principles of public expenditure management discussed in chapter 2: (a) comprehensiveness, (b) contestability, (c) predictability, (d) honesty, (e) discipline, (f) transparency and (g) accountability. Tables 11.3–11.6 below summarize the adherence to these and other

[6] This is what motivated the introduction of the planning, programming and budgeting system in the USA in the early 1960s. Meehan, R. P., *Plans, Programs and the Defense Budget* (National Defense University Press: Washington, DC, 1985), p. 5.

Table 11.2. Crucial steps in military expenditure management in Ethiopia, Ghana, Kenya, Mali, Mozambique, Nigeria, Sierra Leone and South Africa: a summary of the country reports

Crucial steps	Ethiopia	Ghana	Kenya	Mali	Mozambique	Nigeria	Sierra Leone	South Africa
1. Strategic defence planning								
Analyse the security environment	Yes	No	Yes	Yes	Yes	Yes	Yes (since 2003)	Yes
Consider the constitutional and legal frameworks for military decision making	Yes	Yes	Yes	Yes	Yes	Yes	Yes	Yes
Identify the challenges before the military, usually in a defence White Paper	No White Paper	No White Paper	No White Paper	No White Paper	Yes[a]	No White Paper	Yes (in 2003)	Yes
Consider appropriate military capability	Yes, on an ad hoc basis only	Yes, on an ad hoc basis only	Yes, on an ad hoc basis only	Yes[b]	Yes	Yes, on an ad hoc basis only	Yes, on an ad hoc basis only	Yes
Define the size, shape and structure of the military	Yes	Yes[c]	Yes	Yes[d]	Yes	Yes[e]	Yes[f]	Yes
2. Determining what is affordable								
Authorities define the financial ceiling for the military sector within the overall national economic framework	Yes, but the ceiling is not firm[g]	Yes, but the ceiling is not firm	Yes, but the ceiling is not firm	Yes, but the ceiling is not firm	Yes[h]	Yes, but the ceiling is not firm	Yes	Yes[i]

3. Allocating resources

Allocate resources, prepare the military budget and defend it in parliament	Yes[j]	Yes[k]	Yes[l]	Yes[l]	Yes[m]	Yes	Yes	Yes

4. Using resources effectively and efficiently

Implement the planned activities	Partial implementation	Partial implementation	Partial implementation	Partial implementation	Yes[n]	Partial implementation	Yes[n]	Yes
Monitor the outputs	Rarely	Rarely	Rarely	Occasionally	Occasionally	Rarely	Rarely	Highly monitored
Account for expenditure	Occasionally	Rarely	Rarely	Rarely	Rarely	Rarely	Rarely	Yes
Evaluate and audit outputs, report results to parliament and the executive	No; audit reports usually years late	Rarely	No; audit reports usually years late	No	Yes	No; audit reports usually years late	No	Yes, regularly since 1994

[a] However, Mozambique has no strategic plans and programmes from which the annual budget would naturally evolve.
[b] Mali relies on the donation of military equipment.
[c] However, the Ghanaian military is smaller than the recommended size.
[d] Mali's paramilitary forces are included within these limits.
[e] There are conflicting reports of the size of the Nigerian armed forces
[f] A new army is being formed in Sierra Leone.
[g] This is the case even with the donor-imposed restrictions on military spending in Ethiopia.
[h] Mozambique has a donor-imposed limit on military spending of 2% of gross domestic product.
[i] South Africa's ceiling is set 18 months ahead and stays fairly constant.
[j] However, there is no proper scrutiny in the Ethiopian Parliament.
[k] The Ghanaian Parliament does not have the power to alter the budget.
[l] The parliaments of Kenya and Mali act merely as 'rubber stamps'.
[m] The Mozambican parliament's role is limited by donor restrictions on spending (see note h).
[n] There is significant donor presence in the implementation processes in Mozambique and Sierra Leone.

principles in each of the phases of military budgeting: formulation, approval, implementation and auditing.

Comprehensiveness

Apart from a lack of well-articulated strategic defence plans to guide their budgetary processes, the military budgets in all the sample countries, with the exception of South Africa, also lack comprehensiveness in terms of their coverage and the level of resources expected to be available to the military during the year.

The main reasons for a lack of comprehensiveness in military budgets in the countries include a lack of comprehensive regulatory laws for government revenues and how they should be dispensed; the absence of a definition of the scope of the military budget; the creation of special accounts by the state to deal with special situations; the non-inclusion of external military assistance in budget preparation; deliberate attempts by the executive to divert state resources for specific purposes; a lack of honesty in revenue (and expenditure) estimation; and the regular resort to supplementary appropriations. The existence of sources of income for the military other than the annual budget reduces the level of accountability and impinges on the level of transparency.

Although the governments in the countries in this study set annual spending ceilings for the military, as for every other sector, at the beginning of the annual budgetary process, the large off-budget revenues and expenditure in the military sector show that these ceilings are not at all firm. In Ethiopia, Ghana, Kenya, Mali and Nigeria there are a number of income-generating businesses, establishments and agencies related to the military whose incomes are not included in the budget but which have expenditure heads in the military budget each year.

One reason for this lack of comprehensiveness is the lack of any definition of the scope of the military budget: what should it include and what should it exclude? Arms procurement, which is a major part of the military budget and the most capital-intensive part of the budget, is seldom included in the military budgets of the sample countries, apart from South Africa. Yet they all buy military hardware, however infrequently. With a comprehensive budget and defence plan and programme, the cost of major acquisitions can be divided between several annual budgets, depending on the type of system. A lack of prioritization denies the countries this opportunity. Instead, they rush to purchase weapons when there is a perception of an urgent security need for them. This often has a negative impact on their finances and represents the greatest inducement for either off-budget spending on defence or diversion of resources from other sectors to the military.[7] This has happened repeatedly in Ethiopia

---

[7] For a discussion of off-budget spending see Hendrickson, D. and Ball, N., 'Off-budget military expenditure and revenue: issues and policy perspectives for donors', Conflict, Security and Development Group Occasional Papers no. 1, Department for International Development and King's College London, Jan. 2002, URL <http://csdg.kcl.ac.uk/>.

(and also in Rwanda and Uganda) since the late 1990s and in Nigeria since the early 1990s.[8]

Similarly, the cost of peacekeeping operations in West Africa—in which Nigeria has participated fairly regularly since the late 1980s and which consume a lot of its resources—has never been reflected in the military budget nor made explicitly clear in the national or overall budget. It has been estimated that the cost to Nigeria of its participation in the activities of the Economic Community of West African States (ECOWAS) Monitoring Group (ECOMOG) in Liberia and Sierra Leone in 1989–2000 was about $12 billion.[9] This is well above the total Nigerian military budget for this period.

In Ghana the low level of comprehensiveness is demonstrated by the extrabudgetary income that accrues to the military and which has never been brought into the budget. This includes the income from peacekeeping operations, which although small in dollar terms is substantial in local currency and, viewed against the annual military budget, is a huge source of income. The fact that Ghana is one of the most readily available countries for peacekeeping duties means that this source of income has been fairly regular. Other sources of income, such as those from the public use of military hospitals in Accra, have also not been included in the budget as revenue for the military.

The military budget in Kenya does not appear to account for all the financial operations of the Department of Defence (DOD). The cost of military equipment seems not to be included in the budget.[10] The fact that the Kenyan DOD is under the Office of the President ensures that it stands to benefit from the extrabudgetary expenditure to which the authorities regularly resort once the available funds fall short of the usually over-optimistic budget projections made at the beginning of the year. Although appropriations-in-aid (the military's expected income outside the budget) are always indicated in Kenya's annual budget estimates, there is little to suggest that they ultimately count towards the total military budget.[11]

The income from the commercial activities in which the Malian armed forces engage does not appear in the budget. These activities include its engineering works, air transport business and the military assembly repair shops.

In Mozambique the fact that the military budget is not transparent obstructs assessment of the extent of its comprehensiveness. What is known is that the military budget is 2 per cent of gross domestic product (GDP). Although Mozambique receives military assistance in the form of military training, supply of non-lethal equipment and technical assistance from China, Portugal and the USA, it is not clear whether this is included in the military budget.

---

[8] Omitoogun, W., 'Nigeria', *Military Expenditure Data in Africa: A Survey of Cameroon, Ethiopia, Ghana, Kenya, Nigeria and Uganda*, SIPRI Research Report no. 17 (Oxford University Press: Oxford, 2003), pp. 76–94.

[9] Dawkins, W. and Holman, M., 'Obasanjo, leader on a mission for a nation in debt', *Financial Times*, 15 Sep. 2000, p. 6. See also Omitoogun (note 8) and note 4.

[10] Omitoogun, W., 'Kenya', *Military Expenditure Data in Africa* (note 8), pp. 63–75.

[11] Mwenda and Gachocho (note 1), p. 37.

Box 11.1. The medium-term expenditure framework

The medium-term expenditure framework (MTEF) is a tool for linking policy, planning and budgeting over the medium term (usually three years). It is a process of decision making that consists of the top-down imposition of a financial ceiling consistent with macro-economic stability and broad policy priorities together with a bottom-up estimation of the medium-term costs of existing policies. It involves rolling over the exercise each year to reflect shifts in policy.

The MTEF is the last stage in a three-stage process. The preceding stages are: the formation of a medium-term financial framework—which is a statement of financial policy objectives and medium-term macroeconomic and financial targets and projections—and the medium-term budget framework in which the medium-term budget estimates for spending ministries, departments and agencies are made. The MTEF is where the budget estimates are linked to specific activity and output.

Increasingly, African governments are being encouraged to adopt the MTEF in their public expenditure management in order to achieve improved budget outcomes. However, only South Africa and Uganda have succeeded in institutionalizing MTEF principles into their public expenditure management systems. Other countries, such as Ghana and Kenya, have lapsed into old habits after initial progress. Among the reasons for the relapse are a lack of honesty and realism in revenue forecasting at the budget formulation stage and a lack of discipline at the implementation stage. A lack of policy objectives against which output and outcome can be measured is also a problem. The failure to integrate a medium-term perspective in the national budgetary process invariably affects planning in the military sector, where long-term planning is needed.

Sources: World Bank, 'Medium-term expenditure framework debate', URL <http://www1. worldbank.org/publicsector/pe/mtef.htm>; Oxford Policy Management (OPM), 'Medium term expenditure frameworks—panacea or dangerous distraction?', OPM Review Paper no. 2, Prepared for the World Bank, May 2000, URL <http://www1.worldbank.org/public sector/pe/mtef.htm>; and Holmes, M. with Evans, A., 'A review of experience in implementing medium term expenditure frameworks in a PRSP context: a synthesis of eight country studies', Oversees Development Institute, London, Nov. 2003, URL <http://www. odi.org.uk/pppg/cape/>.

In Nigeria the level of off-budget military expenditure is significant. There is a practice of providing for arms purchases outside the approved budget and without legislative approval. Although extra-budgetary spending in Nigeria does not apply to the military sector alone, military off-budget spending has been going on since the era of military rule and does not appear to have been mitigated by the return to democracy in 1999. Instead, new unbudgeted expenditure, which is not routed through the Nigerian Ministry of Defence (MOD), has been made by the executive on behalf of the military without consultation with the National Assembly.[12] Extra-budgetary spending and financial indiscipline were hallmarks of the democratic government in Nigeria during its first term in office, 1999–2003.[13]

---

[12] Olatuyi, J., 'Govt may go bankrupt by Dec. Kuta warns', *The Guardian* (Lagos), 1 Nov. 2002. See also chapter 8 in this volume.

[13] Okocha, C. and Umar, B., 'Financial indiscipline bane of govt—audit report', *ThisDay* (Lagos), 13 Jan. 2003, URL <http://www.thisdayonline.com/archive/2003/01/13/>. See also Eluemunor, T. and

Conversely, South Africa (and, to a lesser degree, Sierra Leone since 2000) has a comprehensive approach to military budgeting, with all the costs of its military activities included in the military budget. Box 11.1 describes the medium-term expenditure framework (MTEF), which has been used to good effect in South Africa. The strong involvement of external actors in the restructuring of Sierra Leone's military establishment, including its MOD, has had a great impact on the military budgetary process, and its budget is now more comprehensive.

Contestability

The principle of contestability in public expenditure management requires that all parts of the public sector compete on an equal footing for funding during budget planning and formulation. In theory, all the countries examined in this study adhere to the principle, especially since their return to democracy. One significant sign of this apparent adherence to the principle of contestability is the dominance of the finance ministries in the budget process. Since all minis-tries, departments and agencies (MDAs) have to pass through the same process of defending their expenditure estimates at the finance ministry, the latter exer-cises considerable control over the process. In practice, however, the political authorities have great influence on the process as finance ministries are forced to favour certain MDAs, of which the defence ministry is invariably one. This influence is exercised principally by exempting military budget estimates from cabinet-level debate. Instead, debate on defence issues (and sometimes national security) is limited to the national security committee, whose membership is highly restricted. The committee's decision is not open to cabinet-level debate in most cases or to parliamentary scrutiny.[14] Subsequent allocations to the defence ministry in either a supplementary budget or extra-budgetary allocation are treated similarly.

Apart from the influence exerted by the political authorities, the finance ministry itself often lacks an objective basis for streamlining expenditure esti-mates submitted by MDAs at budget defence meetings. This is the case because competition for funding by MDAs is not driven by policy. In the absence of any overarching national financial policy framework to drive budgetary allocations, the control that the finance ministry exercises on MDAs is arbitrary, and certain MDAs (with powerful and well-connected heads) are favoured at the expense of others. As a result, the finance ministry is feared rather than respected as an arbiter in the allocation of state resources. In Ghana the extent of authority over the process held by the country's Ministry of Finance (MOF) is reflected in the attitude of MOD officials who have to defend the military budget at the MOF; they take the defence of their estimates more seriously than when they defend the same estimates in Parliament during budget hearings. According to officials

Ezea, K., 'Auditor-General exposes multi-billion naira fraud: Presidency, Assembly, ministries involved', *Daily Independent*, 29 Mar. 2003.
  [14] On Kenya, e.g., see 'Clays's feat', *Africa Confidential*, vol. 45, no. 15 (July 2004), p. 7.

Table 11.3. Adherence to principles of public expenditure management in the formulation phase of military budgeting by Ethiopia, Ghana, Kenya, Mali, Mozambique, Nigeria, Sierra Leone and South Africa

Principle of public expenditure management	Low	Medium	High
Comprehensiveness: the budget encompasses all financial operations of government; off-budget expenditure and revenue are prohibited	Ethiopia, Ghana, Kenya, Mali, Mozambique, Nigeria	Sierra Leone	South Africa
Contestability: all sectors compete on an equal footing for funding during budget planning and formulation	Ethiopia, Kenya	Ghana, Mali, Mozambique, Nigeria, Sierra Leone	South Africa
Predictability: there is stability in policy and therefore a sectoral policy that informs the level of expenditure for the sector	Ethiopia, Ghana, Kenya, Mali→, Nigeria	Mozambique, Sierra Leone	South Africa
Honesty: the budget is derived from unbiased projections of revenue and expenditure	Ethiopia, Ghana, Kenya, Mali, Nigeria	Mozambique, Sierra Leone	South Africa
Discipline: decision making is restrained by resource realities; the budget absorbs only those resources necessary to implement policies; budget allocations are adhered to	Ethiopia, Ghana, Kenya, Mali, Nigeria	Mozambique, Sierra Leone	South Africa
Transparency: decision makers are aware of all relevant issues and information when making decisions	Ethiopia, Ghana, Kenya, Mali, Mozambique, Nigeria, Sierra Leone→	South Africa→	
Accountability: decision makers are responsible for exercising the authority provided to them	Ethiopia, Ghana, Kenya, Mali, Mozambique, Nigeria	Sierra Leone	South Africa
Legitimacy: policy makers who can change policies during implementation must take part in the formulation of, and agree to, the original plan			All

Note: → indicates that the country's adherence to the principle is improving.

of the Ghanaian MOD, the MOF is where their estimates can easily be cut down, whereas Parliament will only discuss whatever the MOF approves.[15]

This power of finance ministries is undermined by the knowledge of the defence ministries, and of the military in particular, that through their direct access to the highest level of authority they could easily resort to extra-budgetary means. This allows them to fund what they consider to be priority projects or, as is the case in most of the eight countries studied, to receive a special allocation from special government accounts to buy major weapons that are not included in the budget. In Ghana this is financed through peacekeeping funds and income from military businesses; in Nigeria it is through special or oil windfall accounts; in Kenya it is under contingencies funds held by the Office of the President; and in Ethiopia, where the activity is more difficult to pinpoint, it could be from the income-generating businesses of the military or specific hidden allocations in the budget.

Predictability

In addition to the general lack of comprehensiveness of the military budgets of the countries studied, there is also a lack of stability in the sector's policies and in the resources provided to achieve set goals, which creates problems for budgeting. The main reasons for this are: (*a*) inconsistent policies; (*b*) unstable and unreliable sources of income, including foreign assistance; (*c*) a lack of realism or honesty in revenue projection; and (*d*) irregular disbursement of approved funds at the implementation stage

The absence of any guiding defence policy in Ethiopia, Ghana, Kenya and Nigeria makes budgeting in the sector ad hoc, while long-term planning is what is required. In Ethiopia, for instance, while multi-year budget planning has been introduced in all other sectors based on sectoral policies, defence is excluded from the multi-year plan. Instead, military sector budgeting is based on 'zero budgeting', which means that budgets have to be prepared from scratch every year, driving out any medium-term perspective. Thus, there is little continuity and long-term planning. The situation is similar in both Ghana and Kenya. In Nigeria, on the other hand, while some of the long-term needs of the military are presented in the National Rolling Plan, these are rarely factored into the national budget. Moreover, the level of resources that is required in order to accomplish the goals of the plan is not made clear. However, the development of a new national defence policy is in progress; in the interim, budgeting in Nigeria remains ad hoc. These examples contrast sharply with the situation in South Africa, where there is a published and highly publicized defence policy as well as a defence review covering the details of the goals of the South African National Defence Force and the means for achieving them.[16]

[15] The Nigerian National Assembly is quite powerful and, as explained in chapter 8 in this volume, members of key committees have been bribed by ministers and heads of government agencies to increase their allocations during appropriations hearings.

[16] South African Department of Defence, 'Defence in a democracy: South African Defence Review 1998', Pretoria, 1998, URL <http://www.info.gov.za/documents/subjectdocs/subject/defence.htm>.

Table 11.4. Adherence to principles of public expenditure management in the approval phase of military budgeting by Ethiopia, Ghana, Kenya, Mali, Mozambique, Nigeria, Sierra Leone and South Africa

Principle of public expenditure management	Low	Medium	High
Comprehensiveness: the budget encompasses all financial operations of government; off-budget expenditure and revenue are prohibited	Ethiopia, Ghana, Kenya, Mali, Nigeria	Mozambique, Sierra Leone	South Africa
Predictability: there is stability in policy and therefore a sectoral policy that informs the level of expenditure for the sector	Ethiopia, Ghana, Kenya, Nigeria	Mozambique, Sierra Leone	South Africa
Transparency: decision makers are aware of all relevant issues and information when making decisions	Ethiopia, Ghana, Kenya, Mali, Mozambique→, Nigeria	Sierra Leone, South Africa	
Accountability: decision makers are responsible for exercising the authority provided to them	Ethiopia, Ghana→, Kenya, Mali	Nigeria, Mozambique, Sierra Leone	South Africa

Note: → indicates that the country's adherence to the principle is improving.

Even where a country has some form of policy and the elements of a medium-term planning system, as in Mali and Mozambique, instability in revenue makes planning difficult. Dependence on external assistance for budgetary support also makes funding of the programme over the medium-term problematic.[17]

The problem of unpredictable income is as much a reflection of the lack of reliable and regular sources of income as it is self-inflicted.[18] Many of the countries lack realism (or honesty) at the formulation stage of the budget, when revenues are estimated for the year. Certain countries, notably Kenya and sometimes Nigeria, have been known to make over-optimistic revenue forecasts at the beginning of the financial year only to announce midway during the year their inability to meet the revenue target and thus their need to cut back on certain approved activities.[19] This has a crippling effect on implementation as it makes it impossible to execute approved programmes. It is the principal reason

---

[17] Most external assistance for budget support usually excludes the military sector as a beneficiary. In fact, debate on aid fungibility always focuses on diversion of aid to the military.

[18] Holmes, M. with Evans, A., 'A review of experience in implementing medium term expenditure frameworks in a PRSP context: a synthesis of eight country studies', Oversees Development Institute, London, Nov. 2003, URL <http://www.odi.org.uk/pppg/cape/>.

[19] Mwenda and Gachocho (note 1).

(along with strong encouragement from donors) for the introduction of cash budgeting by some countries, in particular Ghana and Kenya. The main idea behind cash budgeting is that the country will spend only what it earns. This gives a lot of power to the finance ministry and the office of the president, which have to determine the manner in which revenues will be shared in case of any shortfall in projected income. This power has been used to favour certain ministries, of which the defence ministry is usually one. Indeed, it has been argued that under severe budgetary constraints African governments usually protect the defence allocation while cutting back on approved allocations to other sectors, especially the social sectors.[20] This is common practice in Kenya, as it was in Mali, Nigeria and Sierra Leone under military rule.[21]

In Nigeria in 2001–2003 a major feature of the budgetary process was the great deviation between the approved capital budget and the sum released; the latter was always less than the former. The main reason for this was not a shortfall in expected government revenue; rather, it was the government's own way of controlling graft among its civil servants. In most cases it was the funds allocated for development that were affected, either because they were not released at all or because they were reduced to a fraction of the original amount, about 5–20 per cent. In 2002 the Nigerian MOD received only 15 per cent of its approved capital votes and in 2003 only 20 per cent. This, of course, had a negative impact on budget implementation.

South Africa remains the only country with a clear and tested military sector policy, with goals set over the medium and long terms and with the resources to achieve them. Although some of the objectives set in terms of the ratios of the annual budget that go to certain expenditure heads, such as personnel costs, have not been met, the country has made considerable progress in its planned activities on the basis of its defence policy and defence review exercise.

Honesty

While all the countries studied have tried to correct their lack of comprehensiveness and predictability with the introduction of multi-year planning systems, the new systems are severely weakened by a lack of realism and honesty in planning and revenue estimation. In spite of the annual shortfalls in projected revenues, the countries fail to face up to the realities of resource constraints. Instead, they persist in making high, unrealizable revenue projections and high expenditure plans which ultimately have to be scaled back.[22] In the specific case of the military sector, in order to boost income to the sector this

[20] Gyimah-Brempong, K., 'Do African governments favor defense in budgeting?', *Journal of Peace Research*, vol. 29, no. 2 (May 1992), pp. 191–206.

[21] On Kenya see Kenyan Ministry of Planning and National Development (MPND), *Public Expenditure Review 2003* (MPND: Nairobi, 2004), URL <http://www.planning.go.ke/pdf/per.pdf>, pp. 122–24. On Nigeria see chapter 8 in this volume. Other countries, such as Rwanda and Uganda, have also engaged in the practice.

[22] See Holmes with Evans (note 18).

Table 11.5. Adherence to principles of public expenditure management in the implementation phase of military budgeting by Ethiopia, Ghana, Kenya, Mali, Mozambique, Nigeria, Sierra Leone and South Africa

Principle of public expenditure management	Low	Medium	High
Comprehensiveness: the budget encompasses all financial operations of government; off-budget expenditure and revenue are prohibited	Ethiopia, Ghana, Kenya, Mali, Nigeria	Mozambique, Sierra Leone	South Africa
Contestability: all sectors compete on an equal footing for funding during budget planning and formulation	Ethiopia, Kenya, Ghana, Mali, Mozambique, Nigeria	Sierra Leone, South Africa→	
Predictability: there is stability in policy and therefore a sectoral policy that informs the level of expenditure for the sector	Ethiopia, Ghana, Kenya, Mali, Nigeria	Mozambique, Sierra Leone	South Africa
Transparency: decision makers are aware of all relevant issues and information when making decisions	Ethiopia, Ghana, Kenya, Mali, Mozambique, Nigeria	Sierra Leone, South Africa→	
Accountability: decision makers are responsible for exercising the authority provided to them	Ethiopia, Ghana, Kenya, Mali→, Nigeria	Mozambique, Sierra Leone, South Africa→	

Note: → indicates that the country's adherence to the principle is improving.

weakness manifests itself in underestimation of income (especially internally generated revenue) and overestimation of expenditure.

In Ethiopia, Ghana, Kenya and Mali the expected income of the military (outside the official budgetary allocations) is understated or is not factored into the military budget at all. This leaves more income at the disposal of the military. When there is any shortfall in income, several planned programmes suffer, but the military sector, owing to its perceived special nature, is almost always immune from any general cutback, making it better resourced than other parts of the public sector.[23]

Since most of the countries in this study have no serious guiding policy for military budgeting, projections of expenditure are often exaggerated. There are two ways in which this can be done: by inflating the number of personnel in the armed forces in order to receive additional allocations and by requesting

---

[23] Gyimah-Brempong (note 20). See also Mohammed, N. A. L., 'Militarization in Sudan: trends and determinants', *Armed Forces and Society*, vol. 19, no. 3 (1993), pp. 411–33.

unneeded expenditure items or military equipment.[24] This exaggeration ensures that a high estimate of the military budget is presented to the government. This is done for two reasons. The first is to guard against arbitrary cuts in the military budget by the finance ministry, which has responsibility for reining in the budget estimates of MDAs in the absence of any guiding policy. This is ostensibly in the corporate interest of the military.[25]

The second reason relates directly to the individuals in charge of the military: to ensure that enough funds are available to line private pockets. In Nigeria under the regime of Sani Abacha (1993–98), 500 million naira (*c.* $62 million) was approved for the construction of the headquarters in Abuja of one of the intelligence agencies. Rather than being used for its intended purpose, however, the money simply disappeared into the pockets of those at the highest level of authority.[26] Similarly, conflicting figures have over the years been presented for the size of the Nigerian armed forces. While at the inception of civilian rule in 1999 the new Minister of Defence cited downsizing as a major goal of his administration, a year after taking over he backtracked and said that he had not done enough research before making his initial pronouncement on downsizing and that, after all, the size of the military was appropriate for a country of Nigeria's size and external commitments.[27] His volte-face was generally thought to be a result of the stiff opposition from vested interests in the military who benefit from the status quo.

In Ethiopia the size of the military may be a source of income to fund other aspects of the military budget through the earmarking of a larger than normal allocation for the cost of personnel. This would raise little suspicion from donors. In most of the eight countries studied, personnel costs take more than 70 per cent of the military budget.[28] However, the true strength of the military in most of the countries is not known as very few have conducted any staff audit of their armed forces. Even those parliaments that approve the budgets for the military do not know the exact strength of the armed forces for which they vote money annually.[29]

---

[24] E.g., at the inception of the new democratic government in Nigeria in 1999, the armed forces were asked to submit a list of their urgent needs. The list included hardware that was considered inappropriate for their level of training and for the security environment. See Goldman, A., 'Out of office but still in the picture', *Financial Times*, 30 Mar. 2000.

[25] However, military hierarchies have rarely defended the military as an institution, even under military regimes. For a discussion of African militaries and military coups see Luckham, R., 'The military, militarisation and democratisation in Africa: a survey of literature and issues', eds E. Hutchful and A. Bathily, *The Military and Militarism in Africa* (Codesria: Dakar, 1998), pp. 1–47.

[26] Personal communication with the author, Abuja, May 2002.

[27] Oloja, M., Eluemnuor, T. and Onuorah, M., 'Govt drops plan to trim military', *The Guardian* (Lagos), 24 Dec. 2000.

[28] Omitoogun (note 8). South Africa is an exception.

[29] E.g., Personal communications of a Nigerian parliamentarian with the author, Abuja, May 2002. Another Nigerian parliamentarian, Haruna Yerima, openly admitted the same shortcoming in the National Assembly's work on the military budget at the symposium on Parliamentary Oversight of the Security Sector in West Africa organized by the Geneva Center for Democratic Control of Armed Forces, Abuja, 20 Apr. 2004. Yerima later alleged in a television interview that a lot of bribery took place in the National

Table 11.6. Adherence to principles of public expenditure management in the auditing phase of military budgeting by Ethiopia, Ghana, Kenya, Mali, Mozambique, Nigeria, Sierra Leone and South Africa

Principle of public expenditure management	Low	Medium	High
Comprehensiveness: the budget encompasses all financial operations of government; off-budget expenditure and revenue are prohibited	Ghana, Kenya, Mali→, Nigeria	←Ethiopia, Mozambique, Sierra Leone	South Africa
Predictability: there is stability in policy and therefore a sectoral policy that informs the level of expenditure for the sector	Ethiopia, Ghana, Kenya, Nigeria	Mali, Mozambique, Sierra Leone	South Africa
Transparency: decision makers are aware of all relevant issues and information when making decisions	Ethiopia, Ghana, Kenya, Mali, Nigeria	←Mozambique, Sierra Leone	South Africa
Accountability: decision makers are responsible for exercising the authority provided to them	Ethiopia, Kenya, Nigeria	Ghana, Mali, Mozambique, Sierra Leone, South Africa	

Note: → and ← indicate the direction in which the country is moving on the principle.

In their dealings with the executive on military budgets, most parliaments across the sample countries have been known to engage in collusion to hide the true costs of military activities from the general public and donors of economic assistance. One reason for this is the perceived need to prevent public criticism about 'excessive' spending on defence. Another is the need to give the impression of relatively low spending on defence in order to satisfy donors of economic aid who make aid conditional on low military budgets. In countries such as Mozambique (and also Uganda), where donors have placed ceilings on military spending, the government struggles to fulfil donor conditions and at the same time meet urgent security needs; often, the two goals are incompatible. The result is that all sorts of techniques are used to hide military expenditure, including off-budget expenditure either with the collaboration of the parliament or through manipulation at the finance ministry. Most aid-dependent countries in this study do this, especially Ethiopia, Kenya and Mali and to some extent Mozambique.

South Africa, however, has been positive in its application of the principle of honesty in its budgetary process. Its programmes are based on the defence

Assembly, thus sparking the 'bribe-for-budget' scandal which led to the dismissal of the Minister of Education and the removal of the President of the Senate. For details see chapter 8 in this volume.

policy and the outcome of the defence review process, so there is a solid basis for budgeting. In addition, the MTEF ensures that the cost of major equipment is spread over a period of time. Since the military does not have any income other than what is allocated from the national budget, the principle of honesty is adhered to. The single exception is the payment for the rent and maintenance of state property used by the military, which appears in the budget of the Department of Public Works; this constitutes a subsidy for the military.

Discipline

A common characteristic of most governments in Africa is the lack of financial discipline, especially in relation to security expenditure. Owing to a lack of policy, comprehensiveness and realism at the formulation stage of the budget, governments often find it difficult to adhere to budget allocations made at the beginning of the year. Since they want to protect the military budget, a shortfall in projected revenue or an urgent security crisis often results in either the raiding of the other sectors' budgets or resort to extra-budgetary expenditure for the military's benefit. In Nigeria under the regime of Ibrahim Babangida (1985–93), the use of supplementary budgets became a constant feature of the budgetary process, with the military sector almost always being the greatest beneficiary. Similarly, in Kenya, in spite of the fact that the military sector usually receives the second or third largest allocation, it is also one of the sectors that regularly overspends allocated budgets.[30] Until the introduction there of medium-term planning in the late 1990s, Mali also had a habit of over-shooting the military budget at the expense of other ministries.

A particular feature of the lack of discipline in the budgetary process is that the decision to allocate extra funds to defence usually emanates from the highest political authorities, where the initial military spending decisions were made. This could simply be a result of the lack of policy to guide defence activities, including budgeting, which affects budget comprehensiveness at the formulation stage. More important than a lack of policy, however, is perhaps a lack of political will on the part of the authorities to take tough decisions, especially decisions that will streamline military sector activities in line with national economic realities. The disproportionate allocation to defence in Ethiopia (until 2003) at the expense of other parts of the public sector is an example of this.

Transparency

The level of transparency in all the phases of the budget cycle is low in most of the sample countries, resulting in a huge accountability deficit. One reason for this is the highly restricted number of people involved in the decision-making process; this is a consequence of the entrenched belief that the military sector is a special case that requires a high level of confidentiality since it is central to

[30] MPND (note 21).

the defence of the state. Yet the issue of confidentiality is often overblown, not only in Africa but also in the developed world, in order to deny access to information to those expected to exercise oversight of the sector. As explained in chapter 2, confidentiality need not mean lack of transparency or lack of oversight. It simply requires agreement, through legislation, on what should and should not be kept secret and regulations for a classification and clearance system for those who will exercise oversight of the specifically confidential portion of the military budget or plans.[31] There is a need to explain why confidentiality is needed, what is being kept confidential and what arrangements for accountability are being put in place to check abuse.

In the meantime, the notion of defence as being a special case and requiring the utmost secrecy still prevails across the sample countries, resulting in a narrow decision-making process and the denial of access to information even to crucial actors in the process at the defence ministries, especially the civilian members. Sometimes even unit commanders are excluded from the decision-making process. Decision making is concentrated in a very small circle of people, consisting in some cases of only the service chiefs, the head of government and the defence minister. This is the case in many countries under military rule, and the situation has not changed much after a return to democracy in Ethiopia, Ghana, Kenya, Mali and Nigeria. The myth that secrecy is needed is given official sanction by laws which ensure that revealing information without permission may result in severe disciplinary measures.

The confidentiality issue has been the main reason for the lack of scrutiny of arms procurement in Africa. Recent revelations about security-related procurement in Kenya are further examples of this problem.[32]

The closed nature of the decision-making process prevents proper coordination with other sectors that are critical to state security, especially given the ever-changing nature of the threats faced by states. Increasingly, threats to states are internal rather than external, which makes proper coordination with the internal affairs ministry a logical way in which to frame an all-encompassing budget. Police-related activities in which military participation is required must be identified and costed through such coordination. In addition, the increasing involvement of most of the eight countries in peace operations requires coordination with the foreign affairs ministries. However, the closed nature of decision making makes this impossible, leading to defective planning and, ultimately, off-budget spending on, for example, peacekeeping missions.

During the legislative phase, when transparency is critical to facilitate parliamentary scrutiny and approval, the executives in the sample countries provide little information. Nor is there evidence of public participation in the process. While in all the countries in this study the executives submit information on the budget, it is either too scant to be useful for proper parliamentary scrutiny, as is

---

[31] See chapter 2 for full details; and Ball, N., Bouta, T. and Goor, L. van de, *Enhancing Democratic Governance of the Security Sector: An Institutional Assessment Framework* (Ministry of Foreign Affairs: The Hague, 2003), URL <http://www.clingendael.nl/cru/>, p. 35.

[32] 'Clay's feat' (note 14).

the case in Ethiopia, Ghana and Nigeria, or much too detailed but containing little useful information, as is the case in Kenya.

South Africa is the only country which has enshrined the principle of transparency in its constitution and which has legislation to give practical meaning to this principle. This legislation strictly regulates the process and is adhered to by all those involved.[33] However, the arguments used to justify the country's Strategic Defence Procurement Package show that even here the level of transparency is insufficient. In retrospect, it appears that the implications of the built-in payback mechanisms, such as the offset scheme that made the programme attractive to the legislators who approved the scheme, were not fully understood. This shows that the information provided was not clear enough for its purpose. The corruption allegations that have dogged some of the principal actors in the deal also show a lack of sufficient transparency.[34] Notwithstanding these shortcomings, South Africa's transparency level still stands well above that of the other countries examined in this study.

Accountability

In most of the countries in this study, the level of accountability in the military budgetary process is affected by a lack of transparency and the existence of strong informal networks—within the defence ministry in particular and in the public sector generally. The decisions leading to the final military budget are not necessarily made in the offices created to formulate the budgets; at best they perform only peripheral roles in the process. Hence, it is difficult to identify those to hold accountable in cases of policy failure or an inability to deliver on promises made in the budget. For example, while the Chief Director of the Ghanaian MOD and the Deputy Secretary in the Kenyan DOD are the chief accounting officers for their respective departments, the main power for making the budget in these two countries lies with members of the military: the Defence Financial Comptroller in Ghana and the Chief of General Staff in Kenya. The chief accounting officers are thus subordinated to the military, yet it is the former who are held accountable while defending the budget estimates and during the audit process. Such lack of clarity in roles and responsibilities or lack of adherence to rules makes accountability difficult, not least at the formulation stage.

Even in countries where the rules are clear and an officeholder is held responsible for mismanagement of funds in his or her care, the law is not allowed to run its full course. For example, a former Permanent Secretary of the Nigerian MOD was apprehended for corruption when he allegedly sold the ministry's property. He was charged in court but, before the law could take its full course, the government decided to withdraw from the case, thus allowing him to go

---

[33] Public Finance Management Act (Act 1 of 1999 as amended by Act 29 of 1999), 2 Mar. 1999, URL <http://www.info.gov.za/documents/acts/index.htm>.
[34] See chapter 10 in this volume.

unpunished; he was merely relieved of his duties and suspended from service.[35] This contrasts sharply with the jailing of a former head of the South African Parliament's defence committee who was found guilty of taking bribes in the course of negotiating the country's Strategic Defence Procurement Package.

A legislature that wants to carry out its oversight functions can still be hamstrung by the ambiguity of the law in relation to the extent of its powers or by the limited power conferred on it by the constitution. In either case, it becomes difficult to hold the legislature accountable for lapses in the budgetary process. In Ghana, legislative power over the budgetary process is very limited: Parliament can review the revenue projections but cannot change the estimates provided by the executive, which makes it a mere talking shop. It is no surprise therefore that the MOD officials in Ghana take the annual defence of their budget estimates at the MOF more seriously than that in Parliament. Some have argued, however, that the seeming impotence of the Ghanaian Parliament is due more to its failure to exercise the parliamentary right to scrutiny than any lack of constitutional provision for it to effectively discharge its duties.[36]

In other instances the law is even less clear on the extent of the legislature's power. While the Nigerian National Assembly assumes that it has powers to amend both projected revenues and expenditure upwards or downwards and even to adjust the internal composition of budget heads, the executive claims that the Assembly's power is limited to an adjustment of total expenditure or a downward adjustment of revenue since, according to the executive, it cannot adjust what it does not earn. Thus, in Nigeria it is difficult to identify whom to hold accountable when the budgetary process is poor. In other countries where the powers are very clear and the legislators have the authority to adjust the budget, they have been reluctant to demand details. Thus, in Ethiopia, Kenya and Mali they have not been as effective as might be expected. The negative impact of long years of one-party dictatorships that brooked no opposition and the overbearing presence of the executive in the budgetary process are still evident.

Overall legislative oversight of the military budget across the case studies, apart from South Africa, is weak. The dominance of the parliaments in most of the countries by a single party does not appear to aid positive development of the oversight functions of the legislature. The ruling party often demands acquiescence from its legislators when the executive requires approval of initiatives, including budget proposals. The parliament therefore becomes a tool of the executive rather than a check on the executive's powers. As a result the public perception across the countries studied is that the parliament is a lackey of the executive. Legislative oversight is discussed further in section IV.

---

[35] Reference is often made to this case by those who believe that the current anti-corruption crusade of President Obasanjo is selective. See, e.g., 'Graft: Obasanjo has drawn the dagger', *ThisDay* (Lagos), 6 Apr. 2005, URL <http://www.thisdayonline.com/nview.php?id=13762>.

[36] Fölscher, A., 'Transparency and participation in the budget process: a cross-country synthesis', ed. A. Fölscher, *Budget Transparency and Participation: Five Africa Case Studies* (Idasa: Cape Town, 2003), URL <http://www.idasa.org.za/>, p. 23.

In the implementation phase, in spite of official regulations clearly desig-
nating chief accounting officers and other responsible officers within the
defence ministry, excessive centralization of authority (sometimes in contra-
vention of rules), unclear roles and responsibilities, and informal networks
within the ministry often create a dysfunctional system with no one to hold
accountable for poor implementation of approved programmes. While the
informal channels may not always work to the detriment of the formal decision-
making process, they may easily be abused. The implementation of projects is
also hampered by a lack of regard for established rules for the disbursement of
funds.

In Ethiopia, Ghana, Kenya and Mali there is an over-concentration of power
in bodies other than the respective defence ministries and a lack of effective
punitive measures for offending officials. For instance, in Ethiopia the apparent
over-concentration of power and responsibilities in both the Ministry of
Finance and Economic Development and the Office of the Prime Minister does
not allow for proper accountability as they are not directly involved in the day-
to-day running of the armed forces. Major decisions affecting the spending
level of the Ministry of National Defence are taken elsewhere and there is evidence of a lack of proper coordination between those making decisions for the
military and the (civilian) head of the Budget Department in the Ministry of
National Defence.

In Ghana the over-concentration of authority—including spending powers—
in General Headquarters denies commanders the benefit of being responsible
for the services and units they control and diminishes accountability in the military sector in general. The Ghana Armed Forces has arrears for basic utilities of
billions of cedis (tens of millions of dollars) and no one takes responsibility for
this backlog when these services are budgeted for annually.

In Mali accountability in the budget implementation process is limited.
Although the chief accounting officer is the Minister of Defence and Veterans,
he delegates the power to the ministry's Director of Administration and
Finance. Unlike the other sectors in Mali, where internal accountants are
employed to see to the effective management of resources, in the armed forces
this is done through the appointment of an external accountant, ostensibly to
ensure the prudent management of resources. However, in practice the Ministry
of Defence and Veterans is not accountable to the accounting section of the
Supreme Court, which should audit the final accounts of all ministries and
whose approval is needed before payments can be authorized in the following
year. The ministry can thus act with impunity in financial matters as there is
limited control over its activities.

The situation in South Africa is much better than in the other countries in the
study. The level of accountability is high as there are rules guiding the process.
More important than the rules, however, is the willingness on the part of the

authorities to prosecute anyone who violates them in the process of budgeting.[37] The level of compliance with the rules and regulations guiding the process has been high and this has had a corresponding effect on the level of accountability. The principle of delegation is followed strictly and all portions of the budget are the responsibility of those to whom they are allotted. Sierra Leone has also been following this pattern since 2000, although the influence of donors on the process is considerable. The new system of delegating the powers of the MOD Director-General to implement the budget to those directly under this post in the chain of command and then down to the lowest officers means that anyone can be held responsible for the part of the budget that is placed in his or her trust.

Arms procurement

Arms procurement is a significant, strategic component of the military budget. However, with the exception of South Africa, it is often excluded from the budgets of the countries in this study. One argument employed by many of these countries is that they buy little military equipment. That is true, but they do nonetheless occasionally buy hardware or renovate existing equipment. The military budget that passes through the legislature rarely contains provision for this expenditure or, where it does, the funds assigned are not indicated as being for military equipment. Ethiopian military procurement is rarely reflected in the military budget, yet the country regularly purchases military hardware.[38] Similarly, the military in Nigeria has purchased military equipment without parliamentary approval or the knowledge of the MOD.[39]

All the countries studied have formal rules for military procurement that are not very different from the procurement procedures in the other ministries: the use of tender boards for goods (including military equipment) of more than a certain value and the encouragement of open, competitive bids from contractors. This tendering takes place after the military procurement committee has requested the items, having judged that they are in line with the country's strategic needs. The procurement committee then considers the bids, evaluates them and draws up the contract that is then signed by the minister.

In practice, procurement for both major and minor purchases represents the least transparent component of the military budget and is the most susceptible to corruption.[40] At one point in the 1980s virtually every top military officer in

---

[37] See chapter 10 in this volume; and, e.g., Philips, B., 'Jail term for ANC man', BBC News Online, 19 Mar. 2003, URL <http://news.bbc.co.uk/2/2863531.stm>.

[38] Military spending in Ethiopia is classified as recurrent expenditure following the UN's classification system. The system permits the reporting of spending on military hardware under recurrent expenditure, but it should be indicated as such for clarity.

[39] Olatuyi (note 12).

[40] Gupta, S., Mello, L. and Sharan, R., 'Corruption and military spending', eds T. G. Abed and S. Gupta, *Governance, Corruption and Economic Performance* (International Monetary Fund: Washington, DC, 2002), p. 316.

the Nigerian military was soliciting for contracts for his foreign agents.[41] This situation led to misleading advice on what to buy for the military as each top officer was a front for the overseas contractors who were his paymasters. Ghana had a similar experience with military procurement.

One implication of the poor arms procurement procedures is the overpricing of military hardware because of kickbacks and, of course, the purchase of inappropriate weapons. The purchase of a frigate for the Nigerian Navy in the 1980s was due as much to inter-service rivalry as to the hefty cheques for those who brokered the deal. The purchase of helicopters for the Uganda Peoples' Defence Force in 1998 was similarly motivated by the corrupt deal made by those who negotiated the purchase.[42] The botched 2003 deal for military aircraft involving Kenya and the Czech Republic was also motivated by graft as the Kenya Air Force, for which the planes were meant, had rejected them before the defence minister secretly renegotiated the deal without the air force's knowledge and without parliamentary approval. Tanzania's failed attempt to purchase a radar system from BAE Systems was also done secretly, outside the budget and without the knowledge of the National Assembly. It was only made public by the World Bank, which refused to sanction the deal.[43]

When such a huge part of military spending is not included in the military budget, not only is it difficult to exercise control over resources used for that purpose, but it is also open to corruption. Even in South Africa, which includes the details of procurement for its armed forces in the budget document and makes information on the ongoing Special Defence Procurement Package available to the general public, allegations of corruption have dogged these programmes.[44]

The role of the auditor-general in the budgetary process

The auditing phase of the budgetary process should involve an assessment of the extent to which the approved money was spent for the stated purposes. The auditor-general's annual report is the main instrument for doing this.

The auditing phase is the responsibility of both the auditor-general's office and the legislature, which is supposed to act on the report of the auditor-general. There is no doubt, however, that the primary responsibility here rests with the auditor-general and his or her staff. As a result, the most important question about this phase is the extent of any constitutionally guaranteed power of the auditor-general. Other relevant questions concern the timeliness of the

[41] Adekanye, J. B., *The Retired Military as Emergent Power Factor in Nigeria* (Heinemann Educational Books: Ibadan, 1999), in particular chapter 3, 'The military–business complex'; and Adekanye, J. B., Personal communications with the author, Ibadan, June 2003.

[42] Omitoogun, W., 'Uganda', *Military Expenditure Data in Africa* (note 8), pp. 95–108. See especially p. 103, fn. 27.

[43] Hencke, D., Denny, C. and Elliot, L., 'Tanzania aviation deal "a waste of money"', *The Guardian*, 14 June 2002, URL <http://www.guardian.co.uk/>.

[44] See section V of chapter 10 in this volume for more details of the corruption allegations and the subsequent investigative report.

report and the extent to which the parliament acts on it, and the access of the auditor-general to the necessary information.

The power of the auditor-general

The power of the auditor-general is guaranteed in the constitutions of all eight countries studied, but the extent of that power varies from country to country, especially in relation to the processes of appointment and dismissal and the manner in which the annual report is submitted.

The auditor-general's powers are weakest in Kenya, owing to the manner in which the audit report is submitted. The Controller and Auditor-General has no power to protest about the content of the report submitted to Parliament on his behalf if the Minster of Finance alters the content. The Kenyan DOD, which is situated within the Office of the President, certainly receives good cover in this respect. Several allegations of impropriety in arms deals, for both the police and the armed forces, have never been pursued in the audit reports, nor has the purchase of unbudgeted sophisticated military equipment purportedly bought for the police ever been investigated.

In all the other countries in the study the role of the auditor-general is fairly clear and his or her independence is guaranteed. However, in certain cases the executive has sacked uncompromising auditors-general. In 2001 the first audit of the accounts of the federal government of Nigeria under civilian administration was carried out.[45] The Auditor-General's report was critical of the government in many areas, including revenue collection. The government condemned the report for being too harsh and 'political' since the Auditor-General undertook a value-for-money audit instead of the traditional ordinary audit. The Auditor-General was then fired on the grounds that he was only there in an acting capacity. This raises a fundamental question about how the Auditor-General in Nigeria (and elsewhere) is appointed and dismissed.

Parliament as oversight institution

The parliament is also crucial as an oversight body. In the case of South Africa, where the powers of Parliament are quite strong, parliamentarians' understanding of the several aspects of the military budget enables them to ask relevant questions, which DOD staff have to consider when making the budget. The only factor limiting the effectiveness of the South African Parliament is the fact that a large majority of its members belong to the ruling party.

In other legislatures, however, there have been two main problems. First is the lateness in the presentation of the auditor-general's report, which can be up to five years, as in Ethiopia and Nigeria, or, more commonly, two to three years, as in Ghana and Kenya. It is only in South Africa that the report is

---

[45] Federal Republic of Nigeria, *Auditor-General's Report on the Accounts of Government of the Federation of Nigeria for the Year Ended 31st December, 2000*, part 1 (Office of the Auditor-General for the Federation: Abuja, Dec. 2001).

released on schedule. Second, when the report is eventually submitted to the parliament, it is usually too late for remedial action to be taken for the next financial year and, more importantly, those found negligent are not punished.

Access to information

The amount of available information and the access of the auditor-general to that information also varies from country to country. In most cases the auditor-general is given only partial access to information on the military. The more capital-intensive part of the budget involving military hardware is excluded on grounds of confidentiality.

In Ghana the auditors have been prevented on grounds of security from undertaking a physical inspection of military hardware that is purported to have been purchased. In Mali, while the formal powers of the auditors are broad, in reality they are usually prevented from properly inspecting the accounts of the military. In Ethiopia the auditors have no powers with regard to military accounts on the grounds of national security, although it is claimed in a World Bank report that the Office of the Federal Auditor-General focuses on the accounts of 'those institutions with high budget allocations';[46] the Ministry of National Defence is presumably one such institution.

In South Africa the evaluation and control mechanisms available to monitor output and require value-for-money services from the military sector are perhaps the most effective elements of the military budgetary process. The Office of the Auditor-General is well staffed and an annual audit of the DOD is carried out. The result of the audit is promptly released and is made available both in the annual report of the DOD and on its website. The present Auditor-General has been quite critical of the government or the DOD when waste or deficiency has been noticed in the delivery of its services. He was the first to draw attention to the hidden costs in the Strategic Defence Procurement Package, as he argued that several uncosted expenses would eventually make the bill for the package several billion rand higher than originally planned.[47]

III. Categorizing the case studies

On the basis of certain observable characteristics, the eight countries in this study can be classified according to whether their level of adherence to the principles of public expenditure management is low, medium or high. The performance of the countries is summarized in tables 11.3–11.6.

---

[46] World Bank, *Ethiopia: Country Financial Accountability Assessment*, vol. 1, *Main Report*, World Bank Report no. 26092-ET (World Bank: Washington, DC, 17 June 2003), URL <http://www.worldbank.org/et/>, p. 32.

[47] Engelrecht, L., 'South African MPs left cold by arms deal', Defence Systems Daily, 16 Oct. 2000, URL <http://defence-data.com/>, also available at URL <http://www.armsdeal-vpo.co.za/articles00/mps_left_cold.html>.

Table 11.7. The deviation between the approved budget and actual expenditure on the military sector in Ethiopia, Ghana, Kenya, Mali, Mozambique, Nigeria, Sierra Leone and South Africa, 1999–2003

Country (currency)	Year[a]	Approved budget	Actual expenditure[b]	Deviation (%)
Ethiopia	1999	2 400	5 589	*133*
(m. birr)	2000	5 500	5 075	*–8*
	2001	3 000	3 154	*5*
	2002	3 000	3 000	*0*
	2003	2 130	2 565	*20*
Ghana	1999	158 000	158 060	*0*
(m. cedis)	2000	219 330	277 269	*26*
	2001	231 740	..	..
	2002	297 800	..	..
	2003	439 200	..	..
Kenya	1999	10 503	10 788	*3*
(m. shillings)	2000	12 347	14 439	*17*
	2001	14 948	16 258	*9*
	2002	15 835	17 430	*10*
	2003	18 726	19 921	*6*
Mali	1999	33.3	35.9	*8*
(b. CFA francs)	2000	34.3	41.4	*21*
	2001	34.1	43.8	*28*
	2002	35.5	44.7	*26*
	2003	40.6	47.3	*17*
Mozambique	1999	1 246	1 246	*0*
(b. meticais)	2000	1 414	1 423	*1*
	2001	1 718	1 778	*3*
	2002	2 095	1 960	*–6*
	2003	2 466	..	..
Nigeria	1999	37 189	45 400	*22*
(m. naira)	2000	37 692	37 490	*–1*
	2001	50 628	63 472	*25*
	2002	59 339	64 908	*9*
	2003	76 890	..	..
Sierra Leone	1999	..	..	..
(m. leones)	2000	55 000	..	..
	2001	37 868	..	..
	2002	33 371	..	..
	2003	39 000	..	..
South Africa	1999	10 717	10 717	*0*
(m. rand)	2000	13 802	13 932	*1*
	2001	15 803	16 045	*2*
	2002	18 414	18 835	*2*
	2003	20 286	19 905	*–2*

a Years are financial years, except for the case of Ethiopia, where they are calendar years.

b Actual expenditure here refers to official statistics (including International Monetary Fund figures in the case of Mozambique) on what government officially spent, as opposed to the approved budget. It may not reflect real government expenditure.

Sources: **Ethiopia**: Central Statistical Authority, *Statistical Abstract* (Central Statistical Authority: Addis Ababa, various years); and SIPRI military expenditure database. **Ghana**: Republic of Ghana, *Budget Statement and Economic Policy of the Government of Ghana* (Ghana Publishing Cooperation: Accra, various years); and Ghanaian Parliament, *Parliamentary Debates* (Accra), 2000, 2001 and 2002. **Kenya**: Central Bureau of Statistics, *Statistical Abstract* (Central Bureau of Statistics: Nairobi, various years); Central Bureau of Statistics, *Economic Survey* (Central Bureau of Statistics: Nairobi, various years); and Kenyan Ministry of Planning and National Development (MPND), *Public Expenditure Review 2003* (MPND: Nairobi, 2004), URL <http://www.planning.go.ke/pdf/per.pdf>. **Mali**: Lois de finances [Finance acts], *Journal Officiel* (Bamako), 1999–2003; and International Monetary Fund, 'Mali: poverty reduction strategy paper', Country Report no. 03/39, 27 Feb. 2003, URL <http://www.imf. org/>. **Mozambique**: International Monetary Fund, 'Republic of Mozambique: 2002 Article IV consultation, fourth review under the Poverty Reduction and Growth Facility and request for an extension of the Poverty Reduction and Growth Facility arrangement', Country Report no. 02/140, 3 June 2002, URL <http://www.imf.org/>; and International Monetary Fund, 'Republic of Mozambique: fifth review under the poverty reduction and growth facility and request for waiver of performance criterion', Country Report no. 03/288, 5 June 2003, URL <http://www.imf.org/>. **Nigeria**: Federal Republic of Nigeria, *Government of the Federal Republic of Nigeria Approved Budget* (Budget Office: Abuja, various years); Central Bank of Nigeria, *Annual Report and Statement of Accounts* (Central Bank of Nigeria: Abuja, 2001 and 2002), URL <http://www.cenbank.org/documents/>; and SIPRI military expenditure database. **Sierra Leone**: International Monetary Fund, 'Sierra Leone: fourth review under the three-year arrangement under the Poverty Reduction and Growth Facility and requests for waiver of performance criteria and extension of arrangement, and additional interim assistance under the Enhanced Initiative for Heavily Indebted Poor Countries', Country Report no. 04/49, 3 Mar. 2004, URL <http://www.imf.org/>. **South Africa**: National Treasury, *Estimates of National Expenditure* (National Treasury: Pretoria, various years), URL <http://www.finance.gov.za/>.

According to the World Bank, one standard measure of the degree of adherence to the principles of public expenditure management is the extent of deviation between approved budget and actual expenditure. Table 11.7 shows the degree of this deviation in the military expenditure of the sample countries. The deviations are highest in Ethiopia, Ghana, Kenya, Mali and Nigeria. Deviation is lowest in South Africa, where at no point in the five-year period 1999–2003 was it more than 2 per cent. Mozambique also performs well, deviating by more than 3.5 per cent only once during the period under study. One significant point about deviation is the disruptive effect it has on the rest of the budget, especially in relation to service delivery.[48] The case studies show that a lack of realism or honesty at the budget formulation stage and of discipline at the implementation stage are responsible for frequent deviations, rather than factors outside the control of the state. A lack of sectoral policy is also a factor in this regard.

[48] This point is made in Ball, N. and Holmes, M., 'Integrating defense into public expenditure work', Department for International Development, London, Jan. 2001, URL <http://www.grc-exchange.org/>, p. 13.

Low adherence

This first group consists of Ethiopia, Ghana, Kenya, Mali and Nigeria. These countries performed poorly on all or most of the principles of public expenditure management. The level of transparency and accountability in these countries is very low because secrecy laws inhibit information flow, even to those responsible for making important decisions in the state, such as legislators. Military budgets in these countries are not comprehensive enough, as evidenced by off-budget expenditure, which is common to all of them. While their parliaments have varying degrees of power over the budget, a lack of adequate information and, in some cases, the parliament's own collaboration with the executive prevent proper exercise of authority over the budget. These countries, with the exception of Mali, also lack a well-articulated sectoral policy for defence, which makes planning in the sector ad hoc and budgeting at best incremental. Again, while all of these countries claim that their military strategies and postures are derivates of domestic and foreign policies, there is an apparent lack of coordination between what passes for a defence policy and the policies of the interior and foreign affairs ministries.

An important characteristic of the countries in this group is their long periods of military or one-party dictatorships, which left a mark on the manner in which state affairs are conducted. These states also have a history of providing special privileges for the military. Although Kenya has never been under military rule, during the four decades of rule by KANU the government provided special privileges to the military that other sectors did not enjoy.[49] In fact, those special privileges are at the heart of the avowedly apolitical nature of the Kenyan military.

While all five states are now multiparty democracies, their transitions from authoritarian to civil, multiparty rule were peaceful and without any major transformation of state apparatuses. Although Ethiopia experienced long years of civil war before the EPRDF defeated the Dirgue regime in 1991, the actual change to multiparty democracy in 1994 passed without incident.

Medium adherence

The second group of countries consists of Mozambique and Sierra Leone, both of which have instituted various reforms or transformation programmes that, for various reasons, have not yet taken root. The level of transparency is still low here, too, although efforts are being made to improve the situation through enabling laws and improved capacity. Accountability is improving but is still questionable, especially in the case of Mozambique, where the low level of

---

[49] E.g., in 2001–2003 the salaries of officers of the Kenyan armed forces were raised twice, by as much as 400%. The other ranks reportedly received only a 21% increase and there were no corresponding salary reviews for the other sectors of government. 'Soldiers quizzed over pay protest leaflets', *Daily Nation*, 29 July 2003, URL <http://www.nationmedia.com/dailynation/>. See also Luckham (note 25).

transparency has been attributed to corruption in the system.[50] In Sierra Leone the domination of the political system by corrupt politicians who were active participants in the events leading to civil war in the 1990s is also a source of concern.[51]

The level of parliamentary involvement in the process is increasing in both countries and the budgets are becoming increasingly comprehensive as donors make this a condition for aid. The fact that donors are very involved in the budgetary process in both countries also guarantees some degree of honesty in the process. Mozambique has a limit on spending on defence of 2 per cent of GDP, while the military sector of Sierra Leone is being overseen by the United Kingdom, which has already helped the country develop a defence policy within an overall national policy framework. Mozambique's defence policy is far from ideal, given the process of its development and its incoherent nature: it is also overdue for review.

Mozambique and Sierra Leone are both post-conflict states and their reform processes are being driven by donors. These two cases draw attention to the window of opportunity available to states emerging from conflict. The chance to start from scratch or to initiate a substantial overhauling of existing systems could, when seized upon, provide the opportunity to instil new ways of doing things, including new attitudes and values, and to build new infrastructure and new policies. Since the influence of donors in the two countries is considerable, it is not unlikely that it is responsible for the level of adherence to the good practice principles in these states.

High adherence

South Africa is the only country in the third group; it does well on all the principles of public expenditure management. In fact, its structures are a model for the rest of the continent. Like the post-conflict states, South Africa seized the opportunity provided by the end of apartheid to effect a complete transformation of its legal and political systems to meet democratic standards. Its public institutions, including the armed forces, were also transformed in line with the principles and norms of democratic societies. Proper legislation was enacted that provided for access to information, and high standards of accountability were established.

In addition, appropriate policies were developed for each sector, including the military sector, and now guide South African government activities. Unlike all other countries on the continent, these policies were clearly documented and publicly debated by members of civil society, and a national consensus was reached before they were approved as sector policies. The example of South

[50] Lala, A., 'Democratic governance and common security in Southern Africa: Mozambique in focus', *Journal of Security Sector Management*, vol. 2, no. 1 (Mar. 2004), URL <http://www.jofssm.org/>, p. 5.

[51] Ero, C., 'Sierra Leone: the legacies of authoritarianism and political violence', eds G. Cawthra and R. Luckham, *Governing Insecurity in Africa: Democratic Control of Military and Security Establishments in Transitional Democracies* (Zed Books: London, 2003), p. 246.

Africa shows that leadership and political commitment plus participatory policy review and development processes are more important than donor influence for sustainable reform.

IV. Explaining the level of adherence to good practice principles

As shown in the preceding sections, the good practice principles are not uniformly adhered to by the countries examined in this study. This is particularly so in the military sector, where limited information is available on both the level of and the rationale for military allocation in the budget. This section advances some explanations for the inability of the countries to adhere to the good practice principles. These are: (*a*) long years of military and one-party rule, (*b*) confidentiality in the military sector, (*c*) the attitudes of the elite and bureaucratic inertia, (*d*) strong informal processes, (*e*) limited capacity and lack of political will, (*f*) limited democratic experience and strong executives, (*g*) weak oversight bodies, and (*h*) inadequate regulatory frameworks.

Long years of military and one-party rule

Owing to the long years of military dictatorship or one-party rule in most of the countries in the case studies, and in most of Africa until the early 1990s, military influence on national decision-making processes generally, and on security decision making in particular, has become virtually entrenched. Rule by decree, which usually followed the suspension of the constitution when the military took power, not only created an air of superiority around the ruling military elite, but also made the military an institution that was virtually autonomous from society at large.[52] Similarly, the excessive reliance on the military for support by several one-party states in Africa gave the military special privileges, such as the allocation of a high level of state resources for their maintenance and special remunerations that were not available to other sectors of government. These special privileges have survived to date in countries such as Kenya and are at the heart of the problems of reform in some of the states.

With the return to democracy of most African countries from the early 1990s, efforts to rein in military autonomy and some of these special privileges by applying good practice principles—especially adherence to the law and the twin principles of transparency and accountability—to the budgetary process have, as could be expected, met with only qualified success. Years of autonomous action in budgetary matters by the military and the loss of the power to control and vet military expenditure by both the finance ministry and the auditor-general's office are difficult to overcome with only a few years of democracy.

---

[52] On the issue of military autonomy see Finer, S. E., *The Man on Horseback: The Role of the Military in Politics*, 2nd edn (Pinter: London, 1988). See also Luckham (note 25).

South Africa, with the almost revolutionary transformation of its state institutions, including the armed forces, is the only country that has succeeded in making a quick transition from years of impunity to a democratic and accountable system where good practice principles are applied.

Confidentiality in the military sector

Over the years African countries, and many other developing countries, have developed a culture of secrecy on military matters generally and military spending in particular.[53] This culture is backed by laws in many African countries, which are explicit on the consequences of revealing state 'secrets' without prior approval by a responsible officer. While these secrecy laws were not made specifically for the military sector, it is one of the sectors where utmost confidentiality is perceived to be needed. The basis for this culture is the general belief that, given the military's primary responsibility for defending the country from external attacks, their activities, especially their capabilities and the resources made available for maintaining them, should be kept from the public and, by implication, from enemies. By the same logic, military decision making was restricted to a circle of military officers and a few civilians who were thought to be knowledgeable in military matters or who had to be informed by virtue of their positions (for example, the defence minister) since the prevailing notion was that very few people outside the military circle understood the armed forces and so had little need for information on the sector. Moreover, very few people were trusted to keep confidential the information that military decision making required.

The entrenchment of the culture of secrecy was aided by both the international security environment into which most African states were born in the 1960s and the military and one-party governments that became dominant shortly after independence. A major characteristic of these regimes was their repressive nature. The armed forces were their special instrument for this task.

To a varying degree this culture of secrecy and the claimed need for confidentiality in the military sector is one of the main reasons for the lack of transparency in Ethiopia, Ghana, Kenya, Mali, Mozambique and Nigeria. For instance, in Ethiopia the long years of military dictatorship under the Dirgue regime, which ended in 1991, were characterized by secrecy and official privileges for members of the armed forces in terms of housing and salaries. The post-1991 government of Meles Zenawi has not moved far away from the culture of secrecy of the previous regime, nor has it abandoned the special privileges for the armed forces. Military decision making and, indeed, general decision making in Ethiopia are still highly restricted with only limited, highly

---

[53] Singh, R. P., 'Comparative analysis', ed. R. P. Singh, SIPRI, *Arms Procurement Decision Making*, vol. 1, *China, India, Israel, South Korea and Thailand* (Oxford University Press: Oxford, 1998), pp. 250–51.

aggregated information provided on military spending and the sources of financing for the armed forces.

In Sierra Leone the transformation of the security sector with the assistance of the UK is making this sector generally, and the military sector in particular, more transparent. This is now leading to availability of information on the sector, even if on a limited scale.

South Africa remains the most transparent in terms of the level of information made available on the military budgetary process. This is backed by an enabling law which makes mandatory the provision of such information to the general public on request.

The attitudes of the elite and bureaucratic inertia

Closely linked to the culture of secrecy is the attitude of the country's elite towards the military as an institution and to military affairs generally. The overwhelming majority of the people, including high-placed individuals and groups, regard the military as a special institution whose inner working systems are known to only a few civilians directly associated with it. This attitude emanates from the perceived special nature of the military's task (national defence) and is reinforced by the years of military and one-party dictatorships when the military was the main agent of repression. A major consequence of this attitude was an indirect concession to the military of the right to know, even by the agencies that were supposed to oversee the activities of the military, including the defence and finance ministries, the auditor-general's office and, recently, parliaments. The military became an authority unto itself and, in most cases, special rules were applied to it that differed from those of the other sectors of the economy.

In Ghana, Mali and Nigeria, where the military ruled for a considerable period of time, officials at the finance ministries have become accustomed to approving the annual defence ministry estimates without satisfactory justification of the estimates being given. The grounds cited for this are national security, an excuse not available to the other ministries. Although the finance ministries have the power to cut the military budget estimates, just as they do for other ministries, officials know that the defence ministries could always obtain the full requested budget via an executive order. This practice has become virtually entrenched in these countries even after the advent of democracy.

While some individuals and organizations have campaigned for the right to know what was going on in the military, this did little to change the public perception of the military as a 'special' institution. This entrenched attitude has not disappeared in most of these countries in spite of the introduction of democracy. In fact, since the introduction of democracy most legislators have carried over their entrenched attitudes and notions about the military into the parliaments, and this has affected their role of exercising legislative oversight.

Ghanaian and Nigerian legislators have frequently called for more funding for the military without a corresponding demand for an evaluation of how previous funds were used.[54]

The lack of knowledge of the military engendered by the long absence of any involvement of legislators in the military decision-making process, coupled with subsisting perceptions of the military as a special institution, is preventing a proper exercise of parliamentary oversight of the military.

Strong informal processes

There are strong informal networks of relationships among the various elite groups in the bureaucracies and governments of all of the countries studied. These relationships and their networks exist in virtually every part of the bureaucracy and range from former military officers and guerrilla soldiers now in government to 'old boy networks', township associations and ethnic associations. In several of the case studies, working relationships revolve around these networks of personal relationships rather than operating through legally established institutions of the state. As a result, individuals and groups exercise considerable influence on matters of interest to them, using their contacts in the system rather than established channels.

In some countries this has been put to positive use in the administration of the state. This is the case with the African National Congress in South Africa, where former guerrilla soldiers are now in government and still rely on the former contacts and the trust built up in the bush to foster understanding and to push through government policies. The same also applied in Nigeria after the restoration of democracy in 1999. The new president, Olusegun Obasanjo, a former military leader, appointed a former colleague (and friend) from the military, General Theophilus Danjuma, as Minister of Defence to help in rebuilding the military and the MOD for the new democratic dispensation. The appointment of a former colleague to the highly sensitive position (given the Nigerian armed forces' habit of staging military coups) underscored the significance that Obasanjo attached to choosing a person with whom he shared a vision for the military. The minister helped in maintaining some stability in the military in the period immediately after military rule ended and in repositioning the MOD as the main decision-making centre for the ministry itself and for the military, replacing Defence Headquarters. On the other hand, the old networks have had a negative influence in some other states. In both Rwanda and Uganda, former guerrilla colleagues have used their contacts for corrupt purposes, especially in their activities in the war in the Democratic Republic of the Congo.

Both types of example, however, confirm the general impression about Africa that many activities of the state are carried out at the informal level. This factor

---

[54] See, e.g., *Parliamentary Debates* (Accra), 19 Mar. 1999, columns 4046–49; and Nigerian Senate, *Appropriation Act 2002*, Abuja, Mar. 2002.

has been a major reason for the failure of attempts to institutionalize the decision-making process in a number of African states.

Limited capacity and lack of political will

There is an apparent lack of capacity in key areas of the military budgetary process in many African states that makes it difficult to follow due process. Three critical areas in which capacity is either completely lacking or barely exists are: (*a*) policy development, (*b*) military budget making and (*c*) military budget oversight.

The starting point for drawing up a comprehensive and integrated military budget, which considers both the nation's security needs and the economic resources available to achieve them, is the development of a sectoral policy. The sectoral policy itself will take its cue from the overall national policy framework. Many countries in Africa not only lack sector policies for defence but also lack the capacity to develop one. Although they all claim to have defence policies, the lack of a written or well-codified defence policy obstructs long-term planning and prevents effective annual budgeting. This also prevents proper scrutiny of the budget by the oversight bodies as there is no known objective or target against which success could be measured. This problem is further compounded by the general lack of personnel who are competent to draw up budgets and by weak oversight bodies, especially the auditor-general's office. While all the states have statutory audit bodies, the military sector is only lightly scrutinized owing to the vested interests of high-ranking political leaders such as the president or prime minister.

The countries in the case studies can be categorized in three groups according to the problems of capacity that they face: (*a*) countries that lack capacity at the levels discussed above; (*b*) those that lack the political will to carry through the reform needed (although they may have the required capacity); and (*c*) those whose problem is a combination of the first two. In the first category are Mali, Mozambique and Sierra Leone; in the second are Ghana, Kenya and Nigeria; and in the third is Ethiopia. One fundamental problem common to the three groups, however, is the institutional weakness of their defence ministries, which are supposed to lead the policy development processes.

The countries in the first category—Mali, Mozambique and Sierra Leone— appear to be willing to implement a defence policy but lack personnel with the requisite expertise to develop the policy, manage the sector and prepare the military budget. In Mozambique, for example, the Ministry of National Defence has two people with the expertise to deal with policy development. There is also a general lack of budget specialists in these three countries.

In the second category, Ghana, Kenya and Nigeria do not currently have well-articulated defence policies that can form the basis for integrated budgeting and long-term strategic planning. Yet these countries are not really lacking in the requisite manpower to develop a sector policy, as highly qualified personnel do exist in their various ministries and even in the military, especially in Ghana and Nigeria.[55] What they lack is the necessary will on the part of the political leadership (in the executive and the legislature), especially in terms of creating an environment that allows for policy development. The absence of political will itself could be a reflection of the leaders not wanting reforms to be carried out, since the status quo enables them to use the military to maintain themselves in power. The use of the military for political purposes has been a common practice in these countries, especially in Ghana and Nigeria before their return to multiparty democracy. The Kenyan armed forces were also accused of having been a willing tool in the hands of President Daniel arap Moi during the campaign for the elections of December 2002. In particular, the military were accused of supporting a violent pro-KANU group that terrorized opposition strongholds in the run-up to the elections.[56]

In the third category is Ethiopia, which lacks both the requisite expertise and the political will. One of the main ingredients of integrated policy development that is lacking in Ethiopia is the overarching national policy framework into which a defence policy will feed, as well as the necessary dialogue and interaction among the other sectors with which the military sector naturally interacts: the internal affairs, foreign affairs and finance sectors. The legislature in Ethiopia also seems reluctant to demand from the executive a sectoral policy as the basis for the annual budget considerations. A combination of these two factors has thus prevented the general application of the good practice principles

South Africa is the only country that has developed an integrated military budgeting system encompassing both a well-developed policy for the sector and a planned programme over an extended period of time.

The lack of comprehensiveness in military budgets shown in the case studies can be attributed to the lack of expertise in preparing a comprehensive military budget in some of the countries, especially those with limited capacity to prepare such a document. This has been a major reason for either contingency allocations or off-budget spending when an unforeseen security crisis has occurred or another situation has arisen that could have been taken care of by a more inclusive military budget. This is the hallmark of budgeting in Ethiopia and Kenya. On the other hand, the lack of comprehensiveness in the military budget in countries with more expertise, such as Ghana and Nigeria, would appear to be more deliberate, allowing for misappropriation of funds as off-budget allocations are made to the military. In Nigeria the access of the military to special funds for other activities, such as peacekeeping operations, not budgeted for in the annual budget is a clear example.

---

[55] The Nigerian Army has a well-established financial management training school for its personnel (and those of the other services) in its Finance Department. To that extent, it has the requisite personnel in both the MOD and the services.

[56] 'Kenya police probes army', BBC News Online, 31 Jan. 2003, URL <http://news.bbc.co.uk/2/2714371.stm>.

Limited democratic experience and strong executives

Although all countries in this study are now formally democracies, democratic values and practices have not yet taken root everywhere. This is to be expected given the relatively recent return to multiparty democracy after several years of authoritarian or one-party rule. The lack of transparency of the authoritarian period persists in most of the countries. This is compounded by the emerging trend for the parliament to be dominated by the parties of government. In most cases the head of government is also the leader of his party, and other members of the party, including parliamentarians, are expected to defer to him. This does not make for the effective working of the checks and balances that are a hallmark of democracy. In most of the eight countries the constitution has already made the executive very powerful compared with the other arms of government, especially the legislature. The deference of the legislature to the executive as a result of party loyalty, respect for the office of president or pecuniary gain only makes the executive stronger at the expense of the legislature.[57]

One of the main reasons why good practice principles do not apply in many of the case studies is the excessive strength of the executive, especially the office of the president or prime minister, which wields enormous influence in resource allocation, with few or no checks by the legislature. The power of the executive to dispense resources with little control by other arms of government allows the culture of impunity that was prevalent in the authoritarian era to continue under the new dispensation as due process is only given lip service, not practised. Indeed, until as recently as the early 1990s, most African leaders regarded the notion of public participation in governance as anathema to efficiency. Nigeria is a good illustration in this regard: the dominance of the executive in the whole budgetary process is palpable, just as the lack of proper checks on the powers of the executive by the legislature is glaring. Ethiopia, Ghana and Kenya are other examples of African countries with very strong executives and weak legislatures.

Weak oversight bodies

The ability of a country to institute good practice principles is contingent on its having good oversight bodies. These bodies are very weak in most of the countries in this study. The parliaments, especially their committees on defence, are usually ineffective in the exercise of their constitutional role of oversight of the budget, owing either to deference to the executive, as explained above, or to a lack of capacity to oversee the military budget. The lack of capacity emanates from the legislators' lack of any knowledge of what a military budget should contain and, as explained above, of any previous contact with military decision-making processes. In addition, the parliaments lack the means to employ

---

[57] National Democratic Institute, 'The role of the legislature in defense and national security issues', Seminar report, Dakar, 19–22 Apr. 1999, URL <http://www.pdgs.org/dakar.htm>, p. 14.

experts in order to improve their capacity. At another level, they collaborate with the executive to prevent transparency in the military budget on grounds of national security, or to prevent a true disclosure of total spending on military activities to donors of economic aid who insist on a certain maximum level of military expenditure. This is clearly the case in many aid-dependent countries, such as Ethiopia.

Other statutory oversight bodies, such as the auditor-general and the finance ministry, are also either not properly equipped to do the oversight work or constrained by institutional weaknesses from carrying out their tasks, thus preventing proper monitoring of allocated resources. Mozambique lacks personnel who are qualified to work in this area. Countries such as Ghana, Kenya and Nigeria, which have the advantage of qualified personnel, prevent the proper conduct of a value-for-money audit, fail to act on audit reports or attempt to discredit critical reports as being 'political'. The cumulative effect of this is the absence of proper monitoring and evaluation of government expenditure.

Inadequate regulatory frameworks

Many of the countries studied have obsolete, inadequate or completely absent laws to guide the military budgetary process. In some states the laws guiding the process were made under colonial rule or in the immediate post-independence period and have not been reviewed since then. They thus have little relevance to the modern budget-making process. In others, where the laws have been reviewed, they are not regularly updated to meet modern exigencies, especially the restoration of democracy: those laws that were made under one-party rule or military dictatorships reflected the needs of the time. In a number of other states there is a complete absence of regulatory laws for the process, thereby leaving it subject to the whims of the officers in charge. In such countries, the laxity in the regulatory laws is then exploited for corrupt practices.

V. Summary and conclusions

This chapter shows that there are many gaps between good practice in military budgeting and what takes place in most of the sample countries. These gaps are caused by a number of factors of which the main one is the prevalent political culture—engendered especially by long periods of military and one-party rule—of deference to the military and a belief in its need for special treatment. This is a common characteristic of all the sample countries with low adherence to the principles. While all the countries under study have become democracies, the culture of secrecy associated with military and one-party rule persists and the official secrecy legislation has not been repealed in some countries. This hinders transparency and limits wider participation in the budgetary process. Moreover, it prevents accountability by offering protection to state officials who would otherwise be exposed. The opaque and inadequate or outdated laws that guide the processes in many of the countries also affect the extent of adherence to the principles of good practice as some of their provisions fall short of standards that can guarantee adherence.

However, more important than both the secrecy legislation and the inadequate regulatory framework is the key question of commitment on the part of the political leadership to institutionalizing the military budgetary process. The positive example of South Africa shows that commitment by the highest segment of the political leadership matters for the successful application of good practice principles to the military budgetary process. While sound, adequate and up-to-date legislation is important for the efficient functioning of the process, laws in themselves cannot translate into an efficient, rules-based or institutionalized process unless there is a measure of goodwill and commitment on the part of those who apply those laws. The jailing of a senior member of the ruling party in South Africa shows that that country is committed to combating abuse of the system. Other countries need to follow in its footsteps to be able to establish military budgetary processes that adhere to good practice principles.

Nonetheless, the significance of political commitment as a major ingredient in the success of the system is tempered by what some of the case studies have shown: that the extent of available capacity to manage the process is equally important. The gaps between good and existing practices in the post-conflict countries of Mozambique and Sierra Leone show that a major problem in these countries is the lack of the requisite capacity to manage the process, in both the managing ministry (the defence ministry) and the military, with an even more limited capacity among members of the public to contribute to debates on defence-related issues. This lack of capacity constitutes a major handicap even when the level of political commitment is high. It is therefore important for these countries to correct the deficits in capacity before political commitment can be translated into rules-based budgetary processes. At present international donors are assisting Sierra Leone to fill this capacity gap through direct participation in the process and the training of the Sierra Leoneans who will manage the process. In Mozambique the presence of donors in the military sector is felt both through donations and in the imposition of a spending limit on the sector. What is not clear is the extent to which these countries' fledgling processes would survive the exit of donors. That will of course depend on the amount of local capacity that donors succeed in helping to build and the extent to which they are able to institutionalize the processes in the countries before their exit. Above all, this will depend on the continued existence of high-level political commitment on the part of the leaderships in these countries.

Overall, therefore, for the processes of military budgeting in Africa to reach the ideal level envisaged in chapter 2, the countries will need not only to overhaul the legislation guiding the processes, but also to show at the highest levels of the state a greater commitment to the rules once established, while constantly working with recognized partners to increase the capacity of the state for adequate management and implementation.

12. Recommendations

Wuyi Omitoogun and Eboe Hutchful*

'... defining national and sectoral policies which are clear, affordable and consistent is crucial to the success of any budget process'[1]

I. Introduction

A number of specific policy recommendations follow from the eight case studies in this volume. There are 12 recommendations aimed at national governments and an additional 5 recommendations for the international community.

Three of the recommendations to national governments stand out, as they are key to the transformation of the military budgetary processes in the sample countries; they are also the main factors that distinguish the relatively successful South African experience from the less successful processes in Ethiopia, Ghana, Kenya, Mali, Mozambique, Nigeria and Sierra Leone. The three key recommendations are: (*a*) a well-articulated defence policy should be developed to guide activities in the military sector (recommendation NG1); (*b*) political leaders should make a real commitment to institutionalizing the budgetary process (recommendation NG3); and (*c*) the wider constraints associated with the specific contexts of African countries should be acknowledged (recommendation NG12).

All the recommendations are discussed below.

II. Recommendations to national governments

Recommendation NG1. Develop a defence policy

There is a need to develop a defence policy that will provide guidelines for all activities in the military sector, including budgeting. Such a policy should be developed within the framework of a national security policy and should be subject to public scrutiny. It should have input from critical stakeholders in the sector, including the military, civilian members of the defence ministry, the internal and foreign affairs ministries, and members of civil society. The overall objectives of the military sector and the ways and means to achieve them

---

[1] Oxford Policy Management (OPM), 'Medium term expenditure frameworks—panacea or dangerous distraction?', OPM Review Paper no. 2, Prepared for the World Bank, May 2000, URL <http://www.worldbank.org/publicsector/pe/>, p. 2.

* The authors acknowledge the contributions of Nicole Ball to this chapter, especially section III.

should be spelled out in these policy guidelines. A comprehensive definition of the scope of the military budget should be articulated in both the policy and any subsequent defence plan to avoid confusion of external defence and internal security.

A defence plan should be developed on the basis of the guidelines provided in the defence policy. The means for attaining the objectives in the plan, in terms of both strategy and resources, should also be spelled out. This presupposes that the plan is set within the overall national objectives and economic framework in the first place since achievable defence objectives must take account of a nation's economic realities (see recommendation NG2). As a matter of policy, procurement plans should be integral to overall defence budget planning. The costs of all military procurement should be included in the budget, but costs of expensive equipment should be spread over several annual budgets to avoid undue distortion of the macroeconomic environment. The full life-cycle costs of major equipment should be determined at the time of purchase to avoid incurring unbudgeted additional costs when maintenance costs are eventually added.

Transparency is a fundamental principle that should guide the processes of developing the defence policy and the defence plan. Transparency should not be promoted solely through the involvement of stakeholders in the processes; the policy should also be made readily accessible to the general public through various means, including the Internet and public awareness programmes.

Recommendation NG2. Be clear about the choices to be made

Having a defence policy means being clear about the choices to be made; good policy is about making the right decisions. As indicated in recommendation NG1, these decisions must be rooted in wide public dialogue and consensus. For all the talk about the links between security and development, these priorities are often in competition in the budgetary process. For many aid donors, balancing security and development continues to imply shifting resources from the former to the latter. Conversely, governments, concerned about security and their own survival—and about alienating powerful military establishments—have tended to advocate higher expenditure on security. Military expenditure is thus a significant topic for donors as well as governments and citizens.

A trade-off between security and development is essential in real life because it is far from certain that African countries have the resources for both. Critical choices thus need to be made, including determining the best way of synthesizing the two objectives in resource-constrained conditions. These choices need to be as transparent as possible. An increasingly popular response to this dilemma is to involve the military in development-related missions. One potential effect of this is to further distort the budgetary process. In addition, responses of this kind point more broadly to a lack of clarity about the role of the traditional security institutions in providing 'human security'. There needs to be a debate as to whether the military best contributes to poverty alleviation by involving itself directly in development—as is currently the case under the poverty reduction strategies of many African countries; by providing security (in the traditional sense) effectively and accountably; or through some meaningful and sustainable combination of the two.

Defence reviews can provide an appropriate context for addressing these issues and building consensus, but they should not be seen as a magic wand that can dispel all doubts. Uganda's defence review has not eliminated the disagreements between the government and donors over what constitutes an 'appropriate' level of military spending. In Sierra Leone a scrupulously managed defence review has been completed, but the absence of the resources required to back up its findings and recommendations impedes their implementation. In other words, 'good' policy as recommended above is the beginning, not the end of the process. More to the point, to the extent that it actually integrates security and development, a well-formulated policy can highlight resource constraints, at least in the short term.

Recommendation NG3. Institutionalize the process

In order to develop a defence policy there is a need for a functional institution, with effective processes, that will both deliver and maintain the policy. Thus, the defence ministry, as the main ministry in charge of defence policy formulation, should be strengthened in order to function effectively.

The starting point for this is to have in place relevant legislation to guide the defence ministry's activities. Existing rules and regulations should be reviewed to ensure that they are in line with what is expected of the ministry. The ministry should be properly staffed with qualified personnel who have adequate understanding of the military, especially at the senior management level. However, beyond simply strengthening the institutional structure of the defence ministry, there should be a requirement for strict adherence to the rules and regulations that guide the ministry's activities generally and military budgeting in particular. The degree of adherence to such rules is a major indicator of the extent of institutionalization of the budgetary process. In addition, the political authorities should give the ministry support—including the cooperation of other relevant ministries—to allow it to assert its authority over the process. This presupposes a wider reform encompassing all government ministries and agencies and other major actors in the national budgetary processes. It is only when such an enabling environment has been provided that a proper, all-encompassing policy can be articulated.

Recommendation NG4. Strengthen oversight institutions

Oversight institutions, such as the parliament, the auditor-general's office and the finance ministry, require enhanced capacities to allow them to function at the highest levels in the discharge of their oversight functions.

The parliament needs a well-staffed research unit that will support its defence committee when dealing with the executive on military matters and that will enable it to raise fundamental issues concerning the management of the defence forces. The public accounts committee, of which the defence committee acts as a sub-committee, should be strengthened by enhancing its capacity to perform its functions in the overall national budgetary process. Since the public accounts committee is responsible for reviewing the budget estimates submitted by the executive, it is central to ensuring the wise allocation of resources.

Similarly, the auditor-general's office needs more and better-qualified staff in order to perform its function as government watchdog efficiently, especially in providing timely reports. In addition, there is a need for explicit legislation on the way in which the auditor-general is appointed and dismissed in order to make the office holder immune to any political repercussions of the official audit report. The finance ministry also needs strengthening, both by recruiting qualified personnel to carry out an effective assessment of the military budget during budget hearings and through a general restructuring to enhance the role of professional staff. The latter reform should replace the present system in which support staff dominate, but it should take into consideration the next recommendation.

Recommendation NG5. Make the process simple, with a single controlling agency

Since a major problem in a number of African states is the lack of personnel qualified to handle the tasks of the budgetary process, it is important that the process itself be simplified in order to meet local needs and to stay within the limits of local capacity. This should be done without undermining the main principles: transparency, accountability, discipline and honesty.

A major problem of the planning, programming and budgeting system adopted as part of the analytical framework for this study is the potentially complex nature of its management. The USA developed its planning, programming and budgeting system in the 1960s in response to the specific problems of coordination and waste within the armed services. Since then, it has undergone several modifications to reach its current state. African countries will also need to modify the system described in chapter 2 to suit their local conditions, especially in the areas of perceived weakness. South Africa offers a ready example here, but even this model can be modified to suit specific local conditions, as long as the principles of transparency, accountability, discipline and honesty are not sacrificed in the process.

As part of the effort to make the budgetary process as simple as possible, a central coordinating agency should take responsibility for the process, replacing the current multiplicity of agencies. Experience has shown that, when multiple agencies are involved, overlap and duplication of effort result, causing delays and complicating the process. Conversely, establishing one agency with authority over the whole process will go a long way towards making the process less complex.

Recommendation NG6. Introduce a more comprehensive regulatory framework

Laws guiding the budgetary process should be reviewed, updated or changed entirely, in order to meet modern standards of practice. Budgetary reform in the military sector should take place in the context of an updated, broader national public finance management act that will provide the context for change in all sectors. The availability of a comprehensive regulatory framework is, however, not sufficient as that alone cannot guarantee a good system. It must be followed up with enforcement so that those operating the system comply with both the letter and the spirit of the legislation, and offenders are prosecuted (see recommendation NG9).

Recommendation NG7. Repeal secrecy laws and pass confidentiality legislation

To guarantee transparency and accountability and to encourage public participation in the process, all secrecy laws should be repealed and replaced by legislation guaranteeing the access of citizens to information held by the state. This will ensure that secrecy legislation cannot be used to protect state officials by covering up their misdeeds. Moreover, the new legislation will ensure that the principle of transparency is an integral part of the simplification and indigenization of the military budgetary process (recommendation NG5).

However, in view of the genuine need for confidentiality in certain aspects of defence, there is a requirement for legislation that regulates access to confidential information by certain categories of people or those who are expected to exercise oversight. Confidentiality should not preclude accountability. Instead, the legislation should specify the type of clearance needed for those whose job it is to exercise oversight of the military sector, such as parliamentarians, auditors and so on.

Recommendation NG8. Allow wider participation by civil society

There is need for a wider participation by civil society in the process of defence policy formation in order to form a more representative policy. The participation of civil society organizations in formulating the first South African policy guidelines and the policy review process is a good example to emulate.

The more people from outside government are given the opportunity to contribute to policy formulation or review, the more legitimacy will be conferred on both the process and the resulting policy. Moreover, an inclusive process will eliminate, or reduce to a minimum, the general public's common suspicion of military activities generally and of military spending in particular. Civil society organizations' limited knowledge of the security sector is a problem in this regard. However, several such organizations recognize this deficiency and are increasing their capacity in the area; limited knowledge of the military sector can be overcome once the broad issues involved are public knowledge.

Recommendation NG9. Demonstrate strong political commitment to institution building

There is a need for a strong commitment from the highest political authorities to allowing the budgetary process to function optimally, with strong, explicit leadership. In addition to a coordination role, this requires an insistence from the top that policy be followed. This study shows that this commitment is something that South Africa appears to have but that other African countries lack. It not only allows the process to mature but also ensures that rules guiding the process are adhered to and that no one is immune from prosecution when laws are broken. Such a commitment requires discipline from the leadership, robust checks and balances, and a belief that only a well-functioning process will deliver the desired outcomes.

The countries whose leaders themselves subvert the law, and fail to prosecute corrupt public officials because of their political connections, have weak and dysfunctional budgetary processes that cannot achieve the result they were set up to deliver. Therefore, strong commitment to the process by every segment of the political leadership, in the executive and the legislature, is needed in order to institutionalize the process by which planned objectives can be obtained. The legislature in particular needs to act promptly on the report of the auditor-general so that those accused can be prosecuted according to the law.

Recommendation NG10. Take ownership of the process

The budgeting systems across Africa are changing and this is mainly a result of the influence of aid donors. The introduction of a medium-term expenditure framework in many countries is donor-inspired. While this new approach to budgeting is gaining widespread acceptance among the governments of Africa, its adoption is due more to the insistence of donors, who constitute a significant force in the budgetary processes across Africa. Yet, without a strong commitment to the process by the countries themselves, very little can be achieved. It is therefore important that each country designs a new system to suit its local conditions.

Ownership of the military budgetary process is best guaranteed when the country participates in the design of the system or is convinced that the system represents the best way to achieve set goals. In the present circumstances, the good practice framework adopted for this study, with its emphasis on long-term planning, should be seen as one of several available options. However, it is important to note that long-term planning is a necessity if the armed forces are to be adequately maintained without damaging the economy of the state.

Recommendation NG11. Adopt a sub-regional approach to military issues, including budgeting

In localizing the process of budgeting, there is a need to develop a sub-regional policy so that neighbouring countries take a common approach to budgeting. This has advantages for cost, policy and security in the sub-region.

Given that many sub-regional organizations are already encouraging the development of common defence and security policies as a way out of the perennial security problems in Africa, a common approach to military budgeting will facilitate this process and increase mutual trust—the hallmark of peaceful coexistence in any region. Such an approach will also help to drastically reduce (external) defence budgets, as adoption of a common policy and approach will diminish perceived threats from immediate neighbours.

Transparency and mutual trust are emphasized as major objectives of the African Union's Common African Defence and Security Policy. A sub-regional approach to budgeting will greatly facilitate the achievement of these objectives.

Recommendation NG12. Consider contexts

A narrow focus on budgetary issues and processes that does not acknowledge the wider constraints associated with the specific contexts of African countries should be avoided. Security sector reform has often taken a highly prescriptive, technocratic direction and has in general been agnostic—if not naive—about the historical context and, in particular, underlying issues of power. While the different situations in the countries studied here must be taken into account, their commonalities are at least as pertinent: fragile transitions from authoritarianism; the precarious condition of both state and public security; the weakness of the institutions for managing and overseeing the security sector; significant resource constraints in the security sector; and the reality that military and security establishments retain much formal and informal power—albeit less than in the past—and a corresponding ability to derail democratic transitions. (Many of these characteristics do not apply to South Africa, however.) Typically, these countries also suffer to various degrees from post-authoritarian

272 BUDGETING FOR THE MILITARY SECTOR IN AFRICA

dilemmas: their governments' uncertain legitimacy and the need to contain perceived threats to public order may force democratically elected governments into greater dependence upon their security establishments. In such contexts, reforms, although critical, are nevertheless fraught with political risks and are never straightforward.

Recognizing issues of context and power potentially transforms the way in which issues and processes are viewed, particularly in terms of what constitutes 'rational' and 'irrational' behaviour. For instance, defence reviews and policy frameworks carry both advantages and disadvantages in a resource-constrained context. Reform costs money, which most of these governments have no prospect of raising in the foreseeable future. Thus, governments have to balance the potential benefits of a defence review with the potentially damaging admission that the resources for ensuring security—and for managing security institutions properly—do not exist and may not be available for the foreseeable future. From this point of view, failing to establish a policy framework is a rational response, allowing governments to constantly manipulate their limited options. The alternative approach does not offer easy solutions: realigning security structures and finding the necessary resources require painful and politically challenging decisions and considerable political will.

The price for a political settlement with the military usually includes concessions on the budget and establishing and respecting an appropriate sphere of professional autonomy. This goes beyond 'bribing' the military since it is widely accepted that refocusing the military from internal to external missions is essential for promoting professionalism and civil control. Similarly, some incentives may be required to persuade the military to support greater transparency in the military budget, although resistance to transparency has come as often from civilian as from military officials. As long as it is not seen as a device for marginalizing the military, 'human security' should form a key component of the settlement both as a framework for organizing wide-ranging dialogue among diverse stakeholders and as a means for dislodging oppressive doctrines and encouraging new, more democratic understandings of security.

III. Recommendations to the international community

Recommendation IC1. Factor in the highly political nature of strengthening democratic security sector governance

In common with other components of improving democratic security sector governance, strengthening the military budgetary process cannot be addressed solely by technical measures (see recommendations NG2 and NG12). Rather, it is essential to understand critical political relationships among key actors, how and why decisions are made, and the incentives and disincentives for change. External actors need to develop strategies for supporting reformers and minimizing the impact of spoilers. They also need to look beyond formal legislation and organizational structures to develop a picture of how local institutions actually function.

Recommendation IC2. Ground support aimed at strengthening the military budgetary process in the principle of local ownership of reform processes

While the principle of national ownership is well recognized in the development arena, it is often not applied effectively in practice (see recommendation NG10). In addition, strengthening the military budgetary process involves security actors as well as development actors, and security actors tend to be less well versed in the importance of national ownership. Whereas local ownership requires a facilitative approach aimed at helping countries identify needs and develop their own strategies for meeting them, all too often external actors are highly prescriptive.

Local ownership may be difficult to achieve in military budgeting because of the significant weaknesses in human and institutional capacity with regard to security issues and public expenditure management in many developing and transition societies. Problems often arise when international actors fail to differentiate between responsibility and capacity. Local actors own a process when they have the responsibility for decisions concerning objectives, policies, strategies, programme design and implementation modalities. If capacity is weak, it can and should be built up and, in the short term, it can be supplemented in various ways. Governments can obtain technical assistance, preferably from specialists in local or regional security or public expenditure management.

Weak capacity should not become an excuse for members of the international community to continue to exert control over the activities that they support. However, countries that are frequently heavily dependent on external funding are often not in a strong position to drive processes, since they may think that by taking control they will jeopardize the delivery of assistance. In addition, concerns about local capacity can affect the willingness of local stakeholders to assume full responsibility for reform processes.

Recommendation IC3. Let the pace of locally owned reform processes be shaped by conditions in the reforming country

Strengthening the military budgetary process is a subset of institutional reform, and as such requires a decade or more to consolidate. It must reflect not only human and institutional capacity but also the pace of social and political change in the country in question, rather than arbitrary timetables established by the international community or by funding decisions. This is particularly important for countries affected by conflict, whose political and economic relations have been shaped by wartime conditions and may require substantial time to overcome these distortions.

The weaker the state, the longer the reform process is likely to take. It is extremely important, however, that external actors make the necessary investment. There is increasing evidence that consultative processes that build consensus on both the need for change and the direction and nature of that change are critical for the success of reform efforts. For these to succeed, stakeholders must be allowed adequate time to reach consensus.

While complete consensus on the desirability and direction of a reform process is unlikely, key stakeholders in government, the security bodies, and civil and political society need to support reform if significant changes are to occur. External actors can help to create a conducive environment by making the military budgetary process a regular component of policy dialogue in order to identify entry points for reform (see recommendation IC4 for an example of such an entry point). They can ensure that, where relevant, the military sector is included in work on the public sector and public expenditure management. They can identify and support agents for change within the government and the security bodies and can support efforts to neutralize potential spoilers. They can also help civil society develop its capacity to analyse problems in the current military budgetary process and demand change, as well as provide support for reform. Finally, external actors should explore how they can create incentives for key stakeholders to support efforts to strengthen their capacity to formulate and execute military budgets in line with good international practice.

External stakeholders need to approach such efforts with patience and an ability to facilitate politically sensitive discussions. Unless key stakeholders agree on the way forward, it does not make sense to initiate significant work in the military sector. Rather, external actors should concentrate on developing a reform-friendly environment, through activities such as policy dialogue, support to civil society and capacity building for reformers. Even where there is a high degree of consensus on the way forward, implementation may proceed slowly and the possibility of backsliding cannot be excluded. External actors should neither become complacent themselves when reform processes appear to be moving forward nor allow local stakeholders to become complacent. It is important to avoid the common mistake of assuming that good policy will in and of itself produce satisfactory outcomes and overlooking the need for sound policy implementation.

Recommendation IC4. Donors should exploit a good entry point: deviation from budgets

Aid donors can introduce the subject of military expenditure into their dialogue with a recipient country by pointing out the extent of deviation of actual expenditure from the approved military budget. All the countries that belong to the 'low adherence' category identified in chapter 11 have huge gaps between their approved and actual military expenditure.

Donors need to explain to countries why the military sector should not be treated any differently from other sectors of government. They should also demonstrate the destabilizing effect that overspending in the sector can have on the whole budgetary system, especially at the implementation stage and, critically, in service delivery. When overspending in the military sector damages the whole system of government and diminishes or eliminates the gains expected from donor assistance through budget support, donors should take this up as an issue with the recipient country. Doing so need not amount to setting reduced spending in the sector as a condition for aid; rather, it serves as an opportunity to ask the recipient country to explain the rationale for such high military spending. It may be a good starting point for the encouragement of reform of the sector through policy development or, where a policy already exists, through review. When this influence is exerted in a constructive way, rather than insisting on a reduction in spending without knowing the justification for increased military expenditure in the first place, the recipient country is likely to buy into the idea of reform of the sector through policy review. This will ultimately rein in overspending in the sector.

Recommendation IC5. Encourage partner governments to situate efforts to strengthen the military budgetary process in a comprehensive framework for the security sector

While no reform process can be expected to encompass all of the many actors and activities that constitute the security sector, decisions about priority needs and resource allocation should be made following a sector-wide review of a country's security environment and its broad democratic security sector governance needs (see recommendation NG1). Effecting sustainable change in the security sector will almost always require a focus on one constituent element at a time: defence, public security, justice or intelligence. Within that element, there may be a focus on a specific component or process: for example, the capacity of relevant legislative committees, the courts, the military budgeting system, and so on. However, as the studies in this volume show, in the absence of sector-wide assessments of security needs and governance deficits it will be difficult to identify priorities or to determine how best to prioritize reform efforts.

Although experience is currently limited, evidence suggests that external actors can help reforming governments understand the components of security sector reform and how these fit together. There are two assessment mechanisms that may be useful in this process. The first is the strategic security review which has been pioneered by the United Kingdom in Uganda and Sierra Leone. Regrettably, no formal methodology yet exists and neither experience had been reviewed at the time of writing. The second is the Netherlands' security sector governance assessment framework, although this had not yet been field-tested at the time of writing.

External actors must bear in mind that, while it is important to have ambitious long-term objectives, it is also important to be realistic about implementation capacity. In particular, it is important to develop process-oriented benchmarks to measure progress that reflect the realities of political, human and institutional capacity on a country-by-country basis. Such benchmarks will not only assure external partners that progress is being recorded; they can also help local stakeholders avoid being overwhelmed by the enormity of the reform agenda.

About the authors

Said Adejumobi (Nigeria) is Associate Professor of Political Science at Lagos State University, Nigeria, and Political Governance Adviser to the Economic Community of West African States (ECOWAS). He was previously a Governance Consultant to the United Nations (UN) Economic Commission for Africa during the preparation of the African Governance Report. He has written extensively on governance, conflict and security studies, including *Breaking Barriers, Creating New Hopes: Democracy, Civil Society and Good Governance in Africa* (Africa World Press, 2003, co-edited with A. Bujra), *Leadership, Civil Society and Democratisation in Africa: Case Studies from Eastern Africa* (Development Policy Management Forum, 2002, co-edited with A. Bujra), *The National Question in Nigeria* (Ashgate, 2001, co-edited with A. Momoh), *The Nigerian Military and the Crisis of Democratic Transition: A Study in the Monopoly of Power* (Civil Liberties Organisation, Lagos, 1999, co-edited with A. Momoh) and *The Political Economy of Nigeria under Military Rule, 1984–1993* (Southern Africa Political Economy Series, 1995, co-edited with A. Momoh). He has held fellowships from Columbia University, New York; the Norwegian Nobel Institute; the Social Science Research Council, New York; and the University of Cape Town; and was a visiting scholar at Aalborg University, Denmark.

Anatole Ayissi (Cameroon) is the political adviser to the Special Representative of the UN Secretary-General for West Africa. He was previously Head of the Programme on Peace-building and Practical Disarmament in West Africa at the UN Institute for Disarmament Research (UNIDIR) and worked for seven years as a disarmament expert for the Cameroonian Ministry of Foreign Affairs. He has been a Fulbright Fellow at the Political Science Department of the University of Pennsylvania and a Research Fellow at the University of Paris II, Panthéon-Assas. He has published extensively on disarmament, post-conflict recovery and peace-building in Africa, including *Bound to Cooperate: Conflict, Peace and People in Sierra Leone* (UNIDIR, 2000, co-edited with R. Poulton); *Cooperating for Peace in West Africa: An Agenda for the 21st Century* (UNIDIR, 2001); 'Protecting children in armed conflicts: from commitment to compliance', *Disarmament Forum*, 2002; 'L'ONU et la paix en Afrique' [The United Nations and peace in Africa], *Questions Internationales*, no. 5, 2004; and *Combating the Proliferation of Small Arms and Light Weapons in West Africa: Handbook for the Training of Armed and Security Forces* (UNIDIR, 2005, co-edited with I. Sall).

Nicole Ball (United States) is a senior fellow at the Center for International Policy, Washington, DC, and a Visiting Senior Research Fellow at the Center for International Development and Conflict Management, University of Maryland. She is a member of the Advisory Group of the SIPRI/African Security Dialogue and Research Project on Military Budgetary Processes in Africa. She has worked extensively on issues relating to democratic security sector governance, particularly financial management, since 1978. She is co-editor of *Security Sector Governance in Africa: A Handbook* (Centre for Democracy and Development, 2004, with 'K. Fayemi) and co-author of *Enhancing Democratic Governance of the Security Sector: An Institutional Assessment Framework* (Clingendael Institute for the Netherlands Ministry of Foreign Affairs, 2003, with L. van de Goor and T. Bouta).

Mesfin Binega (Ethiopia), a retired commodore of the Ethiopian Navy, is currently Head of the Administrative Control and Management Centre of the African Union's Darfur Integrated Task Force. He has been with the AU since 1996, acting during that time as a military consultant and as the officer in charge of budget preparation and administration, and of logistics planning for AU peace support operations. He was involved in the deployment of the AU's African Mission in Burundi and the AU Mission in the Sudan. While on active service he was, successively, Deputy Head and Head of the Main Department of Budget Planning of the Ethiopian Ministry of National Defence and economic adviser to the ministry. He is a member of the SIPRI Military Expenditure Network.

Adedeji Ebo (Kenya) is a Senior Fellow and Coordinator of the Africa Working Group at the Geneva Centre for the Democratic Control of Armed Forces (DCAF). He was previously Associate Professor and Head of the Department of Political Science and Defence Studies at the Nigerian Defence Academy, Kaduna, and Guest Lecturer at the Nigerian National War College, Abuja. He has been consultant to the Small Arms Survey, Geneva, and International Alert, London. His research interests include peace and security in Africa, small arms in West Africa and security sector governance.

Osman Gbla (Sierra Leone) is a Senior Lecturer and Head of the Department of Political Science of Fourah Bay College, University of Sierra Leone. He is also a Senior Researcher of the Centre for Development and Security Analysis (CEDSA), Freetown. He was a member of the team of consultants who drew up the Support Document for Peace, Reconciliation, Rehabilitation and Reconstruction in Sierra Leone; the Sierra Leone Vision 2025; and Sierra Leone's Poverty Reduction Strategy Paper. He has written a number of pieces on the civil wars in Liberia and Sierra Leone, including 'Conflict and post-conflict trauma among child soldiers in Liberia and Sierra Leone' and 'Multilateral agencies in post-conflict peace building in Liberia and Sierra Leone' in *Civil*

Wars, Child Soldiers and Post-Conflict Peace-building in West Africa (ed. A. Sesay, College Press, 2003). His research interests include conflicts and post-conflict peace-building, security and security sector reform, and governance in Africa generally and West Africa in particular. He is a member of the SIPRI Military Expenditure Network.

Eboe Hutchful (Ghana) is Professor in Africana Studies at Wayne State University, Detroit, Michigan, and Executive Director of African Security Dialogue and Research (ASDR), Accra, Ghana, and is the co-coordinator of the SIPRI/ASDR Project on Military Budgetary Processes in Africa. He has taught at several other universities in Africa and North America, including the University of Toronto, the University of Port Harcourt and the University of Ghana. His research has been primarily in the areas of militarism and security sector reform and the political economy of adjustment, areas in which he has published extensively. He is the author and co-editor of a large number of journal articles and several books, including *The Military and Militarism in Africa* (CODESRIA, 1998, co-edited with A. Bathily); *Ghana's Adjustment Experience: The Paradox of Reform* (James Currey, 2002); and a forthcoming volume, *Governing Security Establishments in Africa* (with A. Lala). He is current Chair of the African Security Sector Network.

Julius Karangi (Kenya) is a Lieutenant General in the Kenya Air Force (KAF). Since August 2005 he has been Vice-Chief of General Staff. Prior to that, he was Commander of the KAF and Commandant of the Defence Staff College, Karen.

Len le Roux (South Africa) is the Head of the Defence Sector Programme at the Institute for Security Studies (ISS), Pretoria. He served in the South African military for 36 years and, as the Director Strategy for the South African National Defence Force and the South African Department of Defence (DOD) from 1995 to 1999, he was involved in the development of the 1996 White Paper on defence, the 1996–98 Defence Review and the DOD Transformation Project. After leaving the DOD in 2000 he has remained active in the security debate in Africa by supporting the programmes of various non-governmental organizations and universities. He specializes in the fields of defence transformation, civil–military relations, defence management and budgeting. He has contributed papers and chapters to the ISS journal *African Security Review*; *Ourselves to Know: Civil–Military Relations and Defence Transformation in Southern Africa* (eds R. Williams, G. Cawthra and D. Abrahams, ISS, 2003); and *Security Sector Governance in Africa: A Handbook* (eds N. Ball and 'K. Fayemi, Centre for Democracy and Development, 2004), among others.

Lázaro Macuácua (Mozambique), a researcher by training, has worked for the Mozambican Ministry of National Defence for the past eight years. In addition, he is a Research Associate of the Programme on Defence and Security Management/Mozambique, a regional security network. He has participated in various academic forums and has written a number of papers on security issues, including 'O AGP dez anos depois: novos desafios para Moçambique' [The General Peace Accord 10 years later: new challenges for Mozambique], *Estudos Moçambicanos*, no. 20 (Nov. 2002).

Tunde Oduntan (Nigeria) is a lecturer in the Department of History, Obafemi Awolowo University, Ile-Ife, Nigeria. His articles on the Commonwealth and Nigerian history have appeared in the *Nigerian Journal of International Affairs*, *History in Africa* and the *African Journal of International Affairs and Development*. He has been a member of the SIPRI Military Expenditure Network since 2001. He is currently completing his doctoral dissertation.

Wuyi Omitoogun (Nigeria) is a Researcher with the SIPRI Military Expenditure and Arms Production Project and is the co-coordinator of the SIPRI/ASDR Project on Military Budgetary Processes in Africa. He previously worked at the Centre for Trans-Saharan Studies, University of Maiduguri, and Obafemi Awolowo University, both in Nigeria. His publications include 'Arms control and conflict in Africa' in *Arms Control and Disarmament: A New Conceptual Approach* (UN Department for Disarmament Affairs, 2000) and *Military Expenditure Data in Africa: A Survey of Cameroon, Ethiopia, Ghana, Kenya, Nigeria and Uganda*, SIPRI Research Report no. 17 (OUP, 2003). He has contributed to the SIPRI Yearbook since 2000.

Nouhoum Sangaré (Mali) is a Commissaire Colonel in the Malian armed forces. He is a graduate of the École du Commissariat de l'Air, specializing in management and logistics, and of the Centre d'Études Diplomatiques et Stratégiques, Paris. He has worked on several studies on the questions of security, defence, strategy, armed forces and democracy, and promotion of peace in post-conflict situations. After a long career in the armed forces, where he held several positions of responsibility, he is currently the Director of Administration and Finance of the Malian Ministry of Territorial Administration. He is a member of the SIPRI Military Expenditure Network.

Index